In Her Own Time

In Her Own Time

Women and Developmental Issues
in Pastoral Care

Jeanne Stevenson-Moessner, editor

Fortress Press / Minneapolis

In Her Own Time
Women and Developmental Issues in Pastoral Care

Interior Design: Ann Delgehausen
Back Cover Photo: by Todd Tieman. Standing: Jeanne Stevenson-Moessner, Christie Cozad Neuger, Carroll Saussy, Kathleen J. Greider, Maxine Glaz, Carolyn Bohler, Pamela Cooper-White. Seated: Nancy J. Ramsay, Karen D. Scheib, Paula Buford, Bonnie J. Miller-McLemore. Not Pictured: Patricia H. Davis, Mary Lynn Dell, Irene Henderson, Elizabeth Liebert, Judith Orr, Teresa E. Snorton, Carolyn Wilbur Treadway.

Library of Congress Cataloging-in-Publication Data

In her own time : women and developmental issues in pastoral care / edited by Jeanne Stevenson Moessner.
     p. cm.
  Includes bibliographical references.
  ISBN 0-8006-3137-4 (alk. paper)
    1. Church work with women. 2. Women—Religious life. 3. Feminist theology. I. Moessner, Jeanne Stevenson

  BV4445 .I5 2000
  261.8'344—dc21
                                 00-020194

Manufactured in the U.S.A.   1-3137
04   03   02   01   00   2   3   4   5   6   7   8   9   10

In honor of
Maxine Glaz and Carroll Saussy
with gratitude for their lives and contributions to pastoral theology

and

In memory of
Judith Orr
whose breath of life permeates these pages and the field of pastoral care

Contents

Contributors

Carolyn Stahl Bohler, Ph.D., is Emma Sanborn Tousant Professor of Pastoral Theology and Counseling, United Theological Seminary at Dayton, Ohio. She is an ordained United Methodist clergywoman, the mother of two children, and the author of *When You Need to Take a Stand* (Westminster John Knox, 1990), *Prayer on Wings: A Search for Authentic Prayer* (LuraMedia, 1990), *Opening to God: Guided Imagery Meditations on Scripture* (Upper Room, 1977; completely revised edition, 1996), *God Is Like a Mother Hen and Much Much More* (1996), and *CHIPS & SALSA: Children (& Youth) In PlayS—Short and Lively Sacred Action* (1996). She was the pastor of a church in San Diego, California, and was chaplain of Simpson College in Indianola, Iowa.

Paula Buford, M.Div., Th.D. (Columbia Seminary, pastoral counseling), is a Baptist minister who has twenty years of experience in the pastoral care and counseling field. A fellow in AAPC, and a clinical member in ACPE, Paula was a contributor to *Through the Eyes of Women* (Fortress Press, 1996). In 1993, Paula left her full-time position as a pastoral counselor due to disability. She later began Earthen Vessels Ministries out of her home in Stone Mountain, Georgia (an Atlanta suburb). Currently she writes, runs a pottery studio, hopes to lead art and spirituality groups and to begin a small psychotherapy practice.

Pamela Cooper-White, Ph.D., is Associate Professor of Pastoral Theology at the Lutheran Theological Seminary at Philadelphia. She is an ordained Episcopal priest, is a certified Fellow in AAPC, and is the author of *The Cry of Tamar: Violence against Women and the Church's Response* (Fortress Press, 1995) and *Women Healing and Empowering: A Small Group Congregational Resource* (ELCA, 1997).

Patricia H. Davis, Ph.D., is Associate Professor of Pastoral Theology at Southern Methodist University, Perkins School of Theology, Dallas, Texas. She is the author of two books on girls' psychology and spirituality: *Counseling Adolescent Girls* (Fortress Press, 1996) and *Beyond Nice: The Spiritual Wisdom of Adolescent Girls* (Fortress Press, 2000).

Mary Lynn Dell, M.D., M.T.S., Th.M., is a child and adolescent psychiatrist at the National Institute of Mental Health in Bethesda, Maryland, and an ordained clergywoman in the Christian Church (Disciples of Christ). She has also served on the medical school faculties of Emory University and the University of Pennsylvania.

Maxine Glaz, B.S., B.D., Th.M., Ed.D., is formerly the Director of Pastoral Care and Education at HealthONE Alliance, Denver, Colorado. An ordained minister of the United Church of Christ and a Supervisor in the Association for Clinical Pastoral Education, Inc., Decatur, Georgia, Maxine was a member of the first steering committee for the Society for Pastoral Theology. With Jeanne Stevenson-Moessner she co-edited *Women in Travail and Transition* (Fortress Press, 1991). Maxine resides in the Rocky Mountains, Fraser, Colorado, where she skis both down-hill and on skate-skis, and she hopes to progress to skijoring with her dog. She is currently working on developing skills as a pastel painter.

Kathleen J. Greider, Ph.D., is Associate Professor of Pastoral Care and Counseling at the Claremont School of Theology in southern California. Dr. Greider also has a small private practice in pastoral psychotherapy and spiritual direction. An ordained United Methodist clergywoman, she has previous experience in parish ministry and in-patient mental health services. She is the author of *Reckoning with Aggression: Theology, Violence, and Vitality* (Westminster John Knox, 1997).

Irene Henderson is Director of Pastoral Services for Palmetto Health Alliance in Columbia, SC. She is a clinically trained hospital chaplain, an ordained Southern Baptist minister, and a certified ACPE Supervisor. She values her many roles as woman (daughter, sister, wife, mother, administrator, pastor, and friend) as resources for her work and writing. She is married and is the mother of two children, a twenty-year-old son and a fifteen-year-old daughter.

Elizabeth Liebert, S.N.J.M., Ph.D., is Professor of Spiritual Life and Director of the Program in Christian Spirituality at San Francisco Theological Seminary. A member of the Sisters of the Holy Names of Jesus and Mary, she is also on the doctoral faculty of the Graduate Theological Union. She has authored *Changing Life Patterns: Adult Development in Spiritual Direction* (Paulist, 1992; 2nd ed., Chalice Press, 2000).

Bonnie J. Miller-McLemore, Ph.D., is Associate Professor of Pastoral Theology and Counseling at Vanderbilt University Divinity School. Her most recent publications include *Also a Mother: Work and Family as Theological Dilemma*, a co-authored book, *From Culture Wars to Common Ground: Religion and the American Family*

Debate, and an edited book, *Feminist and Womanist Pastoral Theology*. Ordained by the Christian Church (Disciples of Christ), she has also served as a pastoral psychotherapist, hospital chaplain, and minister. Her current research focuses on the imperative for more theological reflection on children.

Christie Cozad Neuger, Ph.D., is Professor of Pastoral Care and Pastoral Theology at United Theological Seminary of the Twin Cities. She is a diplomate in AAPC and a clinical member of ACPE. An ordained United Methodist Minister, she is the editor of *The Arts of Ministry* (Westminster, 1996), *The Care of Men* (co-edited with James Poling, Abingdon, 1997), and the author of *A Narrative Approach to Pastoral Counseling with Women* (Fortress Press, forthcoming).

Judith Orr, Ph.D., was professor at the St. Paul School of Theology, Kansas City, Missouri where she had also served as Dean. She wrote several important articles and chapters on gender and class. She was an ordained minister of the United Church of Christ. Judy died in March 2000. She will be deeply missed.

Nancy J. Ramsay, Ph.D., is Harrison Ray Anderson Professor of Pastoral Theology at Louisville Presbyterian Theological Seminary and former Chair of the Society for Pastoral Theology. She is Co-Editor of the *Journal of Pastoral Theology*. She is an ordained Presbyterian minister. Nancy is the author of *Pastoral Diagnosis: A Resource for Ministries of Care and Counseling* (Fortress Press, 1998) and co-editor with John McClure of *Telling the Truth: Preaching about Sexual and Domestic Violence* (United Church Press, 1998).

Carroll Saussy, Ph.D., is Professor Emerita of Pastoral Theology and Care at Wesley Theological Seminary, Washington, D.C. She is the author of *God Images and Self-Esteem: Empowering Women in a Patriarchal Society* (Westminster John Knox, 1991), *The Gift of Anger: A Call to Faithful Action* (Westminster John Knox, 1995), and *The Art of Growing Old: A Guide to Faithful Aging* (Augsburg Books, 1998).

Karen Scheib, Ph.D., is Assistant Professor of Pastoral Care and Counseling at Candler School of Theology, Emory University, Atlanta, Georgia. She is a clinical member of the American Association of Pastoral Counselors and an ordained elder in the United Methodist Church, with experience in both local church ministry and hospital chaplaincy. She is currently completing a book on the pastoral care of older women.

Teresa E. Snorton, M.Div., Th.M., D.Min. candidate, is Executive Director of the Association for Clinical Pastoral Education, Inc. She is an ordained clergywoman and pastor in the Christian Methodist Episcopal Church and a certified supervisor in the Association for Clinical Pastoral Education. Teresa is also on the adjunct faculty in the Pastoral Care Department at the Candler School of Theology.

Jeanne Stevenson-Moessner, M.A., Dr.Theol., is Associate Professor of Pastoral Theology and Spiritual Formation at the University of Dubuque Theological Seminary. She is an ordained Presbyterian minister (PCUSA), a Fellow in the American Association of Pastoral Counselors, a married mother of two, and a former missionary. She is author of *Theological Dimensions of Maturation in a Missionary Milieu*, co-editor of *Women in Travail and Transition* (Fortress Press, 1991), and editor of *Through the Eyes of Women* (Fortress, Press 1996). She has received specialized training in rape crisis, domestic violence, child sexual abuse, and community mental health. Jeanne is a Henry Luce III Fellow for 2000–2001.

Carolyn Wilbur Treadway, M.S.W., L.C.S.W., has been a practicing social worker, family therapist, and pastoral counselor for thirty-eight years. After twenty-two years of providing counseling, supervision, and teaching at BroMenn Counseling services in Normal and Bloomington, Illinois, she has recently left that agency to open her own private practice—Connections Counseling and Resource Center—which will provide therapy and deep ecology services. Carolyn is Quaker and endorsed by her Yearly Meeting for her ministry of pastoral counseling. She has held various leadership positions in AAPC Central Region and was a founding member of Pastoral Counselors for Social Responsibility and also Quakers in Pastoral Care and Counseling. She and her husband have three grown children. In 1996, she and Mary Kay Himens published *Images: Sights and Insights*, for which Carolyn was photographer.

Acknowledgments

In its own time, this work has progressed. Cynthia Thompson was there for the first steps, Pamela Johnson for the adolescent gait, Michael West and Henry French for the last lap. Many have given technical assistance and spiritual assurance: Lu LeConte, Ann Delgehausen, Sister Carmen Hernandez, Judy Calcari, Linda Wlochal, Faye Key, and friends at St. Mary's Episcopal School in Memphis. Most of all, the stalwart strides are a result of the eighteen contributors who worked not only in collegial fashion but as a sister circle.

In their own time, as this book developed, Maxine Glaz and Carroll Saussy entered retirement. Maxine Glaz was the first person to envision the collaborative possibility of a volume on woman and pastoral care. When no one woman was ready to undertake the project in 1988, she issued the instigating statement: "Let's do it together." Carroll Saussy has mentored many and served as a model of a wise woman in the field of pastoral theology. With dauntless energy, Carroll has investigated topics such as anger and aging.

In sacred time, Judith Orr was taken in death. While awaiting a lung transplant, Judy put the final editorial touches on her chapter. Before going into the hospital with pneumonia, Judy sent in her galley proofs. She never left the hospital. Our beloved Judy Orr will also never leave our sister circle.

Introduction

A woman in her sixties reminisced:

> Divorce was a major landmark in my life's journey. In 1972 I was 34 with three children aged 12, 9, and 5 when my husband decided he did not want to be married any more. 1972 was an awful year for me. A church friend had me (and often my children) to dinner once a week all that year. Sarah and her husband took me to dinner and to concerts. She visited, she called, she loved. I said, "Sarah, I can never repay you for all you are doing for me." She replied, "You'll give to someone down the road. That's the way life is." My gifts of love and nurturing, the gifts I bring to the church, exist because of all the Sarahs God has given me through the years.

Eighteen women come together in this volume with the gifts of our wisdom, clinical training, pastoral experience, and educational degrees. Like Sarah in the opening story, our work in this volume is an attempt to pass on these gifts. We women speak on the topic of religion and woman's life cycle in a way that is authentic, not exhaustive, to our life experience, observations, and research. We are women speaking "out of order" in that we challenge traditional ways of understanding development and the life spectrum.

Rites of passage across the life span have heretofore been primarily described by men. Some examples of these configurations are psychosocial development (Erik Erikson), cognitive development (Jean Piaget), moral development (Lawrence Kohlberg),[1] and faith development (James Fowler).[2] Women have often found themselves "out of order" in these structured theories for the following reasons:

1. The significance of a woman's body to her growth and differentiation has not been adequately integrated into psychosocial, cognitive, moral, or faith development theories. Women develop as embodied selves; it is not feasible to talk of their seasons of maturation without including the body and the interconnectedness of the body-mind-spirit.

1

2. The impact of the societal and cultural context in which a girl or woman matures has been underestimated in traditional life span and stage theories. Women are often aware, even if on an unconscious level, that their development after birth occurs in the context of a society that will not be nurturing. The social construction of their gender has often resulted in feminine stereotypes, models, and paradigms that do not fit. Thus, women's progression through life will always involve mind-body-spirit-*culture*. Implied in this interconnection is a relational emphasis that is missing when the theoretical focus is solely cognitive or psychosocial or moral or spiritual. As women in this volume speak "out of order," that is, apart from artificial stereotypes and generalizations, they offer a challenge to separative, linear notions of developmental and life span theory.

3. Relational authenticity for women calls into question the traditional actualized self or individuated self. Relational authenticity involves not only the mind-body-spirit-culture interconnectedness; relationality in context defies the cult of individualism as a woman sees herself as a "self-in-relation."[3]

4. Complementarity in the life span occurs when the second half of life complements the first half. Whether described in terms of "re-inventing one's life" (Karen Scheib) or "becoming an ancestor" (Maxine Glaz), the nuance of balance and recapitulation leads away from a linear gestalt in the life span.

Images of Passage

Traditional images that depict movement or passage in various aspects of growth have been horizontal, diagonal, or ladderlike. Even the pyramid and the spiral imply forward and ascending progression. As the contributors to this volume challenge separative, linear notions, they are revisualizing development and maturity. No one image suits us all. This fact is informative in itself: women are exploring new models of growth to maturity, and no one depiction can speak for all.

It is not uncommon for the circle, concentric circles (see Pamela Cooper-White), a tapestry (Christie Neuger), or the double helix (see Jeanne Stevenson-Moessner) to emerge as images. The Scriptures offer numerous portrayals of the life span that have a circular, rounded, disklike, or cyclic feature: the golden bowl, the pitcher at the fountain (water to water), the wheel at the cistern, dust to dust, breath of humankind to breath of God.[4] On the theme of development, however, the Scriptures say little. The words used to describe the maturing of Christ are these: he grew in wisdom and in stature. Wisdom is *hochma* or *sophia*, qualities of God imaged by female characteristics.[5] The growth of the boy Samuel (1 Samuel 2:26) is similar: " to grow both in stature and in favor with the Lord and with the people." There are no biblical women whose development is mentioned.

A body of literature is beginning to develop around the image of Sarah's circle. This is a reference to the biblical Sarah, wife of Abraham and grandmother of Jacob.[6] Although there is no biblical reference to a circle of Sarah in the book of

Genesis, this configuration is a counterbalance to Jacob's ladder or Abraham's lineage, as depicted particularly in the book of Matthew. One contemporary rendering of Sarah's legacy is titled "We Are Dancing Sarah's Circle."[7] Whereas there is no record of her dancing, there is mention of her laughter. The various stanzas repeat the words: "Here we seek and find our history. We will all do our own naming. Every round a generation. On and on the circle's moving. . . ." This portrayal is an attempt to veer away from linear formation, upward trajectories, and ladder-like illustrations of maturity.

Narratives of Harm/Narratives of Hope

Throughout women' growth, narratives of harm and narratives of hope interlace their development. Contributors to this volume will give examples of both. Narratives of harm include both intimate and impersonal forms of violence, sexual abuse, rape, exploitation, degradation, shaming, and disempowerment. According to conservative estimates, rape is committed against one out of four women in the United States; one-third of female children and adolescents under the age of eighteen experience significant sexual abuse; and violence occurs in one-third to one-half of U.S. families.[8] Jean Baker Miller summarizes the context of woman's growth: "All women grow up within a context that includes the threat of violence, particularly sexualized violence."[9]

Narratives of hope can also intertwine this process of women's maturation. Narratives of hope include individual and relational stories of affirmation, collegiality, transformation, empowerment, awareness, and illumination. An example of a story of transformation is clearly given *in The Logic of the Spirit: Human Development in Theological Perspective* in the case of Helen.[10] Helen's human spirit had been damaged in childhood after she was rejected by her mother and betrayed by her father. "Helen, conceived as a replacement for her stillborn brother, was the wrong sex. She had been fundamentally and irreversibly wrong from the beginning." After several months of counseling and prayerful intervention, Helen relived the agony of rejection in her birth experience. In guided meditation, Helen not only imaged Christ becoming a child and suffering for her in the delivery room of the hospital, she later imagined Christ holding her and dancing with her as an infant. The gaze of his delight overpowered the parental eyes of disapproval, and she reconfigured her identity as a child of God.[11] Narratives of healing and wholeness permeate women's growth in familial and cultural settings that devalue them.

Sarah and Hagar's Circle

As Susan Wolf has aptly stated in *Women, Culture, and Development*, it is not that there must be a separate norm for women and men in theories of human nature. However, "we must protect against the exclusion of women from the definition, the imagination, the concern of the theory-builders. . . . The way to do this . . . is by ensuring that women as well as men participate in the task of theory construction, that both be sensitive to the history and the dangers of excluding women from consideration, and that both be careful in their reflections sometimes to focus specifically on the real and imagined lives of women and sometimes to focus specifically on the real and imagined lives of men."[12]

As we women seek to give of our insights, as did the Sarah in the opening example, we veer away from linear formation, upward trajectories, and ladderlike illustrations of maturity. Our theory building is not unlike the contemporary song of Sarah's circle mentioned earlier: we seek and find our history; we will all do our own naming—every round generation. Those of us writing for this volume are in our own way dancing Sarah's and Hagar's circle as we seek and find our developmental history. Sarah and Hagar new both exclusion and blessing. Our gifts of naming and nurturing, the gifts we bring to the church, the academy, and the world, exist because of all the Sarahs and Hagars we have been given through the years. These gifts will be passed down by eighteen women, each in her own way, in her own time.

Jeanne Stevenson-Moessner

Part 1

Taking Her Time: Developmental Themes

In due time, women are raising awareness that the body and the culture do affect developmental theory. Jeanne Stevenson-Moessner offers a theological basis for underscoring the importance of women's bodies as a central theme for development and religion. Elizabeth Liebert discusses the limitations of life span and structural developmental theories; both exclude those who are out of the prescribed order of tasks and the "common" progression of life crises. On the assumption that gender, class, race, cultural, and historical contexts shape the course of human development, Judith Orr uses socioeconomic class as a differential for development as she compares a working-class and middle-class population. Christine Cozad Neuger focuses critically on dominant cultural and familial narratives that shape the psychological, social, and spiritual development of boys and girls and lead almost inevitably to physical and emotional abuse in heterosexual partnerships. Pamela Cooper-White asks and answers the question: How does the experience of early trauma, particularly sexual abuse, affect development? Spiritual development is also influenced by the assault of trauma because body and self are one in a child's experience. Patricia Davis uses her research to show spirituality shaping the ways adolescent girls understand themselves and their worlds, including a "gothic view" of the world that includes horror as well as safety.

Incarnational Theology:
Restructuring Developmental Theory

Jeanne Stevenson-Moessner

A few years ago, I was standing in the turnaround in front of Candler School of Theology, Emory University, when a newly retired professor of pastoral theology, Charles Gerkin, was loading the trunk of his car with his theology books. As I watched this leading figure in pastoral care move his office from the seminary to his home, I knew I was observing a pioneer in the field. One of his major contributions was developing the understanding of incarnational theology as it applies to pastoral care and counseling.

Charles Gerkin's contribution to incarnational theology will be augmented and reformulated in this chapter on developmental theory through an examination of the lives and contributions of women. Just as the body and culture of women have been neglected in developmental theory, so have the body and culture of women been excluded from the doctrine of the incarnation, God's becoming flesh. This exclusion has extended from the patristic period in church history to contemporary circles in care and counseling.

First, some background to Gerkin's use of the term incarnational theology. Gerkin claimed Anton Boisen as a "spiritual ancestor."[1] When Gerkin was in seminary in Chicago, Boisen visited an evening class taught by Fred Keuther. Gerkin says of Boisen: "I thought him a strange man with his twisted face, penetrating eyes, and thumping cane. But I was attracted to what he said about the study of 'living human documents' and mental illness as a sickness of the soul analogous to fever in the body."[2] Later, in Gerkin's own work *Crisis Experience in Modern Life*, his own critical theological questions growing out of pastoral work with people experiencing everyday crises pressed him toward "images of a theology of incarnation—God's continuing activity on human behalf."[3] The theological extension I make in this chapter relies on Gerkin's premise:

> Pastoral counseling has long recognized and made paradigmatic use of the
> biblical theological symbol of incarnation as a formative image giving pur-

pose and definition to the relationship of the pastoral counselor to the person seeking help. The analogy of God's incarnation in Jesus here becomes the controlling paradigmatic image for the grace and acceptance the counseling relationship is to embody. It thus provides a structuring image for the intentionality of the pastoral counselor. As a member and representative of the body of Christ the pastoral counselor seeks to embody the quality of relationship that fulfills the incarnational analogy.[4]

The theological reformulation I would like to make in this chapter is as follows:

> God's incarnation in Jesus occurred in the body of a woman. Jesus' maternity was never questioned historically. What was questioned was his paternity. God's incarnation in Jesus Christ of Nazareth occurred in the body of a woman named Mary.

Thus, a restructuring and paradigmatic image for incarnational theology is Mary, mother of God, as God-bearer. What this image underscores is the inseparable unity of spirit and body. God became flesh. God became incarnate in the body of a woman. The Protestant tradition has perpetuated three miscalculations: it has fostered the mind-body dualism, as has the Christian tradition in general; it has devalued woman's experience and her body; it has denied the importance of Mary as Theotokos (God-bearer) as affirmed by the Council of Ephesus (431). Many Protestants stand up each Sunday in worship and affirm in the Apostles' Creed, "I believe . . . in Jesus Christ, God's only Son, . . . born of the virgin Mary," and never incorporate this credal statement into their understanding of incarnational theology. Yet the incarnation was inextricably linked to the body of a woman. Incarnational theology is infused with this connection. Incarnational theology as a biblical theological symbol will inform developmental issues and theory in this chapter.

Mary, Mother of God, as Paradigm

Incarnational theology has traditionally centered on this christological statement: God became flesh (Jesus of Nazareth). Using Mary as she embodies incarnational theology and as a paradigm for the reformulation of developmental theory makes four contributions:

- It gives us a Biblical basis for the mind-body-spirit unity.
- It elevates not only the status of Mary specifically but of women in general.
- It underscores the importance of the woman's body in reenvisioning developmental issues.
- It calls attention to the impact of the culture (that is, the implications for an unwed Jewish woman in a religious tradition of male privilege). Mary's song of praise, or Magnificat, in Luke 1:46-55 underscores this theme of God lifting the lowly.

Before the start of a school semester, I made a retreat to prepare myself. The spiritual director of the retreat, a Methodist trained by Jesuits, asked me to meditate on Psalm 131:2: "But I have calmed and quieted my soul, like a child quieted at its mother's breast; like a child that is quiet is my soul" (RSV). I was to image myself on the lap of God. Then I was to image myself on the lap of Mary. I was to ask for the grace to rest and listen.

I could not emotionally connect with Mary, mother of God. First, I confessed to my spiritual director that it must be her color, for most Marys I had seen portrayed were Caucasian. One of my primary caretakers and nurturers had been a dark-skinned woman like the one depicted in the painting of "The Annunciation" by Henry Ossawa Tanner, an African American. Then I decided I could not connect emotionally with Mary because she was depicted as passive. What I especially found problematic was her helplessness at the foot of the cross. Foremost in my mind was the depiction of Mary by Matthias Grunewald in the Isenheim altarpiece in Colmar, France—a collapsed Mary, upheld by a male disciple, with her hands outstretched and her fingers gnarled and intertwined like a crown of thorns. If I had been Mary, if that were my son on the cross, I trust I would have yelled: "You kill him over my dead body." I would have held his feet and supported him, so his weight would not have borne down over the nails. I would have gotten a small ladder and tried to dislodge the nails. I would have done something. I loathe passive Marys. I could not image myself in prayer in the lap of a passive Mary.

By the end of the retreat, I remembered a traumatic pastoral visit. I had been asked to go to a critical care unit where someone special to me lay in a coma after a car accident. I got there and waited three hours while the nurses and doctors stabilized her. I visited with the parents, who prepared me for what I was to see. They left to go get some rest, and I stood alone in the hallway, waiting and feeling helpless. When the nurse told me I could enter, I did my deep breathing and faced the machines and the tubes and the fragile boundary between life and death. I prayed my pastoral prayer close to her ear and mentioned by name those who loved her and were pulling for her. I touched her pale skin to give her a sense of human warmth, and I made the sign of the cross, invoking the power of the Trinity. I left within forty-five seconds and returned to the hallway where I had felt helpless and passive. I found upon returning, however, that I felt fierce.

Fierceness is waiting when you cannot alter the situation. Fierceness is going into nursing homes and facing senile dementia and Alzheimer's when even the medical profession cannot. Fierceness is staring into the face of suffering, and it has nothing to do with passivity. After I remembered this difficult visit, I was able to connect with Mary at the foot of the cross. I was then able, metaphorically speaking, to climb onto the lap of a fierce Mary.

Only after recognizing Mary's fierceness did I find theologians who had already discovered a Mary of courage. Dorothee Soelle, in *The Strength of the Weak: Toward a Christian Feminist Identity*, portrayed Mary as one who stood against the forces of a violent society, earning the label "madonna of the rogues."[5] A Polish legend is told in which a robber calls on Mary for aid just before the noose is to be put around his neck.

> Mary hastens to him, stands under the gallows, and supports the hanged man's feet for three days and three nights. Presumed dead, the robber is cut down from the gallows, only to run off, rendering thanks to the Virgin. The heroes of such legends are often thieves and robbers—or monks and nuns who have fled the rigors of monastery or cloister—people who oppose law and order and that masculine set of mind intent on domination and regulation.[6]

At the time of Soelle's writing, she as a German also mentioned the view that Mary was seen as a "sympathizer," which in (West) German circles in 1978 meant "one who undermines the power of the ruling classes."[7] Mary has also been presented as a "Woman of Valor";[8] her "passivity and submission" has been reframed as "obedience open to the future," which is supreme activity.[9] Writing on the receptivity of Mary, Rosemary Radford Ruether sees true receptivity to others as only possible for a person with independence and self-esteem.[10]

In her work on Mary, Anne Carr has shown that feminist scholarship traced the contrast of Mary, the sinless virgin mother, to Eve, the symbol of sin and flesh, to the fourth-century church fathers. Thus, only in ascetic virginity could women overcome their corrupt, sexual nature to become virtuous like Mary. The other alternative was to align oneself with Eve in her sexuality and materiality. All women in touch with the real world and their bodies, of course, had to identify with Eve in this dichotomy. In spite of this manufactured contrast, however, women have been reluctant to give up Mary and struggle to see her as a very human figure. Even Mary Daly, at an earlier stage, thought the Marian symbolism might be a prophetic sign of the new woman. The virgin birth suggests that women need not be identified with men.[11] This echoes the sentiment of Sojourner Truth in the 1851 convention in Akron, Ohio. In her "Ain't I a Woman" speech, she commented, "Then that little man in black there, he says women can't have as much rights as men, 'cause Christ wasn't a woman! Where did your Christ come from? Where did your Christ come from? From God and a woman! Man had nothing to do with Him."

If we bypass the body of Mary as Docetics once tried to through the simile of Christ passing through the body of Mary as water through a pipe,[12] we downplay the importance of "the one who gave birth to the one who is God" (Theotokos).[13] If we bypass the body of Mary, we perpetuate the deadly dualism that separates body and spirit, or body and mind.

Women are reluctant to give up Mary. It was explained to me, a Protestant, that Mary stands now in the cloud of witnesses mentioned in Hebrews 12:1. Mary is there, the spiritual director said, as mother of God. Furthermore, she implied, when you enter a hospital room as chaplain or pastor/priest and face hysterectomy, mastectomy, loss of a child, miscarriage, infertility, ask Mary to pray for you—for she knew. She embodied the unity of body and soul. With her the physical was tied to the spiritual.

She illustrates that	hysterectomy	}	
	mastectomy	}	
	child loss	}	
	child birth	}	are spiritual matters.

She further illustrates that	rape	}	
	battering	}	
	incest	}	
	child abuse	}	are religious issues.

The "God-who-became-flesh" was carried in the womb of a woman. Christ was born from the pangs of a woman. It is only by a theological reexamination of these woman pangs specifically and those of women in general that we can articulate, reformulate, and midwife a rebirth and emergence of a developmental theory and theology that evidences a unity of mind-body-spirit-culture.

The Organism and Its Environment

It is not surprising that the woman who was a founder of the Clinical Pastoral Education movement, along with Anton Boisen and Seward Hiltner, exhibited an understanding of the mind-body-culture unity. This woman, Helen Flanders Dunbar, was a medical doctor with a Ph.D. from Columbia University. In 1935, she published a 1,016-page volume, *Emotions and Bodily Changes: A Survey of Literature on Psychosomatic Interrelationships.*

Dunbar developed the interrelationship between the psychic (which includes the emotional) and somatic processes in health and disease. She was ahead of our decade in emphasizing an "outer and inner environment between which there takes place a sort of osmotic interchange."[14] Trying to bridge anatomy and physiology on one hand with psychology and psychoanalysis on the other, Dunbar talked about the "organismal point of view" as the parts of an organism are related to the whole. Thus, the organism is related to its environment as psyche is related to soma.

Dunbar built on the work of Sigmund Freud. For Freud, *psyche* meant mind or intellect while *soma* meant body,[15] and he first replaced speculation with scientific observation concerning psychosomatic phenomena. His study of conversion hysteria did much to combat the equation of hysteria with the "running wild of the uterus (hystera) in the body."[16]

Helen Flanders Dunbar documented numerous clinical cases relating emotions to bodily health and environmental factors. It is intriguing to compare Dunbar's findings in the 1930s with studies at the end of the century. For example, Dunbar's findings in 1935 correlate with a 1996 study on racism's effect on health.[17] In the following case of a sixty-one-year-old woman, Dunbar related blood pressure (BP) and emotional stress in the environment. She illustrated how psychic factors and an unfavorable living situation may influence a serious organic syndrome.

> A woman of sixty-one had been treated for angina pectoris, in the sanitarium under Fahrenkamp's direction, ten years before. She was given a very poor prognosis at that time. In 1924, her husband shot himself in the apartment while the patient was in a neighboring room. Fahrenkamp, who was called, expected, as did the relatives, a fatal outcome for the patient. The BP at that time was between 210 and 240 mm.; the patient would have to stop every few steps because of "pressure on the heart," etc. Two weeks after the burial she came to the office and related that the day after the accident she had done her big laundry herself and that this exertion had been nothing for her, but rather had distracted her from the frightening experience. This "big laundry," says Fahrenkamp, is of symbolic significance, since the patient, who had been strictly forbidden any exertion, was under no necessity of undertaking this hard physical work. Beamingly she related that the big laundry had agreed with her very well, and clinical observation showed her BP decreased to 180 mm., not rising over 200 mm. again. The patient, without ever talking about it, had suffered from her unhappy marriage. To the analytically oriented physician, Fahrenkamp comments, the joy with which the patient related the doing of the big laundry is significant, to the organically oriented physician the fact that she could do it. Under the influence of the improved psychic situation, the patient has remained much better ever since and without her angina pectoris, in spite of her arteriosclerotic myocarditis.[18]

These findings can be compared with a Duke study in which a researcher found increased heart rate and blood pressure among African Americans after racial confrontations. "Participants exhibited blood pressure as much as 40 percent higher during the racial debates than during the non-racial debates."[19] Heart rates were 61 percent higher. "McNeilly's studies on racism build on a large body of research at Duke on the effects of mental stress on physical health. That research has documented that family and work-related stress can increase the risk of heart disease."[20]

Thus, the link among environment, emotions, and health that Helen Flanders Dunbar stressed in 1935 continues to be forged today. Just as psyche is related to soma, so is the organism to its environment.

Psychosomatic Split in the Christian Tradition

German theologian Elisabeth Moltmann-Wendel also underscores the persistent *psyche-soma* dualism in Christian theology, calling our theology "disembodied" in her recently translated book *I Am My Body*. She argues that the influence of the Greco-Roman worldview was a dualism between body and soul, body and spirit; man was associated with spirit and woman with body.[21] Her premise is that the church needs to rediscover the centrality of the body in Jesus' message. Moltmann-Wendel develops the Mark 5 account of a woman who had been bleeding for twelve years. "The bleeding, which is not menstrual bleeding but bleeding caused by an illness and which cannot be stopped, is not a disease. It is associated with emissions, odours, impurity; it is disgusting."[22] A person so afflicted would be unclean and isolated from human company. "This story makes clear . . . how central the body of God (of Jesus) and the human body (the woman's) once were in Christianity. . . ."[23] Yet she argues, the Christian churches have by and large constantly repressed the body and excluded and devalued all that is fleshly, bodily, material.[24] Western dualism has divided body and soul, body and spirit. The church has perpetuated this dualism and has overlaid this dualism with hostility toward sexuality. Christianity has been ambivalent in its treatment of women's bodies: they are both feared and denied, yet the healing of the whole person as woman and man was the center of the Jesus movement. In addition, Christianity has always had an affinity for the suffering body. In Moltmann-Wendel's work on a theology of embodiment, she maintains that the rediscovery of the body could prove to be a turning point in our Western development. She advocates "thinking with the body."[25] Inverse to our culture, however, she begins with violated bodies.[26] When reconstructing developmental theory, we begin with violated bodies. By so doing, we alter developmental theory forever, because we incorporate the impact of both culture and body on a person's progression through life's stages.

A disembodied theology is a theology that devalues the importance of the body. There is no clearer biblical example of disembodied theology than the account of Jephthah in Judges 11:34-35. Jephthah had an egotistical desire to dominate. The son of a prostitute, he was expelled from Gilead by his stepbrothers to the land of Tob. As an outcast, he joined a band of raiders and lived with marauders. Jephthah was a mighty warrior, however, and in due time, the elders of Gilead called him back when the Ammonites threatened them. Jephthah made a vaporous vow to Yahweh: in exchange for victory, the first living thing to come from his house would be sacrificed to Yahweh. The vow led to violence. His only child, a daughter, came out to meet him, dancing with timbrels. In a move that is typical for perpetrators of violence, Jephthah blamed the victim, his daughter: "Alas, my daughter! You have brought me very low; you have become the cause of great trouble to me!" (Judges 11:35). Jephthah never questioned his vow to God. He never realized that to annihilate the body of a woman is to disavow God. And the vow led to violence.

People of faith are able to act as though vows to God have nothing to do with what actually happens to women. Jephthah best exhibits the danger of a disembodied theology, an inability to see that the Creator is devalued when the created is devalued. In the midst of this atrocious event, Jephthah's daughter uttered words that grotesquely parallel those of Mary in the Magnificat: "Do to me according to what has gone out of your mouth" (v. 36). A disembodied theology in Judges contrasts with an embodied theology in the account of the Incarnation: God became flesh in the body of a woman.

Violated Bodies

Using the methodology proposed by E. Moltmann-Wendel, we start our theological reflections with violated bodies. In *Women's Bodies, Women's Wisdom* by physician Christine Northrup these statistics are offered: FBI estimates show one out of
three women are raped, 50 percent of all married women will be battered at least
once in their marriage, and 38 percent of adult women in the United States have
been sexually abused as children.[27] "All women grow up within a context that includes the threat of violence, particularly sexualized violence."[28] It is as survivors of
a violent and misogynistic culture, not as victims, that women reenvision pastoral
theology and its impact on developmental theory.

A video on post-traumatic stress disorder[29] focuses on survivors of Vietnam,
natural disasters such as earthquakes, and sexual violence such as incest. In a discussion about incest, the video illustrates through the story of incest survivor
Michelle Nappi a mind-body dualism and the devaluation of the female body.
After Michelle's marriage and birth of a child, she experienced unsettling nightmares, anxiety attacks, depression, and flashbacks. In therapy, repressed memories
of incest surfaced. She gave birth as a preteen to a baby by her father. The baby girl
was born alive, but her father killed the baby in the bathroom and told Michelle
to dispose of the body in the metal drum used to burn garbage outside. Later, she
gave birth to a boy by her father. She is shown holding this baby in a family photo,
taken when she was thirteen. This baby was put up for illegal adoption. Michelle
says of the family violence: "It is there with me all the time. It doesn't feel like
twenty-six years ago."

Michelle as survivor says: "They [my parents] took enough away from me, and
for me to hand over anything else to them would be something I was doing to myself. I'm not going to hand them any more on a silver platter." This is the type of
self-empowerment that women are choosing. Michelle's story illustrates an extreme violation of the female body and stands in radical juxtaposition to valuation
of the body in portrayals of Mary, Mother of God. Throughout developmental
stages, however, the impact of the culture does manifest itself: "It is there with me
all the time. It doesn't feel like twenty-six years ago."

Developmental theory is challenged at this point. Invasion and abuse of any
sort spiral through developmental stages with varying degrees of healing and scar-
ring. Using the psychosocial stages, for example, of Erik Erikson, the basic trust-
mistrust core issue in the earliest stage of life may not only produce an unfavorable
ratio of mistrust to trust, the imbalance may permeate and rework itself in other
stages. The betrayal Michelle experienced as a child affects not only her psychological and social development, it imprints her body and her soul. It shapes the way
she "is" in her culture. If we start our theory-building with violated bodies, traditional life span and developmental theories are not adequate for the implications
and imprint of violence.

The Role of the Body and the Culture

Women are teaching us that the body is not only tied to emotions, it is intricately linked to self-image and identity. The culture has also sought to shape the way women identify themselves. Theology in general and the Judeo-Christian tradition specifically have often fostered a "sociology of the servant" that has been detrimental to the health of women. As men have been equated with mind (spirit) and women with body (material), it has been women who have traditionally prepared food, cleaned the domicile, attended to material needs, bandaged the wounds, and generally cared for the corporeal well-being of others.

A significant challenge to traditional developmental theory occurred in 1982 with the publication of Carol Gilligan's *In a Different Voice: Psychological Theory and Women's Development*. In the sequence in women's development of an ethic of care, a disequilibrium takes place when care becomes confused with self-sacrifice in the conventions of feminine goodness. In caring for others, the self becomes hurt and neglected.[30] Gilligan also exposes the inapplicability of Erik Erikson's sequence of identity consolidation preceding the core issue of intimacy. Gilligan maintains that many women find their "identity" through the one whom they marry or with whom they form attachments. Gilligan, of course, was not advocating this progression. She raised awareness that established psychosocial developmental theory might not fit the actual life experience of many women.

Women are raising our awareness about the importance of the body and culture on identity formation. Because the culture supports both hidden and overt images of the ideal woman, false measures of self-worth are tied to body measurements, slimness, sexual appeal, color, youth. Following a radical mastectomy, for example, a woman may feel she is no longer attractive. The removal of the uterus is as significant as the onset of menses or menopause in the process of identity formation. Ninety to 95 percent of anorexics and bulimics are women. In *Reviving Ophelia: Saving the Selves of Adolescent Girls*, Mary Pipher attributes these alarming statistics about eating disorders to a dysfunctional culture that objectifies women and worships the trim female body.[31] Carol Gilligan discovered the issue of intimacy has been inextricably linked to women's identity process, and we pastoral theologians are discovering the role of the woman's body and the weight of the culture in her identity formation. Women receive messages from the culture that objectify, falsify, and belittle them. "An inner and outer discontinuity disturb the organization of personal sameness."[32]

In stark contrast, we have the image of Mary, mother of God, receiving the message that she is blessed. In her song of praise, which has become a foundation for liberation theologies, the great reversal is proclaimed: God has brought down the powerful from their thrones and lifted up the lowly. God has filled the hungry with good things and sent the rich away hungry. Theologians have tended to disengage the Magnificat from the culture in which it was delivered, a culture in which adult male Jews recited each morning: "Blessed be God, King of the universe, for not making me a woman."[33] In the Roman culture of Mary's day, power was transmitted through the males in *patria potestas*, the authority of the fathers. A woman was always under the *manus* or hand of the male head of household. Women's bodies were suspected of harboring evil.[34] Women were systematically excluded from the life of mind and spirit.[35] The role of the culture in the way women see themselves and develop cannot be neglected.

Images of Passage

Traditional images that have been used to depict movement or passage in various aspects of growth have been linear or ladderlike. Two established models are depicted below:

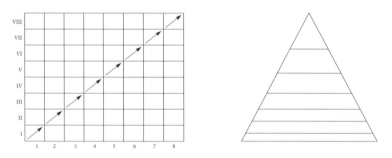

As women revisualize their developmental passages, it is not uncommon for the circle or the double helix (see below) to emerge. One way of imaging life span theory is illustrated in the following modification of the double helix, which is embedded in the milieu of a particular culture.

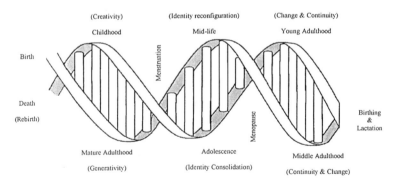

The parallels throughout the life cycle are striking: the creativity of childhood with the generativity of mature adulthood, the identity consolidation of adolescence with the identity reconfiguration of midlife, the change and continuity of young adulthood with the continuity and change of middle adulthood. Birth can be juxtaposed to birthing and lactation, although that is not every woman's choice and experience. Death and the subsequent spiritual rebirth that death brings are positioned side by side with biological birth. The physical passages of menstruation and menopause are indicated. The narratives of harm (such as the life memories of Michelle Nappi) are threaded through the image. Narratives of hope are woven through the life span as well. The entire double helix is embedded in the *culture* in an interactive exchange, thus forming a model.[36]

Mind-Body-Soul-Culture: A Quadripartite Unity

Pastors, theologians, and pastoral counselors have not been convinced of the mind-body-soul-culture unity and our place in that quadrivalent healing relationship. God became flesh in the womb of a woman. It is only through a theological reexamination of this central tenet of the Protestant, Roman Catholic, and Orthodox faith that we can offer an incarnational theology adequate to meet the pressures of a dysfunctional culture.

In the Protestant tradition, why have we stopped short when developing incarnational theology of including the locus of that activity in the body of a woman? Why have we downplayed the role of the mother of Jesus? The cult of the Great Mother had dominated religious devotion in the Mediterranean world at the time of the birth of Christ. The cult of the Great Mother manifested itself in the worship of Artemis, a goddess seen as supreme in divine power. The Ephesian Artemis is most commonly thought of as the polymastoid goddess who was the mother of mothers, the nurse of all, and the divine midwife. The Christian reforms of the time threatened the temple economy and trade, in which statues of the Great Mother were made, sold, and venerated. It is possible that the early Christians reacted to the cult of the pagan Great Mother (Great Artemis) and downplayed the role of Mary, mother of God. In 431, however, the Council of Ephesus upheld Mary's title as God-bearer (Theotokos).

In summary, the importance of the woman's body is a central theme for developmental theory. This theme, the valuing of the body, comes at a time when the woman's body is continually violated, vilified, and degraded through incest, battering, rape, and other forms of violence. Eating disorders and low self-esteem based on body image are contagious in the college population. An emerging developmental theory that is adequate for women's experience will include the following:

- a recognition of the interconnection of body and spirit, body and mind, body and soul;
- a stance that no one deserves to be exploited, violated, degraded or suppressed;
- a resistance to a culture that does so;
- an awareness that the body is a place where God can dwell, which results in actions that respect that holy place;
- a belief that the worth of a person is not based on contour, color, or capabilities;

• a grounding of an embodied theology based on the incarnation of Christ
through the body of Mary. This grounding continually informs our developmental theory and praxis.

Nowhere is the mind-body-soul-culture unity better expressed than in the
Magnificat, sung by a woman of low social status, with body fully and organically
engaged in the message:

> Mary:
> *My soul magnifies the Lord*
> *and my spirit rejoices in God my Savior.*

Blessed are you among women.
Blessed women.

Seasons and Stages:
Models and Metaphors
of Human Development

Elizabeth Liebert, S.N.J.M.

When we use the word *development* in relation to human beings, we all know what we mean. Or do we? We intuitively sense that in some ways, we are not the same person as we were twenty, ten, or even five years ago. We hear ourselves say things such as, "When I was young, I used to think I could do anything I wanted. Now I know that I can't. I don't even want to anymore. I just want to do the best I can with what I have been given." Or, "I can't believe that I used to accept what I was told—as if I had no mind of my own. Now I question everything." Or, "Fifty used to seem ancient. Looks pretty good to me now! I think I am more alive than I even was when I was younger. I haven't yet wanted to be younger."

From another perspective, it is clear that we are indeed the same people we were five, ten, or even twenty years ago. When we use the words "I," "me," and "myself," we mean, somehow, the same self that has endured over time. We notice that our personality has consistency: "I don't get angry in the overt way I used to (when I was a kid, I threw tantrums), but the same frustration is there. Now I just use my feelings to change the situation and smile sweetly while I do it. If I'm lucky, they don't even know what hit them." One of the significant problems in understanding human development concerns accounting for both the sameness and differences in a person over time. Why is it that we do not disintegrate when enormous changes happen to us? On the other hand, why do we change at all?

This chapter will illumine two very different yet complementary meanings of this seemingly innocuous word *development* and point out the domain of each. I will argue that both meanings tell us something important about human beings and that consequently neither meaning should be dismissed. After examining two models, life span development and structural development, I will examine what we can learn about women's development primarily from the second model. This chapter approaches human beings from within the discipline of psychology, but I assume that readers will put this material into dialogue with their various theologies, especially concerning the relationship between God and human beings.

Life Span Developmental Theories

The first developmental model will be familiar to most, at least in its general outline. It entered mainstream thought through the extensive writings of Erik Erikson. Some of the concepts he introduced—life cycle, identity crisis, ages and phases of human development, for example—are now so commonplace that we might easily miss the significance of Erikson's work for the question at hand, namely, what does it mean to say that humans develop? We have grown accustomed to identifying the tasks and challenges we face during each period of the human life cycle. We are familiar with Erikson's eight seasons of the life cycle and the core struggle humans address in each season: infancy (whose struggle centers around the establishment of basic trust versus mistrust), early childhood (autonomy versus shame and doubt), play age (initiative versus guilt), school age (industry versus inferiority), adolescence (ego identity versus role confusion), young adulthood (intimacy versus isolation), middle adulthood (generativity versus self-absorption and stagnation), and old age (ego integrity versus despair). Because of Erikson, we also see that adulthood is not one long, static period commencing as one leaves adolescence and ending with death. Instead, we now recognize that adulthood is characterized by its own advances and retreats, its own crises and challenges, which are no less significant than those of adolescence.

By training, Erikson was a lay (nonmedical) psychoanalyst whose work focused primarily on children. Through his analytic studies under Anna Freud, Sigmund Freud's youngest daughter, Erikson gained access to the inner psychoanalytic circle of Vienna. When the rising Nazi tide dispersed the Vienna psychoanalysts, Erikson moved to Boston, where he set up a practice in child analysis. Soon he was given positions, even without advanced degrees, at Harvard Medical School and the Massachusetts General Hospital. A move to Yale in 1936 introduced him to the Yale Institute of Human Relations, a venue that provided him with the kind of interdisciplinary stimulation that would characterize his own theory building. His first cultural immersion, so crucial to his understanding of the role of culture in human development, came through a 1938 study at the Pine Ridge Reservation in South Dakota. In *Childhood and Society*, published in 1950, we can already see the outline of the theory of human development that he was to expand over the next three decades.

From the perspective of the beginning of the twenty-first century, both the radicality and the incompleteness of Erikson's treatment of culture stand out in increasing relief. His cultural immersions convinced him of the significant role cultures play in the developmental progression of their participants, thereby moving Erikson beyond both then-current orthodox psychoanalysis and theories of development that would develop by the middle of the century. He built this conviction into his scheme by claiming that culture, alongside both biology and ego, played an intrinsic and dynamic role in the process of development. But the nuances and variations between cultures described in *Childhood and Society* get lost in general statements of the theory through the abstraction "culture." In the increasingly postmodern scholarly assumptions at the turn of the millennium, all such generalizations as in the use of the comprehensive word *culture* tend to collapse. For example, how does African American culture shape child-rearing practices? How do the life-tasks, work imposed by circumstance, of Japanese rural residents compare with those of Japanese urban cultures? Laboring class with professional class Italian Americans? Mestizos with indigenous Mexicans? What demands does any given culture place on its members? And how are gender roles and expectations related to cultural expectations? Erikson's move to culture as a function of development, radical in his day, now requires such content-specific questions as illustrated above.

Erikson posited a development based on a series of life crises, which he understood in the Greek sense of "decision." A life crisis offers a substantial opportunity to set the stage anew for the future. These crises occur at the confluence of three factors: the emerging biological organism, a given culture's demands on its individual members, and the individual's own ego (that is, one's personality forged from past decisions, predilections, and so on). If a crisis is resolved in a sufficiently positive manner, the struggle gives birth to a strength, which Erikson calls a "virtue." This strength prepares the individual for the next crisis. A resolution more negative than positive leaves one at risk in the next and subsequent crises, because the necessary personality strength, or virtue, is poorly developed or nonexistent. It is possible though more difficult to resolve a psychosocial crisis at a later time, out of its ordinary developmental season. To do so requires that one rework the formerly unresolved issue in terms of life's present contingencies.

Erikson's crises are age-related because they depend on a biological substratum. Erikson moved past his Freudian roots, however, by positing that the emerging biological organism is moved by more than sexual energies. Erikson's "maturity" transcends Freud's final developmental stage, "genitality," occurring at puberty. Erikson understands development to continue throughout life as one deals with both bodily changes and changing cultural expectations that arise at different points in the human life span. The Erikson developmental paradigm may therefore be called *maturational* or *life span* development.

For example, a particular constellation of issues arise when our children are becoming more independent and our parents more dependent, and when our earlier strivings and successes begin to be judged against the inevitable decline of our physical capacities and the realization that our remaining years are few. These issues can be particularly intense for women, for whom biological rhythms, the culturally required tasks of raising children and caring for parents, and economic realities often collide.

Over the period of a few months, one Roman Catholic sister celebrated her fiftieth birthday, helped move her increasingly frail mother into a nursing home, participated in her mother's funeral a scant five weeks later, finished breaking up her mother's home, and herself moved from a community of six to a community of two, setting up housekeeping from scratch. All the while she was trying to tend to family and community dynamics and adjust to the hormonal changes of menopause. "I thought I was going to be exhausted forever," she commented.

Even if we did not completely deal with the issues of adolescence or young adulthood, midlife issues eventually appear on the horizon, despite our attempts to stave them off. Without the experience of being adequately parented or some chances to practice for parenting, for example, the arrival of one's first child forces the issues of intimacy and generativity. The outcome may be particularly problematic when developmental tasks must be handled out of the ordinary sequence, such as when a twelve-year-old becomes a parent before finishing the tasks of childhood, or when a person beginning the adolescent years faces a terminal illness.

A typical list of developmental tasks of adulthood, this one based on Robert Havighurst,[1] illumines the kind of expectations that our culture places upon us at various places in the life cycle.

Developmental Tasks of Early Adulthood
1. Selecting a mate and getting married
2. Learning to live with a marriage partner
3. Starting a family and rearing children
4. Beginning an occupation
5. Taking on civic responsibility
6. Finding a congenial social group

Developmental Tasks of Middle Age
1. Achieving mature social civic responsibility
2. Assisting teenage children to become responsible and happy adults
3. Reaching and maintaining satisfactory performance in a career
4. Accepting and adjusting to the physiological changes of middle age
5. Adapting to aging parents
6. Developing adult leisure-time activities

Developmental Tasks of Late Adulthood
1. Adjusting to decreasing physical strength and health
2. Adjusting to retirement and reduced income
3. Adjusting to the death of one's spouse

4. Establishing satisfactory physical living arrangements
5. Becoming explicitly affiliated with the late adulthood age group
6. Preparing for one's own death

For most people, the concept of development usually connotes precisely these kinds of issues and tasks.

Developmentalists now recognize the developmental possibilities of the entire life span. Most also recognize that development is multifaceted and cannot be sufficiently understood if an individual is viewed apart from his or her setting, including family, economic status, class, education, work, religion, neighborhood, urban or rural environment, and national government—indeed, the entire complex of dynamic realities we call culture. Yet the power and pervasiveness that the life span paradigm has attained in our culture makes the person who is "out of order" either invisible or painfully visible. The working grandmother who suddenly finds it necessary to raise her grandchildren does not easily fit into the systems designed to help single mothers a generation younger than she. This volume, particularly the chapter by Judith Orr, examines how women may and, in particular, may *not* fit into this general life span developmental plan or into particular developmental concepts. When a person does not fit the common progression, pastors and other caregivers must work harder to notice and validate the unique person and her developmental issues.

Erikson posited a significant role in human development for gender. Although he moved beyond Freud, his resulting theory, consistent with his threefold understanding of the factors that converge in a life crisis, shows its biological grounding nonetheless. Instead of focusing negatively on the presumed penis envy of women, as did Freud, Erikson developed a constructive view that women are aware of having inner space, the womb from which human life emerges. Rather than the derogatory "not male," this endowment entitles women to claim a positive identity of their own. In Erikson's observations, boys' interests usually indicate action, obtrusiveness, and even violence; girls' scenes communicate an interiority, protectiveness, and inclusiveness.[2] Erikson reached this conclusion through many experiments and analyses of children's play and thought it was misunderstood by feminists, who, for obvious political reasons, did not want to see another brick added to the "biology is destiny" pile, even if the brick were contributed by someone who interpreted positively woman's physical body as the ground of her psychology. Erikson could not yet see the radicality of his own theory well enough to be able to question the degree to which cultural assumptions about gender might have already conditioned girls to respond in gendered ways, though he understood that all cultures communicate gender expectations even before the child is born. Nor was he able completely to stand outside his own assumptions about gender and the ways they might have governed what he looked for, what he saw, and how he interpreted it.

We see the particular contribution Erikson-based theories make to our understanding of personality development when we focus on how we resolve life's inevitable demands and tasks. But the life span developmental paradigm has a limitation, too: it has difficulty accounting for the sameness of the individual personality in the face of constant change, both biological and social. Why is it that we do not either disintegrate or metamorphose into different personalities as one developmental crisis after another confronts us?

Structural Developmental Theories

A second developmental paradigm, structural development, offers a way to deal with this problem. We begin describing it by sketching several imaginary women, each at the point of bearing her first child. The age of these women varies a bit, as do some of their other socioeconomic and situational characteristics. For the moment, we shall overlook these variations.

Debbi, talking to a social worker, confides: "I gotta get me an apartment. When the baby comes, I can't keep living with my friends. My mom drinks, so it's no good going there. I got nobody to take care of the kid, so I gotta stay home from school. You know any day care? I got no money for extras, just my welfare check, so it'd hafta be subsidized. I'm going to the free clinic right now, and they said they would show me about formula and that kind of stuff. I really want to be a good mom, better than my mom was for me. Partying maybe, but no drinking. I ain't goin' to hit my kid like my mom hit me. This kid is goin' to be clean and dry. When she grows up, she won't mouth off at other people like I did and get in so much trouble at school."

Ann, meeting with old girlfriends from her church youth group, muses: "Tom doesn't want me to work after the baby comes, and that's just fine with me. We really want to do this right, like, in the Lord's will. So we've been reading the Scriptures and praying about being parents already. Tom's definitely going to be a good father and the head of the family. He's going to be the one who sets the rules. That way the kids won't be able to use one of us against the other. My mother gave me this really neat book about Christian parenting. I've already learned so much. Things I never really thought much about until now, but I can really see how important it is to do it right from the start. You know, about discipline and family prayer and God's plan for the family in Scripture, and everything. Raising a family is the most important thing I can do as a woman, so I want to do it right. So does Tom."

Roberta, newly graduated from business school, over coffee with one of her former classmates, confides: "You know, I never thought I would feel like this. I thought I was getting pregnant just because my biological clock is ticking, and I was getting to the 'now or never' stage. But, it's really made me think. Am I going to be able to take care of somebody else twenty-four hours of the day, seven days a week? What will it do to the child, and to me, and to my relationship with my husband when I go back to work? Will I even want to go back to work? I don't know, but I've sure been thinking a lot and finding whole new parts to myself that I didn't know were there. I think this kid will be teaching me things that I can't even imagine yet."

Sheila, a social worker, talks with her colleagues: "I want to take time off for this child, but another part of me is really pumped to keep working. I look at all these other women who don't have a clue what to do, where to go, who have no support system, and I keep seeing one face after another. I already love this child; it's amazing how you can bond with it even though you're only five months along. But they love their kids, too. The way this system is set up, I'm going to make it, *we're* going to make it, but I just can't see how many of them will. When they've used up their lifetime benefits, where will they be? We all know there just aren't enough jobs for them, even if they all could or should work. I am beginning to think I am in the wrong business. Politics—I hate the thought—is where it's at if you want to change something more than one woman's situation at a time. If enough people like us were in politics, maybe we could change the whole damn system. Anyhow, I've been thinking even more than I usually do about all the rest of the women and their kids."

Four women, each one looking forward to the birth of her first child. The similarities stop there. Their preoccupations around motherhood vary widely. The scope of their understanding of the new responsibilities they will be incurring varies just as widely. Yet all of them, whether they are ready for it or not, are entering the period of human development that Erik Erikson calls "generativity."[3] Debbi, one guesses, has barely left her own childhood chronologically and may never have gained the virtues of Erikson's earlier stages. Sheila, on the other hand, finds approaching motherhood calls her attention beyond her own situation to the structures that work unfairly against some and leaves her wanting to make the world safer and more predictable for other women's children as well as her own.

Jean Piaget first gave us the tools to understand that the kind of variation these women exhibit could have a developmental basis. But here "development" has a very different connotation from Erikson's model. Piaget carefully observed how small children approach and solve problems and began to notice and then trace patterns in their developing ability to think. His "genetic epistemology" eventually revealed an orderly progression in the development of the complexity of thinking processes. This development begins with infancy, characterized by sensorimotor thinking, is followed by preoperational or intuitive thinking in early childhood, concrete operational thinking around elementary school age, and finally formal operational thinking, usually attained during secondary school years. Piaget called each of these degrees of epistemological complexity a "stage." They are achieved in invariant order, from simple to complex, and no stage can be skipped. But once a stage has been mastered, the individual can employ any of the simpler epistemologies, should the situation warrant. Each stage, Piaget stressed, is qualitatively more complex than its predecessor. Consequently, successive stages cannot be achieved simply by repeating the earlier pattern but only through the application of a whole new principle of operation. The development of the neurological substratum of these more complex ways of thinking forms necessary but not sufficient conditions for the employment of the new, more complex thinking strategy.[4]

Let me illustrate from my own experience. As a ninth-grader, I had great difficulty with algebra. Substituting letters where before I had used numbers created a level of abstraction that confounded me. I could do the operations arithmetically, but as soon as I had to replace the numbers with letters and generalize the patterns, I was stymied. Formal operational thinking, the ability to think about the process of thinking, requires us to step outside the literal one-to-one correspondence between a number and an object. But I was reduced to memorizing the ways the operations worked and repeating the pattern every time I wanted to solve a problem. I now recognize that, at fourteen, my ability for formal operational thinking was insufficiently developed to accommodate the level of abstraction algebra required.

Lawrence Kohlberg took Piaget's system and investigated its application to the development of moral reasoning, and in so doing, opened the way for other cognitive structural theories. Soon, the structural pattern broadened from cognitive development into other personality domains. Although less restricted to cognitive functions, these newer theories still followed, with more or less rigor, the pattern traceable to Piaget, namely structural wholeness, invariant sequence, and generalizability across individuals and cultures. Because these theories deal with the organization, style, or inner logic of thinking (or of personality more generally), they can be called *structural* theories.

William Perry, director of the Harvard University Bureau of Study Counsel, investigated the question, "Is there during the college years any fundamental evolution of intellectual process comparable to the childhood stages described by Piaget?"[5] Perry found that there was indeed a comparable evolution in thinking among college students, a finding that ran counter to the received wisdom of the time, which held that maturing intellectual power was complete by the time a student entered college. Perry's work illustrates another important point in developmental research, so obvious after the fact that it seems trivial to us: the research method greatly influences, even determines, the results attained. Rather than dispense questionnaires, as his predecessors had done, Perry and his research associates engaged in conversations held annually over the course of a student's college years. These interviews typically began with the question: "Would you like to say what has stood out for you during the year?" After the students' general statement, they were then asked: "As you speak of that, do any particular instances come to mind?"[6] Their open-ended questioning and attentive listening elicited stories about what mattered to the students and, significantly, how the students themselves understood their lives to be unfolding. In her later study, Carol Gilligan[7] also asserted the importance of research method in the data generated. Among other groups, Gilligan talked to women between the ages of fifteen and thirty-three, diverse in ethnic background and social class, single and married, all of whom were in the throes of deciding whether to have an abortion. Real dilemmas faced by real women revealed a very different kind of moral assessment than did Lawrence Kohlberg's circumscribed choice in a hypothetical dilemma.

As Perry and his associates analyzed the stories offered to them over four years, these stories revealed several stages in the students' thinking. They moved from an initial epistemological strategy described as dualistic, through an uncomfortable and usually brief period of complete relativity to commitments and choices within an inevitably relative world. Only from this latter position, Perry believed, is the student able to understand that knowledge is constructed rather than given, contextual rather than absolute, and mutable rather than fixed. Only then can personal identity and commitment evolve with enough depth to carry one through the vicissitudes of contemporary life.[8] Perry's stages followed the general pattern of Piaget's stages. Their order was invariant, no stage could be skipped, and the pattern seemed generalizable to other people in similar learning situations. Perry's research indicated, however, that an individual could pause for some time at a stage, as if gathering strength for the next epistemological move. We can also turn away from increasing complexity and retreat into an earlier simplicity. To do so once the issues of complexity have been grasped, however, takes consistent and significant psychological energy to maintain the regression. In Perry's sample, undergraduate students engaged in liberal arts education, those students who retreated into simplicity could not tolerate the pluralism and complexity of student life in such rich and competitive contexts as Harvard and Radcliffe. After demonstrating increasing frustration, they dropped out, presumably for a simpler epistemological world.[9] The number of women in Perry's sample, however, was insufficient to test his theory with respect to gender.

Jane Loevinger[10] offers an example of a theory in the Piagetian paradigm that was developed through research involving primarily women and girls. She traced a domain she called "ego," which she understood to be that to which one refers when using of oneself the terms "I," "me," and "myself" (she refers to her stages as I-levels). For Loevinger, a stage is a "frame of reference," a kind of horizon within which one makes sense of one's world. It is revealed indirectly by the totality of one's level of impulse control, interpersonal style, conscious preoccupations, and cognitive style. Loevinger claimed that ego development includes moral development and that it provides a framework within which to understand moral development more inclusive and powerful than either Lawrence Kohlberg[11] or James Fowler[12] has provided. Her rich, impressionistic but reproducible results, gleaned from an open-ended, sentence-completion test, cannot be simply summarized. Briefly ego development follows this progression:

I-1: Symbiotic. This level is preverbal, inaccessible to Loevinger's methods of testing, so she described it only in very general terms: symbiotic interpersonal style preoccupied with self versus nonself.

I-2: Presocial. A person at this stage is impulsive; fears retaliation; is dependent, exploitative, and preoccupied with bodily feelings, especially sexual and aggressive ones; and thinks in conceptually simple and confused ways using many stereotypes. This developmental progression is normal for very young children, but a few adults might still frame reality in this way. Those who remain in this stage long past the age where society will tolerate it are often (and in U.S. society increasingly) found in mental hospitals or prisons.

Delta (a transitional level between I-2 and I-3). A person at this level characteristically operates opportunistically; fears being caught; externalizes blame; exhibits a wary, manipulative, exploitative interpersonal style; is preoccupied with self-protection, trouble, wishes, things, advantage, and control. Many adolescents still show these characteristics, although these development manifestations are age appropriate for younger school-age children. Debbi, herself an adolescent, manifests characteristics of this developmental position.

I-3: Conformist. This stage is characterized by conformity to external rules, shame, and guilt for breaking rules. A person at the conformist stage exhibits an interpersonal style characterized by belonging and superficial niceness; is preoccupied by appearance, social acceptability, banal feelings, and behavior; and thinks with conceptual simplicity, stereotypes, and cliches. Ann defines herself by her religious-cultural image of a good mother; another woman in a different setting that offers different images of mothering will define herself according to her setting's images. Adolescence is the age appropriate time for this developmental stage, although many adults remain here indefinitely, perhaps their entire life.

I-4: Conscientious. Here the locus of authority has moved "inside," and the person exhibits self-evaluated standards, self-criticism, guilt for consequences, long-term goals and ideals. Interpersonal style shows intensive, responsible, mutual concern for communication. Conscious preoccupations include differentiated feelings, motives for behavior, self-respect, achievements, traits, and expression. Conceptually, these people exhibit greater complexity and generate patterned thinking. Roberta's pregnancy is precipitating a good bit of inner work in the manner suggested by this stage.

I-5: Autonomous. A person at this stage maintains all the characteristics of the conscientious stage but adds the ability to cope with conflicting inner needs, toleration, respect for autonomy of self and others, and interdependence. A person at this stage typically conveys vivid feelings, understands the interrelationship of the physiological and the psychological causes of behavior, conceives of roles as distinct from people, and is preoccupied by self-fulfillment and self in social context. This stage is rare before midlife and might not be achieved at all.

Sheila's awareness of the ambiguities and contrasts between herself and some of the women she is working with suggests that she may be heading into this stage.

I-6: Integrated. The research population is very small. Loevinger is reticent to describe the stage. It maintains all the complexity of the autonomous stage but includes the ability to reconcile inner conflicts and to renounce the unattainable. Integrated people cherish individuality and are clear about identity.[13]

These brief sketches do not do justice to the rich detail gleaned from analyzing hundreds of sentence-completion tests, as Loevinger and her colleagues do in the volume that describes the evolution, construction, and use of their testing instrument.[14] Besides her exposition of the developmental vicissitudes of the lives of women and girls, Loevinger contributes a number of significant generalizations about structural theories in general.

Although the following principles are my own formulation derived from a synthesis of a variety of structural theories,[15] they are rooted in Loevinger's theory of ego development and, behind her theory, in Piaget's genetic epistemology.

1. Structural development highlights the formal ordering principles of personality and the way these principles function to organize a coherent outlook on the world. By definition, structural theories deal with abstractions and must resort to a metalanguage to describe the patterns, styles, and principles out of which we act. Maturational theories, on the other hand, tend to describe actions themselves, and therefore can vividly depict familiar and concrete matters.

2. One's ordering system supplies operative assumptions but is itself rarely available for conscious reflection because one looks at the world from within its perspective. The ordering system acts as an unperceived horizon that defines what we see and how we fit these pieces together into a coherent whole. Especially at earlier stages, however, this horizon is entirely self-evident and tacit, seen only when another horizon replaces it. The woman who was quoted at the beginning of this chapter saying, "I can't believe that I used to accept what I was told—like I had no mind of my own. Now I question everything," illustrates the ability to recognize our developmental progression in hindsight.

3. Stages describe qualitatively different styles of viewing reality. Simply summing up prior stages cannot create new stages, but each stage requires an entirely new ordering axiom to account for the new configuration. By itself, more arithmetic did not produce algebra in my concrete-operational mind. Instead, I needed to develop a qualitatively new ability for abstract thinking that could account for both the arithmetic and algebraic operations.

4. The movement to a subsequent stage requires a "higher order of ordering" to account for the increased complexity. Therefore, the stages appear in invariant order from simple to complex. Stages cannot be skipped, but people can understand and use any of the simpler ordering systems they have already transcended. Indeed, in some situations, simpler systems provide the more elegant and commonsense solution.

5. Research shows that people can understand the complexity of a stage that is a half to a whole stage ahead of where they are, but they will reframe any greater complexity in terms of their present stage. Teachers and preachers are familiar with the experience of receiving back from their listeners something less nuanced than what the teacher or preacher originally offered. Television increasingly offers news in the form of sound bites, simplistic reductions of complex situations into short, uncomplicated statements passing for reality. Successful political rhetoric takes this phenomenon into account and uses it for its own purposes.

6. Stage progression is a dialectical movement, with each stage transforming the prior stage and preparing for the next one. Loevinger's more complex stages, above conscientious, do not represent this qualitative difference with as much logical consistency as Kohlberg does his stages of moral reasoning. For this reason Kohlberg[16] calls Loevinger's stage theory "soft," and the logically rigorous Piagetian systems, "hard."

7. Stages are remarkably stable systems, because they represent entire systems of meaning-construction. Change takes place in such a stable structure only when the stage no longer accommodates the contrary data it must absorb. For example, high school students can be notoriously dualistic in their thinking, seeing complex realities in either/or categories, which they often express as "If I am right, you have to be wrong." Eventually, dualistic thinking tends to give way to more relative thinking ("You are entitled to your opinion and I am entitled to mine" is typical of early college years.) and, it is to be hoped, to a considered position within relativism ("You have a perspective very different from mine, and we might learn from each other."). Structural theories with their stable stages can account for the remarkable consistency within the human personality over time. They represent the negative feedback that any system needs to preserve it from flying apart in the face of an unchecked and accelerating pace of change, and they moderate the pace of change to a level the system can tolerate.

8. In a structural system, there is no theoretical necessity for change. Without sufficient dissonance to require a new structure, the person will not change stage. Therefore, stage change does not inevitably result from advancing age. In fact, substantial empirical data suggests that many adults do not change structural stages after their early twenties.

9. When stage change does occur, it is likely to be a protracted process. Not only does stage change take time, perhaps a long time, it is not at all inevitable without an appropriate developmental context. Because stage change in adults is relatively rare, permanent developmental equilibrium is quite possible, and a single transition over the entire period of adulthood is not out of the question. Therefore, though simplistic attempts to move people to more complex stages will most likely prove futile, developmentally sensitive environments can create a context that encourages stage change. We will explore this possibility below.

10. Because the stage at which a person levels off will quite likely provide the frame for a person's life outlook for a period of time, a stage also functions as a distinct personality style. In other words, some personality traits may be accounted for by one's developmental stage.

11. Real people, however, are far richer and more complex than a stage theory can reveal. Individuals regularly use a variety of meaning-systems in response to a variety of situations. Extremely stressful situations generally provoke a return to earlier meaning-system behaviors. Sometimes whole areas of personality may be sealed off from the rest of development and therefore elicit less complex responses. A stage is simply an abstract convention denoting the most complex meaning-system that a person uses consistently in the ordinary circumstances of life. Stage theories are, in fact, metaphors. As metaphors, they may be more or less helpful in explaining the mystery of the human person. A developmental theory, then, ought not be mistaken for the real person, nor the real person reduced to a stage or to a single theoretical perspective.

12. The entire context within which a person lives carries developmental significance. Certain predictable or unpredictable life tasks, such as leaving home or receiving a diagnosis of cancer, may provide a context for constructing a new meaning-system. Sometimes, however, a new system appears in the absence of obvious external causes, especially farther along the structural continuum. Some kind of conflict does precipitate, or at least accompany, developmental stage change, but the conflict may be interior, completely obscured to an outside observer. Conversely, a person might live in a highly conflictual system without any structural change. In some situations, in fact, it becomes far too costly for a person to continue to develop. In the case of a person who lives in a constantly chaotic, unpredictable, oppressive, or dangerous environment, a wary and self-protective stance is both developmentally predictable and environmentally adaptive. Individuals are not isolated automatons but live in complex systems of communities, all of which constantly exert developmental pulls or developmental constraints, both powerful and subtle.

Loevinger also issued some cautions to those who would use structural theories. Investigators almost always overestimate their own structural stage, assuming themselves to be more advanced than they actually test out to be. We also tend to overestimate the developmental stage of whole groups of people, assuming they act out of more complex epistemologies and meaning-systems than, in fact, they do. In Loevinger's research, the modal level for adults in this culture was between conformist and conscientious stages. Advertisers and journalists have grasped this reality better than teachers and preachers!

Several cautions particularly apply to those attending to pastoral care. The first concerns the ability of an individual to affect stage change in another. We often naively assume that our ministrations will bring about stage change, but, in fact, it is rare that they do so directly. We also overestimate the speed in which a stage change can occur. Short-term therapies, although they might be beneficial on many fronts, cannot be expected to be the occasion of stage change, though they may be one of the environmental factors that encourages a stage change. A more constructive posture with respect to stage change is to see each stage as having both strengths with respect to the earlier stages and limitations with respect to later stages, and try to capitalize on the strengths. Second, clergy and religious educators might unwittingly substitute the final stage of the developmental theories for the content of their faith tradition. The developmental theories address the human capacity to apprehend increasingly complex content but do not themselves supply that content. In religious traditions, that content concerns a life increasingly organized around the master narrative of the faith community as revealed through its privileged texts, the history of the community's life of faith and its ethical mandates for living in the world. Finally, the notion of conflict, so central to the structural theories, suggests that it might not always be useful or helpful to reduce conflict, fix things, or make people feel better. This strategy might remove all impetus to develop more complex ways of being in the world.

In 1986, Mary Belenky, Blythe Clinchy, Nancy Goldberger, and Jill Tarule published the results of their attempt to fill in the lacuna around the issue of gender left by William Perry's study of epistemological development. Perry's study, they recognized, was poorly designed to uncover those themes that might be more prominent among women. The other inspiration for their study was Carol Gilligan, who succeeded in bringing to general awareness the gender bias that unconsciously permeated the theory building of most developmentalists up to that time.[17] To begin to redress this bias, Belenky and her colleagues decided to listen only to women, but to talk to women in both formal and "invisible colleges." They went to classrooms of various kinds: a women's Ivy League college, a coeducational adult program serving a rural population widely diverse in social class, an inner-city community college serving a mixed ethnic and less advantaged student body, an innovative "early college" that provides a baccalaureate program after two years of high school, and an alternative urban high school serving students at risk for dropping out of school. The "invisible colleges" were family agencies that offer services and information about parenting. These agencies included one that works with rural teenagers by pairing them with mothers close to their own age, a network of self-help groups for parents working to overcome the effects of family violence, and a children's health program serving a rural population. They elected to follow Perry's phenomenological method, providing women with simple structures to talk about what seemed important to them. Each interview began with the question, "Looking back, what stands out for you over the past few years?" Then they let the interview unfold gradually, at each woman's own pace, moving to questions concerning self-image, important relationships, education and learning, real-life decisions and moral dilemmas, personal change and growth, perceived catalysts for change, impediments to growth, and visions of the future.[18]

After extensive and varied forms of analysis, the interviews were grouped into five epistemological categories:

> ... silence, a position in which women experience themselves as mindless and voiceless and subject to the whims of external authority; received knowledge, a perspective from which women conceive of themselves as capable of receiving, even reproducing, knowledge from all knowing external authorities but not capable of creating knowledge on their own; subjective knowledge, a perspective from which truth and knowledge are conceived of as personal, private, and subjectively known or intuited; procedural knowledge, a position in which women are invested in learning and applying objective procedures for obtaining and communicating knowledge; and constructed knowledge, a position in which women view all knowledge as contextual, experience themselves as creators of knowledge, and value both subjective and objective strategies for knowing.[19]

The research group was quite modest in its claims:

> We recognize (1) that these five ways of knowing are not necessarily fixed, exhaustive, or universal categories, (2) that they are abstract or "pure" categories that cannot adequately capture the complexities and uniqueness of an individual woman's thought and life, (3) that similar categories can be found in men's thinking, and (4) that other people might organize their observations differently. Furthermore, the small number of women in our sample who fell into the position of silence makes these observations particularly tentative and underscores the need for continued efforts to understand the developmental sequences of severe violence and social isolation. Our intention is to share not prove our observations.[20]

One wonders whether the position Belenky and her colleagues call "silence" in fact represents the massive failure of the ordinary human cultural and familial support systems to encourage the development of identity, agency, and voice. It appears to function similarly to Perry's "retreat."

This last judgment raises a difficult and unresolved issue: Does the study *Women's Ways of Knowing* in fact offer a developmental theory? Does one progress from one stage to another? If so, how? The authors did not claim that their findings constituted a developmental theory. They noted that interviewing individuals simply did not provide sufficient data to judge whether a given individual might progress from one epistemological style to another, and if so, under what conditions. Yet basing their work on William Perry's developmental theory and articulating the positions in relationship to one other (ranging from less to more adequate, or less to more flexible) seems to suggest a developmental theory. Women often respond to it as if it illumines a developmental continuum: "The book was wonderful. It was my life and the stages I have gone through and continue to go through. I thought I was the only person that felt the way the women in these interviews did."[21] The authors of the original study have continued to be reticent about the adequacy, maturity, and normativeness of their descriptions and the sequential arrangement, issues raised by developmental theories. As late as 1996, this issue remains unresolved.[22]

Accounting for Change

We now have several maps suggesting the direction of structural development, but how do we go about getting there? It is one thing to describe various meaning-systems; knowing them helps me understand the person in front of me and the balance she manifests in a given context and time. But it is another to understand how the qualitative shift required for a stage change actually occurs. The structural paradigm suggests that development is not automatic, that unless a stage fails to account for the complexity of the data it must accommodate, change will not happen. But can developmental theories move past describing stages to address movement itself? Of the structural theories, Piaget and Robert Kegan offer the most help in this regard. First, however, I will offer a metaphor for non-revolutionary, incremental change, which will also figure into our developing theory of structural change.

In 1965, William Dember published an article challenging the then-common assumption that the human organism seeks to reduce the tension caused by physiological need-states. Dember's research indicated that humans are motivated, at least in part, by complexity and novelty. That complexity must fall in a subjectively judged range, however, one particular to each person in which the amount of complexity is neither too much nor too little. When people are free to choose, they will select experiences within their preferred range of complexity and spend the greatest amount of time on stimuli just a little more complex than comfortable. Indeed, they will seek out such people, things, concepts, values, and relationships that become their own reward. Dember called any stimulus in this ideal range of complexity a "pacer." When summarizing Dember's work, Loevinger concluded that the pacer "appears to be the formula or model for non-revolutionary growth."[23]

Important pacers can include culture (including such socially determined markers as race, ethnicity, class, and gender), socioeconomic status, interpersonal relationships, and conscience. Cultures set expectations about appropriate behavior, which are internalized by the culture's participants as they are gradually initiated into it as adult members. In this way, cultures pace their members to an "average expectable level" of development. Cultures also punish those who "color outside the lines" of culturally acceptable or normative behavior. At this juncture of awareness of the cultural forces at work, structural theories critique the life span theories. Cultures do set expectations for age-appropriate developmental tasks, as the life span theories posit, but these expectations also become unconscious norms internalized by the majority of people, who to the extent that they are conformists are paced at this level of complexity to carry out these tasks.

To move beyond the average expectable level of development requires a pacer cogent enough to counteract the historical-cultural forces working to keep people in step with the reigning system. Within our culture, for example, shifting gender expectations are creating widespread confusion about how men and women are "supposed" to behave. The rising consciousness that women are people in their own right, not merely appendages of significant males, raises a new set of expectations for both women and men, a complexity that can invite both to stretch for more inclusive ways of understanding gender relationships. The unstated (though increasingly stated) rules about appropriate interchange between women and men in the workplace have changed drastically, and those who have not observed the shifts sometimes find out the hard way through a complaint or lawsuit that they are out of step. It is accurate, however, to say that no developmental theory, structural or maturational, has successfully accounted for the interdependent and dynamic relationships among race, class, ethnicity, and gender simultaneously. In fact, none has been able satisfactorily to account for race or class investigated as independent variables.[24]

Interpersonal relationships provide a crucial matrix for pacing ego development. The power exercised by a teacher, mentor, therapist, friend, spouse, spiritual director, or pastor—indeed, the entire network of primary relationships—both to challenge one's assumptions about reality and one's place in it and to support the tentative steps toward greater complexity can be extremely important factors in structural development. (It is equally possible, of course, that these same primary relationships invite one to "settle in" or retreat; they can just as easily thwart development as enhance it.) The notion of pacer provides, I believe, an extremely effective metaphor to guide a variety of caring actions. Coming alongside another, understanding where she is, helping her to notice her deep hungers as well as her needs and to take the next step for herself is the essence of care as understood by both the religious and therapeutic communities.

Just as external factors affect the possibilities and limits of structural development, so too do internal factors. Conscience figures prominently among these internal factors. Somewhat surprisingly for a developmental researcher, Jane Loevinger recognizes that the growth of conscience will, of necessity, be so intertwined with ego development that they constitute a single, complex sequence of events, and that the dynamic principles accounting for ego development overlap those accounting for conscience development. Yet she insists, the two concepts are not synonymous, and neither is superfluous, arising as they do from different realms of discourse.[25]

This datum about the human, that we are attracted to complexity, as long as it is within tolerable limits, provides us a way to understand the possibility of change happening at all within a system designed to preserve the structure (here, personality) from intolerable levels of change. Incremental change, change in such small steps that it appears not to disturb the structural stability that maintains the organism's organization, acts like a Trojan horse, sneaking many small changes into the structure until its stability is undermined. To ground this analogy in developmental terms, we can turn to several concepts from Piaget, namely equilibration, assimilation, accommodation, and décalage.

Piaget assumed that the personality's natural condition is a state of dynamic poise, which he called equilibration. This condition is by no means static psychic inaction. Piaget spoke of "mobile equilibrium," and Loevinger evoked the image of a gyroscope, which maintains its upright position only through continuous balanced movement.[26] A living organism is affected by everything that takes place in its environment. The organism takes each experience "inside," as it were, so that the experience becomes part of the organism's information about its environment. Piaget called this process "assimilation." Each experience also changes the organism, however, if ever so slightly. The organism must "expand" to accommodate this newly acquired information. Assimilation and accommodation are always partners. Most of the time we unconsciously absorb new data into our reigning and also largely unconscious assumptions about reality. In fact, research shows that we overlook or misperceive that which is too unexpected or for which we have no categories or language (part of the reason mainstream research has had so much difficulty even noticing the developmental effects of race, class, and gender). Each assimilation inevitably brings some accommodation along with it, however. After repeated accommodations, the original equilibration or "evolutionary truce," as Robert Kegan calls it,[27] cannot hold all the anomalies it has absorbed. It begins to unravel, and the stage gives way to a transition, that sometimes disorienting period between one equilibration and the next. Eventually, a more complex principle of equilibrium emerges, and the sense of chaos subsides in favor of a new and more complex view of "the way things are"—the next stage. This new evolutionary truce contains all the earlier data and its organizing principles, now subsumed into a more inclusive system.

In an earlier treatment of structural theories,[28] I developed an image to illustrate décalage and its effects. It still seems useful. Imagine, if you will, an expanse of tiered rice paddies constructed stepwise up a gently sloping riverbank. At the spring flood, rising water fills the lowest field. Initially, water spreads across the flat surface, soaking into the earth until it reaches the water table at the level of the river. When it has saturated all the ground at this level, the water again begins to rise, gradually reaching the top of the second embankment. As it tops the wall into the second field, the process of spreading out and soaking in occurs again, flooding the second tier. When it reaches the third embankment, the process repeats itself yet again. The lower paddies, of course, are still submerged, deeper than ever.

Piaget used the term décalage to point out that people can be at different stages at different moments or with respect to different issues.[29] When a new organization of meaning is achieved, one's earlier experience must be reworked in light of this more complex perspective, much like the newly flooded tier first absorbs water until the ground is saturated. Piaget called this recapitulation process *vertical* décalage. In addition, each new organization of meaning is at first confined to a relatively small domain, only gradually expanding to encompass more possible applications. Piaget called this gradual expansion of the system to encompass more experience *horizontal* décalage. In our metaphor, it compares to the gradual spread of the water all across one field before it rises to flood the next.

Through the concept of décalage, Piaget describes the gradual and fragmented process of moving from one stage of meaning-making to another and gives us another way to account for the slowness of the process. Décalage also provides important insights for those who wish to intervene in the development process. In terms of the rice field image, one cannot make the water breach the wall until it has completely saturated its present level. One could take a container and manually lift water into the next level, but the water will soak in and seemingly disappear without spreading out at its new level—until the prior level has been saturated. The implication: structural change cannot be *directly* caused; one may only pose more anomalies to the present system until the system "overflows" of its own accord. The concept of pacer reminds us, however, that the increments of complexity and change must occur within the individual's prescribed range of complexity. Too much complexity offered too quickly, and resistance closes off the possibility of further assimilation and accommodation. When the anomalies are taken into the system, though, their accompanying accommodations prepare the way for a stage change. Yet it will only occur if the anomalies have become persistent, have permeated too many parts of the meaning-system to be walled off and ignored, and have posed questions too deep to be dismissed as trivial. Even then, Perry makes us aware, the outcome is far from assured; stage change always demands a kind of moral courage. When describing the shift his subjects made from dualistic to relativistic thinking, Perry noted:

> Our records suggest that this development becomes a positive experience only where two processes run in parallel: (1) The confrontation with diversity occurs in ways which allow a person to moderate its impact by steplike assimilations and accommodations. . . . and (2) The analytical and synthetic skills of contextual thought are developed . . . to provide an alternative to helpless despair in a world devoid of certainty.[30]

But, says Perry, the community's substantive provision of worthwhile things to care about is not enough. Nor is the provision of an expectation that the student *will* care. The student finds his greatest sustenance, Perry is convinced, in a sense of community *in the risks of caring*.[31] Prophetically, Perry anticipates the recent work of Daloz, Keen, Keen, and Parks[32] by discussing the role of the educator (and, we can add, pastor, social worker, health care provider, parent, or any concerned person):

> The educator's effort would be, then, to increase the student's experience of recognition and confirmation as a member of the community by virtue of the

courage with which he undertakes the risks of care. The communication of this kind of recognition would seem to be both the highest and most profound of social arts.[33]

I will return to this prophetic statement shortly. Before I do, I want to offer several other metaphors that can contribute to our understanding of the laborious and risky undertaking constituting structural (stage) change. These metaphors are all from Robert Kegan.[34] The first, which he calls "a naturally therapeutic holding environment," focuses on the environment in which meaning-making takes place.

Unlike many structuralists, Kegan prefers to highlight the dynamic possibilities in stage conceptions. He recognizes that stages are actually balances; although they are relatively stable, they can "tip over" given the right conditions. In fact, most development actually occurs without much conscious intervention or even awareness on our part. Rather, it often appears to "just happen." Kegan called an environment that encourages structural stage change "naturally therapeutic."[35] He suspected that examining such environments could give us important clues about the dynamics of developmental change. These dynamics, in turn, might offer us a way to understand how complex social groups function to foster development, and indeed how parenting, curriculum building, ministry, and social policy making might collaborate with the naturally occurring developmental dynamic.

Kegan borrows a useful image, "holding environment," from D. W. Winnicott. He suggests we understand stages as matured in a holding environment, which he also calls a "culture of embeddedness." Here, Kegan intends "culture" to carry the connotation of a place provided with appropriate nutrients for the purpose of growing something, like the culture provided for bacteria in a petri dish. Kegan uses these two colorful images to describe the entire psychosocial environment in which personality develops. When holding environments perform three simultaneous and interdependent functions, they become effective as naturally therapeutic environments. First, such environments must recognize and confirm the person as an individual, surrounding her or him with a supportive and caring context. Second, they must foster continued development, encouraging a new level of interpersonal differentiation by providing sufficient disconfirmation to cause movement. Third, they must maintain continuity through this often stressful process of reintegrating one meaning-system into another more complex meaning-system; important figures must "stick around" to provide something solid around which the integration can occur. The chapter by Carolyn Bohler in this volume illumines the naturally therapeutic environments in the lives of the strong girls she interviewed.

For example, using the stage conception I developed earlier,[36] a person whose meaning-system functions at the conformist stage will be embedded in mutuality and in the web of interpersonal systems. A naturally therapeutic holding environment for conformity encourages mutually reciprocal one-to-one relationships. It confirms and acknowledges the capacity for collaborative self-sacrifice in mutuality. It encourages shared feelings. But eventually it should discourage the submersion of self within relationships. It should promote a self that will not be fused with, but still seeks and participates in, transformed relationships. It must gradually begin to demand that the person assume responsibility for his or her own initiatives and preferences. At the same time, the crucial interpersonal partners must remain in place, allowing the relationships to be reinterpreted in a larger context. If significant people, such as a spouse, parent, or pastor, leave or suddenly repudiate the relationship, the reassimilation of these relationships within the new meaning-system will be severely handicapped. When these important players remain constant, however, they encourage the struggle with new instances of complexity. They can act as mentors, cheering-squads, or foils. Over time, they may midwife a new developmental stage.

Each stage provides a different "culture of embeddedness." The confirmations and disconfirmations are stage-specific; that is, they will vary by stage. What constitutes a naturally therapeutic holding environment for the conscientious stage differs from the naturally therapeutic dynamics for the conformist stage. Therefore, knowing the characteristics of each stage encourages the appropriation of the developmentally appropriate elements in an environment. The randomly helpful becomes intentional in developmentally enhanced caring.

Kegan offers one more way to understand the process of structural developmental progression. Standing back from stage change, Kegan realized that each transition shared a common characteristic, namely the progression from being *subject to* or *embedded in* a perspective to standing *outside* that perspective and being able to look at it objectively. That is, one becomes increasingly differentiated from each holding environment in turn, only to be (at least temporarily) embedded in the successive holding environment.

Paradoxically, though stages mark successive differentiations of the self from the environment, they also signal increasing integration with the environment. This dynamic occurs as follows. The perspective within which one understands reality is itself rarely available for conscious reflection. We are aware of the results of our perspective, although we remain unconscious of the perspective that has led to these results. Precisely this embeddedness leads us to project that reality onto the world as our very constitution of reality. We assume "the world is like that." But from the vantage point of the next stage, the assumed reality of the former stage now can be approached more objectively. As Kegan says, referring to the move out of the stage we have been calling conformist, "I no longer *am* my relationships, I now *have* relationships."

At each successive differentiation from the environment, then, we can more accurately integrate the awareness into our own conception of "the way things are." Recognizing that differentiation and integration are two moments of a single psychological event corrects a long-standing and deeply entrenched assumption that differentiation alone serves as the sign and norm of development. This assumption has proven particularly problematic when assessing women's development.

To summarize: structural developmental theories provide a necessary counter-balance to the life span developmental theories. They invite us to think of development in more than one paradigm at once, allowing us a more adequate grasp of the mystery of the human person. They examine a domain different from the life span concepts of development, namely, our meaning-system. They suggest why development, at least of some aspects of personality, occurs slowly, if at all. But the very life-cycle crises of "women out of order," such as those explored in this volume, can be, if recognized and tended, opportune moments for reorganizing our meaning-making capacity in a way more effective for our changed situation. In a sufficiently confirming and consistent context, each life-cycle crisis, be it in or out of order, serves as a crucible in which the contradiction inherent in the crisis becomes the invitation to deal with reality in more complex, inclusive, and integrating ways. As we saw with Debbi, Ann, Roberta, and Sheila, the same life-cycle tasks will be experienced differently by persons at different structural stages. Whether or not structural development occurs depends, at least in part, on the presence of the naturally therapeutic dynamics within the individual's preferred range of complexity.

Structural theories recognize the value of stability to personality organization, and respect this stabilizing function. Although they have tended to focus on describing stages, summarizing the concepts about structural stage change gleaned from various theorists does provide a picture of the process of change even within the relatively stable personality structure. They can suggest the modest yet crucial ways that individuals may participate in fostering increasingly complex meaning-systems, so practitioners of all types can concentrate their interventions where they might contribute most to the developing personality. Finally, they give us another way to look at the effects of culture and other pacers on the individuals who live simultaneously in many systems. It is to this point that we now turn.

Lives of Commitment in a Complex World

In the early eighties, I was doing the research on my dissertation, which involved investigating spiritual direction and discernment through the lens of developmental psychology. I found myself reading many of the developmentalists considered above. Through the years, I have continued to follow their work. All who are still actively producing scholarly work have, without exception, moved away from focusing on the individual person. They have all begun to examine the complex interrelationship between individual development and the communities in which the individuals live.[37] Once they had grasped this important facet of human development, it seems, they moved to questions such as, "So what? What difference will our contemporary times make in human development? What will these years require developmentally if we are successfully to negotiate the challenges facing us at the turn of the millennium?"

In his book *In Over Our Heads: The Mental Demands of Modern Life*,[38] Robert Kegan sets out to look at the "curriculum" of contemporary life in relation to the capacities of the adult mind. He wonders just what our culture demands of us and how we might, in fact, rise to the challenge. How can we make some developmental sense of our cultural predicament? He argues that we unknowingly expect the contemporary teenager to develop the order of consciousness required to participate in a traditional world. Furthermore, our current culture requires of adults a qualitative transformation of mind every bit as fundamental as the transformation from magical thinking to concrete thinking required of the school-age child, or the transformation from concrete to abstract thinking required of the adolescent. We just as unknowingly expect of adults a cognitive threshold open to modernity. But we now live in a world still more complex, often described by the term "postmodernity," and the expectations of postmodernity again require a qualitatively more complex order of consciousness.[39] For at least parts of our lives, there exists an inevitable mismatch between the complexity of the culture's curriculum and our capacity to grasp it.

Daloz, Keen, Keen, and Parks face this dilemma squarely:

> Most of us do not do a lot of thinking about thinking. Usually the work of our mind rumbles along without too much thought of itself. Inescapably, however, whether we are washing the dishes, pounding nails, or surfing a torrent of television commercials, our minds are active. Consciously or not, the human mind is continually composing patterns of order and significance from the myriad encounters, images, words, feelings, objects, smells, dilemmas, and surprises of every day. Consciously or not, the human organism is always organizing meaning.
>
> Meaning does not exist by itself; we create it. A tree may flourish apart from us, but the meaning of that tree does not. Whether we see it as a source of shade, a complex biological system, inspiration for a poem, or as a provider of match sticks, depends in large measure on who we are. Each of us constructs the meaning of that tree differently. In that sense, we are inveterate meaning-makers.
>
> But the conditions of contemporary life assault our meaning-making capacity. The diversity of viewpoints and the complexity of contemporary conditions create an ambivalence that gnaws at the edges of our consciousness, eroding our conviction. Familiar ways of thinking no longer work. We try to understand, to make judgments, even to act. But when we do, . . . we find ourselves confronted by a maze of experts, explanations, and countervailing evidence. Faced by competing perspectives and partial knowledge, we hesitate. We often feel removed from the roots of things and barred from the power to change them.[40]

Recall Perry's foresighted concern, written thirty years ago, about the risks of care, the necessity to create communities of care. How can we, in this increasingly complex world, create effective communities of care where children, women, and men of various races, religions, political convictions, classes, and cultures can peacefully and constructively live together? What kind of human communities will provide us with the conditions of human development sufficient for the challenges of the twenty-first century?

Traditional gathering places, which served in the past to create communities of care, have been transformed almost beyond recognition. Neighborhoods where everyone knew several generations of everyone else's family have yielded in large part to suburbs where neighbors never talk or condominiums where the association impersonally enforces the covenant. Churches are increasingly empty, but individual psychotherapy is flourishing. Family meals have been replaced by restaurants and drive-through fast food. Ball parks have been replaced by video arcades, grange halls and general stores by immense malls, and town meetings by chat groups on the Internet.

Daloz, Keen, Keen, and Parks weave a metaphor for a new kind of gathering place:

> The new commons is global in scope, diverse in character, and dauntingly complex. A radically interdependent world economy has dissolved old boundaries, loosed waves of migrant labor, triggered smoldering cultural conflicts, and forced profound social and political reorganization at all levels. We are simultaneously fragmented into loose and shifting associations of individuals, interest groups, and tribes, yet drawn more closely into a larger web of life.[41]

What capacities might we seek in order to prepare ourselves to participate in the new commons? For a first answer to this question, let us look at uncommon people from the middle of this century, people who risked their lives to save Jews from the Holocaust. In a study of such people, Douglas Huneke isolated seven characteristics.[42]

1. Empathic imagination, the ability to place oneself in the actual situation or role of another person and to imagine the effect and the long-term consequences of the situation or role. This skill can be practiced by even very young children; certainly anyone capable of concrete-operational thinking can be invited to engage in it.

2. The ability to present oneself and take control of critical situations. The primary subject of Huneke's study, Fritz Grabe, began to learn this lesson early. His mother would frequently ask him, "Fritz, what would you do?" as they discussed a critical moment in another person's life.

3. Previewing for a purposeful life, which consists of two subtraits, being proactive and prosocial. The significant adults who surround young children can model these traits for them. The traits can be practiced at developmentally appropriate levels by planning to act in cooperative and responsible ways, by anticipating opportunities for having a positive and beneficial impact in the lives or circumstances of others, and by actively promoting the well-being of others as well as oneself.

4. Significant personal experiences with suffering and death prior to the war. Though we do not plan for death, when it does occur, we can help children and youth be present to it in such a way that they are not paralyzed by it.

5. The ability to confront and manage one's prejudices. This ability requires self-observation and motive for change. It can be modeled, but doing it oneself requires the development of interiority. One is developmentally equipped for this kind of self-reflection only as one moves out of conformity. This level of self-awareness is difficult to come by and will more likely be achieved when communities work together to set a climate that encourages prejudicial behavior to be discarded.

6. The development of a community of compassion and support. Complex and dangerous acts of rescue were seldom carried out alone, and rescuers assembled networks of people who both collaborated in the rescues at their own personal risk and sustained the rescuers through times of extreme stress, fatigue, and depression. The likelihood of remaining in the fray is significantly enhanced when shared in community.

7. The ability to offer hospitality. Again, this trait can be modeled in a child's earliest years by the significant people in the child's life. Those who model the trait communicate that it is normal to bring a variety of people into the family circle, where they no longer seem strange or other.[43]

Daloz, Keen, Keen, and Parks sought out and interviewed a wide variety of people whose lives seemed to be motivated by some form of the question, "How can we be part of creating a more inclusive 'common' good?"[44] Their chapter headings summarize their findings: "Community: Becoming at Home in the World," "Compassion: Living within and beyond Tribe," "Conviction: Developing Critical Habits of Mind," "Courage: A Responsible Imagination," "Confession: The Struggle with Fallibility," and "Commitment: The Power of the Double Negative" ("I cannot *not* do it."). As Daloz and his colleagues unfold these chapters, they bear a striking resemblance to the characteristics of rescuers as uncovered by Huneke. These characteristics also have a structural developmental substrate. For example, in the chapter "Conviction: Developing Critical Habits of Mind," Daloz and colleagues speak of six "habits of mind":

- the habit of dialogue, grounded in the understanding that meaning is constructed through an ongoing interaction between oneself and others;
- the habit of interpersonal perspective-taking, the ability to see through the eyes and respond to the feelings and concerns of the other;
- the habit of critical, systemic thought, the capacity to identify parts, connections among them as coherent patterns and to reflect evaluatively on them;
- the habit of dialectical thought, the ability to recognize and work effectively with contradictions by resisting closure or by reframing one's response;
- the habit of holistic thought, the ability to intuit life as an interconnected whole in a way that leads to practical wisdom.[45]

As Daloz, Keen, Keen, and Parks rightly point out, these practices are closely interrelated and developmentally sequential. Previous habits undergird each successive habit. As each evolves, the preceding ones are integrated but not lost. Furthermore, these habits and their precursors are extremely effective in fostering the structural development with which we have been concerned in this essay. They also indicate the kinds of human virtues we will need for the twenty-first century. Our ever smaller and interdependent world requires such virtues if we are to live side by side with others very different from ourselves.

These virtues are not just "women's virtues," they are human virtues. The actions they engender, however, will disproportionately affect women, children, and any people distanced from the centers of power, either bettering the environments in which they live or, by their lack or misuse, leaving many in increasingly precarious situations. Thankfully, these virtues can be modeled and practiced in one-to-one exchanges and in institutional settings as varied as families, day-care centers, health care programs and agencies, even corporations. Women can learn and teach them. Women can articulate the deeply human and spiritual values that will enhance their life's direction. As these virtues are combined with the life span developmental virtues Erikson highlighted a half century ago, we will be better equipped to make the world safer for all women and their children.

Socioeconomic Class and the Life Span Development of Women

Judith Orr

The theories of Sigmund Freud, Erik Erikson, and Lawrence Kohlberg may explain Western male psychosexual, psychosocial, and moral development, respectively, but they do not explain all human development.[1] At least since the nineteenth century, development has been a central organizing concept in the social sciences. Developmental psychology in particular has captured our interest as we seek to describe, explain, modify, optimize, and determine the meaning and goal of human behavior. Life span developmental theory considers these tasks from the beginning of human life to the end, from birth to death. The prevailing theories of Freud, Erikson, Kohlberg, et al., which describe universal, invariant hierarchical developmental stages, however, have been called into question in recent years.

The normativeness of the male perspective in cultures marked by unequal power relations according to gender has been exposed and critiqued in the past several decades. Taking on this task, feminist developmental theorists Nancy Chodorow and Carol Gilligan proposed that men and women simply develop differently. Yet the use of object relations theory by Chodorow presumes full-time mothering, the nuclear family, and heterosexuality but does not distinguish differing caregiving relations among women of color, lesbians, and working-class women.[2] Gilligan interviewed an admittedly advantaged population of college-age women seeking abortions in her study of moral development—quite different from the life context and decision-making processes of unmarried factory workers with several children also considering abortion.[3] These contextual critiques encourage us to ask how growth and development might best be understood in light of socioeconomic realities. Having grown up in a respectable white, working-class neighborhood,[4] I still remember the feeling associated with not fitting the time-appropriate stage when I first read the developmental theories of Erikson, Kohlberg, and Gilligan. I wondered whether stage theory really portrayed the developmental truth regarding all human beings and whether socioeconomic context influenced development. I wondered whether women of the working class develop differently from women of the middle class, and if so, how? Those questions are taken up here.

Socioeconomic class has been variously defined. Some say that class is self-designated, that people belong to the class they say they do. Others suggest that class is a series of positions on a socioeconomic hierarchy determined by occupation, education, or income. Class is not so much a slot or position, however, as it is a network of social relations of control (or lack of control) over investments and wealth, others' work, one's own work, and consequently reproduction, decision making, and consumption of goods and services as these are influenced by economics. Thus, class is not a place but a process of both situational and historical power relations, which includes the unequal distribution of rights and privileges, duties and obligations in the economic sector.

The working class is expected to take orders rather than give orders and to give deference rather than receive deference.[5] The class includes the blue-collar industrial and trades workers, white-collar clerical workers, and pink-collar service workers who earn wages. On the other hand, the middle class includes professionals as well as the managers who take orders from and give deference to corporate owners above them but also control the work of laborers beneath them. Those in the middle class generally have more education (a college degree), earn more money (receive a salary), and have a wider range of responsibility and decision-making authority about the work and life of others than those in the working class do.

Rather than stage theory, this chapter will use the insights of dialectic developmental theory.[6] The focus is on the dialectical interaction of individual and society; on the influence of biology, environment, and history; and on the self's creative ability to use available resources to negotiate adaptive responses—either progressive or resistive—to life's turning points and conflicts. These conflicts are rooted in unequal distribution of power and the effects such inequalities engender. Adaptive developmental responses are conscious or unconscious attempts to overcome these inequalities. Development, therefore, is the acquiring of various competencies (cognitive, affective, behavioral, motivational, communicational, social) needed for specific race, gender, class, and cultural contexts.[7] Such developmental work presumes the need for change and envisions a reordering of relationships toward the mutual respect that makes true community possible. In such a schema, God is willing to change the world through conflict and adaptive responses and willing to provide rest for all from their labors.

This chapter presents the results of conversations with twenty adult women between the ages of twenty-three and eighty from Kansas City in the U.S. heartland. Because the primary intent was to hear working-class women's stories that might provide patterns and themes for further exploration regarding this less well-known group, fifteen of the women were from the working class. Five middle-class women were also interviewed to suggest class comparisons for further exploration.[8]

The chapter proposes that although there are some cross-class similarities in life span development among women, the unique context, timing, and meaning of events in working-class women's lives make their life span development unique.

Although even the simplest societies distinguish among childhood, adulthood, and old age, this chapter will consider five phases across the life span in the late twentieth and early twenty-first centuries: childhood, adolescence, young adulthood, middle adulthood, and older adulthood. Themes associated with each phase will be developed.[9]

Childhood (Ages Birth to Twelve)

From the time of birth, children develop a particular perspective on reality. According to Minuchin and Fishman the adult-child family subsystem is where the child learns a sense of relative adequacy, what to expect from people with greater resources and strength, whether authority is rational or arbitrary, whether her needs are supported, how to communicate what she wants, what behaviors are rewarded or discouraged, and how to deal with conflict and negotiation.[10] The sibling subsystem is where she learns how to negotiate, cooperate, and compete, make friends and deal with enemies, learn from others, achieve recognition, and belong to a group and make choices. In many cultures mid-childhood (especially ages five to seven) is the time when concrete operational thinking, social productivity, and a sense of competence through achievement begin to develop.[11] From the beginning the child is learning the essentials of surviving and living among those on whom she is dependent and with whom she is a peer.

A woman's development is influenced not only by family (both nuclear and extended), but also by culture and society at large. For example, among the lower working class in particular, poverty means unpredictability. Even if parents have stable employment, it is not assumed to be permanent nor is it taken for granted. In the midst of such uncertainty, childhood can be more worrisome and less carefree for working-class children than for middle-class children. When asked whether they had particular worries as a child, the Kansas City women raised in middle-class homes often reported that they did not. If they did worry, it was often about falling short as an individual—for example, not excelling or being too unattractive to men. Women raised in working-class families had some of these worries, but many worries were related to their network of relationships—an alcoholic parent, whether the family would have enough food at the end of the month, not getting into trouble, keeping the peace, family fighting, joining in and fitting in at school, lack of money and clothes, a sick grandmother who was all this child had. Some women did not recall particular worries, though they remember childhood was bad. Some of those interviewed said they were poor, but that was not too much of a worry, because everybody they knew was poor. By and large, however, working-class children are never too young to worry.

It is during childhood that working-class women as well as racial and ethnic minority women begin to learn adaptive responses to their conflictual, worrisome reality. They learn to live in two worlds, to develop a double consciousness, to become a hybrid person.[12] This skill becomes necessary in any situation of oppression by a dominant group. One develops a pattern or style of living—taking in and expressing information—among family, kin, and one's own kind. One develops another pattern or style, however, for interaction with those unlike one's self, those in power. One struggles to live in two worlds, and learning such dual class roles so early means childhood is a serious time for developing the flexibility, interdependence, and discriminating judgments a dual life requires. Another adaptive response is armoring, developing a protective shield (physical, emotional, social) that allows one greater control over when and how one reveals one's style of living. Nurturing multiple intelligences is yet another adaptive response, referring to the multiple ways information can be processed and communicated, for example, through logic, social skills, emotions, bodily kinesthetics, song, and dance.[13] In other words, there are different ways of being smart.

Family dynamics for children of both classes have changed through several historical and cultural shifts. Regarding family decision-making patterns, for example, both working-class and middle-class Kansas City women born in the early twentieth century remember their fathers as the primary decision maker in the family, and most women born after 1935 remember their mothers as the primary decision maker. The role and authority of women in the family has changed considerably during this century, which has also influenced the way women have entered the paid workforce and raised children.

All children have some basic structure to gender identity in place by the age of two, although sex role socialization continues into mid-childhood through peers and media and is further shaped in the adult workplace.[14] Among the poor and working class, children's sex roles are also formed in the community as the logical outcome of communal norms for survival, bonding, and self-defense.

Among the Kansas City women interviewed, there were some subtle class differences in parental expectations of children as they grew to adulthood. The differences usually had to do with being a particular kind of person or doing something in a particular way, rather than simply with engaging in a particular behavior or role. For example, middle-class parents expected their daughters to marry. Working-class parents expected their daughters to "marry a nice boy," "marry a man with a good job who loved me," or "be happily married." Middle-class parents often wanted their daughters to go to college. Working-class parents wanted their daughters to "not get pregnant and quit school," "go to college, if possible, to go up in the world," and to "not have too many kids." Working-class parents were clear about what could hold their daughters back, probably because it happened so easily in their neighborhood.

Several studies indicate that the mothers of high-achieving children are twice as likely as the mothers of low-achieving children to be employed outside the home.[15] This likelihood is true of both working-class and middle-class mothers. African American women of both classes value achievement highly and have less fear of success and less anxiety about achievement on average than white working-class women. In general there is more autonomy and achievement orientation among women who have struggled with poverty, serious illness, early physical growth, family crisis, or some experience of loneliness or marginality during childhood and adolescence. These conclusions are confirmed by the Kansas City interviews.

The frequency of sending children to preschool and kindergarten is similar in the middle and working classes. Although the extended childhood education of preschool is sometimes used to explain faster rates of cognitive development in the middle class,[16] in the Kansas City study many more mothers of children who did go to kindergarten were working class and employed than were the mothers of children who did not go to kindergarten. Kindergarten might be a helpful childcare alternative for some working mothers.

Yet finally, the factors most influencing whether a daughter pursues work and builds a family as an adult are her evaluation and interpretation of her own mother's behavior, her encounter with other significant people, as well as social options and incentives (such as the availability of birth control and government training programs or work incentive programs). Larger numbers of working-class women modify their goals than do middle-class women,[17] which may reflect their relative lack of control over their own lives or their need always to modify goals to meet changing circumstances resulting from unequal power arrangements.

Working-class children grow up fast and generally do not romanticize childhood. When asked about the age and event at which childhood seemed to end for them, the Kansas City middle-class women usually mentioned a time during mid- to late adolescence—rarely an age less than fifteen years old. Working-class women see the end of childhood differently, saying things such as, "I always felt like an adult," or "I didn't know that anything like that [the end of childhood] happened," or "At age seven, when I got lots of responsibilities for my three younger siblings."

Several of the named transitions out of childhood were the same for both working-class and middle-class women in the Kansas City study. Some of those transitions involved finding one's voice and speaking one's mind with parents. Others were the transitions from adolescence into the adult roles of worker and partner. But there is a sense in which life was somewhat harder and the events more difficult (for example, untimely death, alcoholism, household responsibilities) among the working class. Childhood ended for middle-class girls as they struggled to claim their identity and leave home. Working-class girls claimed their identity as they struggled to keep family together, protect the vulnerable, and survive.

Furthermore, childhood for the working class is in many cases abbreviated. Working-class women get their first jobs and begin earning their own money earlier than middle-class women do, and they begin earning money in order to buy clothes or to contribute to the rent rather than to save for college. Marriage is a marker ending childhood/adolescence for some women but primarily for those who marry just out of high school. Having a child is usually not mentioned by women as the marker ending childhood. Working-class Rita, for example, who had her first child before her first job or marriage, experienced the end of her own childhood long before that child came into her life.

The worry and anxiety of childhood in the working class is a response to the experience of lacking control over one's life and one's future. Worry reflects very real concerns about whether and what one will eat and wear. Finally, however, worry alone does not solve the troubles of the day, give one peace of mind, or extend one's life. To worry is to experience need. To resolve one's worry is to act so that one's needs are met and to learn where to place one's trust—whether in one's self, one's family, one's community, God, or all of these together—in order for those needs to be met in the future.

Adolescence (Approximately Twelve to Eighteen)

Adolescence is a time of much exploration and struggle. It is the period in which girls must adjust to the tremendous physical changes of menstruation, sexual body changes, sexual feelings, and deal with physical attractiveness and growth spurts.[18] Ruth Josselson distinguishes between early adolescence as a time of struggling to fit in with a peer group, and late adolescence as a time of struggling with what to do with one's life.[19] Heterosexual girls begin to think about dating and sex, and about how these fit with marriage and work. Cognitive changes are also occurring as some girls with the aptitude and requisite environmental challenge develop abilities for abstract thinking in adolescence. Adolescence might even include an experience of religious conversion. Adolescence is generally shorter for working-class youth than for middle-class youth, many of whom enjoy the extended adolescence of university education before they work full time or enter a committed relationship.

Erik Erikson called this adolescent time of turmoil the "identity crisis." The men in Daniel Levinson's study[20] resolved this crisis with a sense of self or identity achievement. Judith Bardwick claimed the women in her study drifted in identity diffusion.[21] J. E. Marcia suggests two other resolutions to the adolescent identity crisis. Individual identity might be foreclosed as one's sense of self is shaped by family and communal connections where interdependence rather than autonomy is expected. This experience is shared by many working-class women. The identity crisis might also be resolved with an identity moratorium in which crises are ongoing and commitments are vague.[22] Many working-class women examine their lives but see no choices open to them. Their "lack of identity" stems not from the fear of looking at themselves but from the despair of looking and seeing few or no options. Their crises never let up.

Although class is rooted in economics, it is also associated with a hierarchy of social status and cultural style, and early adolescence is the time when all working-class children become painfully more aware of being excluded from the "in crowd" of the middle- and upper-middle classes. The pain is less acute only if all others in their school or neighborhood are like themselves. The weak association between self-esteem and social class in childhood becomes a modest association in adolescence.[23] These young girls learn lessons about *their place,* and they are often scarred by what they learn. By the time working-class adolescent girls are in junior high school, socioeconomic class has often become forthrightly "soul wounding," because of the shame it engenders.

The sense of differentness is compounded if one's dawning gender identity is lesbian. The normative adolescent interest in the opposite sex does not occur among young lesbians, and their rite of passage begins with the emotional dissonance between heterosexual expectations and their own blossoming sexual feelings. If allowed into consciousness and explored, one's self-identification as "different" from most women can occur as early as adolescence among 40 to 55 percent of all women who later self-identify as lesbian.[24] In some ways the working-class lesbian adolescent may feel less alone than her middle-class counterpart, for it is normative for working-class adolescents to retain many of their same-sex friends even while dating. But it is no easier to "come out" in the working-class community than in the middle-class community.[25] It is difficult for any adolescent to claim who she is when she does not receive acceptance and support. These women seek out friendships in the heterosexual mainstream or look toward young adulthood, when they can find companionship and community in the bars, the military, or the convent. Regardless of the achievement or relational commitments of lesbian adolescents, the experience of marginality is an intense one.

Generally in American culture one leaves adolescence by taking on an adult role. For a working-class woman, this transition usually takes place at the point of high school graduation, followed by employment and/or partnering. If she attends community college, her adolescence might extend to age twenty, or to age twenty-two if she is an upwardly mobile college graduate. Adolescence may also be shortened if pregnancy and parenthood intervene. Some working-class women leave their parents' home earlier than middle-class women. Most also get their first job earlier than middle-class women, even if they remain in the parental home. Some working-class women get their first job as early as fifteen or sixteen. Working-class adolescents do not tend to make long-range career plans, having learned that short-term planning might help organize the chaos of life but that long-term plans will likely be changed by the exigencies of circumstance.

As indicated by these diverse ways of bringing adolescence to a close, there is more than one way of being a working-class adolescent. One insightful portrayal of this diversity is Arthur Shostak's *Blue Collar Life,* which describes three types of working-class adolescent girls in the 1960s: achievers, accommodators, and rebels.[26] His work is worth summarizing here, because the Kansas City working-class women appear in all three groups, each addressing the shame of socioeconomic exclusion and the dilemma of identity in its own way.

The *achievers* make up the smallest group and sometimes grew up in suburban tract homes, the daughters of better educated, skilled workers. They delay marriage and curb sexual behavior in order to expand their options. They are upwardly mobile and try to behave as they believe middle-class girls do. When they do not measure up, they experience much psychological pain. They dissociate from the more traditional working-class accommodators and seek out the college-oriented crowd. But they belong nowhere. Although they are proud of their accomplishments, they are in an unfamiliar world and so are often fearful and suspicious. Their values revolve around achievement, autonomy, and respectability, and hence, they reveal the least degree of sex-role socialization of any working-class adolescent girls. Traditional fathers do not often reward such achievement, however, so the achieving daughter might not have the male approval she seeks.[27]

Achievers who are not college-bound might pursue traditionally male occupations such as the trades. Mary Walshok describes the childhood and adolescence of these women. They were conscious of needing to take care of themselves, because life was not predictable and secure. They assumed responsibility at an early age and knew they had to work for any success and happiness they might get, although they never felt victimized, abandoned, or abused. Unlike traditional women, who grew up watching their parents being victimized by economic uncertainty and their mothers in untrustworthy or oppressive relations with men, these nontraditional women received security from certain experiences, such that their hard living was episodic and not oppressive.

These achievers grew up embarrassed by their homes, their secondhand or handmade clothes and toys, and did not have many friends. They were not unhappy but felt different. They were not preoccupied with their appearance or acceptance and did not date much in high school. They often learned occupational knowledge and skills from men but did not see women as overshadowed by men or vulnerable without a man. These women often left home as early as possible and shared household duties equally with a live-in partner or spouse. They never had the time or money for an elaborate domestic role. They could see alternatives to the norm. They had some self-esteem and were out to make their own security.[28]

Accommodators among working-class female adolescents are often from the traditional homes of semiskilled workers living in stable ethnic neighborhoods. Their rebellion is mild, and they dream of marriage as a solution to financial problems, the need for safety, and not belonging. Individual achievement is discouraged, especially among daughters. Their knowledge about sexuality comes from their mother, sisters, or other female relatives. Premarital sex is handled ambivalently, for "good girls don't do it," but good girls also do not take birth control pills in case they *do* do it. Hence, pregnancy is not an uncommon reason for getting married.[29]

Pregnancy not only resolves the ambivalent parental message about birth control, but also resolves the experience of social powerlessness the working-class adolescent female experiences. Early marriage is expected, although many mothers primarily wish other options were available, so their daughters would not have to marry so early. The middle-class and upper-class phenomenon of mothers being involved in arrangements for the courtship and marriage of their daughters is generally missing in the lower socioeconomic classes and among employed mothers.[30]

These girls are oriented to the high school social system and are the ones who lose interest in academics as they gain interest in boys. Although some attend vocational or technical school after graduation, many women in this group are underachievers. They are more conflicted than any working-class girl about juggling marriage and employment, but unless they have married a tradesman, they grow up knowing they will probably need to find a way to be both wife and employee. They usually have had the role models to do so. Although their mothers might have been factory workers or waitresses, the accommodators consider it an advancement to become clerical workers. They are pro-family and the primary transmitters of mainstream working-class culture.

The third group of working-class adolescents are the *rebels*. They generally come from low-income and more disorganized households of undereducated laborers with uneven work histories living in crime-prone neighborhoods. Alcohol abuse and domestic violence are not uncommon.[31] These girls feel unprotected and friendless, their only source of stability being their mother or another female relative. They are often fearful of puberty, and although they might flaunt their sexuality and begin to have sexual experiences earlier than accommodators, they are not necessarily promiscuous. The high school dropout rate is highest in this group, for they seek escape from dreary working-class jobs or illegal pursuits such as theft or prostitution by getting married. Marriage becomes as much a medium of survival and commodity exchange as a way to meet needs for intimacy.

If marriage fails, having a child might provide the pathway to survival and the need to be needed in a society that acts as though it would rather do without you. Motherhood might soothe the loneliness, helplessness, and anonymity of hard living.[32] By age twenty, 45 percent of African American women and 19 percent of European American women have at least one child. In 86 percent of African American teen births and 30 percent of white teen births, the mother is unmarried, perhaps due to lack of information about sex, pregnancy, and contraception, or to the need for family planning and abortion services. But it might also be due to low motivation to postpone parenting because of weak aspirations for further education, few employment options or plans, and little desire for children within marriage.[33] There is little need for a public persona among working-class rebels, for they are not trying to impress anyone. Their rebellion is a desperate search for dignity.

The transition from adolescence to adulthood is much more the end of a carefree extended childhood among the middle class than among the working class. A number of Kansas City working-class women see the meaning of impending womanhood as "not much fun," "getting married and having kids," "doing dishes, housework, and taking care of kids," "having to work and do everything for people," "being dominated by men" or "being boss while making a man think that he is boss." Most Kansas City working-class women, when answering the question, "If you could change one thing about your life, what would you change?" referred to decisions made during adolescence. They wanted to finish college, not get married so early, not have babies so early, and take time to find out who they are and what they want. There is a sense of hurried tiredness among working-class women who reflect on their adolescence and young adulthood. But a number of working-class women see the end of adolescence and the beginning of womanhood as the beginning of freedom, being responsible for themselves, making their own decisions, being on their own, picking their own friends. A working-class woman's identity is thus embedded in a complex matrix of practices she became more or less competent in and committed to within her family and community. That identity is strengthened as she discovers and exercises what freedom she has—freedom of choice, freedom of spirit—to construct the best life she can for herself with her family and her community.

Young Adulthood
(Approximately Ages Eighteen to Thirty-Five)

Adolescence is a time of exploring and assimilating new experiences, but young adulthood is a time of accommodating and consolidating new demands and responsibilities.[34] It is the time to live out one's choices for adulthood, which intersect in various ways to provide and limit a woman's options and resources for being a worker, partner, parent, citizen.

Before taking on these roles and tasks, however, women in the middle class at least begin to separate from their family of origin. This separation is truncated, and sometimes never attempted, in the working class, where more apparent ongoing connections are maintained than among middle-class young adults. Lillian Rubin suggests why this may be the case:

> There is no time for concern about the issues of their own growth and development that so preoccupy the college educated middle-class youth in this era, no time to wonder who they are, what they will do, how they can differentiate themselves from parents, how they can stand as separate, autonomous selves. Instead, early marriage and parenthood catapult them into adult responsibilities.[35]

It is also hard to be autonomous and separate from parents and other relatives on whom one must rely for child care or other exchanges of mutual aid in the midst of juggling work, family, and community roles.

Whether or not a woman works outside the home as a young adult is an extremely complex matter. Only working-class women in the Kansas City study mentioned working in order to survive, although a few middle-class women indicated they *began* to work in order to support themselves. Some working-class women talked about work in terms of their improved sense of self-confidence, self-esteem, self-respect, and sense of worth and dignity, because work brings a sense of contributing to the family economy, a sense of accomplishment, a link to the wider society, and new relationships. On the other hand, some women shrugged their shoulders in exasperation when asked why they work, for they did not think they had any choice. For women living on the edge, unemployment can cause depression, low self-esteem, substance abuse, and even suicide.[36]

Satisfaction with one's work is a complex matter. It is dependent on the nature of the work, job conditions (pace, noise, workload), skills required, and the network of relations involved. Most important to middle-class women are the intrinsic qualities of work—how interesting work is, the amount of freedom allowed, the chance to help others, the chance to use one's abilities. Most important to working-class women are the extrinsic qualities of work—pay, fringe benefits, the supervisor and coworkers, the hours one works, how tiring work is, degree of job security, degree of pressure on the job.[37]

Work satisfaction is also influenced by job conditions. Women in the working class encounter a number of physical challenges in employment, such as bells ringing and the constant roar of loud machinery. Some are exposed to extreme heat or cold, and still others suffer physical injury from constant standing (retail clerks), lifting (packing), or eye strain (computer terminals). Hypertension has been found to be inversely related to income.[38] Exhaustion is the norm among employed working-class women. And some are exposed to health risks from accidents or chemicals, radiation, and other hazards. Working conditions actually increase working-class mortality, with 20 to 40 percent of cancer deaths due to on-the-job exposure.[39] The poor and working class are less likely to visit a doctor or dentist or engage in preventative health care, and are more likely to consider aches and pains normal and yet to be hospitalized for serious illnesses. Women's bodies are wounded at work in a number of ways. They are not strangers to bodily suffering.

The pressures of much working-class employment—including ever-increasing production rates, wages based on piecework, seasonal employment, split shifts, physical exhaustion, mental boredom, and the lack of recognition—result in the common working-class complaint of "nerves." Such pressures can also create rebellion—either covert rebellion through foot dragging, sabotage, theft, or overt rebellion such as going on strike. As Studs Terkel put it, the worst pressure might be that the jobs of many working-class women are not too big but rather too small for their spirits.[40] The natural creative spirit within all humans is stifled in much routinized work.

Young adulthood is also the time most working-class women assume the roles of wife and mother, which provide some of the privileges and independence of adulthood. Because their vocational alternatives are limited and because so much working-class employment is not found to be intrinsically meaningful, working-class women often invest more heavily in family than employment. Working-class women are likely to be married by their early twenties.[41]

The majority of employed married women are working class, because as many as two-thirds of all married working women have husbands with working-class occupations,[42] and a full 80 percent of working women are clustered in twenty low-paying occupational categories, such as clerical, sales, service, and factory work. Although the goal of having two salaries in the middle-class family is generally to maximize individual opportunities, in the working-class family the goal of having two wage earners is to protect dependent and disadvantaged members through mutual sacrifice and pooling of resources due to shared scarcity.[43] Working-class cooperation and group solidarity (anti-individualism) are rooted, therefore, in economic realities.

When a woman earns a substantial percentage of the family income, her family power also increases.[44] A relative increase in her economic power also means a relative increase in control over her own fertility, extramarital sex, whether-when-whom to marry, freedom to divorce and grounds for divorce, management of the household, movement in the public domain, and access to education.[45] Her power is greatest when her income more nearly equals that of her spouse and is lowest when the percentage of income she contributes is either very high or very low.[46] Women who work out of economic necessity have more power in family decisions than women who work optionally. But women in a bad marriage with low-wage employment might nonetheless feel trapped, with no sense of freedom either to quit work or divorce.

Dual-earner families tend to operate with more mutual decision making, and in single-earner families decisions tend to be made by individuals in different arenas of family life. Hence, the stereotype of the authoritarian working-class family with rigid sex roles depends on the man maintaining a superior position as wage earner. Family power and freedom is attractive to working-class women, and the only cost is a lot of hard work. A woman's family decision-making power is least when she is at home providing full-time child care, which is most common or necessary in young adulthood, when the family has preschool age children.

Increasing numbers of women are single. Some have always been single, with or without children. Others are single again after separation, divorce, or death of a partner. Some working-class women remain single, although according to Daniel Rossides there are relatively fewer unmarried women in the working class than in the middle and upper classes.[47] When men are absent, women become managers of their own and their family's lives, regardless of societal gender roles.[48]

Working-class women today begin working when their children are much younger than was the case several decades ago, with one of the most rapid changes in women's employment patterns being the increase in work outside the home by women with preschoolers. Once children are past the earliest years of life, working-class women begin to develop work patterns similar to those of men.[49] Hence, interruptions in employment usually do not signify the woman has limited commitment to work, but rather that she is tending to responsibilities of family and child care.

Women do not merely seek employment when their fertility allows, but sometimes limit the number of children they have in order to work. Working-class women uniquely experience work conditions that are potentially damaging to their fertility. Dangerous industries often exclude women of childbearing age, which can push women to sterilization or abortion in order to protect their jobs.[50] Moral issues around working-class women's fertility, then, are not abstract and philosophical but are quite concrete and economic at their foundation. The attack against abortion and other aspects of women's reproductive control is not only an argument about individual freedom, but also about family survival. For working-class women, issues of reproduction and economic production are interdependent. There is no clear line between her private and public life.

Employment also affects a mother's relationship with her children. One study found that both working-class and middle-class mothers who are employed foster more autonomy and self-reliance in their children than unemployed mothers.[51] And the more years of a child's life a mother works, the more the child acclimates to developing autonomy and not being the focus of family interest. Of course, more working-class than middle-class mothers work outside the home.

Socialization of the next generation reflects the respective themes of young adulthood that appear in each class. Among the twenty women interviewed, the theme of middle-class young adulthood was personal achievement and preparing children to achieve all that they can. The theme of working-class young adulthood was survival and preparing children for a hard life. Negotiating survival in these economic times of industrial downsizing and expansion of a low-pay service economy is difficult, wearying work. The burden of working too hard for too little—at home and away from home, in private and in public—is exhausting and discouraging. Such work requires a strength that comes from beyond one's self. Such work leads the laborer to seek rest and renewing of strength for the work that still lies ahead.

Middle Adulthood (Approximately Ages Thirty-Five to Fifty)

With middle age comes introspective reflection and life evaluation in which questions about objectives, values, commitments, and choices are considered, according to Daniel Levinson's study of adult male development.[52] It is a time of answering the question, "What am I producing?" Judith Bardwick suggests that a larger number of women than men will evade an evaluation of their lives, because such an assessment would heighten their awareness that they do not determine their life style.[53] This avoidance is also characteristic of the working class, as described poignantly by Tillie Olsen in her 1953 story "I Stand Here Ironing," in which a mother is asked to help an inquirer understand the mother's daughter in order to give the daughter the help she needs:

> You think because I am her mother I have a key, or that in some way you could use me as a key? She has lived for nineteen years. There is all that life that has happened outside of me, beyond me. And when is there time to re-member, to sift, to weigh, to estimate, to total? . . . I will become engulfed with all I did or did not do, with what should have been and what cannot be helped.[54]

The self-evaluation of the middle class is more extensive and introspective be-cause there is time, and the results of such reflection reveal that one has had a measure of control over one's life course.

Midlife is also a time to evaluate one's primary adult relationship. When asked what she valued most in her husband, Vivian, a Kansas City working-class woman, responded in much the same way as the working-class women in Lillian Rubin's study of California working-class families:[55] "He works, he doesn't drink, he does-n't hit me." Although compassion, support, and communication from one's spouse are valued by working-class as well as middle-class women, middle-class women tend to value attributes of being: a good mate is "a person with good standards and a good mind," "supportive, kind, considerate, and even-tempered," "patient," or "emotionally supportive, a good friend and partner." Working-class women, on the other hand, also included action-oriented attributes—a good mate "stands by you through good times and bad," "helps carry the load, loves me, and shows it," is "someone to talk things out with and work things out with, someone who respects me," or being good mates means "working together and being true to each other."

Older married, employed, working-class women experience somewhat less stress with dual roles once the children are older and leave home. Both work (especially higher paying union jobs) and intimate partnerships bring more satis-faction as workers and their children grow older. Women born between 1910 and 1920 were not socialized for a long-term work role and generally saw work as both temporary and secondary to their spouse's work role. Most women born after 1920 *started work* after their children were in school to buy a home and put children through school and *kept working* to retain their independence and retire with dig-nity. So even older women for whom the necessity of working for family survival has passed might continue working, although they become interested in work that allows them to slow down and be more comfortable.[56] Work-related friendships are more important as women move beyond their childbearing years, with some of these friends becoming like kin in certain ethnic groups.[57]

Because marriage in the working class occurs earlier and sometimes under more adverse circumstances than in the middle class, the rate of divorce is also higher, whether divorce occurs in young adulthood or middle age. The single-parent families that result from separation and divorce experience more and longer transitions between periods of equilibrium. Those who remarry often experience even more disorder than those who remain single.[58]

The empty nest created when the children leave the parental home is clearly more of a crisis for women who found the nurture of children central to their identity—usually women unemployed outside the home in both the working class and middle class. Because most working-class women are employed and must juggle two full-time jobs, children leaving home is often met with some relief. For the mother who is unemployed, and especially for women born early in the twentieth century for whom motherhood is the primary source of identity, the empty nest is a greater crisis.

The life theme identified by many working-class women in middle adulthood is that of helping others. They have moved beyond the theme of survival, even though some were single parents and struggled economically, to a point of feeling satisfaction in helping and guiding other people even outside of their family circle. Hence, caretaking and caring are virtues of maturity. This wider social interest was also reflected in the responses of several Kansas City working-class women when asked what they would do if given a million dollars. Some said they would give to some social cause, whether colleges, homes for the homeless, or for some cause of freedom. Other working-class women said they would give some of the money to their church. Middle-class women mentioned none of these targets for their money but talked rather about home, family, and investments.

Older Adulthood (Approximately Ages Fifty and Older)

Some of the life tasks of late adulthood include adjustment to menopause, grandparenting, retirement, caring for parents, and dealing with one's own aging and death. These adjustments become more difficult the lower the socioeconomic class to the degree that economic resources aid coping.

As women become free of some of their former roles (mother, spouse, employee), they often display increased strength, energy, and independence. Especially in ethnic neighborhoods they might become midwives, guides, and advisors of the young, transmitting their wisdom through oral traditions.[59] They might also enter community activism and organizing. They have the time for it and see their purpose as enhancing the living situation of family and neighborhood. Such involvements are in line with the middle adulthood theme of caring for others.

Among the working-class women interviewed, however, the primary life theme in late adulthood was no longer that of helping others. It was learning. They never really felt as if they had "chosen" a theme to live out, but given the cards they were dealt in life, they sought to learn from it all. Rhonda thought her life theme was to "try to get at the truth, to learn, and to better [myself] by rising above the not so nice things of [my] childhood." Stella was inspired by macrobiotic nutrition and wanted to open up some new thinking in that area, except she felt she "didn't have the brains to do so." Although not a teacher perhaps, she did call herself a "hungry learner."

Learning is important to working-class women, partly because the ideology of bourgeois culture suggests that one can move up and be somebody if one knows enough. But education is also something that no one can take away from you. Being deprived of advanced formal education, working-class women also sense that their own development can only proceed to the degree that they continue to understand and integrate the world and events around them. This perception becomes more true as working-class women become older and more free of parenting and worker roles. Learning becomes a way to attain a measure of dignity, to break out of one's private existence into shared communal wisdom, to move beyond survival to the fullness of life.

As women move through late adulthood, losses become inevitable, but managing them is easier, and self-pity, nervousness, and depression are less likely when one has one's health, an intact extended family, a social peer network, financial security, and a meaningful purpose in life.[60] Friendships become especially important in the older adulthood of working-class women as a resource for managing multiple losses. In a mid-1960s study of middle-aged and older adults, Bernice Neugarten found that women rated higher on intimacy than men, especially those in late adulthood, and the working class and lower middle class had higher ratings than the lower class and the upper.[61] These differences might be due to working-class women's tendency to find friends in wide networks of kin, and middle-class women's common understanding that their best friend is their husband.

The loss of death can be difficult, but it is often not the greatest enemy in the working class. Worse than death is lack of dignity, respect, and belonging. Working-class women not uncommonly say that they want to die before becoming a burden to someone else, because they know only too well what burdens in life feel like. This attitude is quite different from the middle-class women, who fear being dependent or losing control as death approaches. The great tragedy and suffering around the experience of death in the working class are the result of death coming too early and systemic assaults on one's dignity and vulnerability.

Death does not wait for the working class. According to Albert Szymanski, white working-class women are 2.04 times more likely to die in a given year than white middle-class women, and 60 percent of those between twenty-five and sixty-four years of age die of poverty-related illness.[62] The infant mortality rate is higher in the working class, and more working-class mothers see their sons killed in war than middle-class mothers do. White working-class women are 1.2 times more likely to die of cancer, 2.4 times more likely to die of heart disease, 2.6 times more likely to die of hypertension, and 3.5 times more likely to die of diabetes than middle-class white women.[63] Some of this variation in death rates is due to downward mobility that illness and unemployment cause, but it is also due to greater stress and trauma from divorce, the death of close relatives, violent crimes, loss of jobs and homes, and having fewer resources to deal with the stress.[64] When the health of aging mothers begins to fail, working-class children wait longer to have their mother move in with them, and she is more incapacitated when she does, because working-class families are generally more cramped for space.

The number of losses and the vividness of suffering was found to be greater among the Kansas City working-class women interviewed than among the middle-class women. Working-class women mentioned suffering from living in single-parent families, having their home robbed, having a breakdown. They mentioned alcoholic parents, the death of siblings, and the death of children. Middle-class women mentioned divorce and racism but also that they really did not endure much suffering.

Late adulthood is a time to understand the meaning of who one has been through life and to assess one's accomplishments or successes. None of the Kansas City women interviewed understood success to mean that someone else did comparatively less well or failed. Both middle-class and working-class women understood success as a particular degree of power and mastery, but only working-class women also understood success and accomplishment collectively to mean a contribution to the group goal or feeling.[65] For example, one working-class woman thought that not only the rich succeed, but "you can be poor and be successful at living, at getting along with people." Another working-class woman understood her own success at setting and reaching goals as something that arose not from within her but from the requirements of the workplace and "everybody pulling together for the same thing." Collective implications of failure can also be detected in one working-class woman's understanding of failure as "letting someone down." There is a clear sense that success can only be properly so called when it benefits the group rather than an isolated individual.

Only working-class Kansas City women attributed success or failure to the environment or fate. Two working-class women suggested that "success is hard work plus luck, failure is hard work plus no luck (or bad luck)." A third working-class woman felt that failure was when "things just don't work out as planned." And a fourth working-class woman, who in her childhood and adolescence came from the depths of poverty, thought that "failure can come from the environment, from lack of role models as much as from lack of skills or not using your God-given talents." Among many working-class women, there is a realistic ability to understand success as more than setting and attaining individual goals. The reality of the powerlessness they experience in the world shapes their consciousness of success and failure in profound ways.

One final theme that the Kansas City working-class women revealed was that of leisure and rest. Amid the weary struggle for dignity and survival, working-class women especially yearn for rest. The alienation of work from its inherent mean-ingfulness is burdensome. So when the Kansas City women were asked what they would do if given a million dollars, many said they would pay off their bills. Additionally, however, they would spend it not only for a social cause, but also for leisure of a special kind—travel or having fun making people happy.

Because there is nothing leisurely about working-class employment, working-class people are keenly aware of the need to get away from it all and how impor-tant rest is for total development. Rest and play nurture creativity and serve to unite a fragmented self, living with a hybrid identity. Rest is more than the absence of work. It is the joyous re-creation into wholeness.

Conclusion

As we listen to the voices of working-class women, several themes emerge throughout the various phases of the life span. In childhood we hear about the per-vasiveness of worry. This is a style and set of behaviors rooted in mistrust—an un-derstandable mistrust in contexts of economic vulnerability. But childhood was also the period during which working-class women learned a double consciousness and other skills to cope with their unpredictable and disparaged context.

In adolescence working-class women struggle with being excluded from main-stream middle-class culture. This exclusion brings on a sense of shame and feeling unacceptable. Working-class adolescents battle with these enemies in a variety of ways. Adolescent achievers often struggle through their identity crisis toward an autonomous self. Believing their problem is merely standing too low on the cul-tural ladder and seduced by the American myth of upward mobility, they hope to move above their current state and into the middle class. Accommodators might experience stunted identities as they require interdependence rather than auton-omy in relation to their kin and community. Rebels might experience identity moratorium as they move from crisis to crisis with never enough time or energy to wrestle with questions of who they are and what they want.

In young adulthood women live out choices regarding work and family in a variety of ways, with the theme of achievement predominating in the middle class and the theme of survival pervading working-class life. The tasks of work and fam-ily give way in middle adulthood to the theme of helping others. This helping might include caring for one's parents, but it also means broadening one's care to include one's community and church. Finally, the themes of older adulthood are learning and rest, providing the concluding dialectic to a working-class life that frequently lacked both.

Listening to women's voices makes clear that women are different from men in some of the developmental issues they face, but there are also differences *among* women in the developmental themes their lives reflect. Certainly gender, class, race, cultural, and historical contexts help shape the course of human development.

The theological assumptions that we are rooted in and created for community and that we must struggle against the absence of such community provide a critical perspective from which to assess both bourgeois individualism as cultural imperative and the autonomous self as the primary goal of human development. An examination of the lives of working-class women, however, helps us to understand the purpose of development as struggling through personal and systemic conflicts with race, class, gender, and culture to overcome intersecting psycho-socio-spiritual inequities to make possible mutually respectful life in community.

The themes of women's life span development that have emerged from this inquiry suggest women's development of several competencies for mature life together, including trust, interdependence, flexible/expanded identity, conflict engagement and resolution, survival, care, multiple learning modes, and joyfully recreative rest.[66] This developmental process involves liberation from domination and movement toward the goal of dignity, liberation from privatization and movement toward the goal of community, and liberation from survival toward the goal of life abundant. These freedoms are rooted in a story that reveals God's forgiveness of past wrongs, God's power for covenantal life in the present, and God's promise of a future with all God's creation. That promise is vital for those who might otherwise give up amid the frequent despair of working-class life.

During the course of the interviews reported in this chapter, I asked Mary, "What is the basic dilemma of living?"

"Greed," she responded. "Greed means we sell our values for money. It means we aren't able to live and work together where everybody earns enough money to live. It means too many have to fight tooth and nail to survive, to put up with crazy people on a job they don't like just to make it from one day to the next."

"Do you think we will always have poor people among us?" I asked.

"Sure," she said knowingly, "Until God decides differently." She paused a few seconds and then continued, "You see, rich people make poor people. And rich people don't ever give up enough to make poor people go away." She paused and reflected a few seconds, then continued, "I stand on the promise that God will change things some day, 'cause the rich won't and the poor can't. Until then, we work hard, love and protect our families, and safeguard our communities for everyone from the newly born to the dearly departed. Yes, God will change things some day."

Narratives of Harm:
Setting the Developmental Context
for Intimate Violence

Christie Cozad Neuger

The purpose of this chapter is to explore domestic abuse, especially partner battering, through a lens of resistance and prevention. My premise is that the way we shape the psychological, social, and spiritual development of boys and girls in our culture makes it almost inevitable that physical and emotional abuse will occur in heterosexual partnerships.

As we will explore, the cultural, theological, and familial narratives about gender in this society shape intimate partnerships between men and women in such a way that family relationships often become laden with abusive dynamics. The chapter will focus primarily on heterosexual couples, although violence occurs in a significant number of gay or lesbian intimate relationships as well. Usually, gay and lesbian children are raised within the dominant gender paradigms assigned to their biological sex and within heterosexual parental structures. Thus, they generally do not escape the gender training nor the relational paradigm based on heterosexual gender stereotypical norms that make violence likely.

This chapter focuses on these norms for gender and family in the hope that pastoral theology can find ways to counter these dominant narratives and thus resist and prevent family violence. I would argue that the primary model in pastoral theology for working with people who are suffering because of domestic violence has been a *response model*. Our focus has been on those who are victims of violence and on providing nurture, care, and protection for them. Although this response, rather than prevention, has been the focus for care, as we shall see, pastoral caregivers have tended to be generally ineffective when providing this kind of care for victims of domestic violence. Certainly the work of adequately responding to victims of domestic violence must continue and improve, but it needs to be joined by the work of resistance—especially resistance through changing the way we raise our children. My hope is that this chapter helps us to (1) develop better strategies for assisting the development of girls and boys in such a way that they will be better able to resist the cultural norms of intimate violence; (2) develop better methods to respond to women and men caught in patterns of physical and emotional intimate violence; and (3) challenge the assumptions of our psychotherapeutic and developmental theories that suggest equality and trust are the normal contexts for girls in a culture that disadvantages them and puts them at risk for intimate violence from the moment of birth.

The Current Picture of Domestic Abuse

Talking about intimate violence as "normal" might seem extreme. It is clear that most religious leaders would prefer to believe that battering in intimate relationships is exceptional rather than normal. After all, most marriages in the United States occur because two individuals fall in love and desire to be good and caring partners with each other. Can we not assume that this motivation for marriage is an adequate antidote to domestic violence in most cases? We cannot. Even in the context of love and well-meaning intentions, the statistics about the occurrence of domestic violence force us to acknowledge its normalcy.

The United States Justice Department recently released a comprehensive study on the price of violence in our society. It attempted to include the costs of domestic violence and child abuse in addition to the kinds of violence more typically studied. The report found that "child abuse and domestic violence account for one-third of the total cost of crime."[1]

According to Margi McCue and the United States surgeon general, "[Domestic] abuse may be the single most common etiology for injury presented by women, accounting for more injury episodes than auto accidents, muggings, and rapes combined. A review of 3,676 records randomly selected from among female patients presenting with injury during one year, revealed that 40 percent of the women's injury episodes were identified as resulting from a deliberate assault by an intimate. Nineteen percent of the women had a previous history of abusive injury."[2] The American Medical Association estimates that four million women suffer severe assaults by boyfriends and husbands each year and that one in four women will be abused in her life. Estimates in a variety of studies range from two million to eight million women assaulted every year by partners and up to one in two women being abused sometime in her life. The American Psychological Association Task Force on Depression suggests that almost 40 percent of women in the United States are physically or sexually abused before the age of twenty-one, and McCue reports that medical personnel in emergency rooms think the number is more likely 50 percent or even higher.[3]

A Bureau of Justice report suggests, "Based on evidence collected in the National Crime Survey, as many as half of the domestic 'simple assaults' actually involved bodily injury as serious as or more serious than 90 percent of all rapes, robberies, and aggravated assaults."[4] And yet, only somewhere between 40 and 50 percent of domestic violence incidents are reported to the police.[5] The reasons given for not reporting incidents were (1) a fear of reprisal, (2) the sense that it was a private matter (the woman often felt that she must be somehow to blame), and (3) the feeling that the crime was just not important enough.

Again, according to the Bureau of Justice, African American, European American, and Hispanic women have approximately equivalent rates of intimate violence. Women who are between the ages of twenty-two and thirty-four have the highest rates of victimization and women who are college graduates have lower rates than noncollege graduates. Women in central cities have about the same rates of domestic violence as those in suburbs and rural environments. Somewhere between one-third and one-half[6] of all female murder victims over the age of fourteen are killed by a current or former spouse (compared to 4 percent of men),[7] although a study by Kesner, Julian, and McKenry says that 75 percent of all homicides of women are perpetrated by a male intimate partner.[8] Obviously many more women need shelter from domestic assault situations than are able to find it. According to McCue, "Shelters for battered women are only able to admit between 10 and 40 percent of women who apply. Shelter personnel believe that for each woman who calls a hotline or enters a shelter, there are at least ten battered women without a safe place to stay."[9]

Despite the prevalence of this crime, many women feel that they are the only ones who are experiencing this abuse. Further, they often feel they either deserve this violence or that they should somehow figure out how to prevent it, especially early on in their experience of battering. This sense of isolation and self-blame contributes to the difficulty women have trying to get out of these violent situations. Battering is a demoralizing, humiliating, dangerous experience. It is perpetrated by one with whom there has generally been an intimate and loving relationship. It frequently embodies a deep betrayal of trust along with the sense of isolation.

The Current Response Patterns of Religious Leaders

Although there are exceptions, the church, speaking generally, does not have a good track record in working with victims of family violence. Religious leaders tend to participate in the silencing of domestic abuse victims and their stories that the culture does. They have used theological justifications, particularly the sanctity of the family, to justify this silencing of domestic abuse victims. They have been in unquestioning collusion with patriarchy, assuming the normativeness (and believability) of males. And they have not wanted to participate in the kind of upheaval that it would cause to advocate actively on behalf of victims, especially because it is often the perpetrators who have the power and authority within local churches. For example, Marie Fortune warns pastors that when a woman comes in to tell you that her husband—who is also the chair of the board of trustees, an active church school teacher, and a large donor—has been battering her,

You will not be able to believe her. No matter how well intentioned you may be, what she is describing to you runs counter to your experience of that individual. What you have to keep in mind is that your experience with that individual is true and real for you and is public. Her experience with that individual is true and real and is private. Now with most of us, in the conflicting face of experience and information, we go with our experience. Remember, however, that in cases where someone is disclosing abuse by someone you know, there is another piece to this story that is the private person. Oftentimes the typical abuser has an exemplary public persona and yet in private engages in all sorts of behavior that seems unbelievable to you. Knowing that, our job is to press ahead and to believe that person—although it doesn't fit with what we know about the abuser—so that we can be present to the victim and ultimately to the offender.[10]

It is usually more difficult for us to side against a person whom we wish to believe is innocent of this kind of behavior than it is to believe that the accusation is a lie.

As we said above, pastors, overall, have not been very useful to women and children who have experienced abuse in their families. Many studies that have been done about the usefulness of clergy in situations of domestic abuse find that clergy are rated as one of the least helpful resources compared to family, friends, psychotherapists, family doctors, and social service agencies. In a recent study, researchers found that clergy effectiveness is consistently low, and they speculated that this was probably due to clergy endorsement of traditional teachings concerning the sanctity of marriage. In addition, a research group sent out a two-page questionnaire to 5700 pastors, and fewer than 10 percent of the questionnaires were returned. The researchers concluded that pastors lacked interest in or were hostile to the notion of domestic abuse. They also noted that the clergy that did return their questionnaires seemed to be concerned about battered women but indicated that they were torn by theological perspectives that seemed to be in conflict with the best interests of the women.[11]

These are very serious issues if clergy are indeed feeling that they are not able to really be very helpful to victims of intimate violence, especially wife battering or spousal rape, because they are trapped by theological doctrine that mandates patriarchal power. Pastoral theology must commit itself to closing this gap between theological doctrine and the well-being of women. It is interesting that when pastors are used as resources in situations of domestic violence, those women who rated their pastors as helpful tended to be from churches that normally addressed social problems in general and that created an environment where women felt safe coming forward with their stories. They were also more likely to rate their pastors as helpful if they were willing to take action to intervene in the violence, not just to listen passively to them.[12]

Women who are committed to their religious traditions often turn to pastors for help when they experience problems in their families. Yet, it is also true that women who have experienced intimate violence are much more likely to leave their religious practices and affiliations than are nonabused women, partly because they have only experienced revictimization through silence and silencing and partly because they experience the church's betrayal as symbolic of God's betrayal. In other words, when churches are silent about domestic violence or use stereotyped images of girls and women that encourage passive responses to abuse, women experience the church (and God) as having abandoned them. We will explore some of these issues further when we explore the power of cultural and familial narratives.

It is important to say, however, that there are some signs of progress in churches' response to and resistance against domestic violence. For example, the Center for the Prevention of Sexual and Domestic Violence, directed by Marie Fortune as an educational ministry, has had considerable influence in recent years. Many pastors, seminary professors, and religious educators have been trained to offer appropriate intervention into situations of domestic and sexual violence. In addition, several important texts in the last few years have indicated that religious leaders and church scholars are viewing family violence as a serious theological and pastoral issue. Marie Fortune and Carol Adams have edited a significant theological sourcebook for religious leaders who are seeking resources for addressing these issues of family violence. The sourcebook looks at theological, biblical, historical, liturgical, and pastoral perspectives on intimate violence in ways that lend themselves to pastoral practice.[13] John McClure and Nancy Ramsay have recently edited a book focused on preaching about intimate violence. The text provides important theological and social reflection and ends with several sermons to guide pastors in this form of intervention.[14] And Toinette Eugene and James Poling have recently written an important book on pastoral care for African American families who are experiencing domestic violence.[15] These texts and the examples they give about ministry in the midst of family violence give hope that the church will soon be able to give appropriate time and energy to this epidemic problem.

The Power of Dominant Cultural Narratives in Shaping Family Violence

I have referred several times in this chapter to the formative power of cultural and familial narratives in people's lives. When I use the word "narrative," I mean more than casual or haphazard stories. I am really talking about core narrative—the story line within us (or within a culture) that shapes the way we encounter, interpret, and make meaning out of all other stories or experiences. Core narratives have to do with the primary sets of assumptions about reality that we carry. Individuals have core narratives, which are formed early and then enlarged and detailed as time goes on. Cultures have core narratives—systems of truth and meaning—that shape how people experience themselves, one another, and the primary systems in their lives.

Cultural core narratives tell us who we are in the context of that culture. Our core narrative tends to form out of early experiences and authoritative sources. That narrative then serves as the filter for interpreting ongoing experience and integrating it into the core narrative. In this way, core narratives both describe the key experiences a person (or a culture) has had and determine which experiences will be seen as primary and worth remembering and which will be discarded or reshaped in order to fit with this core understanding.

If, for example, a person has watched her mother get battered by her father throughout her childhood, that experience will probably form a key lens in her core narrative. Not only will that story be important (although possibly lost from conscious awareness over time), but it will serve as a framework through which to make sense out of other experiences and relationships. It will most likely motivate her to understand other experiences of harm in the ways she learned to understand and interpret those early experiences. It will also most likely serve as a framework for seeing other relational interactions as potential reproductions of that early experience. This is not to say that other powerful experiences will not challenge that core narrative and even reshape it, thus providing new frameworks of interpretation. It is to say that these early core narratives have a lot of power to shape and interpret future experiences without much critical reflection. The longer the strands within core narratives develop without being challenged, the "thicker" they are, and the harder they are to deconstruct. Obviously, personal core narratives develop in the context of the variety of interpretive frameworks to which we are exposed—our parents and families; peer groups; institutional connections such as school, church, clubs, and the media—which probably offer some of the most powerful interpretive frameworks in our culture today.

Cultural core narratives function in the same way. If a cultural story has shaped itself, for example, around a belief in a binary or dualistic system, separating thought from feeling, spirit from matter, men from women, God from humanity—and valuing the first half of the pair over the second, then that core narrative will continue to find ways to support its own claims to truth and will ignore or minimize those experiences (exceptions) that do not fit. In our culture, this dualistic framework is one strand of a powerful cultural core narrative, and it certainly affects our understanding of gender relationships.

I want to make the case that the primary "story we live by," the one within which we make life decisions in the culture, is a narrative that normalizes and even explicitly trains men to harm women in intimate relationships (especially when men feel threatened) and women to find ways to interpret that violence so that they remain in it. I am not making this case in order to demonstrate hopelessness or to posit an inevitable future of domestic violence. I believe that narratives are dynamic and can be rewritten, although not easily. I describe these cultural narratives of violence for two reasons. One is so that pastoral care ministries might be about the task of helping people (both perpetrators and victims) to examine the narratives through which they build and interpret relationships, including violent relationships. The second is to deconstruct and reformulate violence-laden narratives at both cultural and individual levels for the purposes of prevention and resistance.

In our particular culture, a powerful narrative strand suggests certain people are more valuable than others. People are subtly and blatantly ordered according to a hierarchy of value based on various essential qualities (defined more or less at birth) such as skin color, ethnicity, sex, able-bodiedness, intelligence, sexual orientation, and physical appearance. The combination of these factors guide our placement in the value hierarchy to a large degree. The cultural narrative is the story that implicitly and explicitly defines and prescribes this hierarchy and shapes individual, familial, and societal compliance to it. Obviously, this process is not as mechanical or deterministic as I have made it sound. Many factors influence how individuals and institutions internalize and live out the dominant cultural narrative. Nonetheless, the narrative about who we are as individuals and in relationships is a powerful shaper of attitudes and behaviors. I want to briefly discuss two windows into the cultural narrative—popular entertainment and advertising media, and popular religious doctrines.

Popular Media Narratives

There has been an increase of violence, especially explicit violence, in the film industry in recent years. It is becoming more evident that violence against women, even when that violence is not explicitly sexual in nature, causes people to become desensitized to violence in general and to the violence of rape against women in particular. A set of studies by Linz, Donnerstein, and Penrod concluded:

> When subjects are continually exposed to graphically depicted film violence against women, individual feelings of anxiety and depression begin to dissipate. Material that was anxiety provoking became less so with prolonged exposure. Perceptual changes found in the study also proved to be reliable in later studies. Subjects reported seeing less violence with continued exposure. They also rated the material differently with continued exposure. Material once found somewhat degrading to women was judged less so after prolonged exposure.[16]

In this same study, these subjects also judged a rape trial victim more harshly after exposure to films depicting R-rated, nonsexual violence against women.

It might give us an element of hope to know that a later study by Donnerstein and Linz found that when viewers are carefully debriefed after this kind of viewing experience—when they are helped to recognize that the movies are fiction, that rape is a crime of violence, and that assaulting women is illegal—their more positive sensitivities toward women are retained, and that retention was long lasting. Certain forms of consciousness-raising about media depictions of violence against women, then, seem effective.[17]

When we consider both the quantity and quality of violence in today's "entertainment" industry, these conclusions become very important. In addition to film viewers, there are large numbers of pornography readers. (Pornography has been defined very helpfully by Gloria Steinem as sex being used to reinforce or create domination, pain, and humiliation. Violence, dominance, and conquest are the essential ingredients.) Pornography has also become more violent over the past ten or so years, and music videos have joined the violence movement. According to some studies, more than one-half of the music videos on MTV feature or suggest violence, present hostile sexual situations as acceptable, or show male heroes abusing women for fun.[18] In addition, there are more peepshows and adult bookstores in the United States than there are McDonald's[19] (four times as many, say Gary Brooks and Louise Silverstein[20]). One out of eight Hollywood movies depicts a rape theme. By the age of eighteen, the average youth has watched 250,000 acts of violence and 40,000 attempted murders on TV.[21]

In addition, the average American is exposed to over 2,000 ads per day. This sweeping form of education teaches us a great deal about who we are to be. Jean Kilbourne, an expert in the analysis of advertising, says, "Women are constantly exhorted to emulate the ideal of femininity (of young, thin, perfect), to feel ashamed and guilty if they fail, and to feel that their desirability and lovability are contingent upon physical perfection."[22]

Along with the various forms of advertising, television images, in general, are problematic for girls and women. A recent study by the nonprofit organization called Girls, Inc. (an association that has been operating for the past fifty years to improve the self-image of school-age girls) found that girls get their ideas about who they are or who they should be from television. Children in this survey of girls and boys in third through twelfth grades were found to watch television more than twenty hours per week.

The findings from this study are disturbing. Girls, Inc. discovered that the more television a girl watches, the more likely she is to think that household chores are women's work, and the more boys watch television, the more they agree with this assessment. The less television a girl watched, "the more likely she was to focus on career goals."

They also found that, except on public television, most children's shows are aimed at boys. In addition, television programs distorted the realities about women's and men's lives. For example, they said, "In the real world 80% of single households are headed by women, but on television, half of the single parents are men." In addition, they found that for every female character, there are three male characters in the average TV series, and on children's shows more than three-fourths of the adults are men. Finally, they revealed (to no one's surprise) that most of the victims in television shows are women.[23]

These are very serious findings. Television is one of the most significant influencers of self-image and relational expectations. In addition, television and other forms of entertainment media all shape our personal core interpretive narratives *and* reflect a cultural core narrative that portrays violence against women as normative and that demonstrates rigid gender stereotypes and the consequent power differences between men and women.

Maybe what is most compelling about this analysis is that we, as a culture, pay attention and money in order to receive these violence-laden messages. We do not, as a whole, protest these portrayals of unequal power relationships between men and women, nor do we protest the portrayal of violence against and objectification of women. By financially supporting these portrayals we affirm them as accurate and guiding strands of our cultural narrative. (See Pamela Cooper-White's chapter, in which she makes similar points about the culture.)

Popular Religious Narratives

A second illustration of formative cultural narratives might be found in certain dimensions of our theologies—especially as they are interpreted within an already existing cultural story of gendered hierarchy and power. It's important not to suggest that our religious foundations are necessarily negative about issues of objectification of and violence toward women. I believe that our theological heritage has deeply liberating dimensions. Much of our theological formulation, however, has been done in and by a culture already operating out of a normative narrative of patriarchy with all of its negative consequences.

For virtually all theologians interested in issues of intimate violence—much of which is perpetrated by adult men against boys, girls, and women—language and imagery for God has been of central importance. The focus on language and imagery for God reflects the philosophical understanding that language does not just describe cultural reality, but also informs, influences, and to a certain extent determines that culture. How God is named, imagined, and conceptualized significantly affects how we understand ourselves and our purpose, how we order our social and familial relationships, and how we structure our culture. In other words, our understanding of God and our relationship to God, for those of us who have religious commitments, orders and grounds our core narrative. If we believe, for example, that there is a natural order or hierarchy of value that God has ordained and represents, then we create cultural structures that keep that order in place. If we believe that God is male and, thus, that the male is closer to the image of God than the female, then we value males more highly than females, and we claim that males are naturally created to do more "godlike" things than are females. We would use that rationale to develop theories about gender roles and power positions, designating men as dominant and women as subordinate. We would then use these theories to define separate characteristics and even separate worlds for women and men that reflect this similarity and dissimilarity with God. We would also make the maintenance of these characteristics and worlds a matter of divine obligation. We find this ordering of our world in many dimensions of our society today, and we find it very clearly at work in many of the dynamics of intimate violence.

Another theological issue that has been pursued by both male and female theologians exploring the dynamics of intimate violence is that of the glorification of suffering sometimes culled from our theologies of atonement. Jim Poling's research and writing have been important in this work, as has the work of Joanne Carlson Brown and Rebecca Parker and Rita Nakashima Brock. Feminist theology, in particular, has demonstrated a heavy investment in exploring, deconstructing, and reimagining Christian understandings of Jesus' death and resurrection.[24] The investment has hinged, at least in part, on the recognition by many women and men of the epidemic levels of abuse against women and children, and the use to which Christian theology has been put in allowing that abuse to occur. Feminist theorists have long been aware that abused women and children frequently receive messages from their pastors, from Christian husbands and parents, and from "well-meaning" Christian neighbors that there is divine meaning in their experience of abuse, that the abuse itself is salvific or a means to deeper spirituality, that it is their place to suffer, that husbands or parents know best, that they are somehow at fault, or that it is a sign of deep Christian charity to tolerate being abused by a "loved one." The stories about these kinds of messages, told by battered women, incest survivors, and others are legion. Annie Imbens and Ineke Jonker conducted a study in the Netherlands of eighteen women who had experienced childhood sexual abuse and who had been raised in Christian homes and studied how the abuse and the Christian upbringing might be related. They heard over and over again that Christian images of women, the God-given authority of fathers, and the mandates of humility, forgiveness, and submission were contributing factors in both the occurrence of violence and recovery from it.[25]

These studies and stories convey some of the motivation behind feminist and profeminist theologians' exploration into theories of atonement. Obviously, these issues around Christology and the way suffering and redemption are understood are of major import in pastoral care work.

Another theological issue has to do with the qualities that have been defined as valuable for Christians and especially for "good Christian women." As Mary Daly once said, "The qualities that Christianity idealizes, especially for women, are also those of a victim: sacrificial love, passive acceptance of suffering, humility, meekness, etc. Since these are the qualities idealized in Jesus 'who died for our sins', his functioning as a model reinforces the scapegoat system for women."[26]

The theology of forgiveness is an important issue, too. There has been a tendency for churches to urge victims of violence, especially intimate violence, to forgive their abusers. Those who do so are seen as more Christian, more holy. Yet, as Marie Fortune suggests, forgiveness should probably be the last step in the healing process rather than the first. Using a helpful exploration of the biblical understandings of forgiveness, Fortune finds that without justice, forgiveness is an empty exercise. She says, "Forgiveness before justice is cheap grace and cannot contribute to authentic healing and restoration to wholeness for the victim or the offender."[27] Some very important work is being done by feminist theologians on the issue of forgiveness.[28]

As Hedwig Meyer-Wilmes summarizes:

> The religious inculturation of contempt for women is something that Christian women theologians have long criticized, by drawing attention to the fact that an insistence on the father god, the absence of women in positions of church leadership, and the exclusive language of liturgy, provide ideological and social support for violence done to women."[29]

Thus, we have identified significant strands in the culture that both reflect and form personal and cultural narratives that support and normalize intimate violence by men against women. One problem with core narratives is that they function as *truth frames,* usually outside our personal or cultural awareness. When new understandings begin to emerge that challenge the unilateral interpretation that comes out of an unquestioned core narrative, then new narrative strands that allow new interpretations and meaning-making can be constructed. That reconstruction is motivated by the hope that the resulting narrative is less problem saturated or more in keeping with a preferred future. In other words, we need to continue to deconstruct these violence-laden narratives, so we can construct new narratives that work against the likelihood of intimate violence.

Familial Narratives

Cultural narratives are significantly shaped by the dominant narratives of the subgroups to which people belong. For example, subcultural narratives for many people of color intentionally teach their members to be suspicious of many narratives of the dominant white culture. A subculture of radical feminism will hope to help its children to challenge and reconstruct dominant cultural narratives about gender. Churches that are self-conscious about dynamics of power and oppression will help their members to develop counternarratives that are liberating and empowering for all people. In similar ways, individual families and subcultures of families provide more particular narratives for their members that either amplify, support, or negate the core narratives of the dominant culture. Families that reproduce patterns of violence supported by the culture or that reinforce gender stereotypes held as normative in the culture will continue to normalize patterns that make domestic violence likely. Families that challenge traditional gender roles and demonstrate egalitarian power relationships among family members (including children) are more likely to diminish the power of the cultural narrative. Given the strength of cultural narratives to reproduce familiar power relationships, behaviors, and attitudes, counternarratives have to be intentional and have to teach people how to challenge and deconstruct normative assumptions. Only then will people find ways to resist the influence of cultural narratives of power and control.

Gender Narratives

It has been the assumption of this chapter that gender narratives are powerful and formative in our culture. They are binary and polarized. Women and men, girls and boys are defined over against each other. They are seen as opposites. This is one of the first harmful dimensions of gender stereotyping. Gender stereotypes teach girls and boys to relate to one another in ways that do not challenge the power organization mandated by the dominant culture. Girls and boys begin their education about how to fit into the dominant narrative from the moment of birth. Along with their pink or blue hospital caps, they are talked to more or less, played with more or less, and given more or less freedom of movement as determined by their sex.

Sandra Bem's perspective on gender schema theory is helpful for us as we look at the cultural contexts of gender narratives. Bem is most famous for her work in the 1970s on androgyny. She has since rejected her conclusions in that work and moved to a focus on gender schema theory. This theory suggests that children, from a very young age, internalize the lens of gender polarization into their own narrative frameworks. Within these narrative frameworks, people then resist challenge from experiences that do not support them and pay attention to any data or experiences that do support them, thus reinforcing the culturally supported narrative. Bem writes:

> Gender schema theory contains two fundamental presuppositions about the process of individual gender formation: first, that there are gender issues embedded in cultural discourse and social practice that are internalized by the developing child, and, second, that once these gender lenses have been internalized, they predispose the child, and later the adult, to construct an identity that is consistent with them."[30]

She goes on to state that girls and boys have to contend not only with gender polarization, but also with cultural androcentrism and with a mandate to pass this schema on through the culture from generation to generation. The cultural phenomena that reinforce androcentrism and gender polarization include such things as "generic" male language (including male names becoming the "family" name), child-rearing practices, advertising strategies, entertainment themes and images, and so on. Bem argues that gender polarization and its enculturation is so ubiquitous that even feminist theory building (such as the persistent emphasis on women being more relational than men) can perpetuate its legacy.

It is important to note that Bem begins here with assumptions very different from those of many developmental theorists. Her assumption is that children are formed in the cultural soup of gender norms and power arrangements. There is no emphasis here on an epigenetic principle of positive unfolding but rather an affirmation that children use the narrative material of their families, institutions, media, schools, and so on as the raw material for the way they shape their places and identities in those systems. The theory also assumes that girl children are immediately exposed in this culture to narrative messages that deny them, at least to some degree, the ability to develop a comprehensive sense of trust, industry, or even identity, no matter how stable or affirming their family life or personality.

This developmental dynamic of gender shaping is a key factor in the promulgation of violent family narratives. It is important, then, to look at gender development in boys and girls in some detail.

Girls' Gender Training

Lyn Brown and Carol Gilligan have documented that many girls in late childhood and early adolescence seem to lose their "voice." Gilligan and Brown did a longitudinal study of girls moving from age eight into their early teen years. They found that younger girls were in significant relationships with their peers and would speak directly and clearly about violations and injustices done to themselves or to their friends. By the age of eleven, however, these same girls were moving away from their own knowledge, using the phrase "I don't know" much more frequently and expressing implicit and explicit knowledge of the rules they were to follow in order to be acceptable and "in relationship." Gilligan and Brown summarize their findings:

> At the crossroads of adolescence, the girls in our study describe a relational impasse that is familiar to many women: a paradoxical or dizzying sense of having to give up relationship for the sake of 'relationships.' This taking of oneself out of relationship in order to protect oneself and have relationships forces an inner division or chasm, it makes a profound psychological shift. . . .Women's psychological development within patriarchal societies and male-voiced cultures is inherently traumatic.[31]

Women and other members of nondominant groups have thus learned to interpret their own stories and experiences, needs and goals, through the lenses of the other—those they have been taught to please and appease. Often they have lost access to their truths and their honest strengths.

Brown suggests that the girls learn during early adolescence what it means to be a "good" woman, fearing that if they do not follow the rules of "femininity," they will experience abandonment, exclusion, or ridicule. Recently published books of "rules" for how young women can attract men make these rules explicit, but my experience has been that girls and women, almost without exception, know those rules by heart. And those rules about being feminine—quiet, nurturing, relational, supportive, full of caring feelings and empathy but rarely angry, and so forth—teach girls and women how to be part of the supporting cast, rather than actors or authors with voice and authority.

When a young woman does not follow the rules she pays a price, often humiliation or retribution. Maria Harris names the problem:

This dilemma—and the choices it suggests—can be described thus: (a) either to stop or hide one's own voice in order to become, or thought of as, a "nice girl," and so become alienated from oneself; or (b) to refuse to be silent and take the risk, perceived and real in this society, of becoming alienated socially and politically, of being ostracized as, for example, "brash," "loud," "aggressive," "bossy."[32]

Some girls do take the latter choice, refusing to give up themselves or their knowledge for the sake of an idealistic dream about being the perfect woman and the implications of that dream. Studies indicate that African American girls in particular are better able to resist the seduction of this ideal, in part because they are more aware of its falseness, and because they are raised in a community that teaches girls that, in order to survive racism, they need to be able to speak out against cultural lies. For some of these young women, the resistance they are able to express to the dual realities of racism and sexism helps to create possibilities for real transformation in their lives. As Tracy Robinson and Janie Ward discuss, however, there is a difference between resistance for survival, which often offers short-term gains but long-term problems, and resistance for liberation. They suggest that the role of the community is to foster the kind of resistance in young African American women that will lead to long-term liberation, not just survival.[33] Beverly Jean Smith writes, "As an African American, I grew up within a particular cultural context that values voice. African American culture demands that individual voices be connected to the whole and not just to go solo and fly off somewhere." She goes on to say that African American girls do not fall prey to the rules of femininity as often as do European American girls, because they do not fall victim to the myth of "Prince Charming."[34] These writers think that living in an African American community helped them to resist these cultural lies about the promise of true femininity because their voice in resisting racism was encouraged.

Many young women learn in adolescence what it means to be a "good" woman and to "forget what they know." They give up the ability to be in authentic relationship for the sake of being related in ways that minimize the risks of exclusion and abandonment. This process seems to be a subtle one that most girls identify in a positive way—claiming in Gilligan and Brown's studies that their previous answers (from childhood) were "stupid" and that they see things more clearly as adolescents. Many of the young women in their study were able to identify a vague sense of disquiet, that if they expressed themselves honestly, especially in ways that might hurt other people's feelings, their relationships would be lost. Even when there was no evidence that the relationship in question was that fragile, the conviction that honest expression of feelings would lead to exclusion was maintained.

All of these developmental processes put women at risk for violence in male-female intimate relationships. We will look more at this phenomenon in a moment.

Boys' Gender Training

A lot of important, gender-conscious research has been done in the past ten or fifteen years about masculinity and men's psychological and spiritual health. This research has focused on the problems men experience that might well be a direct result of their attempt to conform to male gender roles. Ron Levant writes that these new approaches to understanding masculinity have provided a framework for a psychological approach to men and masculinity that questions traditional norms for the male role, such as the emphases on competition, status, toughness, and emotional stoicism and that views certain male problems (such as aggression and violence, homophobia, misogyny, detached fathering, and neglect of health) as unfortunate but predictable results of the male role socialization process.[35]

James O'Neill says there are six patterns that are a result of gender socialization in men. These are:

1. Restrictive emotionality
2. Socialized control, power, and competition
3. Homophobia
4. Restrictive sexual and affective behavior
5. Obsession with achievement and success
6. Health-care problems

He goes on to say, "How men are socialized produces sexist attitudes and behavior that explains much of the personal and institutional sexism in society."[36] O'Neill suggests that normative masculinity sets up persistent worries about personal achievement, competence, failure, status, upward mobility and wealth, and career success in men's lives as well as a drive to obtain authority, dominance, and influence over others. There is an emphasis on striving against others in competitive ways. Restrictive emotionality suggests that men have difficulty and fears about expressing feelings and difficulty finding words to express basic emotions. Ron Levant says that emotionality (boy babies are more emotional than are girl babies) is socialized out of boys very intentionally and this has four major consequences. First, boys develop a form of empathy he calls "action empathy," which is the ability to see things from another's point of view in order to predict what they will "do" (not what they feel) and is usually employed in the service of the self (different from emotional empathy). Second, boys become strangers to their own emotional life, and most develop at least a mild form of alexithymia (not having words for emotions). Men who are in the presence of an unrecognized emotion often experience only the bodily sensation of its physiological component. Third, boys pour their vulnerable emotions out through the channel of anger—one of the few emotions boys are encouraged to express. Fourth, boys learn to channel their caring emotions through their sexuality.

We need to recognize some of the important negative consequences for men of gender-role strain. For example, probably all four of the gender-role conflict factors correlate positively with depression in men, and restrictive emotionality correlates positively with depression at all life stages of men. Higher levels of gender-role conflict correlate positively with low self-esteem. In race studies, European American, African American, and Hispanic men all reported problems with success, power, and competition; restrictive emotionality; and conflicts between work and family relations. Results of several studies indicate strong correlations between gender-role conflict and negative attitudes toward seeking help.[37]

Other consequences of gender-role strain include the fact that women live, on average, seven years longer than do men, and gender-related lifestyle choices are part of this shorter life expectancy (for example, between the ages of fifteen and twenty-four, men die at three times the rate of women, mostly because of high rates of violent death among male youth). Women are more prone to anxiety disorders and depression, but men show more evidence of antisocial personality disorder and alcohol and drug abuse.[38] Men also participate in violence in very destructive ways that can be clearly related to gender-role training. In a recent study of 518 college men, 34 percent reported that they had engaged women in unwanted sexual contact, 20 percent reported they had attempted unwanted intercourse, and 10 percent reported they had completed unwanted intercourse. Forty-six percent said they were at least somewhat likely to force sex if they would not get caught.[39]

This discussion leads us into the connections between gender training in a world ordered by dualistic power assignments and intimate violence in heterosexual intimate relationships.

Implications for Male-Female Violence in Intimate Relationships

Women who stay in or return to battering relationships, especially early on in the battering, tend to feel responsible for the relationship failure. There is debate in the literature on domestic abuse about how much self-blame women take on in a battering relationship, but it does seem clear that for women who stay in the relationship and for women in relationships in which the battering has not been going on for very long, self-blame is high. In addition, women in battering relationships tend to be and become depressed and to experience low self-esteem.[40] Certainly low self-esteem, which is the reality most closely tied to women's experience in battering relationships, is related to both a lack of a sense of entitlement and a lack of hope for creating something new. These same dynamics also make women vulnerable to the pervasive problem of "hands off" battering, or emotional abuse, which always accompanies physical battering and which might exist in relationships in which no physical battering takes place. (Emotional abuse might also serve as a precursor to physical violence in a relationship.) No matter what the pattern of emotional abuse, the abuse generates deep damage in its victims.

Women who are in battering relationships tend to look diligently for an explanation for a presumably aberrant situation. They engage in mind reading. Lempert suggests that "violence is not a generally expected marital interaction. Cultural expectations of love and marriage do not include the 'stories from hell' that are the lived experiences of abused women. It is the unexpected nature of the violence, its seeming unpredictability, that makes it difficult to assimilate."[41] As a result, women look for an explanation that fits their core narrative. Piera Serra writes:

> If the woman perceives the violence she is subjected to as the expression of her partner's inner world, and she considers the act as a symptom or a message, she will tend to disregard her own suffering and physical helplessness. Most of the women we interviewed who were still living with their partners interpreted their partners' violent behavior as a sign of distress.[42]

The impact of this mind reading and interpretation favoring the other person is that it gets in the way of moral evaluation and self-care. Psychologically, it also gives the woman the illusion that she still has a chance of fixing this problem in the relationship (which, of course, is not a problem in the relationship at all but a problem in her spouse). Lempert suggests that "women in a battering relationship cannot afford to relinquish beliefs that they exercise some control, however minimal, over their lives because their survival depends on those beliefs and on continued use of whatever personal power they possess. With the erosion of these personal and social resources comes increasing demoralization."[43]

Serra concludes her discussion with the statement that women turn to outsiders to help end the violence in order to preserve the relationship. Yet most caregivers, whether police, clergy, counselors, or friends, help only by suggesting that she leave the relationship. They do not think they have the authority or right to make the batterer stop battering. Thus, when the batterer expresses contrition, mild affection, or even just temporarily ends the violence, she takes this as a sign of change, and the bonding between them that might result is usually more satisfying than any outside help has been.[44] In this way, her training to be relationally responsible, to sacrifice self-interest in order to care for others, and to hope nurturing and love will be forthcoming if she follows the gender rules is often temporarily fruitful in the period between violent episodes by the batterer himself.

It's also important to look at men's gender training and its relationship to violence in marriages. Remembering O'Neill's work and Pleck's work mentioned above in the discussion on gender training for men, we can begin to see some connections. Numerous studies have linked the inability to express vulnerable feelings with a strong tendency to engage in interpersonal violence. Other studies have shown clear linkages between socialization for aggression and interpersonal violence.[45] Paul Yelsma, in his work on intimate violence, names several factors that he calls triggers for abuse in batterers. Those factors include: alcohol abuse, need to maintain authority, excessive need for control, high need for power, dependency conflicts, fear of intimacy, poor self-concept, witnessing abusive behavior in family of origin, experience of abuse as a child, a tendency to label all emotions as anger, sex role rigidity, emotional inexpressiveness, intellectualizing of emotions, spouse-specific inassertiveness, tendency to experience suspicion and jealousy, social isolation, low levels of inclusion, and emotional dependency.[46]

Obviously, these factors are not all present in all men, and they take vastly different shapes depending on other particularities such as race, ethnicity, class, sexual orientation, and even age or place in the life cycle. Yet, as Wayne Ewing writes, "When the question is raised, 'who is the male batterer?' the answer is sometimes given, 'everyman!' Without pushing too quickly, let me simply point out here that this observation is accurate."[47] Numerous studies have shown that the psychological profiles of violent men (rapists or batterers) are not significantly different from the psychological profiles of the general population of men. Male gender training, which is facilitated by families and other important institutions, is related to high risk for interpersonal violence. In fact, Ewing goes on to say, "The teaching of violence is so pervasive, so totally a part of male experience, that I think it best to acknowledge this teaching as a civic, rather than as a cultural or as a social, phenomenon. Certainly there are social institutions which form pieces of the total advocacy of violence: marriage and family; ecclesiastical institutions; schools; economic and corporate institutions; government and political institutions."[48] He concludes his article: "I used to think that we simply tolerated and permitted male abusiveness in our society. I have now come to understand rather that we advocate physical violence. Violence is presented as effective. Violence is taught as the normal, appropriate and necessary behavior of power and control."[49]

Certainly not all men (or even most men) are emotionally or physically violent in their intimate relationships. All men who don't engage in family violence, however, must actively resist cultural narratives of maleness that would predispose them toward it. Men must also be willing actively to protest the culture that makes it likely they will be violent with intimate partners. If men want to be seen as nonviolent, it is important that they take a clear stand against family violence.

The issues of power and hierarchy are a foundational part of understanding domestic violence. We must not fall into the mistake that many battered women make of thinking battering is primarily a symptom of their male partners' personal distress or dysfunction. Michael Kaufman writes, "Men's violence against women is the most common form of direct, personalized violence in the lives of most adults and . . . is probably the clearest most straightforward expression of relative male and female power."[50] Joseph Pleck, who has been so instrumental in developing a new psychology of men, notes that men create hierarchies as a key component of the competitive side of male gender training, and those hierarchies determine value between men and over women. This hierarchical power system objectifies women in such a way that it makes violence against them more acceptable and likely.[51] In an interesting newspaper article from the *Seattle Times*, a lawyer is reported to have used the following argument to defend his client from being punished for the crime of sexual assault of which he had been found guilty.

The lawyer said, "Hostility toward women, I think, is something that is culturally instilled in men. It's part of our culture that has been for hundreds of years, that violence against women is not unacceptable. Consequently, my client should not be punished for being culturally male."[52]

Pleck suggests that women are used in male hierarchies in the following ways:

1. Women are used as symbols of success in men's competition. Therefore, when that success is threatened by a woman "failing to meet his expectations," violence is likely.

2. Women play a mediating role and smooth over men's inability to relate noncompetitively with other men.

3. Women provide men a refuge from the dangers and stresses of relating to other males. When she is no longer willing to be a nurturer or best friend, either because of her own needs or in response to earlier violence, violence by him is more likely.

4. Women reduce the stress of competition by serving as an underclass (against whom men do not have to compete). This might help explain why women's successful movement into the public arena in recent decades might be related to escalating violence. It also makes very clear women's "otherness" and objectification.[53]

Ewing writes, "The ruling paradigm for male supremacy remains to this hour, physical violence,"[54] and it is often effective. McMahon and Pence have studied men who batter. They conclude, "When asked, violent men are quite clear about what it can accomplish: 'she would listen,' 'she would drop the order for protection,' 'next time she'd think twice.' Such men benefit from their violence. How much more seductive are explanations that say a man's violence is an expression of his insecurity or impulsiveness."[55]

Gender training within this context of power differences is a powerful narrative for violence by men against women in intimate relationships. It helps us understand that the work of pastoral care and counseling needs to attempt to reshape these cultural, formative narratives, not just work with the idiosyncratic stories of individual perpetrators and victims.

Pastoral Care Paradigms of Response

Pastoral response to victims of domestic abuse needs to include three elements. First, every religious leader who might have pastoral access to battered women needs to understand a basic crisis approach to women who seek pastoral care in the midst of active battering. Every pastor should have a thorough knowledge of the dynamics of battering and battering cycles and the ability to use that knowledge effectively in crisis situations with victims of intimate violence. Pastors should also have the ability to help women who are at risk of future battering to develop a detailed safety plan. The plan should be one the women can put into action when it is needed. Pastors need to have done their homework, so they are not scrambling to find resources (such as women's shelters, legal resources, rape crisis lines, support groups, and the like) during a crisis moment. All pastors need to have a thorough referral list with resources they have personally evaluated, so they can be free to pay attention and tend to the needs of the person in distress. These are basic crisis procedures for victims of intimate violence.

It is common for a woman to come for pastoral care or counseling, however, not during the crisis of violence itself, but as a result of the longer-term effects of the trauma. This fact leads us to the second response element. Religious leaders need to be able to help victims of battering to move through a longer healing process after they are no longer at immediate risk. It is important to remember that the pastor might play many roles. First, healing care is not limited to formal pastoral counseling. Second, the pastor is not the only agent of healing in the church. Third, the pastor needs to be able to work in concert with appropriate community resources for the good of the care receiver. If the church gives clear messages through its education programs, sermon topics and illustrations, support group structures, and use of money (such as having a discretionary fund to help pay for healing resources in the community), then it is more likely that all three of these structures of healing will be able to work together for the good of the victim of intimate violence.

In keeping with both narrative theory and feminist principles, it is important in the healing process to focus on women's strengths and resources rather than assessing deficits and pathology. This is easier said than done. For one thing, counseling has been so steeped in a medical model of sickness and a behavioral model of problems that it is natural for caregivers and care receivers alike to approach counseling with those two lenses. Women who have been victims of intimate violence, however, generally are not in distress (even years later) because they have characterological or even behavioral deficits. They are in distress because (1) they have had minimal opportunity to process and integrate a traumatic history into the rest of their lives, and (2) they have skills and strengths that were of great help to them in surviving the violence but that now get in their way. Therefore, regarding the need to process and integrate the experience, it is important for the caregiver to find the best ways to hear the story of the violence and to believe and support that story fully (rather than to work with a pathology model that focuses on inconsistencies and errors in the story for the sake of symptom assessment). The caregiver also needs to help the care receiver to make sense of and find meaning in the story and to incorporate it into her ongoing life narrative. Regarding the woman's skills and strengths, the care giver needs to assist the care receiver to discover ways that her strengths can be used appropriately for their current context so that they do not cause further distress.

The third element of the response model is to make sure that the batterer is not ignored. He needs to be held accountable and helped to break his patterns of control and violence. Programs are available that combine consciousness-raising about gender roles and power, behavioral relearning, and the development of new strategies for relating that can be very effective for male batterers. The problem is how to get men to stick with programs such as this. The willingness of the church to take a stand against domestic violence without giving up on batterers is key.

Pastoral Care Paradigms of Resistance

Given what we have said here about gender stereotypes and power relationships as contexts for intimate violence, there are three primary strategies for resistance. The first is to bring to greater consciousness cultural narratives that make intimate violence more likely, so the narratives seem less like unilateral, unquestionable truth. This means that we as pastors and religious leaders need to take aggressive stands against gender narratives that make relational violence more likely between men and women. Gender training as it exists in our culture makes death-dealing violence more likely. The church participates in that gender training through its silence, uncritical use of antiwomen and hierarchical theology, complacency about supposedly normal boy/girl and male/female behaviors, and reluctance to boldly and prophetically deconstruct gender assumptions. For the church to stand against the narratives that precipitate family violence, it will have to take gender equality and flexibility seriously in elementary church school classes, junior high youth groups, premarital preparation sessions, adult Bible studies, and everywhere that cultural narratives about gender, power, and control are expressed implicitly or explicitly. The work of resistance against intimate violence requires disciplined scrutiny and the persistent deconstruction of damaging narratives in all church activities, including worship.

The second form of resistance is deeply supporting exceptional narrative strands—strands that work against the core narrative. When those exceptional strands are supported and made stronger, they are more likely to offset the power of the core narrative. So, for example, a key mission of pastoral care in this context would be to support those attitudes and behaviors that go against stereotypical gender roles, challenge unequal power between men and women (or among racial groups, sexual orientation groups, and so on), or immediately stand in the way of interpersonal violence. This support of alternative or exceptional narrative strands in people, institutions, and the culture at large is our most likely avenue for successful prevention of violence. I think domestic violence is one of the most powerful indicators for the mandate to work against sexism at home, schools, our media, and the church. These are not issues of political correctness; we are talking about lifesaving measures.

It is also important to recognize that women frequently engage in small acts of resistance to male violence in relationships and families. Those acts of resistance need to be acknowledged in ways that help women to see the possibilities of their own agency. Religious leaders need to find ways in sermon illustrations, teaching, and pastoral care to affirm all constructive forms of resistance to oppressive and harmful narratives and actions.

The reality is that it is not easy to deconstruct problematic core narratives. We are ambivalent about them, if we become aware of them at all. They make life more predictable and reliable. They fit with our gut experience, which we like to believe is true. They often entitle us to familiar power—to getting what we think we want or need. It is often painful to attempt to deconstruct even damaging core narratives because of their integrative and stabilizing power. Even the intensely negative aspects of our interpretive frameworks are interwoven with those aspects that have given our lives positive meaning. Consequently, when I talk about pastoral care as offering support for alternative narrative possibilities as they occur, what I mean by support is institutional, relational, and personal efforts to affirm and encourage the development of these alternative ways of being and interpreting but not deny the ambivalence in that process. That kind of support means we have to be willing to deconstruct our own violence-laden assumptions—psychological, theological, linguistic, relational, vocational—and to be held accountable when we act out of them. Preventive pastoral care will involve deconstructing and being held accountable for our own violence-laden core narratives (as leaders of the church) and then helping to support the development of exceptional nonviolent narratives in people, church, and society. Knowing how these more overtly violent narratives are interwoven with more subtle strands of stereotypical gender training, our various forms of entertainment, and our theological interpretation helps us to do this deconstruction and restorying at the deep, integrative levels required for change.

Finally, we have to be willing to join with other community resource people who are also attempting to find ways to resist the seductive power of relational violence. Churches and religious leaders need to join with the battered women's shelter movement, legal advocates, educators of all kinds, and others who are willing to speak on behalf of peacemaking in families. In addition, we have to learn how to be open to new expressions of and narratives about gender that break down the absolute dualisms of maleness and femaleness with their assigned roles. We in the church have often been afraid to open ourselves to new ways of understanding roles and relationships, much less gender. We need, however, to find models that help us to break down gender models based on complementarity, hierarchy, and control, and we have to learn from those new models how to live together as people—not just as women and men—with all our potential and all our limitations.

If we are to be true to faith commitments to peace and justice, we can no longer be satisfied with a pastoral theology and pastoral care that focuses only or even primarily on responses to suffering. The contemporary challenge in relation to family violence is to actively and aggressively resist those narratives in ourselves and our world that lead us to do harm to one another. We must settle for no less than transformation of those principalities and powers that seek to separate us from one other and God. We cannot afford to dismiss this transformative work as conformity to political correctness. Lives are at stake.

Opening the Eyes:
Understanding the Impact of Trauma
on Development

Pamela Cooper-White

"And I say, Hey, what a wonderful kind of day, When we can learn to work and play, and get along with each other." Arthur, the latency-age aardvark who wears his baggy jeans and horn-rimmed glasses cavorts on his TV program early each morning. Along with his little sister, D. W., he learns not-too-terrible lessons about friendship, lying, recycling, chicken pox, homework, responsibility, and the death of hamsters. His TV audience of five- to nine-year-olds is brought along with him to learn these lessons gently and vicariously: The world is good. Responsibility is good. Lying is bad. Friends come in all shapes and sizes, but we can all get along. You'll get sick, but then you'll get to go to the fair anyway. Mothers are kind, grandmothers think the best of you, and fathers are honorable, if a little detached. This is the world of children as we adults want to believe it, sometimes remember it, and hope to help our own children experience it. It is also the world of child development as it has been largely taught and written about from Piaget to the present day.

Just as a child moves through the developmental eras of childhood from one evolutionary truce to another and literally cannot conceive of certain aspects of logic or reality that belong to a later phase of development, so our culture has only recently emerged (or, it can be argued, reemerged) from a long incapacity to recognize the reality of childhood sexual abuse and trauma. A quick review of the subject index in each of the developmental texts with which we have become familiar—Erik Erikson,[1] Robert Kegan,[2] and James Fowler's now classic text on faith development[3]—reveals no mention of "trauma," "abuse," or "sexual abuse." These authors occasionally consider the idea of "crisis," but even this topic is generally framed as a naturally occurring disruption or loss that can eventually be accommodated, if not assimilated, as a growth-enhancing experience. Examples of crises include leaving home for the first time or losing a loved one. This exclusion of trauma and abuse is true even of Carol Gilligan's groundbreaking work, *In a*

Different Voice,[4] in which she presents the idea that women's and girls' develop-ment, particularly moral development, might not proceed along the same lines as those laid out by Kohlberg in his study of school-aged boys.

Sexual abuse and childhood trauma were just beginning to emerge into our public awareness in the late 1970s and early 1980s through the work of such authors as Florence Rush,[5] Judith Herman,[6] Roland Summit,[7] David Finkelhor,[8] and pioneering pediatricians Ruth and Henry Kempe.[9] The international journal *Child Abuse and Neglect* first appeared in 1976, and the U.S. Department of Health and Human Services conducted its first studies on child neglect and abuse report-ing in 1978 and 1979. Two landmark empirical studies were published as recently as the mid-1980s, one a large-scale prevalence study of incest in the lives of girls and women by Diana Russell,[10] and another, the first study of sexual abuse of African American girls, by Gail Wyatt.[11]

Two decades ago, the stark revelations of these authors about the nature and prevalence of child sexual abuse seemed at times shocking, subversive, and radical. We now know, as we were just learning then, that from one in five to one in three girls, and one in sixteen to one in eleven boys are physically sexually abused by age eighteen.[12] The work of the Harvard Project on the Psychology of Women and the Development of Girls[13] and the Stone Center of Wellesley College,[14] no doubt because of project members' commitment to the integration of feminist theory, have come the closest in recent years to incorporating an appreciation of trauma and sexual abuse into their theoretical and clinical writings on development. The Kempes' work was also significant, in that it was published in a series on child development and took a strong advocacy stance on behalf of the rights of children and the necessity of a community-wide response.

The split between the domains of developmental theory and the serious study of trauma is reflected in much of the literature up to the present. Both domains can be traced to Freud, but the split begins with Freud as well. Freud can be considered the first developmental theorist; he posited the three well-known stages of psychosexual development (oral, anal, and phallic/genital) in his (1908) *Three Essays on the Theory of Sexuality*.[15] But it is perhaps significant, as developmental theorists remain unaware of the impact of trauma in developmental theories to this day, that this developmen-tal schema evolved as part of Freud's oedipal theory and represented a profound theoretical shift away from the so-called seduction theory of the previous decade in which he attributed the symptoms of hysteria to sexual abuse by a father or father-figure. In this sense, the entire foundation of developmental theory, however accurate a depiction it may offer of certain psychic phenomena, is built on a "closing of the eyes," not against the primal scene, but against the horror of real abuse.

Shift focus: A girl, let us say age eight, finishes watching Arthur and turns off the TV to get ready for her day at school. Last night Daddy came to her room again and did those things that belong to the awfulness of the night. She spent a long time floating somewhere along the ceiling while nightmare things were happening in the dark to her body far below. But that was night, and now it's day. She loads homework and lunch into a backpack and chooses her clothes—the flowered minidress and high platform sneakers. It's the outfit Daddy says he hates, because it makes her look "trampy," and her mother defends: "Have *you* tried shopping for girls' clothes lately?" The young girl likes it because it makes her feel cool, a little more in control, and a little more like the other kids. It keeps her outsides feeling more okay and together when her insides seem to be falling apart in mysterious ways, more and more every day. She will try very hard today not to daydream, not to squirm where it hurts to sit, to pay attention so that she won't draw the teacher's attention to her again, to look and feel "normal," without monsters and terrors deep inside, the way she imagines it is for everyone but her.

It is the purpose of this chapter to return to developmental theories while opening the eyes, and to ask the question: How does the experience of early trauma, particularly sexual abuse, affect development? Does trauma derail or block development as it might be understood against the backdrop of normative developmental patterns? Or does it do something different altogether, creating a new, separate, or alternative pathway—or even multiple pathways proceeding at different rates? Many developmental theories and theorists could be engaged in such an inquiry. For the sake of brevity, I will focus on just three areas of developmental theory, but it is my hope that this examination will offer a method for further examining the impact of trauma and sexual abuse from many theoretical lenses. The areas I have chosen to explore are a number of theoretical perspectives grouped into three broad clusters of ideas. These three groups are: (1) developmental stage theories (including Freud, Erik Erikson, and the more recent author Robert Kegan); (2) relationally focused psychoanalytic theories, which have their own implicit or explicit developmental theory, including object relations, self psychology, and aspects of feminist relational theory; and (3) theories of faith development, beginning with the work of Fowler, which strive explicitly to incorporate a theological and spiritual dimension in development.

This chapter might strike some readers as heavily theoretical. It is my experience, however, that our practices of ministry, including parish ministry, chaplaincy, and pastoral psychotherapy, are subtly and even unknowingly formed by these theories as they trickle down into the culture from generations of psychological research, training, and practice. It is important to know the origins of our assumptive practices in order to be better able to critique them and to choose whether and how to incorporate them into our own practices of ministry.

This chapter is written primarily from the lens of pastoral psychotherapy. Theoretical constructs are ultimately only of use to the degree that they can be applied within the context of real relationships of trust and therapeutic safety. It is my intent, by bringing the all too often hidden realities of childhood trauma and especially sexual abuse into dialogue with developmental theories, to enhance the theoretically informed sensitivity of pastoral counselors and psychotherapists, so that previously unseen truths about trauma survivors' experience might be more readily perceived and empathically understood. It is my further hope that, although the long-term work of helping another to recover from sexual trauma belongs within the realm of a clinically trained therapist, the theoretical understandings offered here will also be of value to parish clergy, chaplains, and pastoral caregivers. Pastoral caregivers' sensitization to the inner dynamics of trauma plays a critical role, aiding in the deeply spiritual healing process of trauma survivors. The absence of such sensitization all too often unwittingly perpetuates cycles of self-blame, premature forgiveness, and retraumatization.

Stage Theories

In a film made late in his life, Erik Erikson talks about the popularity of his "eight stages of man."[16] In a touching personal moment, Erikson proudly shows the filmmaker a quilt or tapestry that someone had made for him in which these eight stages from infancy to old age were depicted artistically in sequential blocks of fabric. Those blocks are the way developmental stage theories are generally thought of and taught—as if they are a series of boxcars, one attached to the next as development proceeds. In such a "boxcar" conceptualization, events that are disruptive to development (whether conceived of as outer or inner events or conflicts) must be understood as impeding forward movement. Disruptive events, from minor challenges to crises requiring major life adjustments, are seen as either slowing development, stopping it at least for a time (as described in the language of "developmental blocks" or "fixation points"), or, in the worst case scenario, derailing it.

In such a conceptualization, the task of care and counseling is focused in linear fashion on getting development back on track. This healing is accomplished by addressing the crisis, perhaps helping the person to acquire new coping mechanisms to deal with what overwhelmed his or her existing capacities, or putting the person in touch with better external supports, so that when the crisis is resolved, development can once again move forward. This model has been taught extensively in counseling programs and has great practical utility, particularly when the disruptive event takes place within the framework of normal, though sometimes intensely painful life crises, such as illness, a difficult move, or the death of a close family member. Is this model adequate, however, when applied to the occurrence of severe trauma?

The term "trauma" is used in many ways. In its broadest sense, based on the original Greek meaning, it is simply any wound or injury. Under such an umbrella definition, trauma can mean any physical, psychic, or emotional insult. In this sense, a person might report to her partner at the end of a long day, "That meeting today was really traumatic!" For the purposes of this chapter, however, I use the term very specifically, following trauma specialists[17] to mean not simply any injury, but rather the deep injury that is accompanied by a feeling of helplessness or powerlessness, an experience of pain combined with the terror of being over-whelmed, and in which normal coping mechanisms fail or are unavailable. This injury might occur as a single terrible event, or it might represent the cumulative effect of repetitive occurrences of abuse or neglect. Children's basic dependence on adults adds to the experience of helplessness and a perception that this abuse or neglect is just how life is.

The experience of acute or even chronic abuse certainly may be understood within the boxcar model as impeding or derailing development. If we take Erikson's model, it rivets our attention to consider the impact of severe neglect, or physical or sexual abuse on an infant whose earliest developmental issue is "basic trust vs. basic mistrust,"[18] corresponding with Freud's oral stage. Erikson considered that "consistency, continuity, and sameness of experience provide a rudimentary sense of ego identity"[19] foundational to all further development and even to the possibility of religious faith in which "trust born of care is, in fact, the touchstone."[20] In the context of a traumatic early environment, the infant's frag-ile capacity for trust is shattered—if it is ever established at all, with devastating consequences for all subsequent development. The absence or destruction of a secure base of attachment[21] is considered by many traumatologists to be one of the deepest, most lasting forms of damage caused by abuse.[22]

It does not take too much imagination to consider the equally devastating con-sequences of trauma as it affects two subsequent stages in Erikson's theory (corre-sponding with Freud's anal and genital stages): "autonomy vs. shame and doubt," "initiative vs. guilt." Abuse can also seriously interfere with developmental tasks at the later stages of "industry vs. inferiority" (roughly the school age or "latency" years), and "identity vs. role confusion" (adolescence). The impact of abuse can be seen through the lens of other developmental stage theories as well. For example, what damage does trauma inflict on a two- to four-year-old child at Robert Kegan's stage of the "impulsive" self,[23] in which the safety of the parental triangle is considered to be essential for the healthy exercise of fantasy, rivalry, and attach-ment, preparing her to meet the challenges around age five of relating to the wider world of reality and culture outside the family?

There is one serious conceptual problem with this boxcar formulation, however: biological maturation proceeds, even if development is damaged. In that process of maturation—simply "growing up"—physical, cognitive, and affective growth does continue, although it might be compromised in some areas, even very prominent areas. If we believe that trauma derails development, how do we explain the sexu-ally abused child who nevertheless becomes an all-A student or star athlete, who perhaps takes refuge in her excellence, or the physically abused child of an alcoholic or drug-addicted parent who nevertheless manages to function somewhat capably as the head of the household by the age of ten? Certainly, some sectors of the per-sonality might be seen as stunted, missing, or suffering great pain, but nevertheless, other parts of the self continue to grow and even to exceed normal expectations.

Two other models might be helpful to place alongside the boxcar conceptualization. First, there is Anna Freud's concept of "developmental lines."[24] This concept is less widely known than Erikson's eight stages but arose from a similar motivation in the first generation after Freud to extend the application of psychoanalytic concepts beyond the clinical treatment of pathology to the consideration of normal development. Through her work with children at the Hampstead Clinic she founded in London, Anna Freud proposed the idea that there is not a single line of development but rather a number of lines running more or less parallel from infancy and on into adulthood. She identified five such lines, not as a definitive accounting but rather as examples: the line from "sucking to rational eating," from "wetting/soiling to control," from "irresponsibility to responsibility for one's own body," from "egocentricity to companionship," and most intriguingly, from "the body to the toy and from play to work."

Today, we might argue with specifics of Anna Freud's examples, which depended heavily upon oedipal theory and the notion of ego, id, and superego formation as central to development, and did not differentiate between boys' and girls' development. Later authors have expanded the concept to include many other proposed developmental lines. What might be most relevant for the study of trauma, however, is Anna Freud's further contention that normal development depends not only on the relatively untroubled progress of each of the lines, but also similar progress along all lines at once. Although she refrained from attributing pathology directly to a "disequilibrium" between developmental lines, she did identify this disequilibrium as a point of vulnerability, a "pathogenic agent."

How might severe trauma in childhood be understood in this conceptualization? Rather than impeding or derailing development altogether, if we think in terms of multiple developmental lines or "tracks," trauma might affect some but not all aspects of development, accounting for the appearance of competence and even precocity in many abused children. This also helps to explain why dissociation, however pathological it might seem later in life, functions to protect traumatized children. If certain experiences are too terrible to be assimilated, they may become encapsulated or frozen on certain developmental lines, while other aspects of development are freed to proceed in relative coordination with maturation. This model might be helpful to pastoral caregivers and counselors by reminding us to consider multiple areas of growth within the same person and to hold in mind both the person's areas of strength or even overdeveloped capacities *and* underdeveloped areas of fragility, vulnerability, and fear.

A second model we might set alongside the boxcar model might be that of the concentric rings of a tree trunk. Using this image, we might imagine experiences during the earliest developmental eras in a child's life as encircled or nested within or beneath later ones. From this perspective, developmental achievements are layered together with the life experiences, joys, and crises of a particular period of time. New growth forms around the old, rather than replacing it. Nothing is left behind.[25] Trauma in this model might then be seen as having a number of manifestations, from being encapsulated like a nodule that later layers of growth cover but leave intact, to spreading throughout a particular layer of the trunk, rendering the whole tree more vulnerable to the impact of disease, cold, and storms. Note that this model replaces the mechanistic image of a train with an organic one. Helping in this model would not be conceptualized so much as getting something back on track, as going deeper, toward the core of the organism to tend enclosed wounds in need of healing and regeneration. It then follows that the earlier the experience of trauma, the closer it is to the core of the person, which could be thought of as the soul itself. Deeper, longer-term work will likely be required for the healing process to take place.

Relational Psychoanalytic Theories

We might gain a deeper appreciation of the impact of trauma on development, particularly very early development, by turning to a different set of theorists whose work, loosely bound together, represents a more relational conception of the development of the self. In this category I am including British and American objects relations, self psychology, the Sullivanian or interpersonal school and its evolution in the feminist work of the Stone Center, and the more recent relational and intersubjective schools of American psychoanalysis. It would be a vast oversimplification to imply that these schools are merely variations on a single theoretical conceptualization. Each represents a rich and complex system of thought that cannot be adequately represented in this chapter. Bearing this caution in mind, however, there are some common threads that are useful for our present purpose, which is to consider the impact of trauma on development and the implications of these theoretical understandings for healing.

All of these relational approaches share two important concepts: the centrality of human relations in development, and the intensely formative impact of the relations between caregivers and children going back to the earliest stages of infancy.

First, let us consider the centrality of human relations in development. Beginning with Melanie Klein in the 1930s, the so-called object relations theorists began to detect the central significance of a drive or yearning for connection with an other (inelegantly termed "object seeking"[26]). In contrast with Freud's theories of drive satisfaction, the object relations theorists began to perceive that the other was not merely a target for instinctual satisfaction, but that connection with the other (both as fantasized and as experienced) was a strong motivating desire in its own right, even replacing sex and aggression as the central motivating factor in human behavior.

Through the work of W. R. D. Fairbairn and others, it increasingly came to be recognized that a variety of significant others, as experienced by the child, to varying degrees came to take up residence in the inner, psychic reality of the child from birth onward as "internal objects." Now not only or even primarily Freud's ego, id, and superego, but a host of satisfying, tantalizing, and tormenting figures or aspects of the self could direct behavior and color perceptions of the external world. These internal objects became the source for inner messages of self-worth, self-condemnation, inner conflict, and projection of old relational patterns onto real, external others. The point of intersection between the inner and outer realities, termed "potential space" by the British theorist D. W. Winnicott,[27] became a rich area for exploration, where fantasy and reality meet in a complex interplay of images and symbols, thoughts, feelings, and behaviors.

Self psychologists, beginning with the work of Heinz Kohut in the early 1960s, although using different terminology, point also to the central significance of the child's lived experience of her caregivers, and particularly the role of an empathic environment early in life, to build the necessary inner psychic structures for self-soothing, self-regulation, and self-esteem. Interpersonal, relational, and intersubjective theorists also generally take the significance of real interpersonal relations as their starting point. Their differences lie mostly in implications for clinical treatment and the relative attention given to conscious vs. unconscious relationship between therapist and patient/client, but all would agree on the centrality of human connection as the starting point for development, clinical treatment, and living one's life in relation with others.

The second tenet of relational theories, particularly object relations and self psychology, is the central significance of the earliest period of development in infancy. Freud's own developmental stage theory spanned roughly the first five or six years of life, beginning with the oral stage at birth, through the anal stage of toilet training and socialization in toddlerhood, and culminating in the child's navigation of the oedipal stage. Developmental stage theories beginning with both Piaget and Erikson spanned even more of childhood, and Erikson set the precedent of examining ongoing development throughout the life span. This lens is an extremely valuable one from which to understand human development. Relational psychoanalytic theories, however, focus us more narrowly but in finer detail on the impact of caregivers at the earliest and arguably the most formative period of development in infancy and early toddlerhood. It might be useful to view Erikson and other stage theorists as providing us with a telescope for understanding the breadth of development over the course of a whole life, and relational psychoanalysts as providing us with a microscope to understand the nuances and complications of the period when the human person is most vulnerable, dependent, and in some senses—though by no means all—unformed and in a state of relative openness with the mother or other primary caretaker.[28]

In this view, in infancy and early childhood, trauma can be extremely subtle because the infant is already in a state of helplessness and total or near-total dependency. Still using the definition of trauma as an overwhelming, terrifying experience, trauma in infancy can be a quite subtle pattern of unconscious inattention, neglect, or hidden hostility. Even a look or the absence of a look can combine with inner feelings and sensations to convey to the infant a message of malevolence, even hatred. In the earliest state of infant-parent merger, it has even been suggested that the infant is able to perceive the unconscious of the parent in a preverbal or presymbolic way.[29] Because trauma can be so subtle, emotional abuse or neglect is desolating, and actual physical or sexual abuse, devastating enough to an older child, can be experienced by a small child as completely annihilating.

One tragic result of abuse in early childhood, in light of object relations theories, is the formation of inner objects that are neglectful, abandoning, and even persecutory. This is a process of mental and spiritual fragmentation. The smaller and more physically dependent the child, the greater the need of the child for some fragile faith in the goodness of the parent. The child, it is theorized, will therefore separate or split good and bad images of the parent in her own inner reality, somehow segmenting off the experience of the terrifying parent from the needed good parent.[30] Often, the child will identify the bad with herself in order to keep the good and loving image of the external parent intact. In a mental process too early for actual words, a preverbal logic asserts itself: "If something is wrong here, it must be me, because the people I depend on must be good." The dynamic of secrecy that typically accompanies abuse, particularly sexual abuse, heightens a sense of shame and aloneness, and concretely results in isolation from others who could help. This negativity can haunt the child into adulthood with feelings of self-blame and an inner sense of damage or basic badness that was long ago separated from its actual origins in abuse. Particularly in cases of severe or repeated abuse, this inner, nonverbal, and potentially damaging logic begins to function as an organizer of experience, a limiting framework from which to understand and respond to subsequent life events.

This process is compounded by the nature of traumatic memory. Neuropsychological research on the effects of trauma is increasingly demonstrating that traumatic experience is not recorded as normal events are, in the form of narrative memory, but rather is encoded in other parts of the brain where the experience remains unsymbolized,[31] and therefore might initially be accessed only through bodily sensations and preverbal, body-based memories; unconsciously driven behaviors that might appear self-destructive; and physical illness. Furthermore, there is little or no differentiation in the early stages of development between the experiences of *body* and *self*. Violations of the body are violations of the whole self, often with disastrous consequences for the development of healthy boundaries and a sense of the integrity of the self.

The implications for healing from this theoretical perspective lie in bringing inner self-persecutory aspects of the self to light. This process is not one of exorcism, attempting to root out negative aspects of the self. As self-destructive as they might seem in the present, they once served a protective function, enabling the person to survive through some capacity for identification with the abuser on whom she depended, and perhaps in some cases later to fight back. Often, however, once the person grows up and begins to establish a life independent of her abusers, these negative functions have outlived their usefulness. Clergy and other helpers can support the person to build a conscious sense of self-worth and purpose, in tandem with more intensive psychotherapy designed to address the deeper, more unconscious aftereffects of trauma. The process of such psychotherapy with victims of sexual abuse and other trauma is one of identifying sensations and behavior that have never been verbalized, or possibly even "digested" mentally in any symbolic form, and helping to move these from unmetabolized raw experiences through symbolization and verbalization to understanding.[32] No single insight will be curative. Over time, however, as understanding grows, the experience of trauma can come to be incorporated as something that happened but that no longer has such controlling influence over the person's experience of herself and over her actions and choices.[33]

Feminist relational models speak similarly of the consequences of violence in terms of voice and the loss of voice. Mary Belenky and her colleagues, in their important study of "women's ways of knowing"[34] interviewed women to investigate how women learn and organize their knowledge, including abstract critical thought and moral decision making but also their knowledge of self, others, relationships, and their whole world of experience. They identified "five different perspectives from which women view reality and draw conclusions about truth, knowledge, and authority."[35] They emphasize that these are not developmental stages per se, although their work does imply a hierarchy of complexity and maturity of thought. The first and most painful perspective they identify is that of "silence," in which women's experience of the absence of validation for their own self-expression, often combined with the presence of violence, created a disconnection between language and authoritative speech. Authority is viewed as external, unrelated, and uncaring. In this view, which complements the object relations perspective, helping must include a commitment to empowerment, of "hearing into speech"[36] by creating an environment of care that is empathic, connected, and deeply respectful.[37]

Interpersonal, feminist-relational, relational, and intersubjective theories all emphasize in various ways the two-person nature of the therapeutic relationship.[38] Rather than a classical stance in which the therapist or counselor is the expert, and the patient or client is the object of treatment, these theories emphasize the mutual influence of therapist and patient. There is a recognition of a shared, co-constructed field of conscious and unconscious thoughts, images, feelings, and even bodily sensations that might arise between them as their exploration of the patient's suffering occurs in the context of deep connection. It is the therapist's responsibility to maintain good boundaries around the work in order to provide a safe container in which this deep work may occur. Within that safe container, a depth of shared experience can richly inform both partners in the therapeutic enterprise about the nature and origins of the patient's pain and the process needed for healing to occur.

Faith Development Theories

Let us return to the story of the eight-year-old girl. School has begun. The first class is on nutrition, and the teacher says, "Good eating is very important. Whatever goes into our bodies can make us healthy or unhealthy." She doesn't know why, but the pictures of fruits and vegetables the teacher shows suddenly make her want to throw up. She's been wanting to throw up more lately. Like when the Sunday school teacher started talking about good and evil. The teacher seems to think they should be able to understand this much more easily now, but for some reason it seems more complicated than ever. She can't figure out how Daddy, who is good, can make her feel so bad. So the badness must be in her. But God's a daddy, too, and he punishes badness.

Trauma ultimately is a spiritual assault. Because body and self are one in a child's experience, trauma strikes at the deepest essence or core of self and source of self-worth and integrity. Beginning as early as preschool age, children's experiences of Sunday school and formal church worship can compound the sense of powerlessness and alienate the abused child from a sense of God as a loving, protective resource. Religious images presenting God to children as all-powerful, all-knowing masculine Lord become easily equated in the child's mind with the abuser who exercises absolute power over them in terrifying ways. Especially when the abuser is the child's father or father-figure, church-authorized language and imagery presenting a powerful, male father-God combines with the lived experience of a powerful, male father-abuser, and both images become mutually reinforcing.[39]

Theologian Jane Grovijahn[40] recently addressed the absence in existing theological frameworks of abuse survivors' experiences of God. For Grovijahn, the body is unequivocally the site of religious truth.[41] She has offered us two new terms for better understanding survivors' embodied theological experiences: "Not-God" and "God-Gone-Wrong." These terms attempt more adequately to represent survivors' felt apprehension of God as "neglectful, abandoning, abusive, hostile or persecutory." As Ana-Maria Rizzuto[42] powerfully demonstrated in a clinical study of psychotherapy patients' images of God, each individual's unique representation of God, or God-*imago*, depends heavily on internalized experiences of early caregivers and other significant others; experiences of oneself that might be invested with calm, conflict, or shame; and the way these experiences interact with the cultural surroundings and the belief system of the environment. She emphasizes that "once formed, that complex representation cannot be made to disappear; it can only be repressed, transformed, or used."[43] Although Rizzuto does not directly address the impact of trauma on the inner evolution of the God-*imago*, the implications are clear: abusive significant others will be internalized, not only as abandoning or persecutory inner "objects," but as the foundation for an abandoning or persecutory God.

James Fowler in his *Stages of Faith* introduced a now familiar and widely used framework for understanding individual differences in not only the content but the formation of religious belief and meaning-making. Fowler's six stages of faith rely heavily on both Erikson's "stages of man," but also on the foundation of Piaget's stages of cognitive development, the premise being that the mode of thought possible for a child at various ages will strongly shape his or her developing faith conceptions. When we put this understanding of faith development together with the perspective of an abused child's inner experience of terror, abandonment, and violation, the overwhelming impact of trauma at the various stages becomes devastatingly clear.

For example, in the first "pre-stage," termed "undifferentiated faith" by Fowler, the "seeds of trust, courage, hope, and love are fused in an undifferentiated way and content with sensed threats of abandonment, inconsistencies and deprivations in a child's environment."[44] This is the normative definition of the first "pre-stage," however, in which an experience of basic care and protection (Winnicott's[45] "good enough" parental holding, both literally and symbolically) is reliably present. This normative definition does not account for an environment in which abandonment, inconsistencies, and deprivations, as well as active violation of boundaries and overwhelming, frightening stimulation are the norm. Abuse and other forms of trauma at this earliest stage therefore undermine not only basic trust, as in Erikson's first developmental stage, but the whole foundation for trust in a caring, reliable, loving God. Because this stage of development is preverbal, traumatic experiences have even less likelihood of being recorded as any sort of symbolic or verbal memory and can lie dormant in inchoate, bodily form for years or even decades.

Trauma has a particular impact at each of the subsequent stages of faith. In stage 1, "intuitive-projective faith," the child, roughly ages three to seven, is susceptible to be "powerfully and permanently influenced by examples, moods, actions and stories of the visible faith of primally related adults."[46] Because fantasy and external reality are fluidly related in this stage, real experiences of abuse and terror combine, sometimes catastrophically, with inner fantasies and nightmare images. God in this stage of imaginative and intuitive understanding of self and world can become a terrifying monster, or an absent, nonprotecting parent who does not care. Perhaps in the best scenario, if there is some adequate caring or protection from an adult other than the abuser—a nurturing grandmother, a parent who learns of the abuse and takes a strong, protective stand—then there might also be some foundation in the child's inner life for imagining a rescuing God or avenging angel.

In stage 2, "mythic-literal faith," located roughly during the school years, the child begins to appropriate the rules, norms, and stories of the wider community of institutions such as school and church. Here the impact of Sunday school lessons becomes formative. This fact points to the necessity for programs of Christian education and formation that reinforce not theologies of dominance and submission, but mutuality, care, hopefulness, and respect for the child's own thoughts, experiences, and perceptions about God, self, and others.

In stage 3, "synthetic-conventional faith," usually corresponding with adolescence, the views and expectations of the wider world, and especially the judgments of peers, are ascendant. This is the stage of emerging ideological belief, but it is often embedded in what others think. The locus of authority is external. Fowler notes that a danger of this stage is that "interpersonal betrayals can give rise either to nihilistic despair about a personal principle of ultimate being or to a compensatory intimacy with God unrelated to mundane relations."[47] Abuse occurring or continuing during this stage is likely to trigger either outward conformity and compliance coupled with an increasing inner sense of theft of identity and despair, or in other cases, intense rebellion, often in the form of self-destructive behaviors and peer alliances. God and religion might become an object of extreme scorn for the abused adolescent. Like the younger child, she will absorb the impact of abuse wordlessly in her body, but she now also has the intellectual capacity for both rationalization and cynicism. She might either rationalize the abuse and identify with the needs of the perpetrator, or she might violently reject faith messages that seem fake, authoritarian, or smacking of collusion with her perpetrator. It should be noted that many people in Fowler's formulation remain at this stage for life.[48]

The remaining three stages occur past childhood and adolescence. Therefore, the occurrence of trauma during these stages falls outside the scope of this chapter. Nevertheless, a history of abuse might condition how these stages will be entered and lived, if at all. Also, the implied hierarchy of the further stages is challenged by the insights of Gilligan, and Belenky and her colleagues: women's and girls' development does not necessarily proceed directly from stage 3 into a more rationally critical stage. The emphasis on critical analysis over emotional relatedness privileges the rational mind and does not give adequate attention to the emotions, bodily feelings, and wordless images as parallel, equally valid ways of knowing, growing, and relating both in connection with other people and with God. As this emphasis on critical analysis interacts with a history of abuse, it tends to privilege precisely the type of knowing that is least likely to provide access to knowledge of the abuse or its full impact. This lack of access in turn colludes with the messages of the perpetrator and the wider society to ignore, disbelieve, or forget that the abuse ever occurred.

Like the developmental stage theories discussed above, stages of faith must also be considered in light of the fragmentation and compartmentalization of survivors' experience into different sectors of the personality and memory. Again, there might be multiple developmental lines, and more than one faith stage might be operative in the person at different times and in different contexts of threat or safety. It seems to be the case that in many survivors' experience, a part of the self containing the memory of trauma is walled off from other parts of the personality. Development may proceed extremely successfully by external appearances. Self-experiences of body and affect might be sacrificed to the task of successful daily living.[49]

Externally, such survivors might consciously give the appearance, both to themselves and others, of achieving an advanced stage of faith and intellectual theological integration based on Fowler's categories. Even a number of clergy and seminarians might fit this pattern. What is often missed, however, is the persistent inner sense of emptiness, fraud, self-doubt, shame, and incipient depression associated with earlier experiences of trauma. The depression of such individuals, sometimes itself masked by extreme industriousness, is a lid covering varying intensities of rage, pain, grief, and terror.

Trauma and Women's Development

Why a chapter on trauma in a book devoted specifically to women's development? Developmental theories have cast male experience as the norm, as reflected in popular culture. Arthur the Aardvark is, after all, a boy, as was Charlie Brown before him, and as are a host of contemporary children's cartoon characters. Female characters have always tended to be secondary, if not goofy, pesty, mean, bossy, or vapid, and there are few strong female figures even in educational television for children. Allowing male development to set the authoritative standard has had the consequence of "normalizing" a lesser occurrence of abuse than is girls' reality. Girls are victims of sexual abuse about three times more often than boys, and the vast majority of abuse (81 to 95 percent) is committed by men against girls.[50] These statistics in no way excuse or minimize the devastating impact of sexual abuse of boys[51] but are reflective of the whole continuum of violence against women and girls that continues to be a characteristic feature of our society.[52] The very nature of many developmental theories might be seen, in contrast to women's ways of knowing, as showing traces of masculine thought process, to the extent that they organize the messiness of human growth into rational, linear taxonomies.

Further, the focus of traditional developmental psychology on *individuals'* development is challenged by feminist models of care that call for attention to the "living human web."[52] Healing of abuse requires not only a sensitized response to individual victims and survivors, but a contextualized awareness and response. In the words of a recent book, we all live in a "rape culture"[54] in which women's and girls' experience is surrounded every day by media messages that female bodies are meant to be used as commodities, and that violations of female body-selves will be ignored, tacitly condoned, or blamed on them. In the privileging of the rational, the sources of women's knowledge of abuse in body, image, and emotion will be discounted, and truth-telling can become a Cassandra-like exercise in futility and ostracism.

The "closing of the eyes" is not only an individual but a systemic and societal response. It is natural to recoil at the prevalence and the horror of the sexual abuse of children. The widespread existence of sexual abuse defies our beliefs about ourselves as a democratic society that is both rational and decent. This unwillingness to see is further compounded in the church, where we want to believe that Christians are loving and nice. Ultimately, our pastoral response must be one not only of care and compassion and belief toward individual victims and survivors—although this is the very least we must offer. We must also make sexual abuse and trauma visible. This step is the first toward changing the social, political, and ecclesiastical contexts that sponsor abuse through denial and inertia. Only in this way will we fully validate the authority of women's and girls' experience and vision. By so doing, we open our eyes and thus open the way to God's own healing and justice making to move among us and transform our world.

Horror and the Development of Girls' Spiritual Voices

Patricia H. Davis

Girls between the ages of ten and nineteen present special problems of interpretation. On the one hand, the evidence of their involvement in witchcraft proceedings is remarkably full and vivid; on the other, there is hardly any evidence about their experience apart from such involvement.[1]

John Putnam Demos
Entertaining Satan: Witchcraft and the Culture of Early New England

Nilla was twelve years old, the sister of three older sisters, and the daughter of the most eccentric parents in her rural township.[2] Their old gray house was set back from a dirt road, surrounded by untidy fields. Their barn was teeming with dogs, cats, kittens, baby pigs, a ragged old horse, and assorted wild orphans. Their back woods were rumored to be the site of cult rituals, and Nilla herself said she had found possible sacrificial remains by the overgrown pond there.

Halloween was the family specialty. On Halloween nights, Nilla's father became a vampire, and her mother became a particularly horrible-looking witch. The combination of the two monsters and their enthusiasm for their roles scared local trick-or-treaters out of their wits on a yearly basis. It was a rare child who had the courage actually to accept the candy offered. For several years members of fundamentalist churches in the area picketed the house in hope of shutting down the family's extravagant Halloween enterprise. Even without the vampire and witch on the porch, however, the house had a spooky aura. Even the family's minister tried not to visit at night.

Despite her family's eccentricities, Nilla had many friends. Usually she looked and behaved like most of the rest of them—except that she got better grades in school. She was, in most ways, a normal kid with strange tales to tell. She loved to tell her stories: of ghosts in her bedroom, and tapping noises in her basement, and candles that would burn without having been lit by human hands. Although neither she nor her sisters or parents attended worship regularly, she had a keen interest in traditional Christianity and was a regular attender at the local Methodist church Sunday school. She was the student who could be depended on to notice the odd subtexts in the Bible stories and the one who demanded explanations of hard passages.

The year she was in sixth grade, she and her parents decided that it would be a good thing for her to be in the church Christmas Eve pageant being organized by the new pastor's wife. This woman wanted to avoid leaving anyone out or casting people in roles they did not want, so she was determined to allow the children to choose their own parts. She assigned Mary and Joseph to two older children, then gathered all the others and began slowly to read the familiar story of Jesus' birth. As she read, the children called out the characters they wanted to play; angels, shepherds, kings, lambs, donkeys, camels all claimed their roles. At the end of the story Nilla had not found a role to suit her.

Mrs. Alexander, the costume manager, tried to coax Nilla into being a king or shepherd, to no avail. Nilla finally asked if she could have the Bible. She took it off to read by herself. For fifteen or twenty minutes she was hardly noticed as she read intently amid all the confusion of trying to find wings and tails and crowns for all the angels, kings, and beasts. After ten minutes, Nilla returned. "Mrs. Alexander, I've found my role."

"Yes, Nilla—who are you going to be?"

"A hit man."

Mrs. Alexander swallowed hard, noticing the upward glance of the minister's wife. "There are no hit men in this story, honey."

"Right here: 'Rise, take the child and his mother, and flee to Egypt, and remain there till I tell you; for Herod is about to search for the child, to destroy him.' I want to be Herod's hit man."[3]

"What would a hit man wear?"

"All black—to hide, and he'd carry a sword."

"You're sure that's what you want?"

"Yes, Ma'am."

"Okay, Nilla. That's you."

On that Christmas Eve night—thanks to Mrs. Alexander and Nilla—worshipers at the Methodist church saw and heard a fuller version of the story of Christ's birth, with both the wonder and the horror intact. In this church, the wise men traveled to King Herod before they arrived in Bethlehem; they were accompanied by a shadowy figure on their way to the stable. Outside the stable, a hit man lurked as Mary cherished the baby and the angels sang. On that Christmas Eve, Nilla's church may have been the only church in Christendom to remember Christ's birth in this more complete narrative, including not only the beauty and glory, but also the fear, the evil, the grief, and the hit man.

Girls' Lives and Voices

Horror. Nilla was an expert. Even girls less attuned to it than Nilla seem to understand it. Television programmers understand the attraction of horror for girls and have capitalized on it. Shows such as *Buffy the Vampire Slayer* and *Xena: Warrior Princess* weekly attract huge audiences of adolescent girls. Publishing houses have also realized the power of girls' fascination with the horrific side of life. The best-selling young adult author of all time, R. L. Stine, churns out little novels authenticating girls' vision of horror on an almost monthly basis.[4] V. C. Andrews writes more substantial novels about girls whose lives are touched by evil and marked by their resistance to it.[5] Books about girls who are addicted to drugs,[6] in love with serial killers,[7] sexually abused,[8] and living with physically abusive relatives[9] are receiving many girls' attention. Both the *New York Times*[10] and *Publishers Weekly*[11] have recently run articles wondering about girls' predilections for such "grim" topics. Girls, even those not as attuned to horror as Nilla, live in a strange and dangerous reality; they know it, and choose entertainment and reading that reflects it.

A part of this dangerous reality is the rate of violence and crime perpetrated against girls. Research on criminal victimization rates of girls has shown that one in three girls will be sexually abused before she is eighteen.[12] Of these girls, 89 percent will be abused by a family member.[13] The Department of Justice *National Crime Victimization Survey* from 1993 reports that girls ages twelve to twenty-four are almost ten times more likely to be raped than females of other ages.[14] Murder rates are also much higher for adolescents (both boys and girls) than for other age groups.[15]

In addition to violence, girls are also subject to such cultural factors as racism, classism, and ageism. Undoubtedly some of girls' appreciation for horror stems from their relatively dangerous social locations in the culture, the reality of which they are just beginning to be able to comprehend.

Why are adolescent girls particularly attracted to depictions of reality that reflect horror? The answer to that question has at least partly to do with girls' realities and their newly forming abilities to comprehend them. Adolescence is a time when girls begin to develop the mental capacities to think in new, more complex ways. Robert Kegan, a developmental psychologist, describes the changes that take place in adolescent meaning-making as girls and boys move from "categorical" to "cross-categorical" ways of thinking and feeling.[16] Young children think categorically, living inside their social realities in such a way that they are unaware that the realities could be different. They cannot imagine things outside of the categories they believe are normal. They cannot understand, for example, that their parents could be different, that their teachers could be more or less fair, that their churches could be more or less open to hearing their feelings and thoughts about God and their faith.

As girls become adolescents, however, they move out of merely categorical thinking and are able to begin to comprehend their worlds at deeper levels, moving toward cross-categorical mental capacities. They begin to develop abilities to reason abstractly, to think about their own thinking, and to understand others' points of view empathically.[17] They also become aware that their realities could be different from the way they are—that violence could be stopped, that abuse and oppression are not normal, that religious people have responsibilities to take action against injustice.

Girls have trouble, however, being understood and taken seriously by the adult world that has so much power over them. Because of their age, gender, inexperience, and relative powerlessness, their awareness of social realities does not often translate into an ability to make changes. Often it does not translate into the ability, or opportunity, or safety even to *speak* of the things they see.

They often feel, in fact, that telling what they think, expressing preferences, lobbying for what they want, or asking for what they need are all hopeless and/or dangerous enterprises. Educators note that this struggle for "voice" arises, in part, because of another cultural factor—a "hidden curriculum"—that teaches girls in subtle ways that they do not matter.[18]

Carol Gilligan writes that because girls' voices are cut off and their visions of life are undervalued or disregarded by adults, many girls retreat to places unseen by others. They seem to begin to live significant portions of their lives "underground."[19] Gilligan's research aims at meeting girls in their underground caverns of knowledge—where they keep their most precious thoughts and insights. Many girls stop talking altogether in the "above-ground" world; they remain silent in classes, church, and their families. They stop talking, but they do not stop watching. They see and understand the reality of the danger and horror around them.

Horror in Our Culture

In 1997 Mark Edmundson, an English literature professor at the University of Virginia, published an excellent volume of provocative popular theology, *Nightmare on Main Street*. In this book he attempts to explain the resurgence of what he calls gothic horror in our culture at large.[20] He writes that he found himself strangely drawn to a whole set of current and cult horror movies—with titles like *Scream, Dawn of the Dead, Last House on the Left, Nightmare on Elm Street,* and *Texas Chainsaw Massacre*. He not only watched these films, he became somewhat obsessed with them. Then he analyzed his obsession.

In brief, he decided that he had tapped into a cultural undercurrent (almost undertow) of horror, gothic horror—"possession narratives"—running from the O. J. Simpson trial, to Oprah, to horror movies, to rumors of ritual cult abuse, to the evening news. Gothic, Edmundson writes, "is the art of haunting. . . . It shows us time and again that life, even at its most ostensibly innocent is possessed, that the present is in thrall to the past. All are guilty. All must, in time, pay up."[21]

Why this undercurrent of horror? Edmundson's almost throwaway answer is that people have stopped believing in God.

Though most of us Americans claim to believe in God, few of us seem able to believe in God's presence. That is, we do not perceive some powerful force for good shaping the events of day-to-day life in accord with a perceptibly benevolent master plan. Most of us don't have a story that we can believe about the way God's designs are unfolding among us. Whatever God is up to, God is not busying himself unduly with worldly events.[22]

How can we escape the horror of a Godless world? Edmundson notes there is another strong undercurrent in our culture, one he identifies with angels and Forrest Gump, and calls "facile transcendence."[23] Forrest is faced with many challenges and heartbreaking circumstances, but none touch his essential goodness. And he is richly rewarded for remaining simple. Edmundson writes: "Through [all his trials] Alabaman Forrest is magnolia sweet.... At the core of Forrest Gump is the sugary fiction that dull virtue in tandem with humble, unresenting poverty is well rewarded."[24]

Forrest Gump is the culture's vacation from horror. He is the respite—to whom we turn when we need a breath of cleaner air. It is not satisfying, because it is honeysuckle sweet. But it is some sort of relief.

My Research

How does spirituality, a topic underrepresented in other research on girls, shape the ways girls understand themselves and their worlds—their experiences of safety and horror? Between 1993 and 1997, I undertook research designed to try to hear (as much as they would allow it) from the underground worlds of girls from various geographic, economic, racial/ethnic, and religious backgrounds. I used a questionnaire and an interview format and talked with girls in churches, community agencies, and schools. The methodological premise was that to understand girls' spirituality, it was necessary to engage and to encourage their voices. During the four-year period, I talked to over one hundred girls from Boston, New York, Philadelphia, Dallas, Denver, Indianapolis, and Atlanta. Interviews took place in church youth groups, dance troupes, prep school lounges, and a church "attic" after an annual youth service. The girls represented diverse religious communities—Presbyterian, Methodist, Episcopalian, Roman Catholic, charismatic, Southern Baptist, agnostic, and those who categorized themselves as "nothing" or "atheist." They also represented diverse ethnicities: Arab American, African American, European American, Eurasian, and Latina.

Some of the girls had very strong spirituality that helped them to develop their voices and to resist many kinds of cultural and personal oppression. They had begun to learn to relate to God in mature ways, tolerating ambiguities and paradoxes—even making sense of silence. For these girls, their spirituality was beginning to give them a positive sense of identity and life's meaning.

Most girls who participated in this study, however, also revealed ways in which their spirituality was troubled. Many of these girls described having deep spiritual questions that arose out of their new comprehension of their worlds. They wanted answers to questions. They wondered whether God listens; they often wondered whether God cares about them. They also wondered what God expects from them and why those expectations are not communicated clearly. They were very troubled about God's seeming tolerance of evil and violence.

Many of the girls I talked to bear witness to a *gothic vision* of the world arising from their own experience, their view from the underground, and their cultural heritage. They are also, however, struggling to find a way to believe in God in this world. They often turn to the church for help in this struggle. But they are startled, unhappy, and disillusioned to find that, for the most part, the God they are presented in church is a God derived from the facile transcendent world Edmundson describes. It is the God of Forrest Gump—present in the world but only capable of the most innocuous goodness. A God who is essentially unaware of evil. A God who seems not to give answers to hard questions.

Two topics that seem to hold special interest and to pose very difficult problems for the girls I talked with are sexuality and violence. Girls have an intuitive sense that the ways they view and are viewed as embodied beings deeply affects their spirituality. For the girls, both sexuality and violence have strong connections to their vision of God and their feelings of insecurity in the world.[25]

Sexuality

Today's adolescents have much more exposure to sex than teenagers of previous generations. From television, to movies, books, and the Internet, sex acts are performed before their eyes and ears, and sexuality is discussed in both healthy and unhealthy forums. Sexuality is tied to horror for girls through first or secondhand knowledge of sexual abuse and rape, their observations about the culture's general attitude about young women's supposed "uncanny" sexual powers, and their observations that, for instance, girls who are sexually active are often the first and prime victims in the sorts of horror movies Edmundson watched.

It is natural that adolescents would turn to the church and to God for guidance on this matter so important to them. It is natural that they connect sexuality with spirituality and with horror as they recognize the new power and vulnerability that is theirs in sexuality, and as they begin to feel the dangerousness of cultural projections about sexuality onto them and their bodies.

Sadly, for many of the girls I interviewed, there is a large gap between what they are being presented by their churches and what they wish would be addressed. Girls want to discuss sex and sexuality with adults who are not embarrassed. They want to learn about the emotional as well as physical aspects of sex. They want help in making decisions. They wonder why their sexuality is not encouraged and celebrated. They wonder what God thinks of them as sexual beings. Even those churches that provide sexuality education for adolescents often miss the point, as far as the girls are concerned, and avoid the questions the girls are really asking about God and their sexuality.

The following conversation took place with a group of six girls at a large Midwestern church the week after they had all participated in a sexuality education seminar called CPR (*Creating Positive Relationships*). The conversation began with an acknowledgment that the class was an embarrassment for most students:

> Liz: Our [church] had a thing on CPR, and we talked about sex and things like that. But most people were embarrassed about it, and they really didn't want to talk about it. But we had this whole lesson. Most of the people really just laughed at it and were very immature about it.

According to Liz (age fifteen), the problem stemmed from the fact that the teacher was uneasy about teaching sexuality and conveyed this attitude to the students. She wonders if she was the only one who thought this ("Am I crazy?"):

> Liz: I could tell the teacher sort of felt uncomfortable in a way. Or maybe it was just me that felt that way. It just . . .

Clair (age fourteen) interrupts and expresses her gratitude for any information:

> Clair: I'm in the eighth grade, and with this CPR thing, I've never heard of this before in my entire life. . . . I never knew any of this, 'til this Sunday and last Sunday, and I knew about saving sex for when you're married. But like, nobody ever explained it to me or anything, and I think a lot of the eighth-graders who are in my class feel the same way. . . . I think it's a really, really good thing to talk about, because it just helps you plan your life, basically.

But Clair acknowledges that the answer to her real question—"How do I know what the limits of sexual activity should be at my age, before I'm married?"—was not provided:

> Clair: We've asked questions like, "How far is too far?" and stuff like that, but our teacher didn't really answer. He just said, you know, "Sex before marriage is wrong," which we all knew that. . . . Well, you know, what do you think about what comes before—like until you can't stop from going on and having sex and stuff? . . . So we really didn't get an answer on that, and I was wondering about that.

Why, she wonders, won't the teacher answer her question? Why did he try to substitute an easy, and well-known, answer for a harder one—the real one?

Missy (age fifteen) agrees that the subject needs to be discussed, because girls her age are not aware that other sexual activities besides intercourse are also, she feels, wrong:

Missy: I believe that we don't talk about the other things that go on, because there's sex and then there's other contacts . . . that are sinful also. And we don't talk about that. [Girls] are like, "Well, as long as I'm not having sex, I'm okay." But I don't agree with that, because in a guy's eyes sex and all those other things are equal. I don't know if you guys believe that or not, but I think if you're doing something that you're not supposed to, it's still a sin. And so I think this is overlooked. And I don't think [sex is] talked about enough in school, and that it's not okay to do that.

When I asked her to be specific about what is sinful and what is not, she responded:

Missy: Well, kissing's obviously not [a sin]. I guess, yeah, don't go on beyond a kiss. Removing clothes or going up someone's shirt or something like that . . . I don't think you should be going beyond a kiss, or whatever.

She begins to hesitate and stumble over words when she hears the rest of the girls disagreeing with her. She thinks maybe she has set the boundary too high. Then she returns to her original argument, stressing the need for people to be told about all kinds of sexual expression, because knowing that it is wrong might make girls think more, although it might not change their behavior much:

Missy: I wish people would know. Because when you think back more, if people actually knew, it would make them stop and think that what they're doing is wrong. And they wouldn't do it. As much.

Where is God in sexuality? For these girls it must appear that God either does not provide answers for hard questions, or that their real questions are too embarrassing to be talked about, or that they are too young to hear. Girls make all sorts of excuses for God and for adults who are not helpful. Even so, it makes them wonder about their God and their church: "So we really didn't get an answer on that, and I was wondering about that."

Violence

Girls who have experienced violence often have a difficult time relating to God and the church. Beliefs about God change, or God begins to fade from their immediate concern. Sometimes they try not to think about religion, because they cannot reconcile the violence they have seen with their images of a God who loves them and the world. Their churches do not seem able or willing to help them in this struggle. The next set of examples has to do with the violence girls experience and the church's inattentiveness to it.

Maria, eighteen, is the secretary of her church, an ethnically diverse congregation in an urban area in the Southwest. Three years before, she had been a member of the youth advisory team and president of her youth group. Then one of her good friends was shot and killed. She talks about the shooting:

> Maria: One of my friends, one of the members of the youth group, was murdered about three years ago. . . . Eric. He was shot. He was the vice president of the youth group and in charge with me. He was in a house, and they broke in, and they shot him point blank, so . . . there was no struggle or anything.

Eric's death was her first real experience of loss due to violence, and it shattered her belief that the world is a safe place. The morals and values her mother instilled in her did not protect her from losing a friend:

> Maria: I've always been and I still am kind of sheltered from everything. My mother is so strict with me, and she's brought me up with morals, and values, and things, and I've always been sheltered from violence and things that are going on. So it was a shock and kind of hard to handle, because that has been the only time I've had to deal with losing a close friend.

In the aftermath of the shooting, she felt close to God and alienated from God at the same time:

> Maria: In this situation, I felt closest to God and distant from him. I think this situation kind of pulled me away from him, but at the same time it made me feel close. I felt closest to God, because I feel that he got me through it. Without him, I don't think I would have, and it was also with friends and family that supported me. But at the same time I felt distant from him, because that's the time that I started questioning him and doubting him, and you know, wondering, "Why me?" or "Why my friend?" So it goes both ways, me feeling close to him and me feeling distant.

Maria continues to attend church and to participate in national youth events in her denomination, but God is not currently an important part of her life. Between the time of the shooting and my interview with her, God had become more and more distant.

> Maria: I'm in this stage, kind of, right now where I feel kind of distant from God. Religion hasn't been that important, hasn't been up there in a long time.

Her problem with God stems from Eric's death and her realization that violence and cruelty are pervasive in her world. She has begun to reckon with the problem of theodicy in her own way:

> Maria: I think I kind of don't understand why, if he is such a powerful God, I don't understand why we have so much crime and so much death and things like that. There's so much cruelty in the world, and it seems like things are just getting worse. They're not getting any better, and, I think, I don't understand. If he's supposed to be so loving and powerful, then why are so many things going on? So I think that's the only thing I have with God.

She has repeatedly asked adults in the church, including her ministers, to answer her questions. She is not satisfied with any of the explanations given and is not willing to forget the questions in order to restore a closer relationship with God:

> Maria: It's been explained to me so many times why things like this happen. But I still kind of have doubts. I don't think it's going to get any better unless someone changes it.

It is up to "someone" else to change the world. She has doubts that God or the church will be much help.

In another interview, I talked with Kim, De Andree, and Vanesia from south Dallas. They are frustrated that the church has done little to change the dangerous situations in their neighborhoods and at school. They describe having grown up with kids who are now in gangs, and having to learn to negotiate relationships with those kids and the gangs. They talk about drugs and weapons in their schools and police dogs sniffing their lockers. They talk about worrying about drive-by shootings and hearing little voices in their heads always telling them to be careful because, "The next time, it could be you."

Kim is frustrated that the church seems to be more concerned with its own peace than her safety: "The church could do something about it, but they're scared."

De Andree believes that God is furious with the perpetrators of violence and with the church. God is also, in her view, shamed by the pervasiveness of violence. She wants to encourage "everybody" to take part in working to change their neighborhoods.

> De Andree: God does not like this—is probably very angry, angry at everybody. I'm *serious!!* He feels disgraced by it. And everybody would have to suffer just because of some people. Everybody needs to work together.

When asked whether the church helps them to stay out of trouble, they respond with giggles. Their community leaders have obviously let them know that gangs, drugs, and other kinds of violence are not acceptable: "They just put the fear in us, so we will know not to do something like that. It would be all over."

According to these girls, the church can help them to stay beyond the reach of perpetrators of violence by encouraging them and standing by them as they resist the temptation to join. It also provides activities for them to "keep them off the streets." They believe, however, that the church will not fight to reduce the influence of gangs and violent people in the community, because it is afraid to be involved. They are grateful for any help they can get in their struggles with violence—grateful that the church is a safe place for them—but they are frustrated and confused about the church's unwillingness to take on the real battle.

For Maria, Kim, Vanesia, and De Andree, who see the reality and pervasiveness of violence in their communities very clearly, adults and the church are disappointments. From their perspective, adult Christians fail them in two ways: (1) by hypocritically denying the extent of the violence, and (2) by failing to "work together" to solve the problem. They are hesitant to talk about God, but when they do, it is clear that they are disappointed with God also: "If He's supposed to be so loving and powerful, then why are so many things going on? I wonder . . . how anyone can allow children to die like that." The explanations given to them by adults do not make sense to them, and this leaves them more prone to doubts about God's power and love. Girls believe that most adults are not able to appreciate the seriousness of their situation.

Conclusion

Girls' voices challenge Mark Edmundson's theory that our cultural undercurrent of gothic horror would be less pervasive if people really believed in God. Research with adolescent girls indicates that the real struggle seems to be to try to find God in the midst of horrors. Girls, if we listen to and encourage their newly developing voices, will help us to see enough of their lives—and our own—to appreciate the reality of horror, violence, and hard questions about sexuality, sexualized violence, and violent sex. Girls—if they are given safe spaces in which to speak the truth, and if their voices are attended to—can give churches an antidote to Forrest Gump theologies. They can clear the air of honeysuckle sweetness.

But girls need something in return. They need models of adults who have wrestled with God, who have experienced and not turned from the horrible questions of faith, who can talk with clear voices about sexuality in realistic and wholesome terms—and help them to find God's grace as well as "sin" and horror in sexual expression. They need adults who will face up to the reality and horror of violence in their lives—and not try to cover it over. More than easy answers, they need adults who will listen carefully, who will not assume they can easily understand, who will try to be empathic with girls' gothic visions of the culture, and who will act to protect them from any identified ongoing violence.[26]

Girls from families and faith communities who address the hard questions will be better able to resist cultural messages that their voices are not important. They will also be better able to live in relationship to God, notwithstanding their important questions. Life can be hard, unfair, and unjust; hitmen lurk, ready to ruin even the most innocent pleasures. For girls who are just developing their voices and just beginning to understand the realities of their world, a God who smells like honeysuckle may be more of a horror than an absent one.

Part 2

Marking Time:
Developmental Passages

Women mark time through developmental passages uniquely their own. This involves not only a linear timetable but multiple dimensions of living as a woman. Beginning with a clinical case, child psychiatrist Mary Lynn Dell discusses how a girl's life, death, and perceptions of family and faith are affected not only by her stage of development, but by the multiple spheres of development.

Seeing themselves as subjects in their own right, adolescent girls can negotiate a complex world and difficult transitions. Using Lewis Carroll's *Alice in Wonderland*, Carolyn Bohler attends to the resourceful and undaunted "Alice" inside all girls—girls who can navigate their centered selves in a world as complex as Wonderland.

From menarche to menopause, biological processes become passages unique to women. In pregnancy, a woman's identity is altered as she experiences time with another life inside her and later with another life to nurture (Carolyn Treadway). Bonnie Miller-McLemore explores the increasingly complex role that birthing and mothering plays in women's development as forceful rites of passage. Frauenzeit, or "women's time," flows through perimenopause and other midlife opportunities (Kathleen Greider), through menopause (Irene Henderson) and into postmenopause (Maxine Glaz). Generativity rewinds as women's biological clocks lead them into becoming ancestors. Karen Scheib closes this section with the passage of widowhood, another occasion to survive and reinvent one's life.

She Grows in Wisdom, Stature, and Favor with God: Female Development from Infancy through Menarche

Mary Lynn Dell

It was after 11:00 P.M., I had been on my feet since 5:00 A.M. and had just settled onto the bunk bed in the female call room when my beeper went off—again. This page was from the school-age unit of the children's hospital where I was on-call as a third-year medical student. The nurse on the other end of the phone said, "Julie's IV came out again and she really needs her fluids and morphine drip. I paged the resident and the intern—they bumped it on down to you. Hope you don't have anything else going on tonight. She's a tough stick and everybody bets you're gonna be here awhile." As I groped for my glasses, donned my white coat, and trudged up the back stairwell to the ward, I thought the tone of the nurse's voice sounded more like a challenge to my fledgling clinical skills than one of concern about the child I was about to meet. Had I been fully awake, the mention of a morphine drip should have alerted me to the girl's condition and probable diagnosis. Little in my medical education, however, could have prepared me for the next six hours of that late winter night.

I arrived on the unit, collected the paraphernalia to restart the intravenous line, and was pointed down the darkened corridor by the night clerk who was monitoring the bells and buzzers at the nursing station. At the far end of the hall, in a small room usually reserved for kids who made too much noise or were behavioral management problems, was a frail nine-year-old girl lying in bed alone in the dark, kept company by three pumps, a cardiac monitor, and a bedside commode. A few handmade get-well cards from school friends were taped to the wall opposite her bed, but the posters, stuffed animals, pillows, pictures, and bedspread from home that adorned nearly all other young girls' hospital rooms were noticeably absent. Julie had a form of leukemia that was resistant to all treatments tried over the previous two years, and the goal of this admission was to "keep her comfortable" until she died. I stood in the doorway, feeling badly that after all this child had been through, she was being subjected to yet another stick and more discomfort by the least experienced person on the treatment team—a third-year student hoping to find a section of good vein in a body tired and disfigured by procedures and chemotherapy. I resisted the urge to wake her up and apologize that I was the only person available to restart her line, not a more seasoned physician. Praying that I would not have to stick her twice, or even more, I restarted the IV on the first attempt, secured it with tape, and made sure the line was patent and fluids were infusing without problems. It was obvious that she might not survive through the night, and she had not opened her eyes or even flinched when I stuck her. I was headed out of the room when I heard her say in a faint voice, "Doctor, can I ask you a question?" Somewhat surprised, I said, "Of course," and pulled a chair close to her head at the bedside.

"Will I have hair in heaven?"

I sat there for what seemed like an eternity, wondering what I should do or say at a time like this, painfully feeling the injustice of a child dying alone at the end of a dark hallway, without family or friends to hold her, and in the care of physicians, nurses, and hospital chaplains too threatened by death to keep her ravaged body within eyesight of their workstation. Julie went on, "I think I will, and it might even be longer than it was when my earth hair fell out last time from the chemo. My friend's mom—she takes my friend and her family to church every Sunday—says everybody gets new bodies in heaven that don't get sick or break down, so I'm sure they have to have pretty hair, too. And my friend's mom knows a lot about God and Jesus and heaven because she's a Christian. I've gone to church with them sometimes. I wish my mom could take us to church, but she doesn't believe in it and always says she has too much to do to take care of us since my dad left. That's why she can't ever come and stay at the hospital with me, so I'm glad they called a lady doctor to restart my IV so I can talk about girl stuff a little."

Julie's conversation was rambling and tangential while her mental status waxed and waned in delirium, but she was able to share quite a bit about herself in the next hour or so. She lived three hours away in a poor household her mother worked night and day to keep afloat. The hospitalizations and treatments were covered to a point by Medicaid, but the hidden costs of missed work, transportation, and additional child care for Julie's younger siblings had precluded visitation by her mother and other relatives. Although her mother probably provided the best she could, it was evident that the woman had little energy and emotional reserve to invest in her children, even before Julie's illness was diagnosed. Julie talked about making a best friend at school who lived in a wealthier neighborhood, had a very attentive mother and father, and was active in a church that sponsored many children's activities. Sometimes she went shopping with her friend, and she especially liked some of the clothes her friend's older sister had given her after the older girl had outgrown them. Clearly, those were the relationships and memories that had given her greatest hope and comfort during her illness and provided her with assurance that better things awaited her after leukemia and death. About 2:00 A.M., she woke up again, reached for my hand, and thanked me for restarting her IV so the morphine could keep the pain away. I stayed with her, holding her hand until she died a few hours later.

"Will I have hair in heaven?"

Those last hours with Julie many years ago were a crossroads in my development as a physician, pastor, and person of faith. I have told this story many times since then to illustrate various teaching points to many different types of audiences, but only now has it dawned on me how much of Julie's life, death, and perceptions of family, God, and heaven, were influenced by her stage of development. Furthermore, her individual personhood was the composite of multiple spheres of development, including physical, cognitive, emotional, spiritual, and social. The events surrounding Julie's death illustrate that development cannot be considered apart from significant cultural, economic, and political influences. Certainly, I realize in a fresh way that the significance of relationships with other females in children's lives is a consideration often overlooked in treatises on childhood development. Clergy, pastoral theologians, and all who work with young girls need to be aware of these issues.

We need to understand and remember that having hair in heaven can be an important concern for nine-year-old girls.

Childhood in the Bible and the History of Christianity

In the preface to *Sisters in the Wilderness: The Challenges of Womanist God-Talk*, Delores Williams states, "I have come to believe that theologians, in their attempt to talk to and about religious communities, ought to give readers some sense of their autobiographies. This can help an audience discern what leads the theologian to do the kind of theology she does. What has been the character of her faith journey? What lessons has the journey taught?"[1] These questions can and should be generalized from womanist theology to the study of children and child development, particularly to the places given young girls in families and cultures throughout history to the present day. What can we learn from the journey of childhood over the centuries? A brief overview of biblical writings regarding children and beliefs about childhood over ensuing centuries enriches the discussion of current developmental theories and the contemporary female life cycle.

The Hebrew Bible contains the stories of many women of varying degrees of faith and character, including Sarah, Hagar, Rebekah, Rachel, Ruth, and Esther. Selected qualities of Eve, Potiphar's wife, and Delilah have become stereotypes for feminine behaviors with negative connotations. Although it can be said that these females, often called "young maidens," were actually girls chronologically, the Hebrew Bible itself does not name or refer to a period of time identifiable as girlhood. In Hebrew culture, as in virtually all of the ancient world, male children were favored and privileged over female children. The single exception may be the story of the deceptive midwives in Exodus 1. After the death of Joseph, the new king of Egypt was threatened by the number and strength of the captive Israelites. He ordered the Hebrew midwives Shiphrah and Puah to kill all male children at birth and allow female infants to live. The women disobeyed, explaining to the king that the Israelite women were so hardy that they delivered their babies before the midwives could arrive with their birthstools. When that did not work, the Pharaoh decreed that all male Hebrew babies be cast into the Nile, setting the stage for Pharaoh's daughter to find baby Moses in the bulrushes. In this particular instance, girls were protected because they did not grow up to be soldiers. They were needed to mate with sturdy Hebrew males to perpetuate a strong slave race. When forced to mate with Egyptian males, Hebrew women involuntarily enriched the gene pool of the oppressing nation. Finally, young Israelite females were protected in ways that guaranteed that they could continue in servitude to support the lifestyle of the ruling culture.[2]

The New Testament speaks of children more frequently and in a kinder light, but does not differentiate developmental issues by gender in the modern sense. That children were loved by God and graced with some form of innocence or receptivity to spiritual truths is obvious by Jesus' words, "Let the children come to me, and do not hinder them; for to such belongs the kingdom of God."[3] Jesus called his disciples "little children,"[4] and Paul and the writer of 1 John later addressed their readers and new Christians as "little children."[5] The only mention of a specific female child is in the story of the healing of Jairus' daughter,[6] but to assert special theological significance to this act of healing a girl instead of or in addition to boys, aside from the fact that Jewish and Greco-Roman cultures of the time were male-oriented, is to read too much significance into this one of many healings and miracles performed by Jesus. While the Bible as a whole has much to say about women and being female, scripture is relatively silent on the state of girlhood as we know it today.

A survey of the history of childhood confirms that neither young boys nor young girls have been viewed or treated as gifts of God to be nurtured and celebrated. Indeed, historian Lloyd deMause notes the following in *The History of Childhood*: "The history of childhood is a nightmare from which we have only recently begun to awake. The further back in history one goes, the lower the level of child care, and the more likely children are to be killed, abandoned, beaten, terrorized, and sexually abused."[7] In many ancient cultures, infanticide was common, as was selling children into slavery. Females were exposed and left to starve much more often than males, although at one point a Roman law dictated that families must raise all males and at least one female born into the household. On a positive note, wealthier Greek and Roman families invested considerable resources in their offspring's development. Both Plato and Aristotle described five stages of childhood. The first stage corresponded to modern babyhood and toddlerhood, from birth until the child was weaned and talking. The second stage corresponded to modern preschool years, when the child became mobile, individuated from the mother, and was able to play alone. Next came a phase during which the child became more social and group-oriented, lasting until approximately age seven. From age eight until puberty, the philosophers remarked about the emergence of competition, especially in boys. The final stage was equivalent to adolescence, although this may have been nonexistent for many females because they tended to marry shortly after puberty.[8]

From approximately 250 until 1200 C.E., parents of all faith traditions and socioeconomic classes in Europe and western civilization had the option of "abandoning" their children, or voluntarily and legally leaving or selling them to other individuals or institutions, including monasteries and the church. Most of these children were adopted into other households or worked for the institutions that housed and fed them. Poor parents were prone to abandon children they were unable to support or believed would be better off if adopted by caregivers with greater resources. Females were more likely to be abandoned than males. This practice did not decline until the thirteenth and fourteenth centuries, when major cities had established foundling homes to provide unwanted children with institutional care.[9] Despite a social climate that often seemed hostile to the best interests of children, medieval writers noted three stages of childhood (compared to the five stages described by the classical Greeks). Medieval experts defined infancy as the period from birth to age two, described the ages of two to seven as a stage comparable to the modern preschool period, and identified puerility as the time from seven to fourteen years of age.[10]

Perhaps the next milestones in the history of childhood with theological significance were the publication of John Locke's *Essay Concerning Human Understanding* in 1690 and *Some Thoughts Concerning Education* in 1693. In these writings, Locke argued against the doctrine of infant depravity, declaring instead that children were born neither good or bad, could learn from experience, and that ideas were not innate.[11] Locke paved the way for Jean Jacques Rousseau, the Swiss-French philosopher and rationalist of the eighteenth century. Rousseau's contributions to the understanding of childhood included *Du Contrat Social* and *Emile*, both published in 1762. He advocated that children be permitted to experience sights, sounds, textures, temperatures, and other physical qualities of the world via all physical senses, not setting physical constraints on the exploration of the environment. Children were to be treated as individuals whose growth and development were to be nurtured. Soon thereafter, the Swiss educator Johann Pestalozzi proposed that child development unfolded in a stepwise fashion from within the individual, that the child was not the sum of environmental influences, and that no gender distinctions were indicated in the education of young children. On a practical level, these new Enlightenment ideas came at a time when pregnancy and childbirth were still concealed, high rates of postpartum and infant mortality were the norm, and the practice of swaddling limited physical interaction between infants and other humans for months after birth. Changing beliefs and practices regarding childhood was a slow process.[12]

The nineteenth-century Victorian era saw the perpetuation of peculiar, erroneous beliefs about young girls, many of which were fostered by physicians and religious institutions. For instance, children's brains, especially those of females, were believed to be unusually susceptible to inflammation until three years of age, with girls at increased risk until older ages. Formal education was thought to exacerbate the risk of infection in the central nervous systems of young girls, disrupting a sensitive physiological and emotional balance.[13] With few exceptions, the role of young girls was to grow up, bear children, and carry the banner of virtue to the next generation.

Childhood in the early industrial United States and Western Europe was difficult at best. The plights of child laborers in urban areas were highlighted in the novels of Charles Dickens. The world saw poverty, hunger, homelessness, and orphanhood through the eyes of Oliver Twist and the Artful Dodger, adding momentum to the work of social reformers. Again, however, girls remained essentially nameless, faceless victims in the early years of reform.

Late nineteenth- and early twentieth-century industrialization did raise living standards for many. In particular, children benefited from the establishment of child labor laws after World War I. Because a more technologically advanced economy required a more highly educated workforce, opportunities for secondary and higher education expanded.[14] Together these developments bestowed greater status upon and generated increased concern for children. Psychological, social, moral, and emotional maturity became as important as physical growth in youth. At the same time, however, as the American economy became more oriented toward mass consumption, businesses sought to develop new markets for their goods. Through newspapers, magazines, motion pictures and, eventually, radio and television, advertisers began to target children as a discrete market in and of themselves. While reinforcing the growing conception of childhood as a distinct period of life, the commercialization of childhood also served to create standards and expectations for what an ideal childhood and an ideal child should be, particularly in a society of affluence. In general, by the mid-twentieth century the lot of most children in the United States had improved in the areas of education, basic physical needs, access to health care, and work conditions. (These reforms notwithstanding, large numbers of children are not cared for adequately according to today's minimal standards of care.) Despite gender inequalities, major and minor, over the past fifty to sixty years, no one can deny that childhood is generally a discrete time period in the lives of most individuals, and that children and adolescents enjoy many educational, health, recreational, and political advantages and protections that were nonexistent in previous centuries and civilizations.[15]

Stages of Normal Childhood Development

Numerous theories and schemas exist to explain aspects of physical, cognitive, emotional, moral, academic, and faith development in childhood. The study of development is an interdisciplinary endeavor and readers are referred to other sources for thorough reviews from the perspectives of pediatricians, and child and adolescent psychiatrists.[16] In addition, existing theories are continually modified and new postulates are put forth to incorporate new findings and research. The following section is a summary and review of major developmental domains of the stages of childhood: infancy, toddlerhood, early childhood, and middle childhood.

Infancy: The First Year of Life

More physical and neurological growth and development occur in the first year of life than during any other life stage. Assuming a relatively uncomplicated pregnancy and delivery and a healthy neonate within normal limits of weight and length, parents can expect the birth weight to double by five months of age and triple by the first birthday. Length at birth will increase by 50 percent during the first year. Invisible to observers is the phenomenal growth of the brain and central nervous system. By the second birthday the brain will attain 70 percent of its full adult weight, its neurons sprouting millions of dendrites. Cortical synapses form extremely rapidly during the first year, then are "pruned down" to the range of the number of adult synapses. During the first day of life infants can track with their eyes and heads drawings resembling human faces, and at two days of age will look at their mothers' faces longer than those of other women. Because neonates have difficulty focusing on objects too near or too far away, they can distinguish their mothers' faces better than the infants' own hands or other body parts. At one week, neonates can distinguish fairly complex visual patterns and movements, respond selectively to their mothers' voices, and discriminate between the smell of their mothers' milk and that of other women. In addition, the senses of touch, pressure, and proprioception are operational at birth, meaning that even newborns can feel and suffer physical pain.[17]

Immediately after birth, neonates have no purposeful reach or grasp but do have a number of primitive motor reflexes that gradually subside or extinguish over the first year of life. By three months of age, they can attend to visual and auditory stimuli for at least three to five seconds, are alert for increasing periods of time, and can focus on individuals who are speaking to them. By sixteen weeks they can hold up their heads, and by five months they have developed characteristic arm and leg movements for contented and angry states. They can sit with support at twenty-eight weeks, sit alone, creep, and pull themselves up by forty weeks, and stand alone around forty-eight weeks, if not sooner. At nine months, babies can gesture intentionally for desired objects or to be picked up. At twelve months, females are able to walk with support, with African American and other ethnicities mastering these gross motor skills earlier than many infants of European American backgrounds. Females often achieve these physical milestones slightly earlier than males. Although babies vary significantly in their sleep-wake cycles, most infants are able to sleep through the night, or at least lie relatively calmly in their cribs, sometime between the sixth and ninth months. As all parents can attest, however, sleep is susceptible to the vicissitudes of illness and other external influences.[18]

Children make significant strides in communication and cognitive development during the first year. Parents of little girls (boys too, but after all, this is a chapter on the development of young girls!) soon learn to distinguish the emotions and needs of their newborn daughter's cries—pain, hunger, fatigue, fear, and need for physical contact. The baby soon learns to communicate nonverbally by smiling, looking toward or away from people or things, and reaching toward desired objects. Solo babbling around four to five months progresses to reciprocal "baby talk" between infant and adult, and by her first birthday the little girl can say "mama," "dada," one or two other simple words, and comprehend very simple commands. In Jean Piaget's cognitive development scheme, the infant is in the first, or sensorimotor stage. During the first four months of life, she demonstrates the first part of the sensorimotor stage, including primary circular reactions, motor reflexes, and behaviors focused on the body. Although the sensorimotor stage seems almost synonymous with motor development in the beginning, cognitive elements become more evident as the maturing infant tries to manipulate the world around her, as she does with increasing mastery in the secondary circular reaction period from the ages of four to ten months. By her first birthday, she attains object permanence, the knowledge that an object continues to exist even when it is out of her immediate sight. At this age, she also enjoys reaching for books, vocalizing and patting the page as she looks at pictures.[19]

Attachment between the infant and her parent/caregiver is a process with important implications for the child's future relationships. Attachment refers to the emotional bond, begun at birth but nurtured for months thereafter, that is enduring, specific to the individual adult and infant combination, and both stimulates and is stimulated by physical closeness. Caregivers who are perceptive, sensitive, and responsive to the baby's physical and emotional needs are usually successful in forming secure attachments with healthy, responsive infants. The caregivers' interactions with the child are influenced, sometimes quite significantly, by the baby's temperament, whether it is easy, difficult, or slow to warm up. After the first successful attachment to the primary caregiver, the infant can generalize the ability to attach emotionally to select others. The dances between attachment, dependency, and nurturance continue in various expressions throughout life, and the first year is crucial in shaping the young girl's ability to make healthy attachments in other relationships. For too many individuals, male and female, inadequate caregiving, abuse, and neglect adversely affect this vital process. In Erik Erikson's framework, the developmental task of this time period is the establishment of basic trust.[20]

The Toddler: Ages One to Three

In young children, gross motor, fine motor, and cognitive development are inter-twined processes related to the maturation timetable of the central and peripheral nervous systems. Neurons are migrating, proliferating, and making more complex connections. Children become capable of more sophisticated communication with the production of neurotransmitters. Myelination, the sheathing of neurons in pro-tective layers of fatty and protein substances, increases the rate of neuronal firing and facilitates faster, more complex signals between brain cells and from the brain to the rest of the body. Of course, good nutrition is crucial to these physiological processes, and early educational stimulation is increasingly appreciated for its role in activating certain neural pathways that might otherwise remain dormant or understimulated. The toddler and preschool periods are times of monumental brain development, continuing a young girl's susceptibility to physical and emotional neglect and abuse.[21]

By two-and-a-half years, the toddler is approximately half her adult height, gain-ing two to three inches and three to five pounds per year. By her second birthday, the young girl walks and runs with ease. By thirty months she can stand for a short time on one foot, and by age three she can climb stairs alternating feet, do a broad jump and ride a tricycle. Fine motor control progresses as well, with a two-year-old capa-ble of stacking six blocks and a three-year-old able to stack ten blocks, use scissors, and copy a circle. They feed themselves readily and have strong food preferences. Language and speech blossom, with two-year-olds commanding a 300-word vocab-ulary, and using two word sentences and even longer phrases, and thirty-month-olds using pronouns properly. By age three, children are extremely conversational and they are good storytellers. Naps may last anywhere from thirty minutes to two hours, with older children in this age range starting to resist this particular daily event. Bowel and bladder functions are regular and sphincter control sufficient enough for toilet training, which typically begins between eighteen and thirty months.[22]

Cognitively, the toddler is in transition between Piagetian stages. The last phase of the sensorimotor stage, the development of the tertiary circular reaction, occurs in the first part of the second year. At this point, the child is interested in producing novelty and engaging a broader array of objects in her environment. Piaget's preoperational stage emerges in the third year as she tries out symbolic thought and representational play. In an object relations paradigm, the securely attached little girl passes through Margaret Mahler's steps of separation-individ-uation, using the primary attachment figure as a base for exploration, realizing her ability to be physically separate from that adult, and becoming comfortable with those short separations. Toddlers are curious about other children, and progress from individual, solitary play (parallel play) to doing the same thing side by side, without significant interaction with each other (associative play). According to Erik Erikson, the fundamental issue of this stage is autonomy versus shame and doubt, and, if all goes well, the desired outcomes are the positive aspects of self-control and willpower.[23]

Early Childhood: Ages Three to Six

Gross and fine motor skills continue their developmental trajectories. Physical growth remains steady, but the rapid rate of growth seen in infancy and toddlerhood levels off somewhat in the late preschool and early elementary school years. The vast majority of children, especially girls, are dry through night by the fourth year and use the bathroom without assistance during the day. Balance improves, and boys and girls can throw a ball overhand, swing on a playground, and skip. Four-year-olds can generally wash and dress themselves (preferably with helpful supervision!), copy a cross, and draw a person with three body parts. Five-year-olds can print their first names and copy an open square with a circle in one corner. These have been the traditional developmental measuring rods, but clearly revisions are necessary—with increased academic exposure in many preschools and homes, a sizable population of late preschoolers are reading and more computer savvy than many adults.

On the cognitive front, Piaget's preoperational stage continues, and the child masters the concepts of classification, ordering, and matching. Thought processes are concrete, and cause and effect are mediated by proximity of events in time. Children in this stage struggle with the concepts of time, and similarities and differences in people, places, and things. Imagination and symbolic play take on lives of their own. As many as a quarter of children in this age group have imaginary companions that usually disappear by no later than age ten. Children at this developmental level are fond of role playing, imitating the adults in their world, and thereby practicing skills important in later life. By the age of six, children with secure attachments and good physical and emotional health are generally capable of successful days at school apart from parents and familiar caregivers. According to Erikson's psychological stages of the life cycle, the fundamental issues of this age are initiative versus guilt, with the desired outcomes of direction and purpose.[24]

Middle Childhood: Ages Six to Twelve

In child development circles, middle childhood is actually better known as "latency." More closely aligned with analytic theory than any of the previous developmental stages, the term has been retained today, even though significant maturation work occurs during these school-age years. Freudian theory holds that sexual drives and conflicts are less evident, or "latent," while the child is engaged in school and other socially sanctioned, age-appropriate activities, hence facilitating ego development and the beginnings of the superego. Latency is often divided into two parts: an early phase, ages six to eight, in which the child's attention is totally directed inward toward herself, and a later phase, ages eight to twelve, during which she becomes more aware of the outside world.[25]

Physically, latency marks the time between the rapid and dramatic growth of earlier childhood and subsequent adolescence. By the seventh year, the brain comprises 90 percent of its adult weight, the process of myelination is largely complete, handedness and dominance are determined, and children can process complex sensory stimuli. They practice and master a broader variety of sports and athletic skills due to improved coordination, balance, and large muscle strength. Fine motor-adaptive skills and small muscle control are refined as well, permitting elementary school children to tie their shoes easily, snap their fingers, and whistle. Although considerable variation in physical maturation occurs due to genetics, nutrition, and other factors, a few generalizations are still possible. Girls and boys are close to the same height and weight until approximately age ten, with girls tending to experience the onset of pubertal changes an average of two years earlier than boys. A noticeable growth spurt begins at age nine or ten, the maximal rate of linear growth occurring around the twelfth year. The early stages of breast development, pubic and axillary hair, and redistribution of body fat characteristic of the female figure follow the onset of the growth spurt. Menstruation heralds the physiological beginnings of adolescence. According to Piaget, middle childhood is the time of concrete operations, during which the child can consider more than one parameter at a time (e.g., length and weight), learns to reverse operations mentally (e.g., addition and subtraction), and understands that changes in shape or size do not alter the properties of a substance (conservation). She is on the brink of abstract thinking. According to Erikson, the fundamental issues of middle childhood are industry versus inferiority, and successful negotiation of this stage leaves her with a sense of competence.[26]

Melvin Levine, M.D., has outlined twelve "developmental missions" for middle childhood, including: (1) to sustain self-esteem, (2) to find social acceptance, primarily with peers, (3) to "reconcile individuality with conformity," (4) to identify and emulate role models, (5) to examine values, (6) to feel successful in the family, (7) to explore the freedom and limits of autonomy, (8) to grow in knowledge and skill, (9) to become reconciled to her own body, (10) to handle fears, (11) to limit and control appetites and drives, including foods, sexual drives, material wants, the seeking of attention, and (12) to "know thyself," or to develop self-awareness. Successful negotiation of these missions will result in the child entering adolescence equipped with what Dr. Levine calls "basic developmental acquisitions." These include: (1) attention, persistence, and goal-directedness; (2) orientation and perception, or the ability to perceive how they relate to aspects of daily life; (3) storage and retrieval, primarily referring to information and memory; (4) interpretation and generalization (another way of talking about cognitive development); (5) expression and production (the processes of exchanging ideas); (6) social reception and interaction, an awareness of the dynamics of relating to others; (7) protective resiliency and strategy formation, including managing success, failure, discomfort, loss, disappointment, and frustration. Other acquisitions include more sophisticated play, a burgeoning sense of humor, and increasingly complex moral reasoning.[27]

Of interest from historical and cultural perspectives is that many civilizations and societies have attributed particular significance to the specific age of seven. At this age, children are mature enough to accept greater responsibilities and learn new skills. The seventh birthday has often been the milestone beginning mandatory schooling. In medieval times and later, seven-year-olds were first sent off to be trained as court pages. English common law has long set the age of seven as the age at which a child is capable of criminal intent. Seven years has also been recognized by the Roman Catholic Church as "the age of reason," when cognitive development permits the understanding necessary for a child's first communion.[28] Obviously, the maturing sense of responsibility recognized at age seven was vital to learning a trade and making a way of life in premodern societies.

Spiritual and Religious Development

Religion and spirituality are riding a crest of renewed interest and enthusiasm in American culture at the present time. In the adult world, available literature includes traditional holy writings, respected theological treatises, stories of personal faith and experience, theories regarding the psychology of religion and spirituality, and a broad array of other inspirational writings. A number of respected researchers are investigating the effects of religious and spiritual attitudes and practices on physical and mental health. Thus far, the empirical research studies reported in youth involve primarily high school students, although that may not be true much longer. Methodologically rigorous studies of children's spirituality, however, are quite few. What does exist are rich interview and case study materials, such as the work of Robert Coles, and several theories describing the development of religious thinking, belief, and practice in childhood.[29]

James Fowler's faith development theory is by far the best known and elaborated of the stage frameworks of religious and spiritual development. Influenced and informed by the work of Erik Erikson, Jean Piaget, Lawrence Kohlberg, Robert Kegan, and Wilfred Cantwell Smith, Fowler's paradigm consists of six stages, encompassing the entire life cycle. The first two complete stages, in addition to what he calls a "pre-stage," are relevant to children from birth until adolescence. In the pre-stage, "Undifferentiated faith," the nurture and care provided in the first year of life allow the child to experience the precursors of love, trust, hope, and courage—all integral aspects of relating to God, others in community, as well as being key components of subsequent stages of faith development. The acquisition of language for the expression of thought and emotion bridges into Fowler's first full stage, "Intuitive-Projective faith." Characteristic of children from three to seven years of age, this stage is notable for the roles of imagination, egocentrism, and the influences of stories and the words and deeds of surrounding individuals on the impressionable preschool/elementary-aged religious life. With the advent of Piagetian concrete operational thinking, the child enters stage two, "Mythic-Literal faith." Coincidental with middle childhood, or latency, children internalize religious stories and moral precepts in a very literal and absolute manner as they integrate themselves into the beliefs and observances of their particular faith communities. The ability to think abstractly and the need to question absolutes hearken not only adolescence, but also the next of Fowler's stages beyond childhood.[30]

Piaget's stage theory of cognitive development has substantially influenced various other frameworks and studies of religious and spiritual growth, particularly in the areas of God images, religious identity, prayer, and religious morality. All begin with spiritual/religious naïveté and pass through a phase of egocentrism to a concrete religiosity of late childhood and preadolescence. Work by E. Harms in 1944, David Elkind in the early 1960s, Ronald Goldman in the mid-1960s, and, more recently, Fritz Oser, along with Fowler's faith development theory, have confirmed the utility of Piagetian thinking in this field.[31] Lest contemporary scholars of religious development be accused of leaning too heavily on Piaget, L.A. Kirkpatrick and colleagues have applied John Bowlby's parent-infant attachment theory to the development of early religious life and have considered potential ramifications for children and adults.[32]

School-aged children, whether raised in religious homes or not, have a fairly complex, though often literal and concrete image of God, and view religious leaders as physical embodiments of God and their religious traditions and communities. Gender differences will be discussed at length later, but God images tend to aggregate by sex—girls like a relational type of God, while boys like an active, rational Creator. In most studies, girls also tend toward an intrinsic religiosity and register greater religiosity when beliefs and/or behaviors are measured or quantified.[33] Family and household factors that enhance the importance and expression of religion and spirituality in the lives of children include the modeling of religious behavior by parents, the amount of time devoted to faith practices and open discussion of religious issues.[34] Certainly, a young girl's participation in religious rituals and traditions enhances moral education and her sense of connection to parents, extended family, and even a larger faith community, all foundations for adolescence and later adult life.

Menarche and Menstruation

Menarche, the onset of a girl's first menstrual period, signals the transition from childhood into adolescence and subsequent adulthood. Usually an extremely meaningful event to an individual girl, and often her mother or closest female caregiver, the first menses has been addressed in medical and psychological literature, but has not received the attention in pastoral theology circles to the same extent as childbirth, general sexuality, or menopause. A chapter on the biopsychosocial and spiritual development of young females would be incomplete without consideration of the biblical attitudes toward menstruation, a review of the physiological events, and accompanying psychological issues.

Menstruation in Scripture and Biblical Times

> Jerusalem sinned grievously,
> therefore she became filthy;
> all who honored her despise her,
> for they have seen her nakedness;
> yea, she herself groans,
> and turns her face away.
> Her uncleanness was in her skirts;
> she took no thought of her doom;
> therefore her fall is terrible,
> she has no comforter.
> "O Lord, behold my affliction,
> for the enemy has triumphed!"
> Lamentations 1:8-9 RSV

Again the word of the Lord came to me: "Son of man, make known to Jerusalem her abominations, and say, Thus says the Lord God to Jerusalem: Your origin and your birth are of the land of the Canaanites; your father was an Amorite, and your mother a Hittite. And as for your birth, on the day you were born your navel string was not cut, nor were you washed with water to cleanse you, nor rubbed with salt, nor swathed with bands. No eye pitied you, to do any of these things out of compassion for you; but you were cast out on the open field, for you were abhorred, on the day that you were born.

"And when I passed by you, and saw you weltering in your blood, I said to you in your blood, 'Live, and grow up like a plant of the field.' And you grew up and became tall and arrived at full maidenhood; your breasts were formed, and your hair had grown; yet you were naked and bare.

"When I passed by you again and looked upon you, behold, you were at the age for love; and I spread my skirt over you, and covered your nakedness: yea, I plighted my troth to you and entered into a covenant with you, says the Lord God, and you became mine. Then I bathed you in water and washed off your blood from you, and anointed you with oil."

Ezekiel 16:1-9 RSV

For better or for worse, interpretations of Hebrew Bible passages such as these from Lamentations and Ezekiel have served to cast the process of menstruation in a negative light, as a blight or curse. These images have perpetuated the age-old association of women with the body and flesh, and hence, sin. The prophets may not have intended to convey this message about menstruation, but sadly it is the understanding too often handed down by religious institutions and internalized by both male and female members.

The Book of Lamentations was written to decry and mourn the destruction of Jerusalem and the temple by the Babylonians in 587 B.C.E. In the first chapter, Jerusalem is portrayed as the wayward "daughter Zion," an accomplice in her own suffering and demise. The uncleanness of her menstrual flow is but one aspect of her humiliation and shame.[35] Ezekiel was deported from Judah to Babylon in 598 or 597 B.C.E. He continued the earlier practice of using female imagery to represent Jerusalem, sin, and unfaithfulness, emphasizing the priestly rituals and teachings regarding women's monthly menstrual periods. In chapter 16, Ezekiel portrays Jerusalem as an abandoned baby saved from destruction by God. When she grew into young adulthood, God married her and spoiled her with food and fine clothes. But she gave herself to other men, namely the Egyptians, Assyrians, and Babylonians, and paid them to receive her attentions. Once again, menstruation is viewed as a liability, a symbol of dirt, shame, and part of the total package that betrayed God.[36]

The substance of the prophets' bewailing of females and menstruation can be traced to the priestly purity codes of the Pentateuch, particularly in Leviticus. The two most detailed accounts of the purity laws are found in two sections, the purity guidelines for menstruants in chapters 12–15 and the Holiness Code in chapters 17–26. "When a woman has a discharge of blood which is her regular discharge from her body, she shall be in her impurity for seven days, and whoever touches her shall be unclean until the evening. And everything upon which she lies during her impurity shall be unclean; everything also upon which she sits shall be unclean. And whoever touches her bed shall wash his clothes, and bathe himself in water, and be unclean until the evening. And whoever touches anything upon which she sits shall wash his clothes, and bathe himself in water, and be unclean until the evening; whether it is the bed or anything upon which she sits, when he touches it he shall be unclean until the evening. And if any man lies with her, and her impurity is on him, he shall be unclean seven days; and every bed on which he lies shall be unclean."[37]

In *Dirt, Greed, and Sex: Sexual Ethics in the New Testament and Their Implications for Today*, L. William Countryman notes,

> One of the easiest purity elements to identify is concern about the menstruating woman. During her menstrual period, she is unclean for seven days, and her uncleanness is so contagious that it can affect others indirectly through their touching any furniture on which she lies or sits. This uncleanness also extends to any woman who has a hemorrhage and thus appears to be in a kind of ongoing menstrual state . . . the normal state of a woman is nonmenstrual, especially in an ancient family-oriented culture where the ideal woman married at puberty and, from then on, remained more or less continually either unclean when menstruating, hemorrhaging, or giving birth (Lev. 12; 15:19-30), for in all these conditions her normal wholeness and completeness is being violated by the loss of something proper to her. Any breach in the ideal wholeness of a being or of its place in ordinary processes thus occasions a diminution of its perfection.[38]

The Holiness Code a few chapters later prohibits intercourse during the menstrual period. "If a man lies with a woman having her sickness, and uncovers her nakedness, he has made naked her fountain, and she has uncovered the fountain of her blood; both of them shall be cut off from among their people."[39] By having intercourse with a menstruating woman, the man becomes unclean also, and both must be expelled from the people of Israel to maintain cultic purity.[40]

Worthy of attention and directly relevant to the development of young girls is the fact that the priestly codes demanded more from a postpartum mother of a newborn female than the mother of a newborn male.

> The Lord said to Moses, "Say to the people of Israel, If a woman conceives, and bears a male child, then she shall be unclean seven days; as at the time of her menstruation, she shall be unclean. And on the eighth day the flesh of his foreskin shall be circumcised. Then she shall continue for thirty-three days in the blood of her purifying; she shall not touch any hallowed thing, nor come into the sanctuary, until the days of her purifying are completed. But if she bears a female child, then she shall be unclean two weeks, as in her menstruation; and she shall continue in the blood of her purifying for sixty-six days.
>
> "And when the days of her purifying are completed, whether for a son or for a daughter, she shall bring to the priest at the door of the tent of meeting a lamb a year old for a burnt offering, and a young pigeon or a turtledove for a sin offering, and he shall offer it before the Lord, and make atonement for her; then she shall be clean from the flow of her blood."[41]

Countryman notes, "Even apart from menstruation, women appear to be a more virulent source of contagion than men." Scholars have not decided upon an acceptable explanation as to why the mother's period of cultic impurity was eighty days after the birth of a female infant, but only forty days if the child was a male.[42]

Judith Romney Wegner asserts that the passage in Leviticus 15 regarding menstruating females has been misinterpreted and it is the erroneous understanding that has perpetuated the view that menstruation and sexuality are dirty and sinful. She reads the priestly code to mean that the flow of menstrual blood itself is unclean, not that menstruation as a physiological reality or sexuality as a whole is inherently dirty or sinful. Judaism values reproduction, the ability to execute the command to "be fruitful and multiply," and regards sexuality in marriage highly. Cultic purity has nothing to do with germs and sanitation, but subsequent interpretations of these texts lacked the advanced scientific knowledge to make these discernments on a consistent basis. In other words, the blame for interpretations of the priestly code that are prejudicial against females does not rest so much in the texts themselves, but in how they have been read, interpreted, and applied over subsequent generations, in biblical and modern times.[43]

The ritual bath taken by the *niddah* (Hebrew for "menstruating female") at the end of her period of uncleanness merits special consideration by Christians. Women were to immerse themselves in the ritual bath, or *miqveh*, twelve days after beginning their last menstrual period and before resuming intercourse with their husbands in the nonmenstrual state. Judith Romney Wegner, bringing a balanced analysis of Hebrew customs involving menstruation and sexuality, observes the following: "The modern mind tends to regard the *miqveh* as an outmoded relic of a primitive idea. Yet what matters is not the physical immersion but its symbolic value. Just as with Christian baptism—a symbolic cleansing from the intangible impurity of sin—so with the *miqveh*, the significance lies not in the physical act but in its spiritual symbolism. While feminists may deplore the one-sidedness of the system, observant Jewish wives and husbands perceive the monthly purification rite as a constant reaffirmation of the sanctity of marriage."[44] On a similar note, the ritual bath into which new converts to Judaism were immersed to become spiritually clean was also called a *miqveh*. If this practice was not the direct source of the baptismal ritual performed in early Christian communities, it was certainly a related practice.[45]

The New Testament is virtually silent on menstruation and female genital discharges with the exceptions of the healing of the hemorrhaging woman in Mark 5:25-34 and the recapitulation of the Levitical priestly code through the eyes of early Christians at the Jerusalem Council in Acts 15. In the first story, two aspects of the bleeding should be considered: the physical and the cultic, or religious. Continual bleeding for twelve years, undoubtedly with compromised nutrition due to the ostracism of women with this type of malady, would leave her weak and anemic. Secondly, the stigmatic nature of the hemorrhage, its relationship to female reproductive functioning, meant that the woman had endured twelve years of ritual or cultic impurity. This perpetual state of uncleanness would have isolated her even more from fellow Jews observing Levitical holiness laws than the actual medical condition and the resultant fatigue. Through this particular miracle of healing, Jesus goes against prevailing customs of the time by ministering to a socially outcast woman and disregarding the Torah's admonitions regarding physical contact with a woman who was ritually unclean due to a vaginal flow of blood.[46]

In Acts 15, menstruation is not the focal issue, and is alluded to as only one of several practices observed by Jewish Christians who, in the first years of the New Testament church, retained their Jewish identity, maintained the priestly code on a day-to-day basis, and believed that the first step in being a good Christian was to be a good Jew—and being a good Jew meant observing the ritual purity instructions set forth in the Book of Leviticus. This conviction was problematic for Christians from the gentile ranks who did not follow the proscriptions on sexuality, food, and blood. The compromise negotiated by Peter, the leader of the gentile Christians, and James, head of the largely Jewish church in Jerusalem, was that gentile Christians would be asked, not commanded, to consider the customs of the Jewish Christians to facilitate table fellowship. Observance of the Jewish purity codes, however, was not a prerequisite for membership or acceptance into the Christian community. Again, menstruation was just one of the cultic purity concerns mentioned in this passage, and the New Testament is otherwise silent on the matter.[47]

So, once again, why this seemingly long digression about menstruation in biblical times in a chapter on the development of girls from birth through the age of twelve? As an area of academic interest, little work has been done in pastoral theology on menstruation and its attendant historical, cultural, and theological backgrounds and attitudes. This relative inattention to the process that essentially defines the major physiological difference between the two sexes and without which God's people cannot go forth and multiply is rather surprising given the greater amount of research and scholarship recently on the implications for pastoral care surrounding childbirth, breast cancer and malignancies of the female reproductive tract, menopause, and homosexuality. These biblical messages, explicit and implicit, accurately or inaccurately derived from Scripture and the authority of religious institutions, and handed down through faith communities over the centuries have influenced western civilization's approach to the development of young females both directly through churches and indirectly through wider cultural means. Finally, this understanding and appreciation of scriptural and religious attitudes is essential to the fund of knowledge of pastoral caregivers if we indeed hope to offer perspectives unique and faithful to our theological training and pastoral calling.

Pubertal Development, Menarche, and the Physiology of Menstruation

Physiological processes and neurochemical elements essential to sexual maturation can be identified during fetal development as early as ten to twelve weeks after conception. Initially, the reproductive tissues in the fetus are undifferentiated, subsequently developing into female organs and the female reproductive system unless triggered to differentiate into male fetal structures and processes by the genetic material from a sperm carrying a Y chromosome. (Each sperm contains either an X or a Y sex chromosome. Each ovum contains an X sex chromosome. A union of X and Y sex chromosomes produces a male, while the union of two X sex chromosomes results in a female.) If the fetus is endowed with two X chromosomes and is to be a girl, the processes and structures necessary to click into action for female pubertal development are largely in place half way through pregnancy. Key organs in this process are the hypothalamus in the central part of the brain; the pituitary gland, which sits at the base of the brain behind the eyes and optic structures; the ovaries, safely tucked away and protected in the pelvis; and the adrenal glands, which sit atop the kidneys. The ovaries have their full lifetime complement of oocytes, or eggs, midway through gestation, as well as the ability to produce female sex hormones if and when they are properly signaled to do so. The ovaries are prevented from initiating "fetal puberty" by the large concentration of hormones secreted by the placenta that keep the maturation process turned off at the site where it will begin several years later—the hypothalamus. This process is an example of *feedback inhibition*. In this case, enough hormones from the placenta are circulating in the fetal bloodstream so that the fetal hypothalamus recognizes that no more are needed and it does not initiate the process of hormone production on its own. When the child is separated from the placenta and maternal estrogens at birth, the levels of circulating hormones in the newborn's bloodstream drop, and the hypothalamus sends word to the pituitary gland to signal the ovary to produce its sex steroids. This "mini-puberty" is not noticeable physically or externally, and subsides in infancy as the baby's central nervous system matures and develops the capacity to inhibit the hypothalamus on its own, thus interrupting the flow of messages to the pituitary and ovaries and postponing sexual maturation until later. This process, however, is never fully turned off during childhood, for trace amounts of sex hormones and very minimal ovarian follicle development can be identified in little girls. All neonates, male and female, are endowed with many different sex steroids at birth. Healthy males have somewhat greater concentrations of testosterone than females, whereas other important hormone concentrations, such as estrone, estradiol, and progesterone, are roughly equivalent.[48]

At approximately age six, the adrenal glands begin to secrete 17-ketosteroids, or adrenal androgens. This process, called "adrenarche," starts in early latency years but is not evidenced until the appearance of pubic and axillary hair during puberty a few years later. Certain enzyme deficiencies in the adrenal tissue and particular ovarian problems can result in an excess of these adrenal androgens, leading to virilization (taking on male characteristics) in females. On occasion, premature adrenarche can lead to the early appearance of pubic and axillary hair and mature female body odors. Fortunately, diagnostic methods are advanced and treatments are available for these problems.[49]

Although much about the initiation of puberty and menarche remains unknown, a key signaling event is the increased secretion of gonadotropin-releasing hormone (GnRH) by the hypothalamus. GnRH acts on the pituitary, thereby stimulating production of follicle-stimulating hormone and luteinizing hormone. These two substances stimulate the growth of ovarian follicles and the production of estrogen. Estrogen encourages the proliferation of endometrial cells, those cells lining the internal walls of the hollow, pear-shaped uterus. The pituitary gland, which has been secreting follicle-stimulating hormone and luteinizing hormone for some time before the first menstrual period, responds to the peaked estrogen production of the ovarian follicle by increasing its production of luteinizing hormone. In subsequent menstrual cycles, when this sequence repeats itself, this part of the cycle is called the "follicular" or "proliferative" stage. Ovulation, or the release of the egg from the ovary, occurs roughly twelve hours after this surge in the level of luteinizing hormone. The luteal phase follows ovulation. What remains of the ovarian follicle after the egg is released from the ovary becomes the corpus luteum. The corpus luteum produces progesterone, which prepares the endometrial lining for implantation of a fertilized egg. If an egg is fertilized, human chorionic gonadotropin is produced and uterine changes conducive to nurturing the embryo are stimulated and maintained. If the egg is not fertilized the corpus luteum regresses, progesterone and estradiol levels fall, and the endometrial lining is shed roughly two weeks later, resulting in menstruation. Anovulatory cycles, or cycles in which a girl may shed the endometrial lining in the form of a period without the ovary actually releasing an egg eligible for fertilization, are the rule for the first one to two years after menarche. Irregular cycles are common during this time until the process outlined above becomes truly cyclical.[50]

While these endocrine and hormonal changes are occurring within a girl's body, she must deal with physical changes externally as well. Puberty, comprised of the accelerated growth in height and weight, an increase in the percentage of over-all body fat, and the emergence of secondary sexual characteristics, in addition to menarche, usually begins between the ages of eight and thirteen years of age. Typically, the first outward sign is the development of breast buds, or the modest enlargement of the areolar area and slight elevation of the breast and papilla. The initiation of breast development is called "thelarche." Pubarche, the appearance of pubic hair, usually follows thelarche, although in a minority of girls pubarche can be the first sign of puberty. These changes are accompanied by a growth spurt in the early or middle stages of puberty. The first menses, or menarche, occurs in the middle to late stages of the pubertal process. The average age for menarche in the United States among girls of European American ancestry is 12.9 years (standard deviation of 1.2 years), and among girls of African American descent it is slightly more than a half year earlier at 12.2 years (standard deviation of 1.21 years). Records indicate that over at least the last century, puberty has been occurring at younger and younger ages. The maturation process has begun three to four months earlier over each decade in Europe this past century. A partial explanation for ear-lier puberty is agreed by experts to be the improved health care and nutrition over the last several generations. With improved public health have come heavier and taller children. One of the set points for triggering pubertal and menstrual onset is the attainment of a critical mass of body fat in the young girl. Many researchers in this field are optimistic that the average age at the onset of puberty will not creep appreciably lower. Some claim that medical care and nutrition have improved to the point that the determinant in pubertal onset and adult height is genetic po-tential only, and if this is true, the ages of maturity and absolute heights will sta-bilize.[51] In general, young girls should be evaluated by their physicians if signs of pubertal maturation are noted before eight years of age, or if no evidence of pu-berty exists by the age of thirteen.[52]

Menstrual-related problems are most common in the perimenarchal and per-imenopausal years, or at the beginning and the end of a female's reproductive years. Young menstruating women experience a variety of menstrual disorders, most of a minor nature with no negative effects on overall health or the ability to bear children later. Four of the most common concerns in this age group include premenstrual syndrome (PMS), dysmenorrhea, amenorrhea, and dysfunctional vaginal bleeding.[53]

Definitions and diagnostic criteria for premenstrual syndrome have varied widely since it was first described in 1931. PMS includes physical and emotional symptoms that begin seven to ten days before menses and usually subside during the first one or two days of menstrual blood flow. Physical manifestations may include breast enlargement and tenderness, weight gain, fluid collection in the lower extremities (edema), abdominal bloating, increased appetite, headaches, constipation, fatigue, and a craving for sweet and salty foods and alcoholic beverages. Psychological manifestations, usually noted more by family and friends than by the girl experiencing PMS, may include increased irritability, anxiety, depressive symptoms, impulsivity, and diminished concentration. The exact etiology has yet to be determined, although several theories have been suggested, including steroid hormone fluctuations, vitamin deficiencies, salt and water imbalances, and a variety of other hormonal and neurotransmitter abnormalities. In addition to ruling out other clearly demonstrable and treatable gynecological disorders, assessment frequently involves the recording of symptoms in a menstrual diary, and looking for psychiatric symptoms that might benefit from various treatment trials. Low-salt, high protein diets, increased exercise, and oral contraceptives have proven beneficial for many females dealing with premenstrual syndrome.[54]

Dysmenorrhea is the medical word for menstrual cramps. The term is derived from Greek words meaning "difficult monthly flow." With a prevalence rate in adolescents approaching 60 percent, it is the most common menstrual complaint of young girls and the leading reason for school absences in that age group. Dysmenorrhea usually begins a few hours before or at the same time as menstrual bleeding begins, peaks during the first day of flow, and resolves by the third day of the period. Lower back pain, nausea, vomiting, diarrhea, dizziness, and headaches may accompany the crampy, lower abdominal pain. Primary dysmenorrhea has an onset six to eighteen months after menarche, corresponding with the establishment of ovulatory cycles. Secondary dysmenorrhea is caused by a diagnosable problem not directly related to ovulation, including congenital abnormalities, uterine malformations, infections, complications of pregnancy, and very rarely in young females, tumors. Treatment consists of addressing the underlying medical problem. Because primary dysmenorrhea is so closely related to ovulation, severe pain may be relieved by treatments that prevent or suppress ovulation (i.e., oral contraceptives). Adolescents who exercise little, and who smoke and drink alcohol have more severe dysmenorrhea, and girls from lower socioeconomic backgrounds tend to miss more school, perhaps due to greater obstacles in obtaining medical care. For years, psychological factors such as immaturity, insecurity, dependency, oversensitivity, and other neurotic qualities were believed to cause painful menses. Recent studies have not supported psychological or personality variables as causes for dysmenorrhea. Physically and sexually abused females, however, report a higher incidence of painful menses, and psychosocial concerns may heighten anxiety, which can decrease pain thresholds in certain individuals predisposed to dysmenorrhea.[55]

Amenorrhea, or the absence of menses, is also categorized into two types. Primary amenorrhea is the failure to begin menstruating by age sixteen in the presence of otherwise normal physical development, or fourteen years without typical pubertal changes. Girls with this condition should have a full medical work-up performed by a physician trained and experienced in this area. Secondary amenorrhea is the cessation of menses for six or more months after regular menstrual cycles have been established. As noted in the above discussion of the physiology of menstruation, several organs and multiple endocrine processes must work synchronously to coordinate the menstrual cycle. Hence, fluctuations in functioning at the levels of the hypothalamus, pituitary, thyroid, and adrenal, ovaries, uterus, and vagina may lead to missed periods. Pregnancy is actually the most common cause of secondary amenorrhea. Other conditions or factors that need to be considered in cases of amenorrhea include chronic illnesses, malnutrition, severe weight loss (especially anorexia nervosa), obesity, moderate or serious athleticism, obesity, chronic or intense emotional stress, and polycystic ovary disease.[56]

The fourth common menstrual problem to be considered here is dysfunctional vaginal bleeding, or DVB. Ironically, the most common cause of DVB in early pubertal females is anovulation. When a girl does not ovulate, the uterine lining, or endometrium, is stimulated by estrogens that are unopposed by other hormones released by the corpus luteum after ovulation. These estrogens cause the endometrial lining to become excessively thick, and eventually excess blood from this thickened endometrium is released from the uterus and expelled through the vagina. DVB is a diagnosis of exclusion, which means that other causes of vaginal bleeding must be ruled out, such as trauma from rape or intercourse, reproductive tract infections, endometriosis, bleeding disorders, or retained tampons or other foreign objects in the vagina. The treatment should be matched to the underlying cause, including treatment with progesterone or oral contraceptives if DVB is anovulatory in nature.[57]

Menarche and Young Girls:
A Brief Feminist and Theological Appropriation

Mary Jane Lupton wrote,

> Menstrual blood is gendered blood—blood that separates and defines women, that has made them the subject of taboo, of exclusion, of difference—whether among the Kolash Indians of Alaska or among subtle discourse communities like the Vienna Psychoanalytic Society . . .
>
> To recognize women's bleeding is to assess the consequences of gender in its biological, societal, and psychological representations; it is also to affirm female productivity and renewal against such traditionally negative psychoanalytic concepts as female castration and female masochism.[58]

Within this passage lies both the best and worst of what cultural attitudes and psychological theories have conveyed to generations of young girls regarding their menarche and similarly, to millions of older females about their bodily processes and menstruation. Historically, western civilization has conspired, both intentionally at times and unknowingly in other circumstances, to cloak menstruation in shrouds of silence, mystery, shame, old wives' tales, and even dirtiness and profanity. Traditional psychoanalytic theory did nothing to enhance the understanding of this vital aspect of femininity, and can even shoulder responsibility for the failure to appreciate the healthiness and necessity of sexual differences in biopsychosocial development. In reaction to the neglect of menstruation in this discipline and related professional psychology circles, or perhaps in reaction to the negativity bias shown when the subject has been raised, most of the available writings on the psychology of menstruation appear to fall into two camps. One school of thinkers emphasizes menstruation as the signal event and process that differentiates males from females, and that this should be celebrated and recast in positive terms as the antidote to the oppressive attitudes of the past.[59] On the contrary, an opposing viewpoint is espoused by groups such as American socialist feminists, who posit that an emphasis on sexual differences can come back to bite the very population it was intended to support. Clara Thompson, an American psychoanalyst, made the following observation in the early 1960s: "Sexual difference is an obvious difference, and obvious differences are especially convenient marks of derogation in any competitive situation in which one group aims to get power over the other."[60] Many secular thinkers have viewed the relatively sparse dialogue on menarche and menstruation as reinforcing sexual stereotypes, and as continuing vulnerability to the painful and oppressive consequences that have plagued patriarchal institutions and disciplines such as traditional medicine and behavioral sciences.

That feminist and womanist theologians would be drawn to this argument seems obvious. Indeed, many of the early writings on the female experience of embodiment bear significant resemblance to psychoanalytic essays published up until that time, albeit with theological language and prophetic tones serving notice to religious institutions that the church was very much guilty of misinterpreting gender differences. Feminist theologians reminded the religious community that the unique female experiences of menstruation, pregnancy, childbirth, and suckling provided perspectives on the nature of God and God's love that could not be found elsewhere. Yet, while these writings were precisely the prescription needed at that time to raise awareness of gender differences and their potential for illustrating theological relationships and understanding God and human relationships in fresh ways, today's readers cannot help but notice an edge or bite in early feminist works mentioning menstruation and other female body processes. For instance, in 1985, Rosemary Radford Ruether wrote:

> . . . we are not talking about women's experience primarily in terms of experiences created by biological differences in themselves but rather,

women's experiences created by the social and cultural appropriation of biological differences in a male-dominated society. In such a society, women experience even their biological differences in ways filtered and biased by male dominance and by their own marginalization and inferiorization. Menstruation and childbirth are interpreted to them as pollution, over against a male-controlled sacred sphere, for example, which alienates them from a positive understanding of their own bodily experiences. Insofar as they appropriate their own experiences, such as the experience of menstruation, as a positive and create rhythm of ebb and flow, they must do so in contradiction to the male hermeneutic of their own experience imposed upon them by the dominant culture.[61]

Was this straight-to-the-point, no-nonsense approach necessary fifteen to twenty years ago? Undoubtedly so. Is it necessary in 2000? Perhaps in some settings and with certain audiences it is helpful. Such passionate debates with tough rhetoric between feminists and their critics, even when feminists are upholding the sanctity of women's bodily processes, may still fall short of the gentler, more pastoral words on menstruation that true feminists really want their own daughters to hear and internalize about their developing bodies, well-rounded femininity, and completeness before God. Women "doing" theological reflection on women's experiences today are seeking to recapture an innate spirituality, and consider female growth and development in the context of theological communities and relationships with other females.[62] Kathleen Greider, Gloria Johnson, and Kristen Leslie have defined the focus of current conversation while simultaneously encouraging the direction of pastoral theology in this area in the next several years: "Female body processes—previously taboo—do not define women, but they do inspire. Women put into print reflections on how their 'unmentionable' bodily experiences—menstruation, pregnancy, lactation, and other gynecological processes—complexify women's ways of knowing and parallel ways in which embodiment shapes (and is shaped by) all human knowing."[63] Gradually, this view of menstruation as a gendered process, one through which God exercises God's creative and nurturant qualities, one inspired by God and ever inspiring, will be incorporated not only into the hearts and minds of mature females, but will permeate daughters and granddaughters, husbands, brothers, and sons. Is that not the message of feminists through the years?

Freud, Conventional Gender Theory, Moral Development, Self-Esteem, Other Loose Ends . . . and Julie

The goal of this chapter has been to present an overview and analysis of biopsychosocial and religious/spiritual development in girls from birth until roughly the age of twelve. Unlike many texts or developmental pieces, I have sought to represent as fully and accurately as possible the growth trajectories of females independently and without comparison to their male peers. Although a big part of me believes that nothing more should be necessary, the reality is that the vast majority of individuals in the practical (and certainly academic) worlds continue to describe the development of girls primarily in terms of how they differ from boys. I am quite resistant to that tactic in a chapter of a book focusing on developmental and pastoral care concerns spanning the life cycle of women. The reality, however, is that one cannot blindly advocate new or different pedagogical ways of thinking in any area without fully understanding the paradigms that one is trying to supplant or supplement. Freud's psychosexual theory,[64] Kohlberg's work in moral development,[65] Carol Gilligan's original work plus her responses to the Kohlberg theories,[66] and explanations of the genetic, biological, psychological, and cultural underpinnings of gender identity, gender role behavior, sexual play and exploration, masturbation, sexual orientation, and self-esteem[67] are indeed important for pastoral caregivers to know and understand well enough to apply in individual and group therapeutic work. Dialogue needs to be strengthened between parish clergy, pastoral caregivers, and the teachers who spend numerous hours with children during formative years. The professional education literature addresses the learning styles of young girls, gender tendencies and differences in the classroom, and strategies for improving educational achievement for all children, irrespective of gender.

While many of the classical developmental theories and schemas have remained relatively unchanged over recent decades, the stresses and assaults to healthy development do appear to be increasing. Greater numbers of children, especially young girls, are growing up in family and environmental surroundings so violent that they genuinely believe and live as if they will not reach adulthood. More infants and children in the United States, indeed in the entire global community, are living in poverty than ever before, compromising education, nutrition, health care, and basic supervision. In my ten-year practice of child and adolescent psychiatry, I can attest to an increase in the number of children who spontaneously report fears and nightmares about floods, earthquakes, hurricanes, tornadoes, meteorite crashes, and other random acts of nature that are capable of destroying their worlds. These concerns, not to mention the issues of racism, medical and psychiatric illness, divorce, multiple family forms, and confusing cultural priorities, are changing the validity and applicability of "tried and true" developmental principles. Once again, we do not really know what we thought we knew, and there is significant work to be done to understand the world in which young girls mature and live, and how pastoral caregivers and religious institutions can minister to and enrich these developmental processes.

Finally, let's return to Julie, the nine-year-old girl at the beginning of this chapter who graced me with her presence of body, mind, and spirit for those few precious hours before she died. I see in Julie's story so much that typifies young female development, as well as the best and worst of adults, institutions, public policy, and cultural concerns that defined the world in which she and other children live and grow to maturity. Until she was diagnosed with leukemia, Julie's physical, psychological, emotional, and educational growth had been unremarkable. Perhaps she could have been read to more often as a younger child, perhaps she could have had a more optimum student-to-teacher ratio in her classrooms, perhaps she would have enjoyed and benefited from more undivided and individual attention from her parent, or perhaps she had too many french fries and not enough fruits and vegetables in her diet—but regardless of these concerns, there was nothing so out of the ordinary about her to warrant extra attention by her physician, an evaluation for special services at school, or a protective services referral. Even at the end of her illness she was preoccupied with normal nine-year-old concerns. Body image is important to latency-aged girls—she enjoyed the nice clothes handed down to her by her friend's older sister, and she wanted to look her best in heaven, especially because the chemotherapy here on earth had threatened her bodily integrity. She had the concrete, anthropomorphic conceptualizations of God, heaven, and heavenly beings characteristic of her levels of cognitive, moral, and faith development. Julie's development was on par in virtually every category.

But, as we all know, "life as usual" can be changed instantaneously by accident or illness, and leukemia certainly upset the worlds of Julie and her family. The illnesses of individuals also have an uncanny way of highlighting and exacerbating the chronic sores and pains of human systems and institutions. Too often, these flaws impinge on the care and services young children so need and upon which they should be able to depend. Like the nurse who first paged me to Julie's bedside and seemed more amused by how many attempts it might take me to restart her line than concerned about the fact that the child's morphine drip and pain relief might be compromised, we sometimes lose ourselves in mechanics and policies and procedures, rendering us less able to focus on the needs of individual children. Like the staff members who put Julie in the room at the end of the hall, farthest from the nursing station, we do not want to see problems "up close and personal." Like sending the least experienced medical student to restart Julie's line in veins thrombosed and scarred by corrosive chemotherapeutic agents, our society relegates many important child-related services (such as day care) to the least qualified, lowest paid workers, without providing these individuals with the training, supervision, and positive feedback necessary to enable them to do their jobs well. The absence of stuffed animals and fluffy quilts in Julie's hospital room reflected the struggles of a young single mother to provide basic material necessities for her children, let alone luxuries such as frilly bedroom furnishings. Julie's overwrought mother, for whatever reasons, was not able to muster support in the way of transportation costs, time off from work, and child care for her other offspring so that she could be with Julie as she was dying. At the very end, even the medical and religious institutions, in the forms of "real doctors" and a chaplain, resisted being available and present with her as she was dying. Just the third-year medical student on call who never had a choice about answering a page.

In the midst of the gloom, however, Julie continues to inspire me. Her story reminds us of the power of relationships with other females, especially for little girls. Julie missed her mother desperately, but sustained herself by remembering better times she and her mother had shared in the past. Julie's relationships with her best friend, her best friend's older sister, and her best friend's mother were more than sustaining, for they modeled the best of what Julie knew and believed about the church, God, and heaven. Indeed, these relationships were expressions of God's care. And, on the night when she could have felt the most forsaken, she believed God had answered a prayer by sending her a lady doctor to restart her IV so she could feel comfortable talking about "girl stuff."

"Will I have hair in heaven?"

I forget exactly what I said to her in my weary, sleep-deprived state that night, but I hope I told her she would have a whole lot more.

Attending to Alice:
The Subjective Aims
of Adolescent Girls

Carolyn Bohler

Mothers standing alongside soccer fields, mothers who are seminary students, mothers in sharing groups told me they were reading *Reviving Ophelia*,[1] a popular book that illustrates how our culture is harmful to girls. In the author's own words, "America today is a girl-destroying place."[2] Pipher, the author, does not suggest that America is unique in its destructiveness to girls. She points out that even ancient myths and fairy tales have described a crisis through which many adolescent girls journey. She quotes Diderot, who wrote to a young woman, "You all die at fifteen."[3]

Pipher observes hundreds of girls in her counseling practice whom she likens to Shakespeare's Ophelia. They are free and happy as girls, then fall in love with Hamlets and lose themselves, living only for the approval of males. Pipher sees girls in our culture as identified with their bodies, pressured into behavior they do not want, and working to please others, especially boys. Her argument is that we should not just support and guide girls but shape a "less complicated" culture that focuses less on violence and is less sexualized.[4]

The tone of Pipher's book is alarm. The mothers who were reading Pipher's book were worried—rightly concerned about the effect of sexist and conformist cultural influences on their daughters. I became alarmed by the alarm. For years, feminists working in psychology and in theology have been articulately stating both problems with and solutions for a sexist culture. Alarm as a dominant mood for parenting is not beneficial; it is probably no better than naivete. Although I agree with most of the recommendations in Pipher's "conclusions," I was concerned that the message parents heard was: "Protect your daughters! 'Hamlets' (males) and 'hamlets' (communities) ahead are dangerous; your girls might not survive intact." I wondered whether a more effective message would be: "Attend to your daughters! A perplexing world lies ahead; help your daughters keep their heads and their courage." The message of fear concentrates on what is outside the daughter—males and the culture—and stimulates parents to be anxious in relationship to their daughters. The message of attention focuses on the gifts of the daughter and encourages parents to be calm as they observe, even enjoy watching, their daughters.

I suggest that we would be wiser to recognize that culture is ambiguous: There are threads of violence, sexualization, sexism, racism, cultural conformism, and other perils for all girls, and these dangers should be named and challenged. There are also hamlets, communities of peoples (families, schools, churches/synagogues, communities, Girl Scouts) that try to provide healthy environments for girls, even in the midst of the dangers. Far too many girls live for "Hamlets" (males) to their own detriment—these cases point to the need to keep working to help, not hurt—girls. Some girls are like Alice in Wonderland, however, often maintaining their centered selves even amidst a complex world. These girls regard themselves as usually able to handle what comes their way. They are, as Lewis Carroll describes his own Alice, resourceful and self-confident.[5] They might cry when confused, but they learn to swim in their tears, as Alice did; they do not throw themselves into the river to drown, as did Ophelia. Perhaps if we attended to the "Alice" in all girls and to those girls who remind us a good deal of Alice, we could discern what is going right and have greater motivation and hope for supporting a culture that fosters a healthy environment for girls. The mood with which we would surround girls would be wonder and courage, not alarm and protection.

To affirm that a person is a subject of her own experience is a theological statement as well as a psychological one. Process theology uses the term "subjective aim" to describe a person's own goal with which she leans to the future. God offers an "initial aim" to every person each moment, whether or not we are aware of it. Each of us, however, as subjects of our own experience, is free to incorporate God's aim—or not. We integrate God's suggestions (usually unconsciously) with all the other influences on us, including our own past and our own anticipated future.

An adolescent girl can let a contemporary Hamlet influence her too much, veering her off what she wants (or what God would want for her). She can acquiesce when the queen says, "Hold your tongue!" But an adolescent girl today can also relate to Hamlet's influence in a healthy way that does not deny herself, and she can respond as Alice did when the queen told Alice to hold her tongue: "I won't!"[6] Both scenarios occur in this contemporary American culture.

My appetite was whetted to attend to adolescent girls for myself. Because our daughter was fifteen and willing to let me interview some of her friends, I decided to use the opportunity.[7] I wondered how these fifteen-year-olds experienced themselves subjectively: Did they consider themselves to be making their own choices or others to be making choices for them? How did they consider their future? Does God enter into their picture at all? I wondered whether or not they felt needed, felt accepted, or had a sense of purpose. I wondered how they liked being themselves and with what aspect of themselves (body, mind, emotions, will, and so forth) they identified. I wondered whether they prefer harmony or complexity.

In experiments, we often call those who are interviewed "subjects." When we think this way, we are making those subjects "objects" of our scrutiny, for they primarily have instrumental value for the researcher. I wanted most of all to treat the girls as people who had their own subjectivity; I did not want to objectify them. Therefore, I tried to create a situation in which their own experience mattered—to me, to them, and to the reader of this chapter.[8]

Because I am European American, I wanted and expected to interview all ten girls with my colleague, who is African American. My colleague took on administrative responsibilities, however, and was unable to participate in this project. I believe the discussion would have been better if it had been led by both a black and a white interviewer. Then, for instance, the white girls would have had to think about race, as did all the black girls facing me.

The choice of girls was not random. Rather, I tried to get a diverse set of girls. Of the ten, seven were fifteen years old, two were fourteen, and one just turned sixteen. Eight had just completed ninth grade; two, tenth grade. To my eye, five are European American; five are African American.[9] Seven of the girls attend a Dayton public school for visual and performing arts (which is 55 percent black and 45 percent white); three attend private schools (two different Roman Catholic schools and one Protestant private school). I knew that two were Roman Catholic (or highly influenced by that tradition), two were Jewish, five were Protestant, and one was not affiliated with a religious institution.[10]

Without inquiring but upon reflection after the interviews, I realized that seven or more of the ten have at least one parent who had been divorced, though several of those have lived with both parents their whole lives; that is, their parents were divorced and remarried prior to their birth.[11] My impression is that six of the girls currently live with a mother and father, three with a mother, and one lives at times with an aunt, a grandmother, or her father.

All of the girls and I live in the city of Dayton, Ohio on the west side of town, within a three to five mile radius of one another.[12] The east side of town is often considered the white side. Our vicinity is the only integrated area in the segregated city.

The most homogeneous attributes of these ten are their attitudes and abilities. As I began to listen to them, I realized that virtually all of them are exceptionally good students, with artistic or athletic talents. I fretted about the nonrepresentative quality of the group until I realized that I had enlisted exactly the girls who were barely represented and called "anomalies" in Pipher's dire picture. These girls "manage to hold on to some sense of themselves in the high winds."[13] The voices I was hearing were those of Alice, not Ophelia. My sample of adolescents came not from a therapeutic context, but from those living in an integrated setting, most of whom attend an innovative public high school that supports each student in his or her creativity.

Because I knew most of the girls and shared the context of all of them, I believe I was granted trust more quickly than if I had been a stranger. There were facts I knew about some of them, for example, what schools and synagogues or churches they went to. I tried not to bring up any of this prior information, but neither did I act naive if they alluded to it.[14]

Regardless of what I might glean from these interviews, I wanted the girls to have an experience of being valued and heard. Even if there would be no major breakthrough in this chapter, the girls would experience themselves as being taken seriously and their experience as mattering. Personally, I enjoyed this adventure a good deal. I was in the presence of caring young women, even theologians (people who think about God and the world and are willing to share their ideas). They trusted me—and the reader—with some of their thoughts.

With the exception of two girls, Toccarra and Charelle, who wanted to be cited, the others are named here with pseudonyms that they either chose or agreed to.[15]

The Girls' Own Self-Descriptions

Who in the world am I?[16]

Near the end of each interview, I asked each girl to describe herself, without myself providing any categories. The girls will introduce themselves with their own responses:

Natasha: I don't like being confined. I'm talkative, free-spirited, intelligent—not stupid. I like to learn new things. Musical, I like music.

Toccarra: Strong, high self-esteem, persevering, generous, tireless. . . . Those qualities make a really good person. Oh, and attitude. Fourteen, fifteen soon, and Baptist.

Chloe: United Methodist; I would check the "white" box,[17] but it always makes me feel uncomfortable, because I don't like to differentiate. I just try to avoid the issue of color as much as possible. Teenager, artist, musician, daughter; I'm a sister. I'm sixteen; I can drive whenever I want to.

Nicole: Happy person, faithful, independent, lovable, fifteen, athletic, interested in school, serious about school.

Elyse: Black, ninth grade, anxious to drive, African Methodist Episcopal.

Jane: I'm white. I would say I'm Roman Catholic, with qualifications on that, "cultural Catholic" is the way my mother puts it.

Three girls added particulars about who they were not, and they did so in a self-accepting manner, as if they had come to terms with their abilities:

Deborah: Athletic, not artistic.

Chloe: I'm not an athletic person at all.

Jane: Intelligent, thinking sort of person, not athletic at all. I guess I'm creative, interested in a lot of different things. I'm not particularly a people person; I don't always know what to say. I'm not like a writing person, but sometimes poetry really gets to the heart of things.

Two specifically commented on not labeling themselves:

Djuna: I don't know that I really want to label myself with certain qualities, so that I don't have any opportunities left or whatever to change. I'd have to say female, fourteen, blonde hair.[18]

Madeline: I'm this and this, but I'm also this and this, so it's unfair to force a choice.

Choice Making

She generally gave herself very good advice.[19]

These fifteen-year-old girls experience themselves as making their own choices. They talked about having been guided by family (and for the majority, synagogue or church) as they grew up. They could now choose to rely on that background as well as contemporary dialogue with their parent(s). A few of the girls at first considered that they made choices independently of others. When I clarified potential ways others might affect them, they extended their answers to include some modicum of influence by other sources.[20]

I did not mention anything about "right" or "wrong," but several of the girls seemed to assume "choices" involve right or wrong. This might reveal adults' tendencies to preach to youth to choose right and to say no to wrong.

On the whole, if these girls are making decisions based on boys' opinions, it is not apparent in their comments to me. At this time, they could be described more accurately as finding themselves than as losing themselves.

Jane: I'd say I make my own decisions; I mean [I] take suggestions. My parents are kind of like, "You know this and this and this. . . ."[11]

Chloe: Well, I think I make some [choices], but I think a lot of people make others for me. My mom has a lot of influence on me. They all [school, community, friends] have the same sort of influence. She's just the biggest one.

Nicole: I feel like I make my own choices. I'm the type of person [who thinks] my idea is the right idea—like if you want something done right, do it yourself.

Toccarra: When I was younger, people always made decisions for me. My parents, or my teachers, or my grandparents, or somebody. But now as I get older and more mature, I see that the responsibility lies on me now to make those decisions and choices, and I have to know right from wrong. My conscience is God. Because you know he tells me right from wrong. You have to have your inside to rely on. I feel like I've played a part or had a role or responsibility in the choices that people make for me. Because they ask my opinion, they talk with me, they make the choices with me rather than for me.

Madeline: I was raised to make sure that I made choices, and I sat down, and I listed every choice before I made the choice, to guard against any rash decisions. Calculating, over and over and over. I analyze everything to make sure that what I choose is what I really want to do. My mind basically makes the decision, then it goes through my body and my heart: "Yes, I agree" or "No, I don't." Then we [the parts] go over everything again. I'm kind of collecting everything I'm learning, and I'm shoving it into my invisible backpack, and then once I need to make a decision, I'll have everything I need. I'll have the years to help make my decision. . . .

Djuna: I feel like I'm pretty independent. My parents have taught me to make my own choices, and if I make a bad choice they usually come in and save me or whatever. They taught me to take my time with it [choices], and if it's really important, or I need advice, I can go to certain people.

Charelle: If I'm sort of working at something and look at the whole picture, I'll look at other people to see what they say. [I consult a good female friend.] My grandmother is a big influence on me. She always taught me to have faith in God and to be thankful for Jesus Christ. She's a cool grandmother. My sister [also influences me]. She doesn't let peer pressure determine her future. If her friends are smoking, she doesn't say, "Well, I think I'll smoke too." My last influence would be my aunt; she's the biggest influence in my life, because she helped me get more interested in education, math, and science, and she's a big person on helping others, and that sort of rubbed off on me. Now I stay with my dad.

Natasha: It depends on what the choice actually is. Like if it's a moral choice, it comes from inside, and also outside from my parents, my friends, my background, where I come from.

Madeline calculates and analyzes, based on what she's been taught; Charelle consults with her grandmother, aunt, friend, or sister, and maybe her dad—in other words, she has a strong network of people who convey some interest in reflecting with her. Some of the girls describe the current relationship with their parents as consultation; at least one is very conscious of her mom's influence. They do not give the impression that they want to—or do—wait until someone tells them what to do. They see themselves as subjects in their own right.

These girls are anticipating driving soon and currently sense their own power. They have made it through the age-thirteen transition, when girls may lose their voices, that is, shift their locus of authority from their own perspectives to that of someone else, in order to please.[21] They are not keeping decisions "in abeyance,"[22] not "giving their eyes away."[23] These girls are quite conscious choice-makers.

The girls believe that their upbringing was useful. They could use their "invisible backpacks," Madeline's term for all that she had collected while growing up. Precisely because many of their influences thus far were helpful, they could move on confidently.

Images of the Future

> It was much pleasanter at home," thought poor Alice, "when one wasn't always growing larger and smaller, and being ordered about by mice and rabbits. I almost wish I hadn't gone down that rabbit-hole—and yet—and yet—it's rather curious, you know, this sort of life!"[24]

Without prompting, when asked about their feelings toward their future, these adolescents used two words, in juxtaposition: excited and scared. A few shared their appreciation of the present time and reluctance to hurry the future.

Chloe: Apprehension, very much. This is all I know and to go off into a strange world is kind of scary. Now I always have my home to hold me, but when I go to college. . . .

Elyse: It's pretty scary.

Nicole: When I think of [my future], I get really happy that I'm getting out and going out on my own, but I'm scared about what's out there.

Madeline: I'm really excited, because I really want the future, and I'm kind of not sure what it holds and scared it holds something not necessarily bad but just something different.

Djuna: I guess I'm eager, but everybody else around me is a lot more eager than I am. I'm really comfortable where I am.

Deborah: I want to go away from my family, but I'm close to my family now.

Charelle: I'm sort of scared of going away. What's really exciting is being on my own, and having to support myself and really learning right from wrong.

Natasha: I'm scared mostly. Well, I'm the kind of person who likes to be in control of things. I have this fear of not living up to what everybody expects of me.

Only two mentioned marriage when I asked initially about their futures. The others responded with thoughts on marriage when I followed up with queries about whether they "saw others in their future at all." Clearly marriage, if that occurs, is expected to be a backdrop to their own lives, not the goal toward which they are striving.

The only girl who immediately mentioned marriage, Madeline, put it this way, "I want a husband, and I want two kids, and I want a great big office on top of some pretty skyscraper. The main thing for me is just to make sure that I'm being the best person I can be. I want a strong family who will be behind [me] with whatever decisions I make."

From what she hears from adult women, and her observation of them, Natasha had gained a strong sense of how marriage could deter her from what she wants to do. She stated articulately the struggle between intimacy and identity that many adult women feel:[25] "I want to do everything I want to do first. I hear all these women out there, 'If I had not gotten married, I would have done this, and I would have done that.' It's not like I'm not interested in it, but when you're married, you're like tied. You're not free. I mean you're free to do what you want, but not really.... I don't know."

The three others who commented, when asked directly about others in their future, named marriage as a far-off concern. Chloe answered realistically, "Yeah, I want to get married and have kids, but not until I'm out of college and have a job and everything. But I know people are always saying that, but it doesn't always happen that way." Jane responded, "I don't know. I don't see myself being married. I can't picture it; it just doesn't seem very likely. But, I guess it's possible." Toccarra said, "I haven't thought that far. I want to get my career or profession on steady ground before I would get into any relationship or have kids, or anything like that."[26]

A striking motif, noticeable in their mood as well as their words, was the sense that they had lots of options. Two girls specifically mentioned that they had so many talents, they would probably let someone down as they made their choices to pursue careers. In other words, they knew that they could not pursue all the talents they were now exploring. Credit should be given to their schools, which enable the girls to explore several talents in depth.[27] Exploration is a typical, appropriate task at this lifestage.

These girls have high goals; all expected to go to college. Natasha commented specifically on the reaction of others to her high—and specific—goals. "When I tell people I want to be a human factors engineer, everybody's all impressed and they say, 'Oh, she wants to be something good.' It's kind of disappointing to me, because it's like people don't expect it of black people, to want to be something higher up. They mostly have a surprised look."

Toccarra interpreted my question about the future in terms broader than her own personal future. "As I watch the news these days, I get really bad feelings. Because more things happen; it gets worse and worse everyday—violence in the schools, towards babies and kids. And then there's kids having kids, and then there's drugs and gangs. It's, like, all too much. It's, like, when is the world going to realize and stop? Come on, we have to work together. So, for the future I don't think so much it's going to destruct itself. There are positive people out there, and positive people can outnumber negative people. The future could be brighter. I think the future is going to be a wonderful time for children like us and for children younger than us, because the generation that's here now, they're setting the example. One day, we'll have to take over. And there are a lot of bright kids these days."

Notice, each girl expects to work hard. They seem to take responsibility for their own lives and are willing to care for others. They are not leaving responsibility to others, and they certainly are not expecting a male to take charge of their lives.

God

Let me think.[28]

All the girls spoke of religion and God with considered thought. Similar to the girls in Davis's chapter, they feel free to challenge what they have heard in church or synagogue.[29] It seems as if Jane, who attends a liberal Roman Catholic church that has used inclusive language for God for a decade, and Madeline, who attends a Conservative Jewish synagogue, are encouraged to think in their synagogue and church contexts.

Elyse, who is African Methodist Episcopal, responded to my question, "How do you sense yourself in relation to God, if you think of God?" quite forthrightly. "Oh yes, I'm very close to Him. I say prayers every morning, and my parents—they're talking about God all the time. He [God] loves me." Natasha, who is Apostolic Pentecostal, said, "I think he's real. I think that there's one God, that he has control over everything that ever happens. He knows what the outcome is going to be, but I can still talk to him. He's nice. I use the name Jesus."

Toccarra, Baptist, engaged in a lengthy theological discussion. "I believe to have a relationship with God you have to be saved. That means having a personal relationship with Jesus Christ the Lord. My dad gave me a choice, because you know you have to confess Jesus yourself, if you want to be saved. Some people say, 'If there's a God, why is he letting all this stuff happen?' It's not that he's letting it happen. He's giving you a choice whether you're going to sit back and let it happen." She proceeded to explain her theodicy: "Even though he knows he's in control, he's trying to give you a little responsibility, to see if you know what you're doing." When I asked, "So everything that happens isn't God's will?" she responded, "Right." When I asked whether we can influence God, she answered, "I don't think so. I think every decision he makes is his decision." Toccarra also commented on naming God: "I wouldn't really get all into political correctness or anything, saying God is a woman or a man, or if he's black or if he's white, or if he's something. I just think that God is spiritual, a spiritual friend, a spiritual guide. I wouldn't think of him as a person, just as spiritual peace."

Charelle has explored several Christian denominations and even Islam and Judaism, but is attracted to Jehovah Witnesses because of the sincere impression the people have made on her. She commented, "I think he sort of guides me. I have an intuition about certain things. I imagine God as a man. I see a 'he,' a strong powerful intelligent being. He always loves you."

Deborah, who is Jewish (Reformed), said, "I know about my religion, but I don't think about religion all that much. I think of my religion as being with my family. We all celebrate together. I think he's [God's] powerful." In contrast, Madeline, who is Jewish (Conservative) and whose family had experienced a serious automobile accident with severe consequences for her family members, questioned strongly: "I'm probably not happy with God at this moment in time, because in the Jewish religion you're always taught that you can purge yourself of all the sins, and nothing bad is going to happen. And then, with the accident, lots of bad things did happen. It's two years later, and I'm still struggling with the fact that there's supposed to be this person up there who's watching over everybody. I mean I've talked with the rabbi, talking about the fact that it just doesn't seem fair. I'm really not too happy with him [God], because it really, really is hard. I think everything that happens, God has had a hand with. It just really, really, really upsets me that we're supposed to be good people. I can't even describe it, it just makes me so mad." I asked whether she had seen the book *When Bad Things Happen to Good People*.[30] She responded, "Oh, we have sixteen copies of that. It's like somebody dumps an answer on you: 'We have to stop asking why.' I can't. I'm trying to, but everything I do, I just keep [thinking] how it would be different if that [accident] hadn't happened. All of your family and faith fosters the ability to ask why, so how can you turn off your rational questioning when that's what you've been told to do?"

Later in the interview Madeline commented that she had "kind of like a knowledge that there's somebody up there guarding over." This girl is allowed to be a theologian in her Jewish context. Her rabbi is in dialogue with her, and I had the impression that her community supports her questioning.

Djuna was strongly influenced by "such a negative experience" in a year at a Catholic school (sixth grade). She experienced what Pipher portrays as pressure to conform, because she and others who did not think as they were "supposed to" were not accepted. Prior to that, Djuna had enjoyed four years at a Lutheran school that "was very diverse, and we had people from Africa, and we had Muslims, and we had so many different religions. It wasn't like we all had to participate, and when we did, it was just about learning; it wasn't about becoming strong Lutherans. That was really good. I got to learn about the Bible without having to make a decision [to believe something]. I was around other people that were really religious, and everyone seemed to be accepting [of each other], no matter what." Now, Djuna says, "Religion is not really even a part of my life, really. I've had the opportunity. My parents told me if I ever got interested in any certain religion, they would take me to church. They're really open to it. It sort of all seems kind of fake to me, and I personally don't think I need it. I respect it in other people, people who need that kind of commitment in their life, that sort of reassurance to go on. I've done fine my whole life without it." Even while doing fine without religion, Djuna has had ample room for thinking about it—numerous dialogue partners in an atmosphere in which it is legitimate to think.

Jane, European American and a member of the Roman Catholic church, and Nicole, African American and heavily influenced by Roman Catholicism, both question. Jane explained, "I would say I'm not really religious: Sometimes I believe in God; sometimes I don't, you know. I don't really know. But I feel, like, yeah, I want to make a difference somehow and to be a part of a global community. . . . I think there should be a purpose in life. You can make more of a difference if you've got somebody else, too, if you're not by yourself. Now, mostly, I don't affect many people. I'm still a kid. Sometimes I feel I should make time for [affecting people]; it's important." Jane is "technically Catholic, baptized and first communion, and everything like that." She is also a budding philosopher, affected recently by her reading of transcendentalists such as Emerson and Thoreau. She thinks she should have some ideas about God. "And sometimes I think I have an idea, and then I decide, 'That's not right.' I change my mind. I just think, not about Jesus, just about God, because I just can't understand different parts of God. Sometimes I don't believe in God at all."

Nicole, influenced a good deal by Catholicism (her mother and dad are both Catholic), thinks independently from what she is taught, too. Nicole articulated these thoughts, "I believe in a God, but I'm not sure I believe in the God that my [Catholic] school teaches. But I believe there is a higher power than me, from the stuff in the Bible. I believe, but I question a lot of it, and I'm not Catholic. I don't need to be. But if I were a religion, that would probably be it. I imagine God is like a perfect person, nothing wrong with him."

Chloe, a United Methodist, began her response by saying, "Well, sometimes I think, 'Gee I'm not doing too well, because I really don't think about God all that much.'" She remembered she disagreed with the minister who taught her confirmation class. One thing in particular "I remember disagreeing about is when he was saying that if you don't go to church, and you say you still believe in Christ, it doesn't count. I said I didn't think that was right. If I love people who didn't go to church, then certainly God could love people who didn't go to church, because he's much more loving than I." When I asked whether she told the minister of her disagreement, she was not sure she "ever actually told him. I think I just asked the question." She proceeded, "I think that he [God] is really easygoing. I would hope so, and as long as he understands that you're trying your best, and while you might not think specifically about God all the time, everything you do is trying to do something good." She interrupted herself, asking herself why she had just said "he," saying, "Why did I say 'he'? It could be a 'she.' I don't know."

As a follow-up question, I asked most of the girls whether they felt they "experienced God." The majority said they had not, but three gave very different affirmative answers. Natasha commented, "I experience him mostly in church. It's this feeling, like this glow. I can't explain it. You're sitting there, and it's, like, you're just, like, 'Wow!' At my church we pray to the Lord, and you'll be up clapping and singing, and all of a sudden you feel so good. It's uplift."

Nicole reflected on experiencing God at a family gathering when her grandfather had died and sometimes when she goes down by the river at night and experiences beauty.

Chloe responded at first, "I don't think I've really experienced him. This book I read, it was really good; it was about some lady in the fourteenth century, but she, like, had this healing power, and he talked to her once. That's never happened to me or anything, but I think just experiencing, like, the world is a good way of experiencing God, because I think it's kind of like the same thing. . . . All of it—nature, people, buildings, art. . . . That's what I said in an essay, 'Art is life, and life is art.' That was my ending to the whole [essay]. I was very proud." I understand Chloe to mean that she sees God within the world as well as beyond it, which in theological language is called panentheism.

All ten of the girls spoke of God as "he." Chloe interjected a question about why she used "he," and Toccarra commented on "political correctness," then explained she thought of God beyond gender. As a pastoral theologian who has strong concern about exclusive use of masculine language for God, I do not rejoice at this very pervasive male god language. I am encouraged that two of the girls at least reflected on their pronouns for the deity, however.[31]

Feeling Needed and Having a Sense of Purpose

> *Alice watched the White Rabbit. . . . Imagine her surprise, when the White Rabbit read out, at the top of his shrill little voice, the name "Alice!"*[32]

After reading Patty Davis's chapter in this volume, I wish that I had asked the girls specifically about violence and how they thought their churches or synagogues were or were not helping. These girls definitely know the world is ambiguous; they live amid violence and evil. Seven walk through a metal detector to enter school daily. All probably eat at the nearby Taco Bell that installed a bullet-proof window.

The girls prefer that people would live peacefully. Virtually all these girls seemed to see themselves as part of the threads of hope, however.

Two mentioned volunteering, and three commented on helping others who had problems.

> Nicole: I think there's a purpose in the world for me, but I have no idea. One of my girlfriends right now is trying to get off drugs; I think she needs me right now. I have a lot of spare time; I don't want to sit in the house, so I'll help somebody else. (She volunteers at a nursing home.)

> Toccarra: Yes, I do believe that everybody has a purpose in the world. I feel needed by my family, because everybody feels needed by their family in some way. My brother needs me as a role model. My parents rely on me to help out. I also feel needed by my friends, to set an example again. I feel needed by peers, family, church because they need you to volunteer for things.

> Djuna: Just recently I've felt that my mom has needed me more than maybe she always has. Maybe I have been fulfilling a need [for my mom] all my life and just not knowing it, or it may be I'm at a point when maybe I'm able to converse with her at a level that she may think I'm ready.

Several tended to think they had a purpose but were too young to know the specifics yet.

> Chloe: Well, I think I have a purpose, but I have no idea what it is. Everybody tells me [my many talents] are God's gifts to me. I think, like, the public does not necessarily need me but needs people like me, you know, to see kids aren't all bad and that we really do good stuff.

> Natasha: I guess there must be a reason why we're here, but as of now I don't have a clue why I'm here.

> Charelle: I see my purpose as helping people in some way; I don't know exactly how. Sometimes my purpose is to gain knowledge.

> Jane *responded humbly:* I think I'm important up to a point. I feel important some of the time, though there would probably be somebody else if it weren't me.

> Madeline *made a statement of independence:* My purpose is for me to be the best person I can be. I really think that nobody is significantly needed by anyone else. I guess I'm just more a big fan of independent people than dependent people.

Being Accepted

So they began solemnly dancing round and round Alice, every now and then treading on her toes when they passed too close. . . .[33]

This set of girls surprised me with their responses to my question, "Do you feel accepted?" They linked that question to the issue of "being oneself." They tended to declare boldly how much more important being themselves was than being accepted. Using rhetorical criticism, one could surmise that because the girls raised the issue of being themselves versus acceptance and were so bold about their opinions, the girls probably have wrestled with the issue and decided acceptance was not going to be their number one priority. This way of navigating the teen years is different from the path of the girls about whom Pipher writes, for whom acceptance by others often seemed to be most crucial. The girls I interviewed evidently faced peer pressure, questioned their identities and their boundaries, and came up with their present attitudes.[34]

Madeline was the boldest, "Well, I really don't care whether people accept me or not, because I'm going to be the person I'm going to be. I'm not changing myself for anybody." Deborah considered reciprocity, "I feel accepted by about everybody that I'm around . . . everybody I accept: school, family, sports teams. I think I feel accepted if they need me."

Three of the five African American girls named specific incidents that involved race. Nicole shared, "I feel accepted by some people; I feel accepted by God. You wrestle with dealing with pain." Nicole explained that people talk about others, and some (referring to herself) struggle with being black, playing a sport that is identified as a "white sport." Natasha discussed being the only black person in various institutions. "Usually I can just talk to people and make friends; it makes no difference anyway. But there [in a once-a-year performance group], it's like everybody knew everybody. Every time we had a break, I sat by myself, and it drove me nuts. So last year I was determined to make friends [and another person I knew was there], and I had fun." Elyse alluded to black and white friendships and dating. "I feel accepted even though, okay, you might have one group over here and you have one group over here. I don't really care, it doesn't matter to me whether I'm in a group or not."

Jane, who reflected on ambiguity throughout most of the interview, faced ambiguity again with this question. "I guess, like among my friends, I feel accepted because they accept me; they talk to me. I think people my age in general don't always feel accepted. I feel weird, just not being interested in a lot of things they're interested in. You know, I'm not interested in clothes, shopping, and make-up and popularity and stuff like that, so I'm not interested in them, and they're not interested in me. Most of the time I can accept that, but sometimes I feel left out. I feel accepted with my friends, and I guess most of us wouldn't be accepted by some others."

Being Me

But if I'm not the same, the next question is, "who in the world am I?" . . . And she began thinking. . . .[35]

Closely aligned with the question of acceptance was the question, "How do you feel being you right now?" This question was near the end of the interviews, and several girls answered briefly:

Deborah: I feel good about being me right now.

Nicole: I don't want to change anything.

Chloe: Most of the time, I like it.

Elyse: I like it. It's kind of boring sometimes. But I like it. I can't wait to be sixteen, to learn to drive.

A couple impressed me by mentioning a desire for some improvement. Notice the trend of thought that Natasha and Djuna developed in their answers.

Natasha: Mostly, I'm glad I'm me. I think I have a sense of who I am and what I can and cannot do. There are certain attributes about me I wish I could get rid of, but everybody thinks that; nobody's perfect.

Djuna: I would really rather be me. There are people I think about [wanting to be like]. I've got improvement [to make], and I've got things I can do. I don't really know the people [whom I think I might want to be] all that well, so I guess it's not a very reliable thing to say, so I'd rather be myself.

Jane, *when asked how she liked being herself, responded with gratitude for her family*: I feel like a really lucky person with my family, which is absolutely great. I would not change to be anybody but me. There's a quote I was thinking of earlier, it's like the best thing parents can give their children is roots and wings. It applies to my parents, because they give you freedom and say, "Go out and experience it."

Connected and Separate

"Nonsense!" said Alice, very loudly and decidedly, and the Queen was silent.[36]

Developing and maintaining one's boundary between self and other is an essential emotional task.[37] Females are at risk for blurring this distinction, at least in part because we are socialized to please or care for the other. Males are also at risk, but their risk in our culture is likely to be to spin off into isolation. To evoke these young women's perceptions, I asked how the girls felt either "connected with others" or "separate from others." How one feels connected or separate does not have to be a psychological question; it had theological, cosmological, and even ethical connotations for some. Four of these teenagers waxed philosophical in their answers.

> Toccarra: That would go back to God, because we're all connected, we all came from him. Basically, even though you have your birth mother, we're all connected spiritually. It just takes a lot to realize that.

> Deborah: I feel a little more connected. There are those that don't want to be connected, but deep down they are connected; I don't think you can be alive without connection.

> Natasha: I have a lot of different ideas. Mostly I think we're connected in spirit. I think we all have the same souls and spirits, and that things happen to us that make us different, our personalities and stuff. We're all connected with God of course. I think we all stem from the same thing.

> Nicole: Some places we're separated; some places we're all connected. I'd like it if we were just one, but we're not there yet. I like to make my own independent choices, but I like for people as a whole [to] respect everyone else's choices more.

> Jane *gave a description of what theologians call self-transcendence*: You are yourself, so you feel separate. I think of myself separately from other people. But you see a lot of other people connected, connected to you and connected to each other everywhere. You can only understand from your point of view, and you're more connected to yourself than you are to other people. If you were outside a person, you would see everybody being connected a whole lot. I think everybody really is connected, but you're connected with yourself most of all.

Chloe and Charelle associated this connection/separate question with the need for space.

> Chloe: Most of the time I feel really connected, but then there are some times that I have to be by myself or I'll get mad.

> Charelle *who has lived with different close family members, explained*: In my family, more as individuals, sometimes knowing when to be in your own space, not invading the space of others. Then with friends, it's sort of the same—our group wants everyone to be different.

Djuna perceived that her parents are connected to each other, but separated a bit too much—for her preference—from their extended families or other friends.

"So I think I'm a lot more connected than they are." She mentioned several times throughout the interview her own valuing of friends.

Enjoyment

> *"Well! I've often seen a cat without a grin,"* thought Alice; *"but a grin without a cat! It's the most curious thing I ever saw in all my life!"*[38]

An element in knowing oneself is the ability to know what one enjoys. Borysenko, the author of *A Woman's Book of Life*, tells the story of a girl named Heidi whose grandmother asked Heidi to vow to claim her own happiness rather than living (as Heidi had been) as a wish-fulfiller for others.[39] I asked these adolescent girls, "How do you enjoy life?" I now realize I could have asked the corollary question, "How do you experience pain or evil?" I might have been reluctant to ask that question for a one-time, relatively brief interview, however. The answers were quick in coming and presented a broad range of being and doing. Madeline responded pensively, "I don't know, on days like today, you know, pouring outside, [the rainy day is] just kind of like life. I think the whole concept of [life] is great, but while you're living it, life seems to be more painful."

The other responses presented a fairly consistent joie de vivre.

> Chloe: Well, I like my friends, and I like my school. I know that sounds funny because most people don't like school. I like summer vacation, too. I like music, art, traveling, and people. People are very interesting. Life would be very boring if there weren't different people. I kind of like all of life.

> Deborah: Lots of ways. Well, I enjoy life, having fun. I also enjoy work. I'm making my own money. [I enjoy having my] family around a lot. I don't know what I'd do without them. My extended family was at my house three times for dinner this week. We have two grandmothers and a grandpa and a step-grandmother.

> Nicole: I enjoy living each day. I like sports and stuff. I like seeing other people happy. I like being happy.

Natasha detailed ways she enjoys resting that include both not thinking and also creative thinking, "I like sitting out in the sun. I like just going out and doing nothing. I have a brain that goes constantly. Sometimes I feel so overwhelmed, I'll just go outside and lie down, close my eyes and not think of anything." Influenced a good deal by her high school creative writing teacher, who also teaches yoga, Natasha explained, "I love to write. When I write, I can do anything I want. I make my characters do things that I really, really want to do, but I know I can't. I love short stories. You can really get in touch with yourself. You just lie on the floor and just relax all your muscles, and you just like sink into the floor [to get ready to write], and I love it."

Djuna relayed her love for adventure and risk-taking, referring to such activities as soccer (boys varsity), wall climbing, spelunking, skiing, snowboarding, and who knows what else in the future.

> Djuna: I enjoy life immensely. I'm having fun. I used to be afraid of dying, and I'm not saying I'm going to go jump off a bridge for fun. I mean, I do somewhat think about death, but it's sort of, like, if I'm not enjoying myself then what's the point? Who cares about dying? I don't think [to myself], 'This could involve death; this could involve injury.' I know other people [who] never would do something, not necessarily because they think they're going to die; they just wouldn't enjoy it."

Toccarra and Jane balanced what could be called extroverted and introverted ways of enjoying themselves, which include being with others and writing poetry.

> Toccarra: I read books all the time. I also enjoy life through writing. I write poetry and stories. I enjoy life through acting. I also enjoy life through wonderful friends. When you find the people who are the right crowd for you, you make the same connections, you make great decisions, you do things together. So I enjoy life through my peers, and also through my family. My family, that's the number one.

> Jane: Yeah, I love boating and the water. Every summer [our family goes] to Michigan.

My impression is that these girls are quite connected to family and friends. Peers are important, but the girls seem, for the most part, to have found peers with whom they have congruent values. They can be themselves and be with the friends. Several gave hints that it took them some time and searching to gather or find a compatible group. Several have developed ways to enjoy themselves when alone, either because they do not have many friends or to supplement their peer time.

Complexity and Harmony

> *For, you see, so many out-of-the-way things had happened lately . . .*[40]

Process theologians suggest that beauty is achieved when there is a good balance between rich complexity and harmony.[41] Some of each is needed to avoid the extremes of disharmony (too much complexity, without enough harmony) or triviality (too much harmony without enough complexity). Mary Pipher argued not only that we should give girls a less sexualized and less violent world (a view with which

I agree), but also a less complicated culture. I find her second goal both unreachable and undesirable.

I was curious how these young women would describe their preferences for complexity or harmony, so I asked, "What do you tend to prefer, most of the time: things that are harmonious, neat, familiar, and maybe even simple, or things that are intense, complex, messy, maybe even difficult?" The answers these girls gave clearly showed that they did not want a life devoid of complications. The complexity they sought included harmony as an element, however. Several messed up my categories, which I admit I presented in a too strictly either/or fashion. Their desire for both complexity and harmony supports the theologians' view that beauty is made up of a rich blend.

> Chloe: Can I mix them together? I think life would be really boring if everything stayed the same. I think challenges and doing different things is good, even if at the time you don't like it, because eventually it turns out good. But it's always nice to know that if you do something wrong, or try something and it doesn't work, that you can go back to where you were and start again.

> Deborah: Well, I usually go for the more difficult, but I do enjoy simple things to get my mind off the difficult. Like, I'll read a hard book, then read [something easy].

> Madeline: I hate to be messy; I hate to be dirty. I love complex things, and I love the fact that I have to figure things out, but I think I almost prefer familiar things. Everyday I wake up, and I like to make sure that my room is the way I like it, that there's food I like in the kitchen.

> Toccarra: [I prefer] things intense, complex, and maybe messy. I like the simple things, sometimes, because you know it gives you peace. I'm a very competitive person. Once you get that rush from a challenge, that intensity, you want to do it again, and so it's wonderful.

> Djuna *answered simply:* Complex, most definitely.

What Do You Mean When You Say "I"?

I know!
I won't!
How should I know?[42]

"Beauty is the defining characteristic for American women," says Pipher.[43] There is much truth to that generalization. Plenty of girls identify with their bodies and doubt that their bodies are beautiful. They may become anorexic or feel as if others—even or especially significant others—care about only their bodies.

Curious about how these teens perceived their situation, I asked, "When you say, 'I,' are you aware what you think most of as 'I': your body, emotions/feelings, your willpower, your mind or brain, your sense of art?" Their spontaneous answers did not fit the psychological stereotype of girls this age. Though my question did not even give the alternative of a holistic response, the majority transformed my options as they expressed something closer to the ancient Hebraic or contemporary holistic viewpoints. No one named only her body.

Natasha: My "I" is everything at once. I am a very complicated person, so when I say "I," I am talking [about], like, everything.

Madeline: I don't really think it's, like, a part; I think it's a whole, connected.

Nicole: It's my whole person, my heart, my brain, my body.

Chloe: I think it's mostly my brain and my heart when I say "I." But, then when I'm trying on stuff [clothes], then it's my body. So I guess it depends on the situation I'm in.

Djuna: The majority of the time it would be my mind and what people would think of, and may see, and that relates to my mind. But "I" also refers to my physical self a lot. I mean, mostly I think of soccer as my physical self, but soccer can be my mind, too.

Jane: I guess I identify more with my mind and my character. I guess it sort of goes together—who I am inside.

Toccarra *named several aspects, then concluded:* I would say it's my feelings, my intuition. Feelings and willpower are all wrapped up into one.

Conclusions

> *She ran off as hard as she could and soon found herself safe in a thick wood.*[44]

For me, the most surprising result was that prior to my follow-up question about how they might see "any others in their future," only one girl mentioned marriage when I asked about their images of their future. I believe that this is a major generational shift in identity development. The vast majority of female baby boomers, when we were teenagers, thought about the future linked with marriage. These girls definitely expect to have a career outside the home; that makes a difference in their age-fifteen outlook. It might be that this subset of teenagers does not represent the majority view in their age bracket, however.

I went through the transcripts and found *no* allusions to boys, period. One mentioned dating in general. Males were not uppermost in their mind in this context when they discussed making choices, their future, sense of being accepted, or understanding of who they were. The only use of the pronoun "he" related to God. In other contexts, males may very well be in the foreground.

Another unexpected outcome was the girls' assertiveness in saying that acceptance by others will not take precedence over being themselves. (I simply asked about acceptance but received the answer about priorities.) Their boldness showed that they had indeed wrestled with this issue. Self won, or they believe self should win. This small sample of what turned out to be strong girls, but certainly not girls in isolation from the complexities of life, convey a picture of adolescents who do not consider themselves to be dominated by others', especially males', authority, approval, or acceptance.

Contrary to a common generalization about girls at this age, these adolescents do not identify overmuch with their bodies. As I noted, when they were asked what they meant by "I," their answers were primarily holistic. Also, their own self-descriptions included qualities (strong, talkative, persevering, independent, faithful); demographics (age, denomination); talents (musical, artist, athletic, intelligent); and preferences (interest in school, poetry). Only three mentioned any bodily description: black, white, and blonde hair. ("Strong" may relate to the body or one's character.)

This group of girls experience themselves as choosers; they are subjects, not objects. Some readily acknowledged the influence of others, especially their parents. Others had to work to think of any constraints on their choices. Only one gave the impression that she held her wishes in abeyance, waiting for another's opinion about what she should do. (That comment was in regard to school issues, about which she let her parents decide.) A few were already conscious that parents—or others—would be disappointed with their future choices, especially in relation to areas of interests they planned to pursue. These girls anticipated that the basis for their future decisions would be their own desires more than the wishes of others.

They were able to say what they enjoyed, though a few alluded to the balance of pain in their experience. They enjoyed family, friends, work, school, sports, adventure, resting, reading, writing, and boating. Notice that none mentioned enjoying making others happy, though one said she liked "seeing others happy." Unlike Heidi in the story that Borysenko tells, these girls do live for their own happiness—but not in isolation from others.

They prefer a balance of complexity and harmony, rather than either alone. The "less complicated culture" Pipher proposes does not seem to be a high priority or even appealing to them, though many said they like to rest or have simplicity in the midst of their lives.

They tended to have rather sophisticated perceptions about how they were connected with others and separate from others. Several believe we are rooted, connected, in God. One explained in her own terms how we would see our connection if we could look from a perspective outside ourselves. None seemed to blur the distinction between self and other. Their preferences for connection were more ethical, theological, or cosmological.

The girls had a sense of purpose, though they were not at all sure what their lifelong purposes would be. Some were humbly aware others could take their place; some volunteer, desiring to make a difference; some considered that their generation would make a better world.

Are there any factors these girls have in common that could instruct us as we try to nurture even stronger girls? One striking common element is that each girl currently, or in the past, had a place where she could think about a religious dimension to life or a belief system. Most talked with their parents or family members; one talked with a rabbi; several talked with fellow students. Their religious views were beautifully diverse. This might suggest that a girl's exposure to particular denominations or faiths might not be as significant for her development as having the freedom to think things through and having her opinions heard.

A key factor for these ten is that in addition to their families, each had at least one other place to belong. Several mentioned finding friends who had similar passions, peers with whom they could be themselves. One girl mentioned church as the one place other than family where she belonged. Others identified several talents and interests, each providing a set of friends. For some, athletics was of supreme importance; some formed groups around intellectual pursuits. Most of them were occasionally in the limelight and received awards; they were acknowledged. Their schools and churches, and in a few cases, the community, provided avenues for involvement in fairly small groups. Not only were these venues available, but these girls were invited, even encouraged, to participate. They felt they mattered and responded by believing they should be responsible.

Clearly, we need to keep hearing the pain of girls. We need to be alarmed by child abuse, by parental self-absorption that leads to ignoring children's needs, by the objectification of girls. We need to be political; to insist on equal rights and opportunities for females; to resist generalizations, stereotyping, and pressure towards conformity. We need to raise the awareness of racism and to move beyond it. We need to be realistic and genuine about sexuality education and to offer it at home, school, and church or synagogue.[45]

As important as being on guard for problems is the need to create a mood of self-trust and curiosity about the world. Giving Ophelia too much power leaves us adults and adolescents feeling futile and desperate. Alice, too, exists, perhaps inside every girl. This mood of trust can affect the outcome positively, for whereas a mood of alarm can become a self-fulfilling prophecy, a mood of trust can lead us to have confidence not only in the girls, but also in ourselves. We can stay calm while remaining alert, enjoying our girls as they become women. Like Alice, they—and we—can negotiate and even enjoy a complex world.

These interviews are a minuscule attempt to listen to only ten girls. I make no grand claims in this brief chapter. This work is a mere probe. Many others who are more adept at research and have more resources than I do need to attend to girls in their own worlds, to hear even more.

Potential Questions Asked

I drew up the following questions to ask the girls and I asked *most* of the questions of each girl, usually in the order in which they are listed. Depending upon the length of time for the various answers, however, I did not insist upon completing the whole list.

- How do you think of yourself making choices?
- I am wondering whether you sense that there is a purpose for you in the world or not.
- How do you feel needed or not?
- How do you imagine your future?
- What feelings do you have when you think about your future?
- How do you sense yourself in relation to God, if you think about God?
- If you experience God, what ways, times, places do you experience God?
- How do you feel accepted or not?
- How do you feel connected with others or isolated, separated from others?
- How do you enjoy life?
- What do you tend to prefer, most of the time: things that are harmonious—maybe neat or familiar or maybe even simple, or things that are intense—complex, messy, maybe difficult?
- When you say "I," are you aware what you think most of as "I": your body, emotions/feelings, your willpower, your mind or brain, your sense of art?
- How do you feel about being you, right now?
- I don't have any "boxes" to check for categories, but if you were to describe yourself with various descriptions, how would you do that?

Two Views on Mothering

Carolyn Wilbur Treadway
& Bonnie J. Miller-McLemore

Becoming a Mother

Carolyn Wilbur Treadway

Twenty-eight years ago I was nine months pregnant and very ready to deliver our second child. I remember this time as if it were yesterday.[1] My husband and I had prepared in many ways as best we could, had taken natural childbirth classes, and were eagerly awaiting our baby's arrival to join our family. When the obstetric exam indicated that labor could start anytime, suddenly and profoundly I knew that from this moment on, we were poised on the edge of newness and irrevocable change. Regardless of the outcome of my labor, we would be forever altered by this baby who was about to come. Somehow, time shifted; the present intersected the future. Somehow, I was swept into the ongoingness of time and creation. With heightened awareness, I felt part of a much larger whole. The week that followed was one of the most incredible times of my life.

As the days progressed, I felt more keenly the interconnectedness of everything in the universe. It was not of my doing. Far beyond myself, I was carried along inexplicably, mysteriously, and powerfully into readiness for the imminent changes the next days would bring. I did not fear giving birth; I had done it before and knew I could again. This time, I felt prepared to give the birthing everything I had, and I knew that I would deal from the depths of my soul with whatever occurred. I was very aware of my increased energy and strength and that it came from beyond myself.

Just at that time, a friend gave me a recording of Helen Reddy's newly released song, "I Am Woman."[2] It electrified me, especially her lines, "I am woman, watch me grow. . . . If I have to, I can do *anything*. I am *strong*. I am *invincible*. I am *woman*. I am *wo-man*" (italics mine). Reddy's lyrics gave vibrant voice to my own experience of that time. Even today, her song still energizes me when sometimes I play it to remind myself who I am and what I have done and can do.

Looking at my huge abdomen so full of active life, I felt like "Mother Earth" or some primitive goddess of fertility. I was radiant and aglow. People sensed it. Everything I did that entire week, even the most mundane task, was full of meaning and power, rippling out from within me to affect others who in turn affected yet others. I was perhaps more fully alive than I had ever been. The new life I felt within was also without, everywhere in life. Everything, *everything* about life was sacred. I felt it, and somehow I lived it. As we Quakers would say, it was a week of "living in the Light."

When the actual birthing came, my husband and I were graced with a magnificent experience. Breathing, relaxing, pushing, releasing, taking control, yielding control, turning myself over to the tidal forces of labor, entrusting myself and our baby to God—all these melded together as body and spirit united powerfully to help our baby down the birth canal. This culminated in the incredible joy of meeting our beautiful, vigorous daughter face to face for the first time! All these years later, I remember it as a peak experience for my husband and me. I also remain in awe of how my body, of its own accord and far beyond my knowing, acted exactly as it needed to in order to bring forth a child. Giving birth changed my whole concept of my own body. It also made me feel connected to every other woman who had ever given birth and deeply part of the miracle of birthing since the beginning of human time. Childbirth is simultaneously primitive or elemental yet transcendent, an earthly yet beyond-this-realm, unique experience. It can be an ultimate, life-changing event. It is awesome—in mystery, in energy, in travail, in connection with the forces of the universe and the power of God.

Childbearing, Change, and Experiential Knowing

Childbearing changes us. It is hard to comprehend before having a child just how fundamentally we, the parents, will be changed by doing so. We tend to think we will "just" add a baby to our current life. Not so! New life is created for the adults, even as it is for the child. Conceiving, gestating, birthing, nursing, and nurturing children are profound experiences that affect our sense of ourselves and our relationships with others and with God. The inner physical, emotional, and spiritual changes go hand in hand with the tremendous changes a baby brings to our external lives. As we deal with these changes over time, we grow. During and after each pregnancy, we must achieve a new sense of ourselves (as parents!) and develop a new concept of "normal" for our own and our families' lives. It is a big task, a task that too often we do not anticipate and do not prepare for as well as we could. If we realized fully that nothing will be just the same ever again, we would seek to learn ways of adapting to change at the same time as we learn baby care!

Women know about childbearing viscerally and experientially.[3] Pregnancy, childbirth, and lactation are uniquely female experiences. Men cannot physically experience these states nor know what women experience bodily. Yet men's experience and consequent ideas have dominated our culture, defined our norms, and framed our world. Women's own experience and ways of knowing have been questioned or rendered invisible. Some experiences, however, like childbearing, are so profound that we simply know what we know, authentically and powerfully from within.

Ellen's story exemplifies this. Ellen was a devout and unquestioning Catholic at the time she first became a mother. Filled with the awe and wonder of her beautiful baby, she was horrified to hear the priest's concepts about sinfulness applied to her newborn child during the baptismal service. Suddenly she profoundly knew that babies—hers or others—were not sinful and that the concept of original sin could not be true. Ellen's theology changed dramatically and permanently after this experience, as did her view of herself and her world. Coming home to our deepest experiences and to our own knowing can reframe our inner world and our relationships to self, others, church, and God.

Sharing Our Stories

Naming and sharing life experience can be a powerful way of learning for women, providing identity formation (naming and claiming who I am and what my life has taught me) and connection through sharing the wisdom thus learned. For listeners also, such sharing offers identity development and connection: "Yes, I too have learned from my own life experience, and I also can convey my own wisdom."

Through sharing some of my own experience, I invite readers of this chapter to claim and share the knowing of their own experience. From the beginning, women have supported and taught each other about the mysteries of childbearing. We who now give birth need a circle of women around us, and a lineage of women before us, to help us find our (new) way. In our modern culture, too often this support is missing.

Every childbirth is unique; every childbirth is universal. Each woman who has given birth has her own story to tell about that particular birthing. Some births are transcendent experiences, and others are not; the character of the experience cannot be predicted. Each woman who has not given birth also has her story to tell. Giving birth, choosing not to, or not being able to are events that deeply affect the hearts and souls of women—and of men. Each woman's differing story, often told with great energy, deserves deep and respectful hearing and can teach us much about what it means to become a mother.

Gestation and Generativity

What can possibly be more generative than creating—or raising—a child? Pregnancy offers a unique time of heightened awareness of being an active part of God's creation, even of cocreating with God. It offers a time in the image of our relationship with God, when mother and child are one yet two, joined but separate, together yet apart, in profound, life-giving relationship. It can be an ultimate time of incredible shared relationship as woman and couple dream of, extend themselves toward, and await their coming child. Or it can be a time riddled with problems and shrouded in fear, as the following story illustrates.

Susan described her experience:

> I went through my whole pregnancy, and I wasn't even there! We got pregnant soon after our marriage because my parents pressured us; we didn't choose to. The doctor was in charge of the pregnancy, and I was "out" during delivery. When they first handed me the baby, he was a stranger to me. I was scared to death to take care of him. I had no idea how to, nor did my husband. We had a very hard time getting used to having him as our child.

The first pregnancy can be especially overshadowed by natural concerns: What will pregnancy be like? Will the baby be healthy? Can I handle labor and birth? Can I really care for a child? To maximize the experience that pregnancy offers, prospective parents can learn and prepare, be actively involved in all aspects of the pregnancy and coming birth, and develop a community of support for this process.

Pregnancy is a time of altered emotional states and deep inner focus. Each trimester brings its own psychological tasks.[4] Pregnant women are deeply in touch with the cycles of life; birth and death are juxtaposed. Fear that something could go wrong might loom large. Even a healthy live birth brings the "death" of the pregnancy. Surprisingly, this ending can be experienced as a real loss. Pregnancy seems to last interminably, then suddenly this precious, very special, and unique time is over. This pregnancy is gone forever.

For every second of nine long months, another person is part of the pregnant woman, inside her. There is no getting away from this "other," this two-in-one. This degree of intimacy, which is unlike any other, is overwhelming, scary, and sacred indeed. It teaches us relationship, commitment, and oneness with God. It gives us time to form attachment to the baby and to prepare to become a mother—as if anything could really prepare us for the glory and wonder and frustration and tedium of it all!

Early Mothering

Our first child was born when my husband and I were living in a developing country, Turkey. We were thrilled to be pregnant but rather anxious about giving birth in a different culture, under less than optimal conditions, and far from "home." Labor was difficult physically, my husband was not allowed on the maternity floor, and I had to battle against medical procedures I did not want and felt might harm our baby. When our son was finally born and laid in my arms, I remember my incredulous amazement that he was safely here, that we had conceived a child this beautiful, and that my imperfect body had borne him into this world in such a perfect state. I eagerly and willingly gave over my life to caring for him. Little did I know what a shock the difference between my idealized idea of motherhood and the actual reality of caring for a baby would be!

Our son was beautiful, wonderful, precious, and totally entrancing. But twenty-four hours a day, seven days a week he was there and needed attention and care! Never before had I experienced such sweet but incessant demands. Uninterrupted sleep vanished into oblivion, and exhaustion dimmed my joy. Breastfeeding was incredibly beautiful and connecting, but I was totally unprepared for the energy and stamina it took just to produce milk, let alone deliver it around the clock. It seemed that my role in life was mainly to feed and care for our baby. After awhile, I felt as if I had just disappeared. It would have been difficult for me to give up my own identity and professional life to be at home with a child if we had stayed in the United States and my external circumstances had remained the same. But to be in a Moslem country where men are supreme, and to have a male child, which sealed my fate and determined my role as his devoted caretaker at least until his adulthood, was just unreal! I was unreal; my individual adult self seemed to be gone. Everything about my sense of myself and my marriage and our family seemed altogether new. Much as I loved and cared for our baby, it took awhile to perceive of myself as "mother." When our son was two months old, we attended an American event where Mother's Day was noted. I thought about my mother, half the world away, but was totally surprised when someone pinned a corsage on me! Incredulously, I looked at my corsage and then at our baby in my arms and then back at the corsage. Oh, I am a mother! Perhaps my internalized concept of myself as mother shifted in that very moment.

Gradually, I learned what it is like to be a mother, to care for a child, and still to be "myself." I learned to change my ideas, behavior, and priorities, so that I would have energy not only for the baby but for myself and for our marriage as well. I learned to cherish and to relax into the serenity of the many times of breastfeeding each day and night. Lactation provides profound and singular connection, where the rhythms between baby and mother move in synchronous dance. Our hungry baby cries, and my body changes in response (that is, it lets down milk). The baby grows, needs more milk, is hungry, sucks more, and within a day or two, my body produces an increased volume of milk. Baby and mother are so joined that we can be apart only a few hours before the baby is hungry and I am in pain. Yet despite this symbiosis, we are very separate individuals. Part of my task as mother is to learn who my baby, this particular baby, is, so that I can better help him or her grow.

The Fourth Trimester

In order to prepare for the postpartum time, we can think of the months following birth as a continued "gestational" time, or as an open-ended "fourth trimester."

Mother and baby continue to experience physical and hormonal changes, but the entire family goes through a time of enormous new development, change, and growth. Parents need to realize it takes at least another "trimester" to develop a new sense of equilibrium. Often we are ill-prepared for this. Prechildbirth classes teach us Lamaze and baby care but do not teach about the impact of a baby on the mother's sense of self (and consequent reformulation of her identity), the parents' relationship as a couple (which can easily get lost in the demands of child care), or the balance of baby, self, family, and work (each of which is important). Through their stories, we need the counsel of experienced others and a broad base of support, especially for difficult times.

Our own third child was born prematurely and precipitously and hovered between life and death for some days. Labor and delivery with her were times of danger and distress, because things were not as they should have been. I will never forget her faint, mewing cry, which announced that she had been born alive! Nor will I ever forget the La Leche League mother who appeared at the maternity floor only hours after our daughter's birth, bringing vials of fresh breast milk from several women to feed our baby (to help prevent allergies to cow's milk) before my own milk came in. Nor will I forget the care of family and neighbors during the month our baby was hospitalized, as they nurtured our bodies and souls by providing food and child care, and even cleaning our bathrooms! It was community that sustained us and made so much difference in our experience of again forming a new family constellation.

Enhancing New Life

How can we prepare to become mothers in ways that enhance the totality of our childbearing experience? We can become well informed regarding pregnancy, birth, and early parenting. We can take excellent care of ourselves during pregnancy. We can enter fully into all experiences of childbearing and share them as much as possible with our partner. We can learn from the experiences of others who have already become mothers. We can set up support systems to help us in many different ways throughout the entire early mothering time. (Church congregations and groups can be very helpful here.) We can lobby for relevant services to assist new parents, such as postpartum parent groups or new parent hot lines. We can plan for fundamental life change even as we take care to ensure continuity with our old lives and relationships.

Becoming a Mother

Becoming a mother means that we have received that most profound and sacred gift—the gift of a child. We mothers are entrusted with awesome responsibility and opportunity. Our children become our teachers. They open the spirit for us, give us new ways of seeing life, reshape our identity. By having to resolve the issues of how we were parented in order to parent them, our children help us grow up or come of age. Through caring for them, we learn about relationship, responsibility, commitment, discipline, determination, and faith. Children remind us to slow down our fast-paced lives to see the world with eyes of awe and wonder, as they see it.[5] Children teach us gratitude and peace and joy. Through them we come to learn what love really is. As they grow, they teach us to fine-tune the balance between guidance and control, between responsibility and letting go. If we are wise, we learn to savor these opportunities for our children's and our own continual growth and to cherish and make the most of these precious years.

Postscript

All too soon the childraising years fly by. In retrospect, the children are gone so quickly. We realize the deep truth of Kahlil Gibran's statement that children "come through you but not from you, and though they are with you yet they belong not to you."[6] After having learned so profoundly how to be in relationship, having learned to be a mother and to care so deeply and responsibly for our children every moment for so many years and years, we then have to learn to let them go—into their own lives, *not* under our care, for heaven's sake! Bit by bit, we have to divest ourselves of the myriad ways we have been so involved each day with our children and all aspects of their lives and replace these energies with different activities and ways of finding meaning. Once again, we mothers must go through a whole new process to remake our identities: who am I (now) if not mother? The concept of the empty nest does not begin to convey the changes that occur once the children are gone nor the changes that happen each time a child visits home again and is so different from who he or she was when last seen. Young adults change rapidly, and family relationships thus must be constantly reworked.

We hope that as our children depart from home, we will have the remembered joys of precious years so richly shared. We hope we will have deep satisfaction in our own generativity through bearing them, nurturing them over all the years as best we knew how, and launching them with our blessing into the world, to make it a better place because they are there.

Birthing and Mothering as Powerful Rites of Passage

Bonnie J. Miller-McLemore

"Giving birth is one of the most powerful rites of passage that women experience," observed a student of mine who was expecting her first child any day. Unfortunately, popular culture in the United States has lost a sense of the pivotal and even sacred or spiritual dimensions of giving birth. This is true not only within secular society but also in many religious settings.

In society at large, medicine, technology, and the market shape prominent understandings of birthing just as they have shaped dying. Although many people lament the hazards of dealing with the funeral "industry" and the "American way of death," only particular organizations, such as Lamaze and the La Leche League, challenge the "American way of birth," focusing primarily on contesting medical control. Hospitals continue to define where and how birth will happen, largely restricting its meaning to physiological and emotional dynamics. The market further defines the moral and religious parameters of birthing by producing and promoting the material goods that one feels pressured to obtain to mark the entrance into parenthood.

Christian communities have done little to question these dominant cultural perceptions. The Christian tradition has a checkered history of mixed regard for sexuality and the body, sometimes identifying women as the temptress or the source of evil. In classic theology, women literally taint their children with original sin in the very act of generation and require purification following childbirth. Christianity has at the same time, however, sometimes equated female salvation with childbearing (1 Tim. 2:15) and defined women almost solely in terms of their destiny as mothers. In unfortunate ways, patriarchal religion has depicted female embodiment as either threatening, peripheral, or all-consuming. Through the symbols and rituals of baptism and eucharist, male priests have symbolically taken over the power of female biology, replacing the uterine waters with the "living waters of the Holy Spirit," baptizing children into "new life," and invoking the presence of a male God who gives his body and blood for his children. Activities central to birthing and mothering women find little affirmation in traditions that have only haltingly allowed the leadership of women, pregnant or otherwise. This omission leaves many parents without the means to claim the pivotal place that parenting plays in their own moral and religious development or without adequate pastoral care in moments of need. Although many churches focus on family ministry in a general sense, the sacred is seldom seen as residing in the everyday passages of women's lives, especially the physical event of childbirth and the concrete demands of rearing children.

Almost all women who have experienced pregnancy and birthed a child or become a mother through other avenues, however, know that these life-changing, body-altering processes have powerful moral and religious meanings. Moreover, in the past few decades, women have begun to influence both developmental and religious theory. Recent scholars dispute traditional views of mothering as the only avenue to fulfillment, on the one hand, and modern views of mothering as simply a leisure activity, on the other hand. Mothering plays an increasingly complex role in women's development that demands further study.

In this chapter, I will explore some of these new psychological, moral, and religious understandings of the role of mothering in women's development in the United States, concluding with brief reflections on vocational implications. My immediate intent throughout is to present the complex problems and amazing possibilities of birthing and parenting as powerful religious rites of passage. My broader intent is to enrich the practice of pastoral care with women. As with the other topics addressed in this book, the history of pastoral care written from the perspective of men has not dealt with many developmental transitions of central importance to women. Women need support, pastoral and otherwise, to weather well the difficult demands of parenting and to realize its often hidden transformative potential.

Although I have particular interest in the revelations of pregnancy and childbirth, I do not want to restrict my remarks about parenting as a rite of passage to biological mothering alone. I believe that adoptive mothers encounter many comparable transformations as well as unique spiritual insights of their own. Partly as a result of my desire to include adoptive and "othermothers," I will not comment extensively on the acute physical demands of bearing and rearing children, such as alterations to the body, hormonal changes, fatigue, and so forth, except as they affect moral and religious aspects. Whereas a plethora of self-help literature elaborates the physical changes of pregnancy, sometimes month by month or even week by week, few sources attend to my central interest in this chapter—moral and religious changes.[7]

Changes in the Contemporary U.S. Context

Before proceeding, I want to note briefly the shifting contemporary context of birthing in the United States in terms of age, family situation, gender roles, and social status.[8] First, only a few decades ago, most people assumed that women's development followed a single pattern: the heterosexual couple giving birth in their early twenties. Today, the age at which women give birth varies radically, with the extremes of early teen and late adulthood pregnancies. Such situations raise difficult ethical and political dilemmas. Minimally, they force questions about adult responsibilities toward children. Does a teenager, for example, have the maturity and other resources to care adequately for a child? Does the artificially-enabled birth of a woman in her fifties guarantee she will be able to provide for her child over the long term?

I raise these questions less to answer them than to illustrate that pluralism in childbearing underscores my central contention that complex moral and religious issues surround contemporary birthing and parenting. Birthing is even more of a moral activity than modern society has assumed. In between these extremes in age, a rich variety of patterns have emerged. Women still give birth in their early twenties, but more women wait until their mid to late thirties and forties, sometimes making pregnancy more difficult and infertility more likely. On the other hand, working-class women of diverse ethnic backgrounds sometimes have children at an early age and then seek education and training. Political theorist Iris Young has pointed out the importance of recognizing the "plural childbearing cultures" in the United States when making public policy decisions.[9]

Second, women give birth in a variety of family situations. Children are not conceived only through heterosexual intercourse. Lesbian partners as well as heterosexual couples initiate pregnancy through medical technologies. Again, diversity and innovation only further demand that people grapple with parenting as a moral, political, and even religious event. Valuing lesbian experiences demands that the public begin to recognize the differences between heterosexual and gay and lesbian parenting. The very question of what term should be used to identity those who raise children, for example, is more complex from a lesbian perspective. Sandra Pollack advocates the use of "parent" rather than "mother" to include nonbiological parents, such as coparents, step-parents, adoptive parents, and others responsible for raising children.[10]

Third and related to the first two observations on age and situation, in the first half of this century, gender roles of the dominant culture were rather rigidly prescribed. Many women adopted common roles of wife, mother, and possibly paid worker in sequential order. Today, most women attempt to combine several, sometimes conflicting, roles. Fewer women move in some straightforward, chronological fashion from one identity to another, from youth to adult, unmarried to married, wife to mother. Rather, people experience what one study calls "role proliferation," a coterminous, continuous, and additive combination of multiple, disparate roles (domestic, occupational, marital, parental) to which one has equally high commitments.[11]

In addition to the profusion of roles, women also experience what Mirra Komzrovsky describes as the "scarcity of resources for role fulfillment" when combining work and family roles.[12] Headlines lament that women no longer believe they can "have it all." This kind of media coverage inadvertently encourages mothers with aspirations beyond having children to curtail their supposedly inordinate desires. Lesbian mothers face a double role rejection, finding themselves no longer a part of the childless, politically focused gay community but still not entirely welcomed by the mainstream.[13]

Many couples attempt to redefine conventional gender roles. New ground rules involve far more than role reversal and instead require a complicated process of role sharing. With less precedent and cultural support, gay and lesbian couples have an even greater range of options and challenges when exploring relational roles in family formation. Some studies show that gay and lesbian couples are quick to refrain from assigning either person the role of homemaker or economic provider.[14] This role flexibility is increasingly true for heterosexual couples as well. In general, increasing numbers of women lead complex lives for which previous sex-role socialization has not prepared them. Given the increased diversity, women have fewer peers with whom to share similar experiences than women had in previous eras. In some instances, negotiating the hurdles of childbearing and childrearing becomes a strikingly solitary enterprise for couples and partners, despite the greater visibility and participation of childbearing women and mothers of all sorts in public arenas.

One final area of cultural diversity and ambiguity is worth mentioning: the shifting social status of parenting as a "coming of age." All of these changes in the contemporary context challenge age-old cultural patterns of identifying the act of birthing as a critical movement into genuine adulthood, even if these changes do not fundamentally alter the patterns. Such cultural assumptions still hold enough sway that those who neither marry nor have children often have to find alternative ways to mark adulthood. Although the women's movement strongly contested the centrality of motherhood as an essential and singular means for womanly fulfillment, in some subcultures in the United States and certainly in many cultures outside the country, giving birth remains a prestigious sign of "coming of age" and a status symbol, even though the nature of women's status as mother remains subtly ambiguous.

In certain contexts, this premise goes hand in hand with the prizing of the birth of a male child to perpetuate the male family name and patriarchal lineage over that of a female child, a premise with a long religious history reflected as far back as early biblical traditions. Some subcultures continue to elevate fertility and birth in adherence to religious understandings that define the main purpose of sexuality as procreation. Certainly there are poverty-stricken cultures in which childbirth is more a liability than a gain. Yet even there women and even girls sometimes see motherhood as one means to secure love, security, and advancement, despite conditions that sometimes seriously jeopardize all of these desires. Although the remainder of this chapter attempts to examine birthing and mothering as important rites of passage, we must remain aware of the ambiguities that surround religious and cultural views of birth as a status symbol. It is within this complex context that we consider the ways in which mothering instigates and shapes women's development.

Psychological Dimensions

Of the many psychological dimensions of birthing and mothering, I will focus primarily on those that pertain to my thesis that birthing and mothering are powerful rites of passage. The intent is to be suggestive rather than exhaustive.

Anthropologists who have studied religious rites of passage in other cultural and religious contexts observe that they are characterized by three stages—separation, liminality, and reaggregation or reentry.[15] Liminality is a potent term that captures the state of being suspended between former conventional expectations and social norms and new expectations and norms about one's identity and place. One is "betwixt and between," neither here nor there. Often other people do not know how to regard those caught in liminality. Likewise, a person in a liminal state experiences disorientation in relation to self, others, and common social mores. Contemporary society cleaves to a few popular rites of liminality, such as the honeymoon, as a means to adjust to radical transformations in identity, in this case the shift in status from nonmarried to married. Other scholars of religion have depicted the ways in which religious rituals create sacred space and sacred time within the liminal phase. People experience a different flow of time; time may slow down or even stop, creating a sense of the "eternal now." [16] Place and space as well as particular objects acquire sanctified power and meaning.

Pregnancy and birth contain many of these liminal elements in an acute fashion. Adoption has analogous, even if sometimes less obvious, liminal dimensions. From the moment of recognition of conception or news of a possible adoption, the perception of time changes. One begins to live with a sense of end time. Approaching the end time heightens awareness of time. During birth itself, time stops. The intense and prolonged pain of labor seems both instantaneous and eternal. One loses a sense of time; minutes become hours, and hours become minutes. The duplicity of one's identity is seldom as acute as when one is simultaneously one and two persons, containing in oneself the other almost but not yet born. Julia Kristeva identifies pregnancy as a publicly subversive state, "a continuous separation, a division of the very flesh." In the pregnant body the self and the other coexist. The pregnant woman is both herself and not herself, hourly, daily becoming more separate until what was a part of her becomes irrevocably "irreparably alien."[17] Women have different reactions to entering the liminality of pregnancy. Some are eager to be recognized as one who is both one person and yet the beginnings of a second. Others choose to harbor the knowledge silently, even secretly, until the sheer protrusion makes the becoming of a second person visible. Some resent the disappearance or submergence of their own selfhood in the eyes of others who now attend only to the child.

Using Jungian psychology rather than anthropology, Kathryn Rabuzzi argues that birth is a powerful transformative spiritual event in a woman's life that men in religious realms have "stolen." For a variety of reasons, birth offers the potential for a genuinely ecstatic experience, a reality from which Christianity has shied away. Developmental psychology has, in somewhat analogous fashion, shied away from the complex interconnections between transformation in the mother and development in the child, choosing instead to focus on the latter, as if it could occur separately from the former.

However, as Rabuzzi recounts from her own experience, giving birth involves a "'dying,' 'being born,' and giving birth" simultaneously.[18] Emotional preparation for birth also resembles processes of preparation for death. Some women experience an acute sense of life's finitude and an embodied awareness of the proximity of death. As Penelope Washbourn notes, the woman faces several kinds of literal death—the dying of the old self, the end of the relationship to the fetus, and the transformation of prior relationships to others.[19] Perhaps the biggest, and some-times least suspected, change happens within the couple itself, as each person assumes a new role in relationship to the child, becomes absorbed to different degrees in the care of the child, and hence experiences new and sometimes dis-turbing dynamics in relationship to one other.

Biblical scholar Tikva Frymer-Kensky wrote *Motherprayer: The Pregnant Woman's Spiritual Companion* precisely out of her own existential distress and anger about the lack of childbirth literature that celebrates biological life processes as "occasions for spiritual growth and communication with the divine."[20] Her book seeks to retrieve the birth incantations from such sources as ancient Sumerian and Akkadian texts, the Jewish prayer tradition, and prayer books from eighteenth-century Italy, and includes prayers, meditations, and poems of protection, concep-tion, and safe delivery. These texts confirm that modernist notions of birth as merely a medical condition are limited at best.

Alternative religious communities of women, perhaps most evident in Jewish circles, have begun to recreate rituals designed to acknowledge the fears, ambiva-lence, emotional turmoil, physical pain, and spiritual travail of pivotal passages of women's lives, including birth and mothering. Healing rituals incorporate expres-sion of emotions such as anger, attend to women's spiritual needs, and affirm women's experiences. Some women have particular needs. For example, women with histories of sexual abuse might find that birth or parenting of young children activates disturbing unconscious or preconscious memories. For all women, how-ever, giving birth and raising children can bring repressed material to the surface. The importance of these passages has yet to gain adequate expression in pastoral or ritual contexts.[21]

A great deal more can be said about the broader experience of mothering as a transformative experience than space allows. Adrienne Rich was the first to declare boldly how little is known about the experience of the mother compared to what we know about the "air we breathe, the seas we travel"![22] Much of what has ap-peared on mothering in the past two decades is merely a footnote to her pivotal treatise, *Of Woman Born*. There is perhaps no better treatment of the internal ex-perience of motherhood and no steadier attack on its distortions as a social insti-tution controlled by men. Suddenly, as if a veil had been lifted, gaps and omissions in the literature appeared where before they went unnoticed.

As I develop at greater length in *Also a Mother*, in developmental psychology in particular, mothering has not received adequate exploration as part of the adult life cycle.[23] In a book that seems designed more to be read by the popular parenting audience than to reshape the directions of psychological theory, Daniel N. Stern and Nadia Bruschweiler-Stern contend that motherhood is a process of birth for the mother as well as the child. Early in the book, however, Stern is quick to admit that despite his training and work with children, this idea was entirely new for him, one to which others, including his wife, have had to alert him. In contrast to prominent mental health views that motherhood requires only a "slight variation in the already existing mindset" and has little role in the development of children, Stern and Bruschweiler-Stern argue that a woman "develops a mindset fundamentally different than the one she held before, and enters a realm of experience not known to non-mothers."[24]

Few developmental theorists have attempted to explore and fit into their theories the many and varied ways in which bearing or adopting and raising children causes major changes in one's self-concept and relationship to others as well as one's moral and religious values. Many developmental theories in the psychoanalytic tradition, from Sigmund Freud to recent object relations theories, do not even look past early childhood to understand adult behavior, even though the theories of analysts such as D. W. Winnicott and Heinz Kohut might be used suggestively to identify the intrapsychic shifts required in mothers to attend to children. Freud actually derided the desire to bear children as one further demonstration of the woman's desire to obtain a penis and identified childbearing status as the best women could hope for developmentally, given their bereft state.

Theories who do move past childhood development—such as Erik Erikson's "eight stages of man" or Carl Jung's "stages of life" or, more recently, Daniel Levison's "seasons of a man's life" or James Fowler's "six stages of faith"—either simply do not include women or, if they do, fail to understand women as subjects, truncate expectations for women's development to complement male development, and generally give extremely limited space to the impact of bearing or raising children. Some life cycle theorists have actually treated childbearing as a parenthetical dimension of adulthood, implying that raising children is an activity that adults do on the side. Through these various theories, valuable as they are in other respects, we have learned a great deal about the development of such adult attributes as autonomy but little to nothing about the development of attributes crucial to securing the lives of the next generation.

For a variety of reasons, however, the latter concern was of earnest importance to Erikson. He gave the care of children greater visibility through his concept of "generativity" as an important stage of adult life in which one must choose between creativity and stagnation. He understood crises of generativity—"a biological, psychological, and ethical commitment to take care of human infancy" or "concern for establishing and guiding the next generation"—however, as arising in the second to last stage of the life cycle and as building on the resolutions of previous stages that seem more focused on the development of self-identity than on the evolution of relationships with others.[25]

This conceptualization does not accord well with the lives of most women. Most women do not and cannot wait until later in life to resolve questions of generativity. Most women encounter acute questions of generativity at much earlier stages in life than Erikson supposed, during stages which he characterized as focused on the search for identity and intimacy.

For many women, the biological generativity of childbirth and childrearing often becomes a means to resolve what Erikson understood as earlier life crises of identity and intimacy. Moreover, the stages prior to generativity, as Erikson conceives them, focus on the development of values that do not necessarily enhance one's ability to care for a child—independence, autonomy, self-assertion, and so forth. This development of values fails to account for the emergence of the adult capacity to nurture children. By contrast, in studies of the development of girls and women, researchers have discovered that they tend to focus as much on the quality of their relationships as on the advancement of their own individual identity. Ultimately, as I have argued in *Also a Mother*, contemporary motherhood has developmental and cultural implications that reach beyond anything Erikson understood when he characterized the stage of generativity.

Fortunately, educational theorist Carol Gilligan's research on moral development (to be discussed in the next section) and the work on intellectual development of psychologists Mary Field Belenky, Blythe McVicker Clinchy, Nancy Rule Goldberger, and Jill Mattuck Tarule has opened fresh discussion of the impact of pregnancy and childbirth on women's growth. In the eye-opening book published by the latter group, *Women's Ways of Knowing*, several women whom they interview name attending to children as a practice that provides fresh categories of meaning. In order to grasp alternative modalities of knowing, the researchers intentionally interviewed women both inside and outside formal academic settings shaped by male assumptions. Hence, they talked with women in three different kinds of family agencies to determine how maternal practice shapes women's thinking and development. When asked about the most important learning experience, many women identified childbirth. For women who have been especially silenced by their particular life circumstances and by fear of external authority, the responsibilities of parenting have the power to move them out of silence and into a place of voice and mind. In a word, becoming a mother initiates an "epistemological revolution," dramatically transforming the way a woman thinks and responds.[26]

Moral Dimensions

The rites of passage of pregnancy, birthing, adoption, and childrearing occasion at least two kinds of moral developments for women: the reorientation of self-love and love of others and the reassessment of justice in the distribution of domestic labor.

More than any other scholar, Gilligan has enhanced our understanding of the power of choice in pregnancy as a key factor in moral development. Her book *In a Different Voice* traces a shift in self-understanding from self-centeredness to other-centeredness to a third stage of interdependent care of self and care of others.[27] Granted, pregnancy, childbirth, and especially childrearing present acute moments and prolonged situations of other-directedness, self-denial, and self-sacrifice. Yet each of these rites of passage also has the capacity to move women to the complex moral stage in which one sees the strong interconnection between sustenance of self and the flourishing of the other. Acknowledging oneself as a person with rights and choices—realizing that it is legitimate to consider the interests of the self—can initiate a dramatic moral shift in which women recognize that responsiveness to others and to oneself are not mutually exclusive. A pregnant woman in Gilligan's second stage, in which the "good" is seen as taking care of the other at one's own expense, disregards her own needs at the peril of both her own and her child's survival. The third stage of moral development emerges when a person recognizes the high costs, both to herself and to others, of ignoring her own needs. Rather, acting responsibly toward oneself and one's needs will sustain connections with others rather than impede them.[28] This realization can be amazingly helpful for women and mothers, even if it does not answer completely a further question encountered keenly by mothers about what to do when conflict arises between one's needs and those of the other.

As a pastoral theologian, Brita Gill-Austern has a greater sense of the importance of this question. She vividly depicts the hazards of love understood solely as self-sacrifice and self-denial. Socialized to give and give, women put the needs of others ahead of their own because they devalue themselves, economically depend on others, or even feel biblically compelled to submit. As a result, women are often more inclined than men to lose a sense of their own self and their unique God-given gifts, leading to resentment, anger, diminished esteem, overfunctioning, strain, and further exploitation. The solution is not to eliminate self-giving entirely, however, for raising children requires an inevitable degree of self-denial. Human fulfillment itself demands that one put trust in a purpose larger than oneself and one's desires. The key question is whether self-giving is life-giving or life-denying, that is, whether it enhances the "capacity for love and care for self and other" or reifies "patterns of exploitation and domination."[29]

Gill-Austern stops slightly short of proposing a second moral development sometimes occasioned by childbearing and childrearing: the recognition and demand for a more radical justice in the distribution of domestic labor both within and beyond the private family. Mothering, women must recognize, is not merely a personal activity; it is a social and political activity essential to the survival of humankind, requiring fair allotment of its demands among family members and citizens. When pregnant, a woman experiences in an immediate and literal fashion the acute link between satisfying her own need for food and rest, and ensuring that she has met the need of the other within her. After birth, the ability to satisfy one's own needs while meeting those of the infant becomes ever more difficult. The mother faces daily conflicts between desire and need. Balancing her own sustenance with the prosperity of her child requires ongoing support from partners, wider family and neighbors, the religious community, and the work and political community at large. Once the care of children enters the picture, talk between partners about accomplishing the labor internal to the household becomes even more critical and complex than before children.

According to economist Rhona Mahony, having babies creates a major crisis in negotiating domestic responsibilities equitably between mothers and fathers. Women tend to slide down the slippery slope from birthing children to assuming an ever-growing proportion of child-related tasks. In Mahony's economic terminology, the "headstart effect" of biology, pregnancy, attachment, breastfeeding, and immediate child care, on top of socialization and cultural expectations that child care is solely a female task, reduces a woman's bargaining power and initiates a process that eventuates in her heavier investment in children and house. Nearly all couples need some form of "countertipping." In effect, men need "extra time with the baby to catch up": the "more solo time with the baby . . . the faster he will move along his curve of emotional attachment."[30] Although Mahoney has a truncated theory of human nature as inherently competitive, and a limited understanding of the changes needed in social structures and cultural ideals, she has a clear grasp of the important pragmatic mechanics of fostering justice in the household.

Religious Dimensions

Exploring psychological and moral aspects of the rites of passage to motherhood thus far touches on various religious developments—the experience of the ecstatic, the ritual phases of pregnancy and birthing, the claim of a higher aim within which love of self and love of other are nurtured. This section will briefly identify two further religious components of the developmental transformations in parenting: evolving new God imagery and cultivating alternative modes of contemplation. Of course, neither of these is necessarily or exclusively linked with parenting. However, parenting might provide a ripe opportunity for these developments.

Theologians have used the term "cocreating" to describe the shared responsibility of human participation in God's divine action in the world. Parenting is a powerful experience of cocreating. In *Models of God*, Sallie McFague contends that becoming a biological parent is the closest most people come to an "experience of creation, that is, of bringing into existence" and of passing on life. The act of giving birth inspires a sense of having glimpsed the very heart of things.[31] Parenting also provides grounds for developing a religious commitment to care and preserve life beyond oneself. Christian theology in particular has identified children as gifts who point toward the kingdom of God. This theological claim requires gratitude and respect for the child as well as proper perspective on the crucial, albeit largely transitory role parents assume in a child's care. An adoptive parent might have an even sharper sense of a child as a pure and unadulterated gift.

Moreover, the experience of parental cocreation evokes fresh revelatory metaphors for understanding divine action. McFague presents the model of God as mother as a rich and neglected metaphor for rethinking Christian understandings of God's love, creation, and justice. Physical acts such as giving birth and feeding the young provide new ways to think about creation as issuing forth from the "womb" of the divine and about love as the desire to nurture the most basic needs of the other and to seek its flourishing.[32]

By having children, women experience the twofold dynamic that Margaret Hebblethwaite describes as "finding God in motherhood, and finding motherhood in God."[33] Writing out of her own experiences as a mother of three small children, she shows "how God can bring meaning to the experience, and the experience can bring meaning to God." Regarding the latter, she finds her mothering experience evokes encounter with "God as female." Analogies from her own maternal knowledge reveal many new possibilities: through her captivation by the charming quirks of her children, she learns that God finds our very gaucheness endearing; through the weight of the child in her womb, that God is even closer to us than most other images presume; through the immense frustrations of daily caregiving routines, that God finds ways to bridge both the idealism of the past and the disillusionment of the present; through endurance of the inconsolable storms of a child, that God remains ever present despite our distress; and through her desperation in the midst of the demands of her children, that in God lies rest and refreshment.

Hebblethwaite turns from her thoughts on God to her thoughts about religious practice or the spirituality of motherhood, the second component on which I would like to comment briefly. Long traditions in contemplative practice have emphasized the role of silence and solitude. Although contemplation does not require retreat from the world and a few wise spiritual leaders have attempted to articulate models of the interaction of prayer and an active life, few have turned to motherhood as a model of contemplative practice in the midst of life. Yet the rite of passage into parenthood is full of potential for alternative contemplative practices waiting to be reclaimed. Parenting is the "ascetic opportunity *par excellence*," according to Elizabeth Dreyer. In a manner similar to, but distinct from, the monastic in seclusion, a parent encounters unexpected opportunities to practice the disciplined religiosity that lies at the heart of asceticism's loving self-denial: "A full night's sleep, time to oneself, the freedom to come and go as one pleases—all this must be given up. . . . Huge chunks of life are laid down at the behest of infants. And then, later, parents must let go."[34]

Equally important, through the unpredictable and yet constant demands of mothering, one must learn to encounter God through conversation and relationship, and not simply through silence and solitude. Although parents find little guidance and support for spiritual practice that reclaims the chaos of family life as a viable source of encounter with God, this scarcity of guidance should not derail parents' pursuit of alternative contemplative modes or prevent future explorations of the prayerful potential of the parenting life.[35] Seeing a child grasp the power of language confirms the place of conversation alongside silence and connection alongside solitude as vital sources of spiritual centeredness. Again, this experience is not unique to mothering but finds in mothering a paradigmatic instance of a broader tension in the conceptualization of spirituality.

Through long hours of arduous practice, mothers actually begin to acquire what Sara Ruddick identifies as an entire metaphysical "discipline of thought."[36] The discipline she describes has affinities with theological doctrines of creation and care that she does not note from her perspective as an agnostic philosopher. Genuine care of a small being demands finely tuned "metaphysical attitudes" that I would identify as significant moral and religious virtues long upheld by biblical and religious traditions: the priority of holding over acquiring, humility and a profound sense of one's limits, humor and resilient cheerfulness amid the realities of life, respect for people, responsiveness to growth, and ultimately the capacity for what Ruddick calls "attentive love." By this term, she refers to a loving without seizing or using that is akin to that of divine love for human creation.[37]

Vocational Dimensions: "When the Minister Has a Baby"

An article by pastoral counselor Anne B. Abernethy, written from her own experience and study of the dynamics of women negotiating motherhood and ministry begins with "When the minister has a baby."[38] As with previous sections, this final section can only allude to some of the topics needing further exploration.

Helping professionals, such as those in counseling and ministry, must take seriously the impact of pregnancy or the adoption of a child. Psychology has the tools through which to analyze projections, transference, and countertransference issues. A study entitled *The Therapist's Pregnancy: Intrusion in the Analytic Space* describes the intensification of people's emotional projections onto the mother in response to her pregnancy.[39] The pregnant helper, in this case the therapist, arouses feelings of dependency, competition, envy, devaluation, idealization, and rage, depending on whether the image of her pregnancy evokes projections of the abandoning mother, the idealized disappointing mother, the sexually engulfing mother, and so forth.

Such strong reactions to the physical presence and broader implications of pregnant women in positions of authority previously occupied by men catch most participants off guard. Although more subtle, the minister, counselor, or professor who makes her adoption or her commitment to her children well known and part of her speaking, writing, and presentation of herself faces similar reactions. These are not reactions that people have learned to anticipate or have acquired the capacity to understand. In addition, self-disclosure of intimate sexual activity can hardly be avoided if one's own pregnant body displays the consequences. Considerable anxiety still surrounds maternal sexuality and maternal involvement in complex roles of paid work and mothering. Furthermore, as the expecting mother weathers physical fatigue, emotional extremes, and the self-absorption and maternal preoccupation with embodied changes, she confronts head-on the limits of her empathy—that she "cannot be all available" to either her clients or to her own child. [40]

Analogies between counseling, ministering, and parenting are both enlightening and troubling. Abernethy left her first parish exhausted by the challenges of combining responsibilities for her two young children and the requirements of ministry. Birth and mothering can lead either to "stress and a resulting fragmentation of self-identity and professional purpose" or "a more complete and less conflictual integration" of self, family, congregation, and God. [41] For most mothers, the sheer physical and emotional exhaustion of parenting is a constant theme. In widening concentric circles from a woman's body to family to congregation to connections with the divine, Abernethy describes the conflicts as well as some guidelines for making parenting work, gleaned through twenty-five interviews with women who became mothers while engaging in ministry.

How does one survive, on the one hand, internal dynamics such as role conflicts, contradictory and unresolved feelings about mothering, involuntary personal exposure, stress and the physical limitations of pregnancy and mothering, and heightened dependency needs? And on the other hand, how does one cope with external pressures on the part of the congregation, such as anxiety about desertion, repressed anger, denial of the implications of competition for the minister's energy, and overidentification? Minimally, mothering ministers must be able to set limits and order priorities. Beyond this, successful integration requires several other components: open and honest communication, careful negotiation with one's partner about domestic demands, planning for leave time, modification of expectations, creation of a wider support system, establishment of clear boundaries and a foundation of trust between minister and congregation.

Of course, some of these practical guidelines pertain not just to ministers who mother but to most mothers who resume any kind of paid employment, particularly service occupations in which one of the primary tools is the personhood of the mother herself. As important, however, one must remember that these are simply strategies. Although helpful, such strategies should not fool people into underestimating the difficulty of a broader ideological and cultural change they presume. The strategies contest the validity and the value of the age-old myth of the ever-present, unconditionally loving mother, and make the way for mothers who are "good enough," present in realistic ways, and loving as they are loved.

Unfortunately, many congregations find this change in ideals as difficult as allowing adequate leave time for both men and women. Few role models exist for combining parenting and ministry (or other professions for that matter). All this occurs within the context of wider social and political structures that fail to support adequate parenting and families through governmental leave policies, health care benefits, child-care subsidies, and so forth. The United States lags far behind other developed countries on each of these scores. And few congregations have seized the opportunity to act as political prophets for the sanctity of parenting and the centrality of social structures necessary to secure its success.

Ultimately, despite evidence of grave failures and serious disappointments in parenting, Abernethy ends where we began: the minister who is also a mother has the potential to draw on a powerful human experience as a source of encounter with mystery. As she concludes, childbearing is "not simply an experience of the body, but one of the soul as well. The miracle of birth, the embodiment of spirit, leads those who feel its power to rediscover the presence of the divine."[42] A reinterpretation of pregnancy and mothering as rites of passage becomes an important step in claiming the goodness of the body and sexuality, the power of God as mother, and the grace of alternative modes of spirituality that emerge from the contemplative chaos of childrearing.

Perimenopause and Other Midlife Opportunities

Kathleen J. Greider

When I was thirty-nine years old, I started to experience episodes during which the skin of the top half of my body tingled, turned red, and felt hot. ("Allergies?" I wondered.) I began to have trouble sleeping through the night: sometimes I awakened for no apparent reason and was unable to return to sleep for hours. ("Stress," I assumed.) Other times I was awakened by a soaring internal temperature and perspiration—like a car engine on the fritz, my body overheated and overflowed. My energy level was less and less reliable. ("Disease," I feared.) My capacity for memory and concentration seemed to be diminishing. ("Early Alzheimer's," I fretted.)

Sheepishly, I reported these experiences to my physician. I was lucky. She was informed enough to suggest that these might be signs of the hormonal changes leading to menopause. I was dumfounded. "At thirty-nine? But I'm too young." As the signs and symptoms continued and increased, my doctor's speculative diagnosis was confirmed. I was experiencing—and completely ignorant about—*peri*menopause.

This chapter explores women's experience and care in the coincidence of perimenopause and early midlife (approximately ages thirty-five to fifty).[1] My thesis is that wholistic[2] awareness of and response to the passage of perimenopause and related midlife markers will considerably increase quality of life and care for women in the second half of life. Two goals shape this chapter. One pragmatic goal is to persuade and equip readers—women and their pastoral caregivers—to go beyond this chapter to educate themselves about the health issues of perimenopause. I introduce readers to this way of framing women's midlife passage by providing an overview of the concept of perimenopause. Discussion of perimenopause in five interrelated dimensions structure the chapter: soulfulness, culture, body, relationality, and care. Additionally, to guide further reading, the chapter introduces readers to the burgeoning popular literature on perimenopause by concluding with an annotated bibliography. A more essential goal is to show that perimenopause presents to midlife women and their caregivers opportunities for growth and maturation that are more comprehensive than is suggested by books on perimenopause focused on nutrition, exercise, disease prevention, or aging. The result, I hope, will be some guideposts for soul care during women's passage to menopause—information about perimenopause knitted into soulful, centering, collective wisdom for wholistic, midlife living. In contrast to the frequent characterization of perimenopause and midlife as "wake-up" calls, this essay frames perimenopause as a period of possibility, "a transformation, so that a woman gets to become—physically, emotionally, and spiritually—the best that she ever was."[3] Information and strategies are available to women and the people who care for them through which perimenopause and other midlife experiences can be experienced less as startling alarms and more as heartening opportunities.

The term "perimenopause" entered the medical lexicon in the late 1970s when a few maverick researchers set out to study *menopause* and, to their surprise, discovered *peri*menopause, where "peri-" designates the period of time preceding the event of menopause. Historically, the term "menopause" has been used laxly. Strictly speaking, "menopause" refers to a distinct event—the occasion of a woman's last period, the "permanent 'pause'" in a woman's menses.[4] Before this major female life cycle event recently came to medical researchers' attention, however, the years before and after the menopause were assumed to be a simple decline in women's ovarian and hormonal production. Therefore, "menopause" also has been used to refer to indiscriminate periods of time both before and after the actual cessation of menses. Because the average age of women at menopause is 51.3 years,[5] and because it was assumed that menopause happened in a relatively short period of time (two to three years), women were assumed to be "too young" to be "in menopause" until their late forties or early fifties.

Study of the event of menopause led to the discovery of the process of perimenopause. The hormonal fluctuations and their effects that presage menopause were found to occur much earlier and more gradually than had been assumed. The term "perimenopause" is most helpfully used to refer to the transitional hormonal stage that begins at about age thirty-five, when a woman's production of estrogen and progesterone begins to be irregular. Perimenopause ends when a woman's body is no longer ovulating, which causes the cessation of menses—the hallmark of menopause.[6] Perimenopause and menopause share some characteristics, but there are also important differences. Most notably, although menopause is marked by declining production of the hormone estrogen, perimenopause is characterized by fluctuating levels of two hormones, both estrogen and progesterone. Given average age at menopause—about 51.3—women can spend fifteen years in perimenopause, during which fluctuations in hormone production have critical systemwide effects on a woman's body.

In some women's bodies, these changes are "silent": there are no outward indications. Most women, however, experience signs and symptoms of perimenopause by their late forties. Most typical are menstrual irregularity, hot flashes, and insomnia. More than a few, like me, experience such signs and symptoms as soon as the hormonal changes begin, in their mid-thirties. But whether these fluctuations are silent or overpowering, whether or not signs and symptoms ever appear, responding to these fluctuations—rather than rebuffing them—can greatly increase women's quality of life in midlife and later. Neither perimenopause or menopause are illnesses or pathological. Evidence is growing, however, that hormonal fluctuations during midlife have effects on women's bodies that, unrecognized, can lead to problems in fertility, medical care, and postmenopausal health.

With or without signs or symptoms, women's bodies go through these significant hormonal changes at midlife, an under-researched passage that is critical to women's development and care. Long glossed over by scholars, midlife is coming to be understood as a period of complex development. Indeed, some developmentalists now argue that, more than any other period, midlife carries with it an unsurpassed range and depth of personal and relational responsibilities, quandaries, and challenges.[7] To name a few, midlife is typically a time of intensive caring for children, elderly parents, and other people reliant on the midlife adult; reassessment of one's primary relationships and commitments; mounting responsibilities or declining opportunities in the workplace; expectations for participation in community life; increased awareness of unrealized or disappointing life goals; and, almost always, increased confrontation with human mortality. Each woman navigates these enormous relational and psychospiritual challenges of midlife— often overwhelming in themselves—in a body that is changing profoundly, with or without her awareness.

Many women and those who care for them (intimate partners, friends, pastors, physicians, counselors) are not yet aware of—much less benefiting from—research findings about perimenopause and its coincidence with midlife. This lack of awareness might seem benign, because this research is in its initial stages. To the contrary, given the significance of women's choices in this period, it is not an overstatement to say that this lack of awareness can lead to unnecessary suffering. Women uninformed about and unresponsive to the changes of perimenopause are likely to have more physical and spiritual health problems in menopause and beyond. Fortunately, information about perimenopause and other issues in the care of women in midlife is becoming plentiful and more easily accessible to the average woman.[8]

Information about perimenopause is critical not only because it represents a watershed in our understanding of the maturing female body, but because the demographics of midlife are making perimenopause a quickly growing phenomenon. The so-called baby boom generation in the United States is maturing. Women between forty and sixty are the fastest growing segment of the U.S.

population.[9] A huge wave of women—more than ever before in history—is in or approaching perimenopause. One source estimates that approximately 31 million women are currently perimenopausal. The youngest boomers turned thirty-five in 1999, and the boomers are entering and completing their transitional years at the rate of about two million women a year.[10]

Complementarity: Perimenopause and Soulfulness

With all the other things women have to do, how can our hearts—not to mention our schedules—be open to the opportunities of midlife? With all the emotional and physical demands of midlife, the formation of a spirituality adequate for perimenopause and midlife is suddenly an overwhelming and crucial question. With the many pressures of contemporary living, only a *soulful* understanding of perimenopause and midlife will provide enduring motivation to attend to the priorities, adventures, risks, and disciplines available in this season of life.[11] Even as women and their caregivers practice respect for personal variety in soulfulness,[12] there are common human explorations that can promote soulfulness, whatever forms of spirituality, theology, or religion a woman embraces. At midlife, one such exploration is essential and especially promising for the increase of soulfulness: the exploration of psychospiritual complementarities. That midlife is often experienced as a turning point—welcome and traumatic, subtle and dramatic—is elucidated by the concept of psychic complementarity.

Midlife literature often traces its roots to Carl Gustav Jung's essay "The Stages of Life."[13] Jung starts out to discuss the maturation of human consciousness through the life cycle by way of an analogy: consciousness can be compared to the course of the sun from rising to setting. The majority of the essay, however, is devoted to midlife, the stage Jung calls the "afternoon" of life.[14] The psyche at midlife is like the sun at midday:

> At the stroke of noon the descent begins. And the descent means the reversal of all the ideals and values that were cherished in the morning. The sun falls into contradiction with itself. . . . We cannot live the afternoon of life according to the programme of life's morning; for what was great in the morning will be little at evening, and what in the morning was true will at evening have become a lie.[15]

It is because of complementarity that the psyche—the afternoon sun—appears to "fall into contradiction with itself." Complementarity, in Jung's view, is a principle of the (collective and personal) psyche: Jung argues that the psyche has a tendency toward wholeness, an inborn inclination to assert unconscious dynamics that will fill out or complete whatever principles dominate consciousness. Just as the sun appears to change direction at midday, from rising to setting, the psyche appears to change direction at midlife, from whatever was consciously affirmed to unconsciously affirmed values.

At this point, unfortunately, Jung corrupts his own argument. He goes on to prescribe not balanced complementarity but specific gender-biased complements:[16] more flexibility and less rigidity, more interiority and less social adaptation, more searching and less opining, more shedding and less accumulation. The complements Jung prescribes are unconsciously gendered and laden with assumptions about social location and personality. Much midlife literature, especially Jungian approaches to midlife spirituality, tends to overlook Jung's assumptions and elaborate on these same complements.

Jungian midlife literature—like Jung himself, I dare to say—fails to see the essay's most brilliant, challenging, and soulful point regarding midlife. Note well: the principle of complementarity disallows specific prescriptions for midlife, except to say that it is a time for attending to the unconscious with particular openness to encountering values, impulses, thoughts, and emotions that will fill out—make more whole—our conscious midlife positions, and complements the things that through the first half of life we have held most central in awareness. In the first half of life, because of both nature and socialization, we develop some aspects of our humanity and not others. The principle of complementarity does not imply that we should think we are immature if we arrive at midlife without wholeness. To the contrary, a lack of psychic balance at midlife is not only nearly inevitable but useful. Whatever the specific social, familial, and personal requirements of maturation at our time in history, they will shape our psychic development in some directions and not in others. This shaping has functional aspects, but it also means that most people get to midlife with out-of-balance psyches.

At midday, though we are most conscious that the sun begins to set and the day to end, it is also true that the moon rises and the night begins. Similarly, though midlife appears to be a change of course, in actuality it is the reassertion of courses initially open to us but not chosen. Subtly but surely, the unconscious brings to bear on consciousness the reality that we have reached the chronological midpoint of the average human life span: "We know we are middle-aged when we find ourselves counting the years from the end rather than from the beginning."[17] "Counting from the end," growing less sanguine about our time and our mortality, our psyches' tendency toward wholeness causes undeveloped aspects and unchosen paths to wield renewed power. For better and—if we are naïve—for worse, the psyche's tendency toward wholeness ensures that midlife will present itself as an opportunity to redress the imbalance. To the degree that human beings respond to this psychic need by bringing to consciousness dimensions that have been unconscious, we experience life as challenging but meaningful. To the degree that we resist wholeness, the principle of complementarity degenerates into the push-pull of the tension between opposites. We live a life characterized by flatness, chaos, or a cycling between both. We ignore this opportunity for midlife *metanoia* at our spiritual peril: "Whoever carries over into the afternoon the law of the morning . . . must pay for it with damage to [her or] his soul."[18]

This wholeness is what is at stake, for those of us needing motivation for increased attention to soulfulness. Carrying into midlife only youthful values and habits will damage the soul. By themselves, the laws of the morning are strictures on the soul. Sometimes the damage—like other potential damages of perimenopause—is silent, evidenced only by constricted hearts and withered relationships. Sometimes the damage is, indeed, a midlife crisis, in which hearts and relationships explode. Increased attention to soulfulness at midlife makes these tragedies largely avoidable.

What might an adequate spirituality for perimenopause, guided by the principle of complementarity, look like? A spirituality for perimenopause prepares women (and the people who care for them) for a change in direction. Interwoven with the changing directions of the female body in perimenopause—from the values of menses to the values of menopause—the soul is urging a change of pace and the kind of restfulness such change brings. For example, if the conscious self has lived in the country of extroversion, the soul might agitate for a vacation in introversion. Or, if the conscious self has overworked the muscle of emotion, the soul might wish to exercise the cognitive muscle. If the conscious self has worn herself out either from basking in answers or wallowing in questions, the soul will seek respite in paradox. Indeed, as the sun at midday appears, as Jung puts it, to "fall into contradiction with itself," so the changes in body and soul at perimenopause are likely to appear to be contradictions—not just pleasantly distracting contradictions but fundamentally metamorphosing contradictions—and, thus, to be avoided. In actuality, however, these are not contradictions but the gospel of ambiguity. It is in perimenopause and midlife that we might finally have the life experience (in body, soul, and relationship) to fathom the strange, good news enunciated by Jesus of Nazareth that in order to find our lives, we must lose them. Thus, a spirituality adequate for perimenopause cultivates a tolerance for mixed feelings. From a psychospiritual point of view, perhaps the healthiest perimenopause and midlife is one in which we allow ourselves a heightened engagement with ambivalence, paradox, contradiction, and ambiguity.[19] Perhaps it was at midlife that the writer of Ecclesiastes penned the confounding and yet reassuring poetry of complementarity: "For everything there is a season, . . . a time to be born, and a time to die; a time to plant, and a time to pluck up . . ." (3:1-2)

Yet at the midpoint of life expectancy, a spirituality adequate for perimenopause also cultivates agency amid ambivalence. Ecclesiastes 3 is an ode to action as much as to acceptance. A spirituality adequate for perimenopause enables us to treat the signs of midlife not simply as signs and symptoms but, in Eugene Bianchi's marvelous phraseology, as "angels of annunciation."[20] Like the parent of the prodigal child, we do not fight our impulse to run, welcome, and meet again that which is part of us but had been temporarily lost. We cultivate—and women who garden or farm know that cultivation is backbreaking labor—an attitude of receiving and reverencing the harbingers of midlife and perimenopause. With what do we cultivate the soil of our souls? Perhaps most important, we fashion from our particular humanity, with our loved ones and communities, vital questions that break the crust and plow the loam of our souls. In the now classic expression of Rainer Maria Rilke, we "live the questions" that stir our souls, stretch our communities, families, and selves beyond assumptions.

Perimenopause and Culture

Perimenopause is a common experience among women, but the signs and effects of perimenopause cannot be universalized. Cultural and cross-cultural studies comprise only a small amount of the fledgling research in peri/menopause,[21] but already differences have been observed in women's experiences of this transition, not only within but among cultures.[22] I am using the term culture in its broadest sense—any dimension of human experience wherein patterns and rules that identify values, expectations, and acceptable and unacceptable behaviors are produced. At least four interdependent factors appear to give rise to observed differences among women of different cultures: personality, lifestyle, ethnicity, and attitude.

Typical discussions of cultural influences and their contributions to women's experience of perimenopause do not include cultures of personality. Indeed, "culture" is usually used to refer to everything outside a person, patterns of social behavior and value manifested beyond the individual. Such an understanding of culture, however, is based on a misunderstanding of personality, which is significantly constructed from factors beyond the personal. First, even allowing for diversity within type, there are cultures of personality type—groups of introverts and extroverts, for example, create very different patterns of expectation and behavior.

Perhaps more obviously, personality is affected by the culture of a person's family of origin: every family and household structure (biological and otherwise) has patterns and rules that identify values, expectations, and acceptable and unacceptable behaviors. These rules ("the way things ought to be") and patterns ("the way things are") usually have roots in (both upholding and undermining) the family's historical or contemporary religious identity. Moreover, every family of origin has an emotional culture. Every family formulates rules and patterns regarding what feelings are allowed expression, the meaning and value of emotions, and how experiences such as pain and suffering should be navigated. Thus, if a woman and her caregivers are to navigate perimenopause with maximum benefit, they must identify the culture of her personality, how it is shaped by the emotional culture of her household and family of origin and, in turn, how those affect her approach to perimenopause. In her family, how is a woman expected to behave and feel, especially about her "change of life"?

Cultural patterns related to lifestyle also appear to be linked to differences in women's experiences of peri/menopause. The most frequently referenced research relevant to this factor was conducted by Margaret Lock and her associates, who studied the peri/menopausal experiences of 1,141 Japanese women between the ages of forty-five and fifty-five.[23] Only 15 percent of these Japanese women reported experiencing symptoms associated with menopause, in contrast to perimenopausal women in the United States, 80 percent of whom report having such symptoms.[24] This difference is widely attributed to differences in lifestyle between Japan and the United States. Japanese women's lifestyles tend to include four health factors that other studies have shown to have a positive effect on women's aging: Japanese women tend to eat a low-fat diet rich in soy and low in milk products, exercise throughout their lives, consume little alcohol, and be nonsmokers.[25] Other lifestyle factors—overall stress levels, frequency of leisure activities, cultural valuation of meditation and prayer—affect women's experience of perimenopause. The degree to which women's lives reflect positive lifestyle factors varies according to women's national, ethnic, community, economic, and family of origin cultures. It is important to note, however, that money does not buy perimenopausal well-being: the higher a woman's income level, the more perimenopausal symptoms she is likely to report.[26]

It might also be true that genetic characteristics associated with ethnicity have an effect on women's experience of peri/menopause. In general, statistics suggest that women living in urban areas tend to report a higher incidence of perimenopausal symptoms than women living in rural areas. Yet a 1990 study that followed two groups of Indonesian women, one of which migrated and acculturated to an urban lifestyle, showed no increase in symptoms related to the transition toward menopause.[27] This study suggests that cultural differences in perimenopause cannot be fully attributed to differences in lifestyle.

The most widely noted cultural factor in women's experience of perimenopause is that of attitude—especially values associated in a culture with aging, women, and aging women. In short, research suggests that to the degree that a culture attributes respect and value to aging and women—and it must be noted that such respect and value is quite exceptional—aging women in that culture report fewer problems associated with perimenopause.[28] Several factors are at work in this phenomenon. To the degree that a culture values aging, midlife women and their caregivers are supported in treating perimenopause more as a developmental phase to be anticipated and less as a disease to be cured. To the degree that a culture values women, women at midlife and older are more likely to be making vital contributions to that culture, whatever their physical abilities, and less likely to be dominated by the denigration of mature womanhood associated with patriarchalism, sexism, and misogyny. To the degree that a culture values aging women, the signs and symptoms of perimenopause are more likely to be experienced as symbolic of a passage that marks women's increasing wisdom, freedom, and social stature, and less likely to be viewed as embarrassments to be alleviated or problems to be solved.

Because at this time studies on the interrelatedness of perimenopause and culture are too small and infrequent to support definitive conclusions, only lightly drawn implications can be inferred. It seems fair to say that strategies undertaken to affect cultural patterns in the direction of increasing the respect given to aging and to women will ease women's passage through perimenopause. They also suggest that if one is functioning in a culture in which women and aging are accorded respect, the experience of perimenopause is not only less likely to be viewed as a problem, it might be welcomed. If, on the other hand, one is functioning in a culture in which aging and women are not accorded substantial respect, midlife women experiencing perimenopause might benefit from seeing how the social fabric may increase their discomfort and sense of dis-ease.

The North American context in and for which I am writing provides ample evidence that its dominant cultural attitudes toward aging and women increase women's perimenopausal discomfort and sense of dis-ease. Athletic programs for girls and women, so beneficial for their health, still lag behind athletic programs for males—in equipment, facilities, funding, and public interest. Most measures of stigma against peri/menopause and aging women are not funny, but Sheehy reports that her landmark book—*The Silent Passage: Menopause*—is on the list of the ten most shoplifted books in the United States.[29] Increasing menopause research has spawned a sprawling industry that markets solutions to the "problems" of aging to women and their doctors. Yet despite the amount of research and related capitalization, women and their gynecologists tend to be relatively uninformed about their options for preventative health care during perimenopause.[30] Evidence shows that physicians tend to undertreat or overtreat women's hormonal changes during perimenopause. Overtreatment is most dramatically documented by the numbers of women in North America who undergo surgical menopause—hysterectomies. More than one-third of women in North America have hysterectomies (more than twice the number in Great Britain), and the majority of these women are ages twenty-five to forty-four.[31] Evidence of undertreatment is more anecdotal. Women in early midlife (ages thirty-five to fifty-five) frequently report that when they have told their physicians about signs and symptoms associated with perimenopause, their physicians have declared them "too young" to be going through menopause. On the other hand, women over fifty are not infrequently "too old" for treatment. Older women's discomfort amid hormonal changes might well be minimized by caregivers, characterized as aches and pains of old age to which a woman can only adjust.[32]

These brief observations about the interplay between perimenopause and culture remind people living and ministering in North America to attend seriously to the ways in which cultural values might inhibit women's well-being in perimenopause. In a more general way, they provide yet more evidence that any adequate analysis of women's development and well-being includes paying attention and responding to the cultural factors that help construct development and well-being.

Perimenopause and the Body

Having noted in the previous section some ways that culture contributes to diversity in women's experience of perimenopause, in this section, I describe the more general processes and qualities of perimenopause. What is happening in the average female body during the process of perimenopause?

Because it has been discovered that the cessation of menstruation happens gradually, cyclically, and irregularly, perimenopause is often characterized as "puberty in reverse."[33] "The menopausal passage is almost the mirror image of the transition to adolescence for females."[34] Put another way, the process of perimenopause is to menopause what the process of puberty is to menstruation and maturity. Just as puberty involves general processes that each girl experiences distinctively, so perimenopause involves general processes that each woman experiences distinctively.

To understand fully the physiological context of perimenopause, however, it is helpful to see that perimenopause is part of a larger process that begins before the female child is born. Interestingly, a female's supply of eggs peaks and then decreases slightly before birth, in utero.[35] At birth, the ovaries contain all the eggs a female will ever have (and far more than she will need). They are stored there until a girl's hormone levels change and begin the transition toward puberty. The hormones estrogen and progesterone are the main ones in the physiological passage, though other hormones are also involved. The primary marker of puberty is that a girl's hormone levels begin to fluctuate but gradually increase, and eventually she begins to menstruate. These fluctuations become more and more pronounced: during the period of hormonal turbulence we call puberty, most (not all) girls' cycles are irregular, their emotions (in which hormones play a role) unusually fervent, their relationships acutely tempestuous, their bodies disturbingly unpredictable. These "symptoms" are temporary, of course. It takes a few years, but eventually most girls' hormone levels even out and their menstrual cycles become regular. After puberty, hormone production, fertility, and menstruation continue without major changes until a woman is about age 35.

Mirroring the years of puberty, the primary marker of perimenopause is that women's hormone levels again begin to fluctuate, this time gradually decreasing, and eventually menstruation ceases. Between the ages of thirty-five and fifty, these fluctuations become more and more pronounced. Echoing puberty, during the period of hormonal turbulence we call perimenopause, many women's cycles are uneven and their emotions more stormy, relationships unusually trying, and bodies maddeningly variable. Because more women who wish to bear children are choosing to become pregnant in early midlife, there are an increasing number of women for whom the turbulence of perimenopause is multiplied by the turbulence of birthing and nursing children. All the "symptoms" of perimenopause, however, like the signs of puberty, are temporary. It takes a few years, but a woman's hormone levels do even out, and regularity is reestablished as menstruation ends.

Though both estrogen and progesterone are fluctuating during peri-menopause, one of the most significant effects of this hormonal fluctuation is decline in estrogen production. At about twenty-seven or twenty-eight, a woman's production of the hormone estrogen peaks and then begins a decline so slight as to have no negative effect on a woman's body. In her mid-thirties, how-ever, the amount of estrogen produced begins to be less than the amount needed for maintaining her body, and this decline continues to the menopause. Though best known for its role in the reproductive system, estrogen affects approximately three hundred bodily processes, and thus fluctuations in hormone production affect the body in many ways. Given estrogen's many roles in the body, it is quite understandable that our bodies are temporarily thrown out of balance when the production of estrogen starts to dip.[36] Possible effects in three general areas need the attention of women and their caregivers: fluctuations in fertility, observable signs and symptoms, and silent predisposition to long-term health problems.

During perimenopause, hormonal fluctuations cause fluctuations in ovulation which, in turn, cause fluctuations in women's fertility. These changes lead to problems in conception for women trying to get pregnant and unintended preg-nancies for heterosexual and bisexual women who have mistakenly thought that missed periods mean they are no longer fertile. "Call it Murphy's Law of Perimenopause: the women who want to get pregnant, can't, and those [hetero-sexual women] who don't want to get pregnant, do."[37] Because the number of women in perimenopause is increasing, so is the problem of unintended preg-nancies. Between the early and late 1980s, the rate of unplanned pregnancies among heterosexual women forty to forty-four increased from 24 percent to 53 percent of all pregnancies. As many as 50 percent of women over forty undergo elective abortion; only teenagers have a higher rate of abortion.[38] On the other side are the increasing numbers of women who want to become pregnant in their thirties and forties, which, unbeknownst to many of them, is the time of peri-menopausal hormonal fluctuations. Many of these women are unprepared for difficulties they have getting pregnant during perimenopause. As noted in the bibliography, several new books on perimenopause offer extended discussions of these complicated problems in fertility.

Approximately 10 to 20 percent of women report no observable physical signs, symptoms, or discomfort during perimenopause. The other 80 to 90 percent report that they experience one or more of the signs of hormonal fluctuation. Of those who experience signs of perimenopause, 10 to 35 percent experience enough discomfort from these signs and symptoms that they seek treatment for them.[39] When they occur, observable signs and symptoms of perimenopause range from mild to severe. The signs and symptoms resemble those common to premenstrual syndrome, except that for some women they can appear at any time of their cycle. Some women with more severe symptoms describe the experience as "PMS all the time" or even "PMS from hell."[40]

The most common and diagnostically reliable signs or symptoms of perimenopause are changes in menstruation—changes in length of the cycle (number of days between periods); changes in flow (consistency of the uterine lining, more or fewer days of bleeding, heavier and lighter flow); intermittent spotting or bleeding; missed cycles. The second most common are hot flashes and night sweats—hormonal fluctuations might play havoc with body temperature, causing the top half of a woman's body to become hot, prickly, red, and suddenly drenched in perspiration. A third common sign or symptom is insomnia, which is worsened if the woman is also being awakened by night sweats. Neurological changes such as difficulties with memory, concentration, mood lability, and fuzzy thinking cause a surprising number of women to fear—as I did—that they are experiencing early signs of Alzheimer's disease, but these too are signs of hormonal fluctuations. Researchers rightly deconstruct the misogynist myth that menopause causes insanity. For example, it has been documented that women in their fifties who have passed through menopause have the lowest rate of clinical depression compared to all other women.[41] Hormones indisputably affect emotion, however, and women can experience a range of emotional signs and symptoms that, like physiological and neurological signs, can range from mild to severe.[42] Some women who suffered from depression or anxiety previous to perimenopause report some increase in their discomfort during perimenopause. Some women experience changes in sexuality, such as vaginal dryness, fluctuations in sexual desire, and decreased genital sensitivity. The more sexually active a woman is, however, the more these changes are moderated. Other possible signs or symptoms include breast changes, fatigue (often secondary to night sweats), changes in hair texture, headaches, heart palpitations, weakening urinary control, weight gain, bloating, food cravings, and increased appetite.

Finally, hormonal fluctuations in perimenopause can increase some women's risk of serious long-term health effects, especially heart disease, osteoporosis, and breast cancer. It is crucial to note that the effects of perimenopause that contribute to serious disease are often silent—without any observable signs or symptoms—and thus can do damage before women are aware of it. Though most women do not consider themselves at risk for it, heart disease is the number one killer of women, accounting for half of all female deaths in the United States. Because estrogen protects against blood vessel damage, most women do not have heart attacks until after menopause. Health regimens begun during perimenopause can assure that one's blood pressure, cholesterol levels, and heart muscle are in optimum shape, so that the decrease in estrogen at menopause does not stress an already weakened heart.

Osteoporosis is more widespread among women than stroke, heart disease, and breast cancer combined. Sheehy's name for osteoporosis—"embezzled bone"[43]—is very apt. It is a disease in which decreasing bone density leaves women at risk for brittle, broken bones and other forms of impaired mobility. The calcium levels that assure women of strong bones peak in early perimenopause (ages of thirty to thirty-five), because the hormones that help the body absorb calcium are also peaking at that age. After her early thirties, a woman's bone density will gradually and "silently" decrease unless she sets in motion a health program that includes at least weight-bearing exercise and adequate consumption of calcium. These steps can dramatically slow the loss of bone density. Prevention is critical, because recovery of bone density is a very slow process.

Finally, there are many unanswered questions about the relationship between hormonal changes, hormone replacement therapy,[44] and cancer. Statistics indicate, however, that a woman's risk of breast and other forms of cancer increases as she ages. Instituting a preventive self-care plan in perimenopause is a proactive way women can navigate both the fears and incomplete information regarding this dreaded disease.

Insofar as the signs of perimenopause cause women to be proactive about these "hidden thieves,"[45] one team of writers assures women that "the symptoms of perimenopause can be your best friends."[46] As we will explore more fully in the section on perimenopause and care, during and after perimenopause, a woman has many options for self-care as these changes occur in her body. Attention to the effects of midlife and perimenopause on relationship, however, will help nurture contexts supportive of a woman's self-care, and it is to some of those effects that we now turn.

Perimenopause and Relationships

Where one or more of the partners is in midlife or perimenopause, sexually intimate relationships are likely to change. Whether these changes are welcome or not, whether the relationship is lesbian or heterosexual, they challenge both partners to ever more intimate levels of communication—verbal and nonverbal—if the relationship is to thrive. (Unfortunately, despite the myriad changes occasioned by midlife and perimenopause, there is no evidence that mind-reading or telepathic skills increase!) Men and women have the special challenge of communicating across the differences between male and female bodies. Even lesbian couples, however, will find that their sexual similarity might make empathy easier but, because of the enormous variations in perimenopause and midlife experience, will not override the need for new levels of communication. Given the pressures of midlife, realistic expectations about such communication is especially grace-full. Partners often will need to have such intimate communication in fits and starts. Busy couples who wait for luxurious communication opportunities—weekends off, romantic getaways, long vacations—lose mundane but day-to-day opportunities to glimpse (at least) each other's worlds. Moreover, for most people, talking about one's spirituality is at least as challenging as talking about one's aging body, so we must be intentional about communicating changes not only in our bodies but also in our souls. How can we keep even fleeting communication between physically intimate partners lively and vital? Mentioning details, risking embarrassment, and cultivating a sense of humor all help. Couples that have made a lifelong commitment have a special resource in that promise. Such covenants contextualize perimenopause and midlife and give us perspective. Covenants of commitment remind us to take a long view of the challenges faced in any one part of the relationship's life span.

Our relationships with friends and family are also affected by midlife and perimenopause. Not overloaded with the dynamics of sexual intimacy, friendships with other women might prove to be our most reliable relationships in midlife. Though some women fall prey to "menophobia"[47] and shun any female over thirty, most women enjoy increased sisterhood in midlife and are nourished by being comrades in the passage through perimenopause. Although our relationships with friends might be hitting their prime in this period, family relationships are less likely to be smoothing out. Earlier I noted that because many women are waiting longer to start families, more women are getting pregnant during perimenopause. Perimenopausal mothers in previous generations were typically rearing school-age children. Now, however, many more women are coping simultaneously with vocation and career, pregnancy, mothering infants and toddlers, and the fluctuations in physicality, emotion, spirit, and intimate relationship associated with perimenopause. This additional pressure on mothers is dramatic enough in itself, and it is but a small part of the overload most parents carry. We know that it takes a village to raise a child, but we have yet to be as conscious of what it takes to uphold a family. Of course, grandmothers (biological and otherwise) have long played a significant role in holding up their daughters' families. Contemporary perimenopausal women entering motherhood, however, are as likely to be caring for their aging (or dying) mothers as being cared for by them. As always, mother-daughter relationships bear much of the weight associated with the confluence of perimenopause and changing family structures and needs. Research and reflection that shows us how to better uphold relationships between perimenopausal women and their mothers is urgently needed.

Although the term "relationships" might at first suggest to us personal commitments, women's relationships at work might also be significantly affected by perimenopause and other midlife changes. A woman whose perimenopausal changes are silent, without signs and symptoms, is relieved of the struggles most women have working through—literally and metaphorically—the effects of perimenopause. To the degree that a woman experiences problems in concentration, memory, or energy level, however, she finds herself working harder—and not always successfully—to maintain previous levels of productivity. In work environments in which women's aging is at best a nonsubject and at worst a subject for derision, women who experience hot flashes will find themselves yet again set apart in the workplace. With silence and stigma about it so common in the workplace, perimenopause is a stealth factor in statistics comparing women's and men's workplace productivity and achievements. Until standards for achievement and evaluation in the workplace become less callous toward employees' physical well-being and family life, wise working women will prepare themselves for a period of disjunction in their employment, where biased attitudes in the workplace, more than the effects of perimenopause themselves, impede working relationships.

In religious communities, there is just as much silence and stigma associated with women's perimenopausal and midlife challenges as in the workplace. Clergywomen and other female religious professionals for whom the church and its representative agencies are the workplace will find themselves faced with the challenges we have just enumerated. At the same time, in their own faith communities, women and their pastors can claim more agency to make change—collectively, locally, and relatively quickly. That rituals and religious education for women in midlife are not yet found in worship-books or church school curricula is no reason not to get started. Information in this chapter alone gives clues to the enormous usefulness of faith communities sponsoring, for example, classes and clinics on women's midlife health issues, special worship opportunities for women's spiritual nurture, respite care (and, as needed, emergency funds) for women who are rearing children or caring for aging relatives, easily accessible retreats for self-care and the building of compassionate connections between midlife women in faith communities, and; pastoral care and spiritual guidance rigorously attuned to women's particular midlife worries and wisdom.

Perimenopause and Care

The self-help health books in the annotated bibliography at the end of this chapter give expert and extensive attention to specifics of care for one's body in midlife and perimenopause. If self-care or pastoral care in perimenopause and midlife is to be adequate, much less transformative, readers must engage the expertise and depth of one or more of those books. Rather than thinly recapitulating those books, this discussion of care gives attention to a question largely neglected in self-help health books: how can women fit into their already full lives care for midlife and perimenopause? Self-help health books are filled with statements about what we "must" do: exercise, educate ourselves, log our signs and symptoms, find an informed doctor, plan health care, fine-tune our nutrition, break unhealthy habits, rest more, play more, meditate more. As I read these books, my reactions to these admonitions alternated between giddy illusions of perfection and guilty illusions of sure failure. "Must" changes nothing. Some pathways, however, are simpler, more inviting, realistic, and empowering than "must." These pathways are most transformative when they combine solitude and meaningful connections with other women who are navigating or have passed through midlife and perimenopause. My discussion of these pathways for care are addressed to women's self-care. Caregivers will easily glean guidelines for pastoral care.

1. We begin with the acknowledgment that the "musts" of these self-help health books are seductive and not easily kept in perspective. If you must do something, do one thing. To the degree that a woman finds herself nagged by the "musts" of perimenopausal self-care, the wisdom of those recovering from addiction is a gold mine: one "must" at a time. One expert on perimenopause urges us to set priorities,[48] but I think it is even more realistic and self-merciful to set *a* priority. Rather than making mental to-do lists, make one choice. Then temporarily put the self-help health books back on the shelf. Because urgency and practicality often motivate and enable us, use of those criteria helps us identify the one urgent, practical thing we will do.

2. Practice self-appreciation for whatever self-help you have accomplished. For example, after you have done the one thing discussed in the proceeding paragraph, meditate on and otherwise celebrate your achievement.

3. Self-help health books on perimenopause are filled with admonitions to educate ourselves about the issues of perimenopause. This practice is ideal, and some women will find self-education the one thing they decide they must do. This process is time-consuming and, for many women, daunting. Therefore, for many women, finding a savvy physician—one interested in and informed about mature women—is time and effort efficiently and therefore wisely spent. Choose and build relationship with a physician who knows or will learn about perimenopause.[49]

4. For most midlifers, rest is, ironically, both essential and rare. Therefore, early in your efforts to provide self-care, it is helpful to learn to rest in one-minute intervals. Resting in one-minute intervals will take practice, but not much. (Sheehy suggests five-minute intervals of rest[50] but, in my personal and pastoral experience, this sets the bar too high for most of us beginners.) Once we have attuned ourselves to their availability, one-minute rests can usually be fit into a busy schedule. Moreover, they require no equipment but only the willingness to take a few deep breaths, meditate briefly on some real or imaginary beautiful thing, and otherwise do nothing for sixty seconds.

5. Another relatively easy pathway to perimenopausal well-being is to be mindful about balancing your attention to discipline with at least occasional, intentional indulgence in simple luxuries. For Christian women, the occasional need for luxury has at least two biblical explanations: in the assurance that Jesus came that we might have life and have it abundantly,[51] and in Jesus' strong and public advocacy for a woman's bathing, drying, kissing, and anointing his feet.[52] This truth is plain enough: simple pleasures are part of holiness. Perimenopausal care that is effective will increase in women's lives the abundance of simple pleasures: play, treats, laughter, beauty, joy.

6. Laughter is a characteristic of God's deliverance.[53] Cultivation of our own sense of humor, as well as appreciation of others' humor, prepares us for delivery from perimenopausal (and other midlife) panic and for the presence of the sacred.

7. Contemplate aging women. Really see aging women—their mixtures of strength and vulnerability, knowing and learning, well-being and suffering, courage and fear, happiness and unhappiness. This pathway offers enormous potential for learning and a sense of community, and it makes of us only one major demand: that we allow the presence of aging women gently but persistently to confront our denial of aging. Self-help health books on perimenopause abound with "musts" concerning breaking through our denial about the effects of aging. No more sure remedy for denial of our aging exists than mindful contemplation of aging women's complexity.

8. Trust your own midlife intuitions. The next best thing to self-educating book-learning about perimenopause and other midlife issues is self-education rooted in honoring our intuitive wisdom about our own body and its connections to mind and soul. Because signs and symptoms of perimenopause can exist silently, quietly, or obscured by stigma, our intuitions are both diagnostically valuable[54] and handy. Practice respect for your intuitions about midlife problems, needs, and solutions.

9. Do not just exercise, kindly move your body! Among all the "musts" of midlife and perimenopausal self-care, none is more statistically authoritative than those that support exercise. Correlatively, among all the "musts," no admonition is more ineffective than the admonition that a woman must exercise. If a woman is not already exercising regularly, no amount of telling a midlife woman that she must do this for her health will help her add this unbeatably valuable pathway to her life. Spiritual wisdom opens up a more realistic and transformative pathway. The fourteenth Dalai Lama is said to have put the wisdom this way: "My true religion is kindness." Less focus on exercising your body and more focus on showing kindness to your body just might lead you to the surprising pleasures of movement: "One of the kindest things you can do for your body is to move it around," and "moving our bodies in ways that let us enjoy our strength and power"[55] is an especially inviting pathway to self-care. For some women, movement that "let[s] us enjoy our strength and power" might be as simple as stretching or walking. Where movement is physically impossible or dangerous, we are fortunately reminded that stretching the mind and soul is at least as healthful as physical movement. Whatever your physical abilities, move—kindly.

10. In all things, pray. Let me be clear: only slightly less pointless than admonitions to busy midlife women to exercise more are admonitions to pray more. Consequently, the pathway of "praying in all things" is not praying more often but prayerful mindfulness of the sacred in more of the things we already do. Although times set aside for prayer might well be one of the luxuries to which we treat ourselves occasionally, praying while doing something else—grocery

shopping, reading for class, driving to work, answering e-mail, or whatever other tasks the day holds—can be a remarkably enriching thing to do for yourself and your world. Praying while grocery shopping can become an experience in gratitude for daily sustenance. Praying over a reading assignment might increase your openness to, and thus your retention of, what you read. Praying while driving is likely to decrease rage and profanity. Praying while answering e-mail is an opportunity for intercession. To whatever tasks your days hold, prayerful mindfulness brings care.

Annotated Bibliography

Books designed to help lay readers educate themselves about the health issues of perimenopause are proliferating, and readers should watch for new publications. This annotated bibliography is intended to help readers identify those books and make informed choices for further reading. All the books on this bibliography describe the physiology of perimenopause, provide detailed explanations of the "symptoms" of perimenopause, discuss the three major diseases in which estrogen decline is thought to play a part (heart disease, osteoporosis, and cancer), and present the pros and cons of common treatment choices (nutrition, exercise, complementary medicine, hormone replacement therapy). The annotations focus on each book's distinctive characteristics.

Bender, Stephanie DeGraff, with Treacy Colbert. *The Power of Perimenopause: A Woman's Guide to Physical and Emotional Health During the Transitional Decade.* New York: Harmony Books, 1998.

Written especially for women in their forties by a specialist in women's health issues and the founder of Full Circle Women's Health, Inc. in Colorado. Wholistically oriented, makes suggestions about the role personal and communal spiritual practice can play in vitality and self-care. Offers a chapter to help women assess where they are in the perimenopause process and an appendix on "what men want to know" about perimenopause. Extensive attention to self-care.

Cortese, Bernard J. *What You Need to Know about Perimenopause.* Freedom, Calif.: The Crossing Press, 1998.

The most straightforward of the basic books. "Fast Fact" charts for each subject summarize and help the reader learn major points. Provides helpful forms and hints for keeping a symptom diary. Extensive questionnaire provided for the reader's use in preparing for a consultation with her health care provider.

Doress-Worters, Paula B., and Diana Laskin-Siegal. *The New Ourselves, Growing Older: Women Aging with Knowledge and Power.* New York: Simon & Schuster, Touchstone Books, 1994.

This collaborative project of the Boston Women's Health Collective has become a classic guide for women over forty. Addresses a broad range of health and relationship issues from a wholistic perspective. Lively, organized around snippets from interviews with 350 women. The distinction between perimenopause and menopause is barely mentioned, but basic information needed for perimenopausal women is inspiringly contextualized in women's stories of "aging with knowledge and power."

Futterman, Lori, and John E. Jones. *The PMS and Perimenopause Handbook: A Guide to the Emotional, Mental, and Physical Patterns of a Woman's Life.* Los Angeles: Lowell House, 1997, 1998.

A registered nurse and a psychotherapist, Futterman gives more attention than most authors to the connections between women's mental and physical health, communication issues, and relational dynamics. Distinctive for its focus on the transition from premenstrual syndrome to perimenopause, though this emphasis leads the authors to date perimenopause unnecessarily late. Numerous case examples including lesbian and heterosexual women bring the issues alive. Helpful worksheets for self-assessment and keeping records of signs and symptoms.

Gittleman, Ann Louise. *Before the Change: Taking Charge of Your Perimenopause.* San Francisco: Harper San Francisco, 1998.

Offers a focus on nutrition and herbal remedies as a proactive means of responding to hormonal changes and distressing symptoms. Nutrition guidance is based on the 40/30/30 concept (40 percent carbohydrates, 30 percent fats, 30 percent protein) and, thus, might be especially practical for women already committed to that way of eating.

Goldstein, Steven R., and Laurie Ashner. *Could It Be . . . Perimenopause?: How Women 35-50 Can Overcome Forgetfulness, Mood Swings, Insomnia, Weight Gain, Sexual Dysfunction, and Other Telltale Signs of Hormonal Imbalance.* Boston: Little, Brown and Co., 1998.

Cowritten by a specialist in obstetrics/gynecology and a freelance writer, perhaps the most emphatic discussion of the hormonal differences between perimenopause and menopause and the ramifications of those differences for treatment. Updates readers on birth control pills and their potential for easing the symptoms of perimenopause. The only book to offer a full chapter on Internet resources. Fascinating epilogue, "Medicine in the New Millennium."

Houston, James E., and Darlene Lanka. *Perimenopause: Changes in Women's Health after 35.* Oakland, Calif.: New Harbinger Publications, 1997.

At 394 pages, the longest and most thorough of the books that specifically focus on perimenopause. More technical and detailed than many readers need or can navigate, it also offers extensive discussions not found in other books: how thyroid conditions can mimic perimenopausal symptoms, choices among cosmetic and reconstructive surgeries, gynecological surgeries, and other medical treatment for unusual symptoms and problems.

Lawrence, Marcia. *Menopause and Madness: The Truth about Estrogen and the Mind.* Kansas City, Mo.: Andrews McNeel Publishing, 1998.

Combining reporting on medical research with first-person accounts (including the author's personal experience), argues that for a minority of women, gradual decline in estrogen precipitates psychiatric illness. Important for providing challenging and balancing perspective to books that, seeking to undo myths and stereotypes about female hysteria and menopause causing mental illness, claim that hormonal fluctuation has no effect on mental health.

Love, Susan M., with Karen Lindsey. *Dr. Susan Love's Hormone Book: Making Informed Choices about Menopause.* New York: Random House, Times Books, 1997, 1998.

Written by a renowned specialist in breast cancer, important and controversial for emphasizing the unanswered questions about hormonal fluctuations and hormone replacement therapy (HRT). Though rarely explicit about the distinction between perimenopause and menopause, offers serious discussion of the lifestyle, nutrition, and alternative medical approaches that can be used proactively in perimenopause. One chapter, "The Medicalization of Menopause," is widely referenced. Contains unusually extensive tools for self-assessment and decision making, as well as appendices and notes to guide readers to other resources. Does not assume its readers are heterosexual.

Lucks, Naomi, and Melene Smith. *A Woman's Midlife Companion: The Essential Resource for Every Woman's Journey.* Rocklin, Calif.: Prima Publishing, 1997.

Rightly called a companion, because this is more of a workbook than most texts. An ideal choice if one's attention span and time available for reading are short: presents information in brief and digestible paragraphs and features a playful format. Chapters are fully cross-referenced. Multiple lists of resources.

Reichman, Judith. *I'm Too Young to Get Old: Health Care for Women after Forty.* New York: Random House, Times Books, 1996, 1997.

Written by an obstetrician/gynecologist whose practice now focuses on mature women and whose accessible style frequently lands her on the Today show as a health contributor. One chapter specifically on perimenopause, but notable for giving extensive attention to issues of contraception, fertility, and pregnancy after forty and for its inclusion of an unusually wide-ranging "woman-care checklist and health plan."

Sheehy, Gail. *The Silent Passage: Menopause.* Rev. ed. New York: Pocket Books, 1998.

The 1998 revision of a 1991 landmark bestseller adds a chapter on perimenopause. Based on interviews with a diverse group of women; goes beyond mere mention of cultural differences in menopause and offers occasional observations of how class, race, and region affect women's experiences in what she calls women's "second adulthood."

Teaff, Nancy Lee, and Kim Wright Wiley. *Perimenopause: Preparing for the Change: A Guide to the Early Signs of Menopause and Beyond.* Rocklin, Calif.: Prima Publishing, 1995, 1996.

Good for beginning education in perimenopause. Slightly more technical than Turkington, with many of its advantages. The last chapter offers "a support group on paper"—glimpses into six women's experiences in perimenopause. Admirable for being one of the earliest books on perimenopause, but be sure to combine this book with one more recent, because medical research is ongoing. Written by a specialist in reproductive endocrinology and her former patient, who has authored other publications on women's health issues.

Turkington, Carol. *The Perimenopause Handbook: What Every Woman Needs to Know about the Years Before Menopause.* Chicago: Contemporary Books, 1998.

Excellent for beginning one's education on perimenopause. Provides basic information in nonintimidating language. Makes few assumptions. For example, though most of these books recommend meditation, only this one gives instructions. Especially helpful chapter on finding the right doctor. Explains the range of medical specialists that care for mature women and provides a list of questions for interviewing and choosing among prospective doctors. Organization of the book makes it easy for readers to link symptoms with possible treatments. Extensive glossary.

Betwixt and Between *Again*: Menopause and Identity

Irene Henderson

Menopause has been referred to fondly and fearfully as "the change." The many physical and emotional shifts inherent in this midlife phase of a woman's development can also bring about a spiritual change. This change occurs as a woman comes to terms with the reality of being an aging and finite female creature "fearfully and wonderfully"[1] made in God's image and design rather than according to society's current youth-biased definition of femininity and beauty.

This chapter focuses on menopause as a journey toward a refined identity as a woman. The actual journey will be as varied as the individual women taking it. As a woman passes through menopause, she undergoes many physical, hormonal, emotional, relational, sexual, and spiritual changes and has to assess and define who she is in the midst and as a result of the differences. This chapter offers a pastoral guide for helping women and those who provide pastoral care to them acknowledge transitions in identity and sexuality that come from dealing with the losses and gains inherent in menopause.

Connection to Perimenopause

The word "menopause" is often understood in two ways. The technical use of the word signifies a single biological event; the ending of a woman's menstrual cycle.[2] The more common use of the word refers to a developmental phase or transitional time period in a woman's life. In *The Silent Passage: Menopause*, Gail Sheehy counters the single-event definition by describing menopause as "a much more gradual, stop-start series of pauses in ovarian function that are part of that mysterious process called aging."[3] The term "perimenopause" (*peri* meaning "around the time of") is being used more frequently to describe the myriad of physiological and emotional changes a woman experiences as her body approaches menopause.[4] Because of the comprehensive presentation on perimenopause in the previous chapter by Kathleen Greider, I have chosen to build on that body of knowledge rather than repeat portions generally associated with the broader understanding of menopause.

In the Fullness of Time . . . Again!

I find it providential that as I work on this chapter, my daughter and I share overlapping coming-of-age events in our identities as women—her waiting, with increasing impatience at age fourteen, for menarche; and me, at age forty-eight, for menopause. The anticipation, awkwardness, grief, and excitement my daughter and I share each month watching and wondering what our bodies will tell us about our development and identity as women, either by the beginning of a monthly flow of blood or by its cessation, led me to the title of this chapter on menopause. Our cojourneying as women at opposite yet very similar ends of the menstrual continuum reminded me firsthand of the similarities between puberty and menopause. Both are times of tremendous change brought about by the inner workings of a woman's reproductive cycle.

In early adolescence, I fondly remember being helped by a book that dealt with the problems teenagers encounter when they are caught "betwixt and between" being a child and becoming an adult.[5] The book offered me comfort by normalizing the myriad of conflicting emotions I was experiencing at the time. As I prepared to write this chapter, I was reminded of the comfort of those words and the common need for a sense of normalcy in the midst of transition. Menopause is also a "betwixt and between" time as a woman reexperiences hormonal shifts that usher her and her body into the next developmental stage.

Menopause: What Is It?

Menarche, the onset of the menstrual cycle,[6] is easily recognizable. One day soon, my daughter's wait will be over. She will discover the unmistakable proof that her periods have begun. Once it happens, we will mark that day and celebrate with her in a way that ritualizes the significance of the bodily changes in her identity as a woman. Even if it takes a while for her periods to become regular, she can still claim with assurance that she has begun menstruating. How we as a family help her celebrate the significance of this transition of femininity will set the stage for how she embraces her menstrual cycle as part of her femininity, and how she will later approach her own transition into menopause.

Knowing when menopause occurs is not that simple. Even the definitions of menopause cause confusion. In its simplest form, menopause is defined as "the last menstrual period."[7] The World Health Organization formally defines menopause medically as "the permanent cessation of menstruation, resulting from the loss of ovarian follicular activity."[8] Because the body is no longer producing eggs, "menopause marks the natural end of a woman's reproductive years."[9] Unless they have a hysterectomy, women do not know when they are having their last period. In most cases of natural or nonsurgical menopause, a woman is declared to have reached menopause after she has ceased to have menstrual periods for twelve months. Therefore, menopause is declared after the fact or "in retrospect."[10] These medical definitions see menopause as a recognizable "point in time,"[11] a life event or milestone similar to menarche. They also remind us of the complexity involved in knowing just when the event has occurred.

Although women tend to enter menopause about the same age as their mother,[12] each woman's experience is uniquely her own. Most women experience menopause through the natural ending of their menstrual cycle around age fifty-one.[13] Some women enter menopause earlier due to surgery or as a result of medications such as chemotherapy or radiation therapy taken for a life-threatening illness. A small percentage of women experience "premature menopause," which is menopause occurring before age forty due to "spontaneous early failure of ovarian function."[14] Women who experience premature menopause and women who have had hysterectomies generally "report more severe symptoms than women who have experienced natural menopause."[15]

When the ovaries are removed surgically or cease to function naturally, the body no longer produces estrogen. An important decision menopausal women face involves how they will replace or make up for the need for estrogen, especially to prevent osteoporosis from loss of bone density. Many women find themselves caught in the middle of a debate between the pros and cons of using hormone replacement therapy (HRT) versus naturally replacing estrogen through nutritional changes and supplements, and exercise and weight-training regimens. Some women are ineligible for HRT due to other health concerns and need accurate information regarding their remaining options. It is not within the scope of this chapter to address the pros or cons of any of the current methods of dealing with estrogen loss; however, it is important to say there are many good books on the market that address all options. I encourage readers to familiarize themselves with the available resources for their own knowledge and for use in providing resource materials to others.[16]

The complexity inherent in the definitions of menopause as well as the waiting associated with it contributes to the identity confusion women (and their partners) might feel. The term "perimenopause" helps give legitimacy to the changes preceding menopause, yet that term is relatively new and still lacking in public awareness and validity. A pastoral approach to women in the menopausal phase of life (including perimenopause) is to encourage them to define for themselves what they are experiencing and to make speakable their questions, problems, joys, and pains. Churches can facilitate and process this by providing classes on women's health and sexuality that recognize menopause as a healthy and significant life transition, support groups for menopausal women (and their partners), and worship rituals that incorporate the transition of menopause into a woman's awareness of her spirituality.

Menopause: A Loss of the Familiar

Common euphemisms for a woman's menstrual cycle vary from the notion of being visited by one's monthly "friend" to having "the curse." Regardless of whether a woman's menstrual cycle is experienced as positive or negative, it is normally a given in her life for approximately forty years. A woman's perspective on her menstrual cycle is an important part of her identity as a woman, whether or not she has taken the time to evaluate its significance. Similar to other life events, the importance of a woman's period might not be recognized until after it has ended, thus adding to the complexities of menopause.

For as long as I can remember, one of the constants in my life has been my menstrual cycle. Even during the years before I started my period, it was still a constant as I anticipated its arrival by paying attention to every imagined sign and hopeful symptom. Because I started later than most of my friends, I began to agonize as to whether or not it would ever come! Well-meaning friends and relatives would say, "Just wait until you start. Then you'll be wishing you didn't have it any more!" Their words sent the clear message that I was not supposed to like having a period. There are many women who never come to see or experience their period in positive terms. Somehow I did not inherit that mindset. Instead, my period became a significant life companion—helping me to understand, sometimes enjoy and sometimes simply endure the many bodily, emotional, and sexual changes that accompanied each phase of the monthly cycle. The monthly repetitions of the various manifestations of my cycle found their way into my journal writings. Over time, I learned to navigate my life with an increased awareness of the mind-body connections that go with being a bodied self. For example, I learned that on day seventeen of my cycle, I would be doing myself and everyone around me a favor if I stayed as far away from them as possible! In addition, I learned when I could count on happy moods, when not to panic about the sad ones, and when to expect the ups and downs of my sexual energy. I knew who I was as a woman primarily by living life from within the framework of a predictable monthly cycle.

A few years ago, the predictability changed as I entered into perimenopause. I could no longer count on the certainty of a day seventeen. Some months had none, and some months felt like they were filled with nothing but day-seventeen-like moods and symptoms! The cycle was unfamiliar and erratic, but it was still a cycle. Then I went five months without a period. At first, having never missed a period in my life and in denial that I was "old enough" to stop having my periods, I feared something was wrong. After being reassured by my mother that she had stopped having her periods when she was my age, I began facing the fact that I might be moving toward menopause. I was in deep grief. *I wanted my period!* I found myself experiencing surprising feelings of grief as it began to dawn on me that I would no longer be buying tampons, pads, or cramp medication—paraphernalia whose importance had been lost in the regular routine of my monthly ritual of womanhood as I had come to understand it.

With each passing month of not having a period, I felt myself moving toward a resolution—a newfound sense of freedom that I had not expected to enjoy. I began to embrace "the change" and moved toward redefining myself and my life without a period. Then, with no warning, the periods returned. I was in grief again! I felt as if my body had betrayed or tricked me, because I had thought I was well on the road to claiming "real" menopause—one year without a period. I am once again living in the suspense of the waiting and watching routine, learning to listen anew to the sometimes predictable and sometimes erratic rhythm of my body. Writing this chapter has been difficult, because I felt as if I had not earned the authority to write about a stage in life I could not yet fully claim as my own. Unlike the writing of this chapter, which is governed by an external time clock, my body is still in the process of honoring its own rhythm. Short of an unexpected hysterectomy or illness, I am reminded of the importance of honoring the rhythm of my own development; fully knowing that this too shall pass . . . and that the various passings are also part of the rhythm.

Even though menopause is a common biological phenomenon, each woman will experience it in her own way. It is often connected to how she felt about her menstrual cycle. Some women gladly welcome the ending of their menstrual cycle and move into menopause with a sense of immediate resolve. The menstrual cycle can represent pain, a lack of cleanliness, discomfort, or even shame. The ending of such a cycle can bring about a sense of relief. Other women have viewed their period as a connection to creation that includes but transcends themselves. For them, menopause signifies a lack of biological fertility and can evoke deep feelings of sadness or regret.

Either way, whether menstruation has been primarily a positive or negative experience or a combination of the two, the ending of one's menstrual cycle is a significant change in a woman's life. Although recognizing my vulnerability in articulating my story, I share it to raise the awareness that each woman has her own menopause story. Many times, these stories are not valued or shared, because they are considered too insignificant, too embarrassing, too private, or too sacred. Pastoral care to women includes helping women value the significance of their own life stories including the experience of menopause and the ending of her menstrual cycle. Inviting women to honor their experiences and feelings, and to share them in relationships where appropriate trust exists helps to connect the woman to herself and the larger story of Life. It also validates menopause as a normal and speakable transitional milestone within the community of faith.

Menopause and Identity

In the movie *Fried Green Tomatoes*,[17] Evelyn, a middle-aged woman, goes through the emotional changes of menopause with the unexpected guidance of Mrs. Threadgood, an elderly woman who moves from being stranger to mentor and midwife. I have used scenes from this movie and others[18] in classes on menopause and sexuality. Watching the drama unfold before them within a group context can invite people to make these issues speakable at personal levels. The relationship between Evelyn and Mrs. Threadgood is a powerful testimony to the impact women, and their stories, can have on one another. The intergenerational gifts given and received by each woman in the story can be duplicated by formally and informally established pairs in church settings, where elderly women are invited to mentor midlife women through the menopausal phase in life.

Like many women in midlife, Evelyn is trying to "find herself," because she no longer seems to know who she is. Her son has grown and left home, her husband seems preoccupied, and her body seems to be carrying her on waves of emotion. In one poignant yet humorous scene, Evelyn attends a women's encounter group and is invited within the context of a women's support group to examine her vagina with a mirror. Her inhibitions prevent her from participating, and the group leader asks her in a less than inviting tone, "Do you find this threatening? . . . Do you have a problem with your sexuality?"

While it is easy to laugh at the scene in the movie, it raises two powerful questions for women facing menopause. Menopause can be threatening, because women are often faced with accepting and defining a new sense of "normal" regarding their bodies and their sexuality. The old ways no longer work, and the new ways, which have yet to be discovered, have often been dreaded because of myths and stereotypes about what it means to be an older woman. The physical changes of the aging process occur in the midst of relational and emotional changes, creating an environment for a true midlife identity crisis.

In other words, it is not uncommon for menopausal women to ask a core question similar to one faced earlier in adolescence: *Who am I?* Yet unlike adolescence, when women were embarking on a world that in many ways was theirs to define (that is, a world of education, career, partner, decisions regarding children, and so forth), menopausal women are faced with asking that question joined with an equally poignant one: *Who have I become?* It is often in the uncertainty created by physical and hormonal changes associated with menopause that women have both the need and the courage to rediscover who they are by facing who they have become and are still becoming. The task becomes complicated when they attempt to answer both questions in the context of the life they have created via the myriad of decisions and intimate relationships that have helped shape and define them.

Sometimes, the freedom and the pain of menopause comes with the discovery that *who I am* does not fit with *who I have become* or *who I am with* (relational identity) or *what I am doing* (vocational identity). Then "the change" associated with menopause turns into a life-changing period of reassessing one's life and making new choices that can include changes in primarily relationships, vocation, and lifestyle (nutrition, exercise, approach to medicine, and so on). Changes of this magnitude are often preceded or accompanied by a renewed sense of spirituality when the woman allows the sense of awakening[19] that can occur at menopause to serve as a pathway to her soul.[20]

This process of life review or assessment calls for facing reality in ways that are initially painful but ultimately freeing. In addition to facing *who I have become,* menopause also presents the opportunity to face *who I did not become.* In this time of self-discovery, a woman can deal honestly with dreams that never materialized (that is, being pregnant, marrying, going to school). Through personalized grief rituals, a woman can experience healing that comes from not only accepting but also letting go of past losses. This ritualizing facilitates a sense of empowerment that enables her to make decisions regarding her future by dealing courageously with her past.

To further complicate matters, midlife is a time when many women experience changes in their relational environment—such as the death of parents; death, illness, or divorce of spouse; the empty nest created when children leave; the entrance of grandchildren, and the like. These significant life events and relationship transitions invite, and sometimes force, changes in the woman's identity that she might or might not have chosen for herself. Recognition of these losses can facilitate the task of grieving *who I was* as a way of once again moving more boldly into *who I am.*

This process of life review and decision assessment that can accompany menopause can also offer a time to determine with an increased level of honesty which regrets are true losses and which ones are actually postponed decisions lying dormant. The character Evelyn in *Fried Green Tomatoes* personifies this type of letting go and taking new risks that opens her life to new possibilities. For me, Evelyn's character demonstrates the process of finding the inner peace and empowerment that come from employing the guiding principles in the "Serenity Prayer"[21] as part of the daily expression of one's spirituality.

Menopause and Empowerment

An increasingly popular saying found on bumper stickers and T-shirts that is related to menopause and hot flashes goes, "I'm not having a hot flash—I'm having a 'power surge.'"[22] In addition to the humor intended to reframe hot flashes, this type of slogan proclaims an important paradigm shift in a woman's understanding of productive channeling of her energy and personal power.

In her book on personal power, *The Wish for Power and the Fear of Having It,* Althea Horner describes three stages of development important in exercising power.[23] The first is identity ("I am"), in which a woman is invited to claim for herself how she defines who she is. The second phase is mastery ("I can"), in which a woman assesses what she is capable of doing. The third stage is intentionality ("I will"), in which a woman combines commitment and determination with her abilities and makes a conscious impact on herself, others, and her environment. The process of claiming and using personal power is ongoing as the woman incorporates changes in each of the three phases and allows changes in one area to integrate with and affect the other two.

An important pastoral approach in working with women in menopause is helping them to feel empowered to initiate change, rather than only to receive it. Many women fear their power or get stuck repeatedly "keeping their light under a bushel."[24] Teaching classes on personal power in the context of the faith community is a helpful pastoral care intervention. Encouraging women to explore and expand their theological and sociological understandings of power can serve as a catalyst for their moving more confidently into a sense of self that embraces rather than discounts being a person of worth and power. As stated earlier, menopause is a time of decision making in a woman's life. She needs to make medical decisions regarding loss of estrogen (that is, whether or not she will use HRT or natural methods such as nutrition and so forth). She might also need to reassess vocational and relational changes. Facing these decisions and changes from an empowered position is a way of being a responsible steward of the selfhood given to her by her Creator.

Identity and Body Image

Another paradoxical similarity my daughter and I share is the physical changing of our bodies. Hers is a time of emerging from the cocoon of a little girl's body into a young woman—developing breasts, physical firmness, well-defined curves, facial maturity—and evolving womanly beauty in the context of a society and family that welcomes and blesses her changes with excitement and awe. The changes of midlife are often less thrilling, less welcomed, and less valued by society. As firmness emerges into an aging softness, as skin tone becomes less taut and facial maturity includes wrinkles and facial hair, a woman evolves into another stage of feminine beauty that generally is not valued by our society. Instead, we unfortunately live in a society that elevates femininity as defined and expressed through youthful sexuality, slim bodies, and flawless beauty.

Beginning in adolescence and continuing through early adulthood, most women are haunted by internal and external comparisons between the realities of their body and the portrayal of "real" femininity as depicted by media. This pressure to conform to societal definitions (often internalized and believed by women themselves) can have adverse affects on women's physical and emotional health. Manifestations of this cultural demand for thinness and perfection can be seen in the growing numbers of women suffering from eating disorders, such as anorexia and bulimia in young adults, and increased requests by older women for cosmetic surgery as they attempt to postpone or alter the natural aging process of the body. The cultural pressure can also make menopause and the changes associated with it harder to accept and bless. In *Women in Context*, Ellen Cole states, "We need a new standard of beauty, or at least a more flexible standard, so that a 50-year old woman can be herself without the pressure to look like her daughter."[25]

As is true in all other developmental stages of a woman's life, each woman's body will age in its own way. Common physical changes experienced by women at menopause include a rounding of stomach and hips as the body attempts to store estrogen, changes in breast shape and firmness, nipples becoming less erect, vaginal dryness, the clitoris becoming less responsive, decrease in bladder control, less frequent orgasm, increased facial hair, the appearance of facial lines or wrinkles, particularly around the mouth and eyes, increased occurrence of migraine headaches, changes in muscle tone and strength, and loss of bone density.[26] The way a woman views the aging process will affect how she accepts (or rejects) the natural changes taking place within her body. It is not uncommon for women to experience a sense of loss or sadness as they see their bodies changing before their very eyes.

Women at menopause are also vulnerable to other nonrelated physical changes that affect body image, such as breast cancer, arthritis, diabetes, lupus, and other diseases that can affect women of this age category. The combination of dealing with the changes of menopause and the affects of chemotherapy or body-altering surgery can cause additional stress and emotional complications. A pastoral care approach to women dealing with multiple changes at once, whether from illness or from other midlife crises, is to help her to recognize the magnitude of her combined stressors and to develop a strategy for moving through them at a pace that works for her. It might also involve helping her, and those close to her, to recognize the need for increased patience toward herself and others.

Most women move through these transitional body changes and begin to experience a new level of freedom as they find the courage to accept themselves as they are, rather than striving for society's view of perfection. Some women begin exercise and nutrition programs to help deal naturally with losses of estrogen and bone density, and discover a new appreciation for themselves as an able, active bodied self. A pastoral approach to physical changes of menopause and midlife is to invite the woman to voice for herself how she defines beauty and what her body and its changes mean to her. Possibilities for expression include journaling, poetry, art (for example, drawing her changing body image), writing a prayer about being an aging bodied self, and so forth. Whether or not these tangible expressions are shared with anyone or kept for personal reflection does not alter the validity of the exercise and can keep a woman in touch with her own sense of creativity. A powerful example of this type of expression can be found in Marcia Woodruff's poem "Love at Fifty" in *When I Am an Old Woman, I Shall Wear Purple*. After expressing the physical changes she and her lover have gone through in time, she ends by saying:

"We are real" you say, and so we are,
standing here in our simple flesh
whereon our complicated histories are written,
our bodies turning into gifts
at the touch of our hands.[27]

Identity and Sexuality

In *The Menopause Sourcebook*, Gretchen Henkel states, "In many ways, issues about sex and sexuality are at the center of our anxieties about menopause."[28] Without exception, all the books I have collected on menopause have at least one chapter set aside to deal specifically with sexuality and menopause. Women at menopause wonder how their sexual ability, sexual energy level, and sexual attractiveness will be affected by the physical and hormonal changes. These are valid concerns and should not be dismissed nor exaggerated. Empowerment includes taking a more direct approach when dealing with sexual questions rather than being ashamed of them. Many women are initially afraid to voice their sexual concerns about menopause and therefore needlessly suffer in silence. There are a multitude of resources available in print, video, and on the Internet that can help women feel normal about their sexual concerns and provide helpful information. Most sexual problems associated with menopause (that is, vaginal dryness, changes in sexual energy levels, changes in body responses, and so forth) can be addressed through alternative solutions that can help a woman maintain an active, fulfilling expression of her sexuality. Accepting these solutions usually requires redefining for herself a new sense of what is now "normal," rather than holding her body or her partner to previous expectations.

An important transition in midlife is the movement toward a more inclusive definition of sexuality. Many adults have been taught to define their sexuality based primarily on their understanding of sexual function (what we "do"). When the ability to "do" is changed—by the natural process of aging, or changes in themselves or their partner as a result of illness or medication, or the loss of their primary sexual partner through death or divorce—women at menopause often have to redefine themselves as a sexual being. This redefining might include discovering new expressions of sexual energy that place less emphasis on traditional intercourse and more focus on expressions of sexual and emotional intimacy. The movement into new forms of sexual expression can include a preliminary time of grief for the losses that have precipitated the change. This grief can include intense feelings of anger and sadness. Working through the grief of sexual losses is an important step in clearing the way for new forms of sexual expression to emerge and become satisfying.

Sexual losses are often complicated by the fact that there are fewer places available for these losses to be expressed and explored. Many women are not comfortable talking with their partner about changes in their sexual energy and functioning, much less their friends, physician, or pastor. Many pastors are uncomfortable or untrained in addressing or even listening to sexual concerns and might overlook an important area of pastoral need by not attending to the important connection between sexuality and spirituality.

In the context of my work as a pastoral educator and chaplain, I often have opportunity to teach about the relationship between sexuality and spirituality. I am continually amazed at most adults' lack of reflection and questioning regarding their sexuality—not just their failure to ask questions about the physical, using mirrors as in *Fried Green Tomatoes,* but their lack of cognitive and emotional reflection as well. Yet I am equally amazed and encouraged at the responses I get from people who give themselves permission to explore their sexual history, values, sins, wounds, joys, and hopes.

In the appendix I have included a questionnaire I use in classes on sexuality and menopause to invite women to begin the process of introspection regarding what it means to them to be a bodied, feminine self. These questions are designed to spark a woman's thought process as she begins thinking about and giving expression to her sexuality in ways that are connected to her spirituality and her sense of self.

Menopause, Creativity, and Fertility

A woman's monthly period implies the possibility of fertility. Likewise, the ending of her monthly cycle implies the end of her biological fertility as a woman; she is no longer capable of producing physical life within her. Women experience this aspect of menopause differently depending on their personal history. Experiences range from various degrees of mourning to expressions of joy. For example, some women who for whatever reason have never been pregnant might reexperience wondering "what if," regardless of how resolved the issue had once been. For other women whose primary identity has been that of childbearer, the loss of fertility can bring about an equally painful loss of identity. Sometimes women experience a sense of relief or freedom that comes from not having to worry about birth control. This change can result in an increased level of sexual energy, rather than the expected (and some times dreaded) reduction in energy that is sometimes associated with menopause.

Part of the pastoral care offered to women at menopause is recognizing the significance of this biological loss of fertility while also inviting the exploration of new avenues for expressing creativity. Biblical narratives such as the stories of Sarah and Elizabeth[29] can be used symbolically to show the possibility of creation and new life after a woman has been labeled "barren." A metaphorical rather than literal understanding of these narratives can be used to invite women to embrace a more inclusive and less biological understanding of their fertility and creativity.

Menopausal women can give birth to new dreams, careers, and expressions of their spirituality and sexuality. As Sue Furman states in *Turning Point: The Myths and Realities of Menopause*, "Menopause is not an end. On the contrary, menopause is a new beginning—just as puberty, marriage, a career, motherhood, and all the other roles a woman undertakes represent new beginnings."[30] Because women in our society are living longer and healthier lives than in previous generations, this renewed sense of creativity and inclusive understanding of fertility can undergird a long and prosperous life.

The Pastoral Care Giver and Menopause

As in any other life event for which a pastoral care giver is offering support, it is important for the minister to examine her or his own beliefs and knowledge regarding menopause to gain an awareness of how these assumptions and beliefs are affecting their ability (and inability) to give healthy support and guidance. It is difficult to help a parishioner celebrate something that we ourselves do not value. The pastor's acceptance of aging, views on women's issues, and understanding of menopause as a life transition rather than a medical condition all affect his or her pastoral care. Many well-written and up-to-date books about the medical, physical, psychosocial, and spiritual components of menopause are available for the pastor's use and for inclusion in a church library. Making "menopause" a welcomed word in pastoral conversation and church programming is an important beginning for inviting and nurturing a wholistic approach to menopause. Learning to hear sexual concerns in a pastoral way is a gift to yourself and to those you serve.[31] Preaching sermons from texts that portray aging as part of the creation process and women as productive other than for childbearing purposes can counter the current culture's antiaging emphasis. In other words, helping a woman "chose life"[32] is dependent in part on the pastor's awareness of the options of abundant living[33] available for women at menopause and beyond.

Conclusion

Menopause is both an event and a developmental phase in a woman's life journey. At menopause, women are "betwixt and between" who they have been and who they are becoming. As in any life transition, there are opportunities for simultaneous expressions of grief and loss, as well as new experiences of creation and the possibility of new life. Well-informed pastoral caregivers can serve as guides, encouragers, and prophets and prophetesses as they help women, and the church, embrace and celebrate menopause as a healthy and significant transition and event in defining a woman's identity, sexuality, and spirituality.

Appendix
Sexuality and Intimacy Issues in Midlife

Self-Assessment Guide
Reflect on the following questions regarding sexuality and intimacy in your life:

1. One of the things I enjoy about being a woman is
2. One way growing older has affected this is
3. One of the things I dislike about being a woman is
4. One way growing older has affected this is
5. One trait I admire in other women is
6. One trait I least admire in other women is
7. The age group of women I admire or appreciate most is _____ because
8. The age group of women I dislike or fear most is _____ because
9. My favorite age so far has been _____ because
10. When I was in my twenties, I thought "sexuality" meant
11. Today, "sexuality" means
12. One way menopause or aging has affected my sexuality in a negative way is
13. I have grieved or need to grieve this by
14. One way menopause or aging has affected my sexuality in a positive way is
15. I have celebrated or need to celebrate this by
16. One thing I like about my body is
17. One way growing older has affected this is
18. One thing I don't like about my body is
19. One way growing older has affected this is
20. One way I would like to improve the area of intimacy/sexuality in my life is

On Becoming an Ancestor: Continuity and Change at the End of Life

Maxine Glaz

Becoming an ancestor appears to be a process not very different from the process of becoming a person, although it is said to include a sense of relinquishment to a greater and more explicit degree. The primary psychological task as we enter the later years of life is thought to be one of facing loss—acknowledging and preparing for limitation, pain, and death, and putting one's affairs in order. At least this is a view of aging that dominates gerontology, reflecting in main the stigmatization of aging in American culture and perpetrating a view of the elderly that, however well intended, emphasizes loss and victimization over change and development.

Erik Erikson was the first theoretician to describe issues of late life psychology.[1] In his epigenetic view, the ego develops through eight psychosocial crises, five of which occur in childhood and young adulthood. The struggles at the center of the three adult stages are: (1) intimacy vs. isolation, (2) generativity vs. stagnation, and (3) integrity vs. despair. The theory is said to be epigenetic because the outcome of each crisis is determined in large part by the quality of the resolution of previous crises but provoked by ascendant psychological concerns related to age. In the Eriksonian view, late life confronts the older adult with the opportunity to develop a sense of wholeness and acceptance of self, one's past life, and finally death.[2] According to Erikson, it is only at the end of life that individuals will finally be able to resolve feelings about death, and only after they have successfully completed each of the earlier life phase crises. Erik Erikson's theory first peaked interest in the psychological processes of aging. Theoreticians after Erikson have tended to focus on his description of the final crisis of integrity vs. despair as a late life concern that has at its core the psychological preparation for death.

Embedded in Erikson's description is a view that seniors look at life from a retrospective framework rather than within a prospective vantage point that asks how one might contribute to the care of others, including those younger than oneself. Seniors successfully negotiate the crisis of old age to the extent that they resolve the final existential question, "Has my life been worthwhile?" not the more immediate question that occurs at midlife, "How shall I contribute to the lives of others, to my children and grandchildren?" This view is furthered in the work of Robert Butler[3] on the importance of reminiscence in aging, in general works on the social-psychology of aging, and to a lesser extent was the basis of my own research, *The Construction and Validation of an Ego-Integrity Interview*.[4]

It is apparent that the postwar impact of existentialism influenced the social-psychological theory of Erik Erikson and then Robert Butler and other students of aging. Existentialism did not always contribute to an overall understanding of the psychological processes of aging, but it was consistent with our prejudices concerning the importance of loss in late life and the value of coming to terms with the possibility of meaninglessness. One can easily see how the philosophical view of existentialism, understandable in the aftermath of World War II, began to shape an understanding of the psychological goals and development of late life when each intellectual concern surfaced in the same time period. These theories in turn marked much of the psychological research on aging that followed. Gender differences or gender perspectives on aging were for the most part not considered and are only beginning to be explored.

Is there an alternative? Certainly death is an issue for the elderly who are dying, just as it is for younger people who are doing so. Preparation for death in one's later years, however, is not necessarily a pervasive preoccupation or a dreaded experience. As a chaplain, I have talked to many women and some men who were more than ready to die. In fact, more than a few have been impatient for death to come. When loss has accumulated and health finally begins to fail, when an older adult feels that life is a burden or that she or he might be a burden to others, when loneliness sets in, relinquishment might seem natural and desirable. "I've already lived a long, full life," these seniors sometimes say. "Chaplain, why won't God take me? I'm ready." Other elders, though, less ravaged by the fragility of age, hardly seem to think of death at all. So, why do we believe that older adults often worry about death or that they should come to terms with it in order to achieve integrity?

Those who do not believe they are in the last years of life might consider the prospect of preparing for death as an older person to be a daunting or consuming task. Wishing to remain somehow outside the subtle developmental processes of later life, we imagine what the psychology of aging will be like, and we assume a catastrophic reckoning in which questions of personal significance predominate. Understanding is limited by our inexperience, influenced by a philosophical framework, but is also colored by the cultural stigma of aging and by a uniquely American perspective. We are a culture formed in rebellion against authority, the power of kings, and the traditions of our elders, suggests David Gutmann.

> Gerophobia runs deep in the American grain, part of the founding myth of a nation whose Founding Fathers were in truth Founding Sons, rebellious sons, refugees from patriarchal gerontocracy. Most Americans are immi-

grants or the children of immigrants; we descend from those who fled the ways of the "old country," the stifling traditions monitored by forbidding circles of chiding, gossiping elders in claustrophobic villages. America has been a collecting point for this planetary elite of prometheans—self-selected Americans, contrapatriarchal individualists before they ever saw this land— whose private myth has it that they fled the elders of the old land, and in so doing stole their power and brought it with them to fuel their achievements in the new. The immigrant's personal myth of rebellion matched the founding American myth of a revolutionary brotherhood that had broken from the tyranny of a king, the ultimate gerontocrat, and that had shared out his royal manna, his charge of sacred power, among the democratic comrades, in order to create a new, participatory aristocracy.[5]

Small wonder that we are ambivalent about elders, fearful of the power they might exercise over us if they turn against us. As a nation, we are not comfortable with the notion of strong elders. Better to topple a monarch than to remain beholden for gifts that might be bestowed.

Geropsychologists are not immune from this cultural bias. They have played "down the developmental possibilities of later life,"[6] says Gutmann, who suggests that the psychology of aging does not center on coming to terms with loss and death but on completion, on the phylogenetic requirement that we sustain our children and community through three generations with the wisdom and intellectual resources of a long life. The psychology of late life is not considered by Gutmann to be crisis-free but might include a threatening period of psychological self-revision in order to serve humanity in the years beyond the time in which our primary psychological identification is in parenting. Gutmann also believes that women achieve this state of readiness for late life in a manner different from the way men do. Although men grow psychologically into a less aggressive posture toward the world and demonstrate a greater interest in caring for the young, women develop late life interests beyond the home and toward greater self-expression.[7] To the extent that one has given up parts of the self to manage the responsibilities of parenting, each sex might reassert underdeveloped parts of the self as the parental crises subside. This reassertion of the self who will be an ancestor, however, evokes the revisiting of issues of gender identity that might rock the marital relationship before a new equilibrium is achieved. The equilibrium has as its social aim a renewal of the whole self to serve better the needs of a now altered world and life beyond raising one's children. This view of aging holds that seniors are essential to instructing the young and encouraging their appetite for learning. They are protectors of the evolutionary potential of the neocortex through loving instruction and through nurture of their own children's struggle to be parents.[8] Gutmann's work raises this question: Is the psychology of aging has been as little understood by this generation as the psychology of early childhood was by the generation before ours?

It was once commonly believed that the infant entered the world through a window of autism, a protective cocoon that was given up when a good-enough mother provided consistency, nurture, and warmth.[9] An interest in the study of autistic children had been the foundation for early research in infant development and colored interpretations of the babies' experience of the world[10] as surely as Freud's relationship with his own mother colored his interpretations of infantile sexuality and the creation of the oedipal theory. He was not entirely wrong about the basic sexuality of children, but his was a decidedly slanted view, however important it has been in the development of a broader psychological theory of human experience. We now understand the beginning of life to be psychologically rich, extraordinarily receptive and active.[11] It is a time of rapid learning and intense involvement by the newborn with the environment. It bears little relationship to the state of autism. Similarly, we have had very little understanding of the psychological realities of late life. Social science research is biased by deeply held prejudices against the elderly and a contemporary tendency toward a psychology of victimization. Seniors are inevitably viewed as powerless in the present, helpless, and in need of our ministrations, however demeaned they might be by our good intentions![12] Certainly the potential richness of aging and the potential contribution of our elders is diminished in this worldview.

Nor should we be sanguine that research on aging sufficiently isolates psychological factors and psychological development in seniors, especially if it begins with the catastrophic premise that aging is primarily about loss, as my 1981 study did. Add a questionable theoretical perspective to the general problem of method in social science[13] and the specific problem of research in a high anxiety subject such as death,[14] and you will understand the importance of being cautious about what I can say with certainty as we return to examine this work.

At present I am skeptical that reminiscence and death anxiety are the crucial psychological realities of the elderly. In graduate school I was less convinced by the theory than I was persuaded I was hostage to the politics of graduate education. I now look back at my findings with renewed interest while acknowledging the work began from a theoretical framework I no longer believe is valid. These research results suggest to me the variability of psychological predispositions among the aging, the pervasiveness of certain psychological problems and personality styles across the life span, and something of the wonderful richness of human experience into advanced age. More intriguing than my results and the immediate data that are themselves interesting are stories describing the experiences of two women I interviewed at that time. Their integrity and vitality has stayed with me all these years, more than justifying what has seemed like an inordinate effort to "collect data." These two women, Margaret Anstine and Josephine Clark (not real names), best portray the resilience of women who negotiate the postmenopausal years to become contributors to life and to their communities. On the road to becoming ancestors, they lived well and thoughtfully, each with dignity and force, making their own aging respectable, even while living in a culture with little respect for those who become old. First, however, I turn to the general research design and results.

A Study of Seniors and Death Anxiety—Research Design

In 1981 my doctoral research *The Construction and Validation of an Ego-Integrity Instrument* was complete. It was designed as a study of the elderly, sixty-five to ninety-five years of age, both women and men, and their attitudes toward death. The study was informed by Erikson's concept of ego-integrity vs. despair, and its premise was supported and extended by Robert Butler's research on reminiscence in the elderly. It includes the validation of a research interview[15] (see appendix A—an Ego-Integrity Interview—at the end of this chapter) to be used in the assessment of identity formation among seniors. Expanding Erikson's position that seniors either achieved a sense of integrity at the end of life or ended life in despair, I adapted the identity-status research of J. Marcia[16] on early adulthood to modify the Eriksonian view of late life psychology.

Marcia found that young adults could be categorized according to four basic patterns of adaptation to questions of identity. These four patterns, the Identity Achieving, Foreclosed, Moratorium, and Diffuse, were said to organize around two criteria: (1) degree of crisis, and (2) degree of commitment on identity issues.

Early Adulthood Adaptation to Identity[17]

Identity Achieving	enter crisis/yes
	commitment to identity/yes
Foreclosed	enter crisis/no
	commitment to identity/yes
Moratorium	enter crisis/yes
	commitment to identity/no
Identity Diffuse	enter crisis/no
	commitment to identity/no

Marcia discovered that Identity Achieving young adults enter a crisis about identity and evaluate their commitments and values in order to achieve it. Other young adults might enter a crisis and remain uncommitted. Overwhelmed at the prospect of choosing values and goals, the latter remain in Moratorium. Some young adults do not seem to enter a crisis. Instead they adapt their parent's values and goals and remain traditional in their outlook on life. They are said to be Foreclosed on identity issues; a biased way to describe the matter. Still other young adults do not enter a crisis, but rather than retaining a clear sense of values based on tradition, they are unable to articulate an organizing sense of meaning or direction. These young adults Marcia described as Identity Diffuse.

My research began with the theoretical assumptions that seniors might be at least as complicated as younger adults in their approach to commitments and values, and in the ways that they resolve the later integrity crisis. Thus I developed the interview noted above to assess whether or not seniors experienced a crisis around aging and death, involved themselves in reminiscing, and had a clear sense of who they were whether or not they had entered a crisis. My work confirmed that just as Marcia's younger research subjects had or had not experienced an identity crisis, seniors might or might not experience a crisis around aging. Both seniors who do experience such a crisis and those who do not might hold a strong sense of integrity.

I categorized the seniors I studied as Integrity Achieving or Despairing, using Eriksonian categories, and Foreclosed or Dissonant.[18] Delineating a Foreclosed group of seniors follows the same category designation as in Marcia's work with young adults. These are seniors who were found to have a clearly developed set of values but who had adopted them almost entirely from their forebears and did very little reexamination of the assumptions that sustained them earlier in life. The use of the Dissonant category, however, diverges from Marcia's work. It borrows something of the notion of being "in crisis" from Marcia's Moratorium identity status but examines what is currently occurring to the senior as an integrity issue. Previous questions of values might or might not have been settled before later adulthood, but these are difficult to evaluate separately once the older adult states that she or he is currently examining the meaning of life. There is also a marked sense of dissonance throughout this process of reevaluation. As developed within the research protocols, the Dissonant status might therefore include both those who achieved a sense of identity earlier and those who might not have done so. Thus, seniors who expressed the sentiment that they were in the process of reexamining the question of meaning, whether brought on by a change in situation such as a new residence or a recent bereavement or because increasing age provoked such exploration were placed in the dissonant category.

A Study of Seniors and Death Anxiety—Results

Both the Identity Achieving seniors and the Foreclosed seniors were almost equally satisfied with the lives that they had led.[19] Both groups were able to face death and plan for it, and neither was more successful at avoiding death anxiety. Whether by adapting parental and traditional religious views or by breaking from them, older people with a strong set of values seemed to take death in stride. In fact, Foreclosed seniors who had been more accepting of their parent's values and had adopted a more traditional sense of identity were somewhat less anxious and felt more prepared to die than the Identity Achieving.[20] Those who tend toward reflection on values rather than on the acceptance of traditional values do little better at managing the vicissitudes of aging than those who do not. Many of the seniors I interviewed blithely accepted parental values at a young age and proceeded happily to live out those values over their life span. They had few regrets and felt they had missed little in life. They were resilient in the emergencies of life and found comfort in living as their parents had taught them. Perhaps children from happy, even denying families had reason to be content with their parent's approach to life. Being untroubled about who they were and who they had become was not a grave disadvantage on any mental health or anxiety measure I had chosen to evaluate. The Foreclosed seniors, perhaps using denial, had an awareness of finitude and reported satisfactory levels of well-being. They had undergone significant preparations for death and had reasonable levels of death anxiety.[21] Although gross scores on these measures using six statistical tests were not quite as high as for the seniors categorized as identity achieving, there were no significant differences between the groups. Both the Identity Achieving seniors and the Foreclosed seniors, however, had significantly higher scores on measures of life satisfaction than did the Dissonant seniors and the Despairing.[22]

The adults who were classified as Dissonant were the ones I judged to be currently in an emotional crisis. They presented a variety of concerns that centered around current loss and adaptation. They were often gravely distressed. One woman said she had not felt much discomfort about the advances of aging until the wintry day when she had been mugged in her own driveway. It was difficult to recover from that, she said, for it had made her feel frail and frightened. More than a year had passed since this event and, whereas previously she had considered her single and economically poor life as a seamstress lovelier with the years, now she felt the incident had sapped her of her reserves. She believed she was weak and not so capable of defending herself in the world as she once assumed. She said simply, "I *feel old* now." Other seniors in the Dissonant group faced change of one kind or another. Often they were moving out of or into a new household; some were recently widowed. One woman was slowly going deaf. Her husband said, "It's awful. I've always loved her very much, but we can't have a decent conversation anymore, and she's become very suspicious of everyone."

Many people in the Dissonant category felt they were ruminating about life, but this rumination did not appear to exemplify the quality of reminiscence described in Butler's theory, which suggests that remembering and telling stories about one's life further strengthens the senior's capacity to feel positive about herself or himself and prepares the person for the last years of life and eventual death. In fact, these seniors resembled my friends then in midlife crisis, although the aging adults were not oriented toward the future and toward professional goals. Instead they were working hard to assimilate into their life plan a sense of themselves as physically diminished, more frail, older, more limited in their contribution by immediate circumstance. The older seniors sometimes acknowledged they had to come to think of themselves in a new and less flattering way. The reorientation was hard work! At the same time, many of these older adults recollected a time in their lives when they had faced adversity, suffered, and recovered. Those who did were confident that they would regain a sense of footing and that they could manage what they had to manage. They realized they were in the grip of an adjustment that was taking its toll. Although some of them admitted to being painfully worried, they did not necessarily think of themselves as failures or failing. Some knew they would survive and grow toward a new and older sense of self, although the experience certainly was not an easy one.

I judged from their candor with me that too few of these seniors had anyone to talk to about their feelings about themselves in the midst of this change. I recall my eighty-two-year-old father and his frustration with his physician when he tried to say he was not feeling vigorous any more. The physician did not yet know the extent of my father's nightly dancing and daily golf routine, nor of the cancer that was quietly ravaging his body. This physician said too swiftly, "Well, Mr. Feliks, you are getting older, you know!" I think many of the seniors I interviewed also thought no one wanted to listen to their distress because, after all, they were "getting old, you know!" The passage to being elderly has some of the same qualities as all other life passages, but it might be made harder by the fact that we are disparaging of age and do not want to bother listening to the lamentations of those who are aging. Whereas in adolescence and in midlife we have come to expect a bit of momentary despair by people in life passages, many people seem to hope that elders will remain sanguine through adversity. If theorists missed the real import of early childhood because children could not speak for themselves, it is just as likely we miss the reality and import of aging because we do not care to listen to the elderly. As a pastor friend once said, "I always dread visiting my parishioners in nursing homes, but you know, once I do it I have a great time. I always leave with a lighter step. They seem to care for me."

Finally, the Despairing were the least well functioning of the elderly in my study. Because my research was not a longitudinal study, I could not substantiate my assumption of a connection between Marcia's Diffuse Identity adults and my category of Despairing seniors. Yet these seniors were those who seemed without a sense of meaning or self-efficacy. They rarely agreed to be interviewed. When they did, they readily acknowledged despair. They circled round the trials of their lives like hawks on prey. They relentlessly disparaged their situations and their families, if they had any. They were less likely to report their own limitations and their own conflicts, but it was clear to me as an observer that these people had serious, undiagnosed emotional problems. They reminisced but in very negative tones. Yet I had no sense that things were about to change for them.

One of the Despairing seniors I met lived in a rural home with over fifty dogs. I was greeted at his residence by many of them, which were barking madly. He calmed them down and invited me inside, where I worked hard to follow my interview protocols. The depth of the trash, the smells, and chaos are still beyond description. This man's home was falling down around him, but he spent money on dog food and veterinary care, and he loved his pets. He had been the elder brother of a child with cerebral palsy; his brother's protector and defender until the brother died. When he lost his brother in the middle of his own life, he began to take in dogs; any dog, any time, without thought for himself. He had no intention of changing this largely unconscious commitment, and his world-view did not include people abandoning dogs and condemning his house while it fell down around him. He was openly bitter about life, disparaging about all others, and absolutely terrified at the thought of dying. He was completely iden-tified with his brother's suffering and extremely irritable about what life had delivered! I could applaud his concern "for the underdog" and lament its impact on him at the same time.

Another senior, a woman who lived alone and in isolation in a senior high-rise, was angry with everyone and everything about her life. Her children had long since lost interest in her, and she reported that she had never been happy. She remained a vitriolic woman, I suspect a victim of post traumatic stress disorder. Something had gone terribly wrong for her—perhaps early, persistent, and severe child abuse. She said nothing about it, of course, but her life and her despair spoke volumes. She lived a terrible and perhaps terrifying experience, and it seemed to me she wanted someone to repay her for it *now*.

The Despairing seniors I interviewed left me with the same sense of helpless-ness that had marked their own existence. They were frustrated, even anguished about who they were and what their lives had become. The most extreme of them, such as the two I've described above, did not seem to me to be normal seniors. They possessed a quality of psychological frailty and an absence of resilience in their thinking that seemed chronic, not contextual. They were not despairing be-cause aging forced them to reconsider the past and they decided they had found life wanting. Their lives were wanting, and they despaired. This despair did not seem to be about coming to terms with age poorly but about coming to terms with life poorly. They recounted litanies of failures that had plagued them for many years. Childhood was painful, school had been treacherous, work had not gone well, important relationships, if there were any, had gone sour. They were certainly unhappy now, but they had been so throughout their life. It seems to me that late term reminiscence is unlikely to change the course of psychological events that led to such profound despair. Such unguided reflection does not seem laden with possibility.

Thus, my systematic review of the literature on the psychology of aging, reminis-cence, and death anxiety, but more importantly the process of interviewing forty sen-iors and my results, slowly changed my understanding of how we come to terms with advancing age and the prospect of death. Ultimately it has also altered my view that this psychological reality is, in fact, the central theme in the psychology of aging. The research experience itself led me away from the premise that the prospect of death is preeminent in organizing late life experience. Many adults age successfully and come

to terms with their prospective death without a life review. These seniors talk somewhat cheerfully about the past and take pleasure in any audience they find to listen
to them, but they do not seem to understand this as a crucial review of their life
needed to determine its final value. For Foreclosed seniors, life has always been
meaningful. The prospect of death makes it no less so. Life has been as good as they
have been loyal to the values, ideals, and goals their parents set before them. I have
come to think of these seniors as fortunate, not simply Foreclosed. They might be in
denial, if one follows a theory of defenses, but they are certainly functioning well into
the later years of their lives, even if they are in denial. If they seem happy, can we say
that they are not or that they are missing something?

Other adults are less sanguine about adopting their parents' values, and they
seem deeply thoughtful about the end of life. These Identity Achieving seniors report going through an Eriksonian-style existential crisis in which they stop for a
period of time to take stock of what they have done, who they have become, and
explicitly to consider life's meaning. They end up being quite satisfied with who
they are and the values they have lived by. They do report having suffered some before arriving at this positive conclusion, and that suffering appears to strengthen
their reserves for coping with death and preparing for it.

Seniors I evaluated as Dissonant might be on their way to achieving a renewed
sense of integrity, but the quality of this experience in process is neither comfortable nor consoling. These people are in a crisis related to loss and relinquishment
and thereby to situational distress. The condition is usually not brought on solely
by the recognition of aging but by explicit loss and change. I did not envy these
aging adults the process of dealing with an emotional crisis and a corresponding
sense of being threatened and potentially diminished. They were actively suffering
when we talked. Few if any said they felt helpless in the midst of their crises, and
they did not seem to be reviewing their lives as much as they were trying to find
the resources for managing the changes they experienced. It sounds very romantic to me to call this transitional period a life review; it seems more like a review of coping strategies. These seniors talk about problem solving much as
younger adults do, and they talk about bearing the emotional distress of the present, not the past and its glories. Doubtless the quality of the past helps them manage the present. Previous successes in particular are used as a resource to bear the
emotional weight of the present and their hope for a tolerable or happy resolution
to their discomfort. These are very contextual reminiscences, however. The seniors are not reviewing personal history for the sake of putting it in order. The
order already exists in their minds; they draw on it to manage the present, even
when they could not make orderly the senseless aspects of aging. They generally
accept age with its physical changes and losses as a biological given, although they
do not always find it agreeable.

Finally, the Despairing seniors suggest to me the difficulty of changing a tumul-
tuous or disturbed past. Age is but an added burden to this group, whose lives had

been most circumscribed. It is hard to change what has been difficult in one's story unless someone or something can intervene to shed new light on experience.

Thus I doubt that loss and coming death is the predominant psychological reality for elders most of the time. The quality of what is achieved psychologically earlier in life sustained most of the seniors I interviewed well into late life. I believe this finding is the common psychological way to state an important theological truth. The final word about life is not death's victory but about human meaning and renewal. We learn about meaning, relatedness, and renewal early in life and revisit it with every developmental stage.

The seniors who allowed me to interview them taught me once again that the differences among people within groups, in this case the variability among people ages sixty-five to ninety-five, are greater than differences between groups, say between seniors and those who are much younger. There was considerable variability in these seniors' approach to life and in problem-solving styles. The Integrity Achieving, Foreclosed, and Despairing face the reality of growing older in distinctive ways. Some elders consider death for a period of time, but some do not, and among no group except the Despairing was death and loss a predominant concern; for them, it was oblivion. Other seniors did not seem focused on loss or much concerned about meaning and meaninglessness. They found themselves in the present and enjoyed the perspective of a long life.

Elder Tales: A Portrait of Two Women

When I completed my doctoral research by polishing the statistical reports, I had a dissertation, received a doctorate, and published a journal article.[23] One wise faculty advisor, a Harvard statistician, commented that I had lost everything important in my work in order to meet departmental requirements for quantitative research. He hoped I would publish a book about what I had really learned during those interviews. He was correct, of course, but I did not write the book.

Instead I will tell two of these elders' tales, so that the quality of senior involvement in life, and particularly the changing focus of women's late life experience is evident. I have kept alive the image of two women whose lives suggest something of the strength of human character, the ways we develop a sense of who we are, how we struggle to cope with change, and the potential for sheer beauty in advanced old age. Of course, these women stand out for me because I identified with them as women but also because each one had a clear notion of her values and because they exemplify the kind of wisdom and nurturing presence that elders bring to those younger. The life experiences of these women were very different from one another. One was learned and had been a mother. The other was not schooled and had never had children. Both, however, were vital and engaging well into an advanced age. Even as they lived alone, in the too solitary style of the

American experience of aging, they lived for others and they lived with a freedom to express their own voices with clarity and gusto.

Margaret Anstine

Margaret walked into my life about the time I launched my research project. She was a neighbor who lived one-half block south of me. I met her at her own garage sale while she was clearing out her extraneous life possessions. My dog, Camus, made her acquaintance before I did. I recall that she was thrilled that my big Bernese Mountain Dog had so distinguished a name, and she was delighted to find a young neighbor who knew of the French philosopher. I was also pleased that someone other than my divinity school colleagues could pronounce my dog's name. Margaret was in her late eighties. Tiny and artistic-looking, her home was strikingly different from the others in this lovely older neighborhood. It was, she said authoritatively, Bauhaus International School Modern.

Margaret Anstine painted her fingernails with polish as red as her lipstick; purposefully applied but somewhat askew. It was worn in the way of women whose eyes are no longer sharp and whose hand-eye coordination might be failing. She was fascinated that I was studying aging and seniors' attitudes toward death. "A very important subject," she confirmed. I was pleased by her interest and affirmation.

Margaret told me she was Episcopalian and European in background and had been the wife of a now deceased history professor. They had built their home, architect-designed, to reflect their unique tastes and the aesthetic and intellectual values they cherished. They had furnished it with the best modern appointments they could buy, and she still loved it dearly. "So simple compared to the other houses on the block, you know." My own appreciation for such architecture was indeed piqued, but I could not bring myself to ask for a tour, dog in tow. Her family, two sons, had been raised in this avant-garde home, studied at important universities elsewhere, and gone on to successful careers in other parts of the country. Margaret and her husband had entertained intellectuals in this house, and she was well acquainted with philosophy and psychology. She inquired further about my research, so I knew she was genuinely interested. She revealed that she herself was not happy about growing old, although she accepted it. As with her lipstick, she dutifully applied herself to managing the loss aging had brought. Her garage sale was a current testimony to that. She did not want her children to have to figure out which furnishings were valuable and which were not. She was taking care of that for them. She never spoke about her husband further. I never learned when he had died.

Margaret was disturbed to learn that perhaps some seniors would age without thinking much about the meaning of life or death. Hers was a life of the mind. "But how," she asked, "can anybody age without an existential crisis? This is not a good thing!" I explained my theory of aging psychology based on the research of early adult identity crisis resolution. Some people seemed to foreclose their identity, moving quickly to internalize the parental values they had been taught without much consideration of the alternatives. My research was designed to see whether further along in life some aging people would do the same if they did foreclose, would it affect them negatively. You should have seen the look of consternation, even alarm, on Margaret's face. "Well, do they foreclose?" she inquired. I could see she was hoping to learn and to sharpen my thinking. "Yes," I replied, "it seems to me some do." "Oh dear," she lamented, "this is so American. We Europeans live and feel our loss and our changes. We do not ignore them." Living happily ever after was not something Margaret believed in. She was a student of Sartre, Kierkegaard, and Camus. She had known a very good life, she said, but life was more satisfying because there were so many wonderful ideas to ponder, so much meaning to consider. How terrible to miss out on all that, she thought.

There was a note of certitude and confidence about Margaret and an intellectual acumen worthy of note. I was sure I was not going to catch up with her. Importantly, however, I gained the distinct sense that she wanted me to. She seemed hopeful I would. She responded with pleasure to the name I had given my dog and to the nature of my dissertation. She pursued the basis for my thinking, the significance of my findings, the importance of the study. She was not helpless in organizing her own life on behalf of her children, and I had the sense that I had her support and blessing as well.

Josephine Clark

Josephine was a study in contrast when compared to Margaret Anstine. Josephine had nothing in the world except herself and the small apartment she rented on a Social Security check. Still, nothing stopped her. Whereas Margaret was cultured, sophisticated, and caring, Josephine plugged along and lived abundantly. At moments, given my research premises, I thought she must be in total denial about the losses in her life, yet she remains the most remarkable of the many seniors I interviewed. Even today, I am in awe of what she told me about herself.

Josephine was ninety-three years old when I met her. She was poor, living only on Social Security, as many elderly women do. She lived alone in her apartment and had no living relatives. She did not drive because she had never learned to do so, thinking that an automobile was an expense she and her deceased husband could not afford. Josephine lived by simple rules. One of them was that depression was unfitting to her or any senior; something you brought on yourself by letting yourself be unhappy. She despised self-pity. She was confidently happy with very little support and believed it was very important to take care of yourself. "How do you do that?" I inquired.

"Oh," she said, "it's so simple. You must get up every morning and throw open your curtains. You have to let the light in! That's especially important in a climate like ours, you know." Josephine was referring to her hometown of Rochester, New York. "So many of the residents in my building complain all the time about how gray and dull it is. But they keep their blinds shut all day. They don't go outside or look outside. That doesn't help. You have to keep your blinds open! It makes such a big difference to open yourself up to the world, whatever it has to offer."

Josephine described her daily activities. Because she had never driven a car, she was wonderfully self-sufficient without one. She walked miles every day; sometimes to the grocery store, sometimes to the library, often to her favorite coffee shop downtown, many miles from her home. Inclement weather did not affect her plans. Nothing short of a full-blown blizzard would keep her home. With her blinds open, she could still enjoy the light. She was still in excellent health; doubtless the long walks kept her very fit.

Josephine did not constrain herself to life in Rochester, New York. At ninety-three, she still saved money to pay for her annual trip to the Big Apple, a place she adored. Going there had been a ritual for many years; age was not about to stop her. She went alone to catch the red-eye special from Rochester to New York City. The train would arrive in New York and drop her off at Grand Central Station, where she would stow her luggage, find a place for breakfast, and then proceed to walk to the Metropolitan Museum. After a few hours, including lunch at the Met, she would window-shop and spend the afternoon with a visit to the Rockettes. Finally, she would pick up her luggage, proceed to her hotel, have dinner by herself, and get a restful night's sleep. The next day she hit the bookstores and Macy's, filling her time with whatever struck her fancy until it was time to catch the early afternoon train home.

The only disturbing event Josephine reported about her trips to New York had occurred the last time she went to check in at her hotel. "They told me they could not register me without a driver's license," she said. "Can you believe that! After forty years?" When the staff insisted that she needed a driver's license or a credit card or some ID before they could check her in, she protested that she carried cash! Why should she need a credit card? She then asked to speak to the hotel manager. "I told him that if they would check their records they would find I had been their guest every year for many years and that I had never needed a driver's license before." The manager softened before Josephine spoke about sleeping in the street or calling for a police officer to mediate. I had no doubt that had she needed to, she could resort to high pressure tactics to get the room she wanted. In the morning, however, the hotel manager apologized, provided a gratis breakfast, and told her to return any time. She must have caused quite a stir among the service personnel and administration that evening. The manager was sure his staff would not forget her next year. She was welcome without a driver's license. They would look forward to her annual visit. "Well, thank you," Josephine said. "I won't be looking for another hotel. I've always liked it here."

Josephine also loved her birthday. She said she did not feel old, and she found them rather exciting. The elderly women in her apartment building were a little too retiring for her taste. They struggled to manage each birthday *alone* and could not be expected to party, but she loved to celebrate. She did so with her friends at the coffee shop, who provided a cake and a big to-do about her on the occasion. Every year was special for her, but her ninetieth was more so. After the usual party at the coffee shop, she was invited to go out with a businessman who often visited at the shop with her. For her ninetieth, he wanted to do something special with her. He took her out for dinner. He arrived at her apartment with a corsage and a small gift. They drove off in a well-appointed limo to one of Rochester's better restaurants. She was a very lucky woman, didn't I think? I thought she was extraordinary. Because she continued to see him weekly, she was hoping the gentleman who had taken her to dinner might repeat the treat when she turned one-hundred. He said he would. She planned to be there.

The only sad note in our conversation was Josephine's recollection of her husband's death at sixty-seven. His health had not been good for several months. One morning he was in the bathroom but quiet for far too long. When she went to find him, he was lying dead. He had died without warning her. She remembered those moments vividly. A few tears splashed down her cheeks. "Since we had no children, he was all I had; my best friend. We had lived together for many years with my mother in our home. He was wonderful with her, too. When she died, he was it for me." But that was some time ago now, and being physically active and keeping her blinds open had softened the loss over time. She said it was just great being ninety-three, especially considering the alternative.

"What's the alternative?" I asked, stepping far beyond the design protocols.

"Beyond death?" she came back, "I really don't know, do I?" she twinkled at me.

Elder Tales and Spiritual Being

These two women elders each told their own tale. Margaret's perspective on aging was marked by the same philosophical and existential beliefs that inform much of the literature on gerontology. Yet as an elder, her conversation with me was organized by a keen interest in things of the mind and a rapid, if boundaried, involvement in and support for my work. She was as invested in the present and future as my younger mentors at the university and divinity school. Nor was Josephine, at ninety-three, a doddering, self-preoccupied senior. She was as vital as her excellent fitness allowed her to be and she wished to be interviewed in order to help my project. Like many other of the seniors I visited, she hoped to make a contribution to my work and to the community to which she belonged. This orientation to life is hardly retrospective. How could one think of Josephine as helpless and victimized? Both Margaret and Josephine had achieved a deep inner sense of integrity and the clear, forceful voice that Gutmann describes as the psychological accomplishment of women in their later years. These two women rose to the challenge of aging; to contribute to the support of those who are younger, to aid the next generation as they seek to be effective parents, to develop the wisdom of the sage, of elders, of healers. Compassionately related to all of life and strong of spirit, they lived to live and would die well in good time.

Each of these women lived her spiritual truths, but spirituality was something neither of them spoke about easily. Josephine's was a very practical spirituality. Love your family, be friends with the world. Use common sense. Walk a lot; it beats indebtedness. Stay open to the world, let the light in. Be glad for what you get. She was eager to pass on her wisdom to me, not only by words but by example. She would have hated my pity and had absolutely none for herself.

Margaret, on the other hand, practiced a different kind of spiritual truth. Be responsible. Let ideas in. Seek authenticity and integrity above all. Keep learning. Keep your mind open to the truth, even if it hurts. Accept what is. Contribute to others.

These do not strike me as particularly complicated ideas, but they are representative of the spirituality I often heard from my senior interviewees. They are not Christologically laden, theologically profound statements about what matters in life. Most of the seniors I talked to were greatly aware of the biological givens of aging but not absorbed in thinking about loss and death. They felt a long life had a profound meaning, even when it was sometimes obscured by loss. They were generally glad to be alive, and only the most despairing actually feared death; perhaps as they feared life. Few seniors lamented the realities of aging except when it caught up with them in ill health or loss. Then they cheerfully and often humorously acknowledged how irritable it made them to feel more limited. There might be less celebration in the holidays, and they sometimes felt lonely thinking about family members and friends who had died before them. Some elders looked forward to a reunion with the deceased; few, if any, counted on it. None spoke about eternity or spoke confidently about an afterlife, even among the more traditional of my sample. For the most part, whether religious or not and whether in crisis or not, the seniors I met faced their age not so much graciously as gallantly, simply, and with good-humored wisdom. They enjoyed life, were grateful to have reached an old age, and when confronted with death, faced the thought of it and managed. They were not particularly eager to talk at length about their thoughts about the matter. I was, after all, posing as an academic researcher. All of them, however, maintained their composure, seemed glad to be of help to me, and wished that others felt more comfortable having a serious conversation with them about life. What came through most powerfully was their investment beyond themselves; their readiness to give support and guidance to a young woman who was trying to learn about them; their quiet energy for the good life, families, friends, community; their investment in what the future would bring; and the predominance of satisfaction even among the poorest of them.

The end of "a long life well lived" seems to me to be marked by an appreciation of life's complexity and the acceptance of reality. Margaret Anstine might say,

"Nothing is so comforting as reality." For us, it is possible to learn from seniors by drawing closer to them and avoiding them less. A simple life can be a very happy one. A thoughtful life has a wonderful seriousness about it. Integrity is possible, although we will not always feel better for it.

Age does not make us other than who we have been, with or without a life review. The end of life poses challenges to be faced in whatever ways we usually face challenges. Do not tamper with what works. Be compassionate toward those whose lives have known misery. Age does not change us, it refines us, though, like fire. Keep your blinds open. Rely on your feet, not your wheels, as much as you can. In age you will likely be what you have already become, only more so. You are becoming an ancestor.

Appendix A
Ego-Integrity Interview

General Introduction and Description of the Study for Participants

The purpose of this interview is to learn how older adults understand their lives and how they solve problems. It includes general questions about your attitude toward life, how you solve problems, your response to loss, and your attitudes toward death. These matters are important to those who are trying to understand and learn about aging. You can help by agreeing to be interviewed.

The interview would take about forty-five minutes of your time and could be conducted either here at the nutrition center or in your home, as you prefer.

Consent Form

Construction and Validation of an Ego-Integrity Interview
Principal investigator: The Rev. Maxine Walaskay,
Doctoral candidate, University of Rochester

I have been informed that the purpose of this study is to learn about the attitudes and feelings of older adults toward life and solving problems. I know it will require that I spend forty-five minutes talking with the interviewer. I also understand that the information I give will henceforth be used anonymously without my name attached and that an additional person beyond the interviewer may listen to the tape recording being made of our conversation. All written records from the interview and questionnaire will be kept by the researcher and will be used only to prepare a report of the study and for teaching purposes.

I give my written consent to be studied, knowing that I will be asked to describe myself and my feelings about life. I am also aware that the interview and questionnaire include questions about loss and death, items that might be uncomfortable to discuss. I may refuse to answer any question I find too disturbing or personal, and if I wish, may withdraw from the study at any time without prejudice. If I do choose to withdraw from the study, I am aware that all the information I have given will be destroyed. I have also been informed that many people who have answered these questions about life and death in the past have found it to be enjoyable, experienced some relief from the conversation, and found it to be helpful. I am aware that the interviewer is qualified to discuss these matters with me and has experience as a hospital chaplain and as a counselor.

I have been informed that I have the right to ask any questions about the study I choose. Those questions I have asked have been answered.

Respondent's signature	Date of consent

(The Rev.) Maxine Walaskay, doctoral candidate and Assistant Professor of Pastoral Care (Colgate-Rochester Divinity School) Rochester, New York
Dr. Susan K. Whitbourne, faculty advisor
The Graduate School of Education and Human Development
The University of Rochester, Rochester, New York
Sponsored by the Department of Helping Services
Graduate School of Education and Human Development
The University of Rochester
Rochester, New York

Interview Schedule

Part 1

a. How would you describe yourself? What kind of person do you think you are in general?

b. What would you like others to think of you?

c. How have you felt about your own aging?

d. How would you say you resolve your problems?

e. Each of us is unique. Different people describe themselves as having their own personal style. These are the characteristic ways they see life, make decisions, and resolve their problems.

Let me describe four different styles people seem to adopt: (1) a person who looks only at the "bright side"; (2) a person who sees both the good and bad in life; (3) a person who gets discouraged, "down in the mouth"; (4) a person who weighs things in the balance and "takes forever to decide." Which of these is most like you at this time?

Part 2

a. Do you feel that you are or were important to family, friends, church, neighbors, fellow workers, community?

b. If you could, how would you change things in your life?

c. Do you often find yourself thinking, "I've had the best (darn) life!"

Part 3

a. Do you find you feel quite critical of any of the people or agencies that are important in your life, such as family, spouse or home resident, church, government?

b. Do you have any pet peeves about these groups? What are they?

Part 4

a. Have you gone through times in your life when you've done a lot of looking back at your past?

b. Do you find yourself now in one of those periods where you are thinking and looking back?

c. During the times when you have thought about life, do you ever feel strongly, "What does it mean? What is life about?"

d. Do you ever feel strongly, "Why bother, it's not worth it!"

Part 5

    a. Have you ever lost a significant person by death? (Assess closeness of relationship, and how recent a death.)

    b. How would you say you feel about this loss? Would you say: (1) I was surprised, but kept busy and tried to ignore the absence; (2) it really bothers me; it's got me thinking a lot about my life right now; (3) it really hurt and took time to learn to create new relationships without him/her; (4) I've never been the same; I've just about given up.

Part 6

What would you like others (younger people in general, perhaps those preparing for retirement) to understand about how you are feeling about the end of your life? What would you say to others who will be facing this experience in thirty years or in fifteen years?

Appendix B

Ego-Integrity Interview

Table 1: Summary of Hypothetical Characteristics on Dimensions

Status	Crisis	Resolution	Characteristics
Dissonant	In Crisis	Unresolved	1. Reminisces frequently 2. Negative affect about reminiscing 3. Ambivalent about past experiences 4. Negative psychological well-being 5. Moderate death anxiety 6. Some involvement in preparing for death
Integrity Achieving	Crisis	Resolved Positively	1. Reminisces frequently 2. Positive affect about reminiscing 3. Positive about past experiences 4. Positive psychological well-being 5. Low death anxiety 6. High involvement in preparing for death
Foreclosed	No Crisis	Resolved	1. Reminisces infrequently 2. Negative affect about reminiscing 3. Positive about past experiences 4. Positive psychological well-being 5. Moderate death anxiety 6. Some involvement in preparing for death
Despairing	Crisis	Resolved Negatively	1. Reminisces infrequently 2. Negative affect about reminiscing 3. Negative about past experiences 4. Negative psychological well-being 5. High death anxiety 6. Little involvement in preparing for death

Older Widows:
Surviving, Thriving,
and Reinventing One's Life

Karen D. Scheib

I think that television shows widows pretty much like they do old women
. . . being forgetful and impatient. But they also show them needing help all
the time. Like if there's no man in the house, the woman can't get nothing
done by herself. It's true that I can't do any heavy lifting or anything, but neither could Bill if he was here now. The other thing I can think of is that they
show widows as bitter or angry. Like if there's ever a Halloween show, some
old woman is in a spooky house, and all the kids are scared of her—it's always a mean, angry, very strange widow woman. There's never a husband in
those houses, only an alone woman.
    –Carrie Jones, age ninety-one[1]

What images do we have of older women who are widowed? Do we expect
older women to adjust successfully to widowhood, not only to survive but to
thrive? Too often we anticipate that older widows will either "die off or dry up"—
turning into the stereotypical image of the "strange widow woman" described by
Carrie Jones. This stereotype suggests that a widow is unable to adjust to the death
of her husband in such a way that allows her to care for herself while relating to
others and continuing to be fully engaged in life.

The good news is that for a majority of women, the experience of widowhood
does not conform to the social myths about widows. Prominent sociologist Helena
Lopata states that widows do not fit the myth of leading "very restricted, isolated,
or dependent lifestyles in a limited social life space."[2] If we contrast the lived
experience of many older widows to stereotypical societal expectations and media
images, then these women are often adjusting to widowhood in their own time
and way. A view of widowhood more accurate than one based on media images,
social stereotypes, or anecdotal observations is needed.

A central purpose of this chapter is to provide such a picture of older women's
experience of widowhood. After briefly defining the scope of this study, I will

examine myths and realities of widowhood in light of some of the current social science literature on older widows. The findings of this research challenge stereotypical images of older widows. I will also review several studies that identify some of the relevant factors that allow older women to survive and thrive following the husband's death.

After developing a more realistic picture of widowhood, I will explore how a woman's understanding of herself might change as a consequence of taking on the identity of "widow." This understanding of self involves both psychological and sociological dimensions. These psychological dimensions of self include the way the self is experienced and defined in relation to or apart from others. The psychological dimensions of this new self-understanding will be explored in light of feminist critiques of developmental theory. Feminist revisions of self provide a helpful lens for understanding the changes in identity that many widows experience.

The sociological dimension of self includes what Lopata calls "self-concept."[3] Lopata identifies the reconstruction of self-concept as a central task of widowhood. Self-concept is composed of both the woman's thoughts and feelings about herself and her social roles, such as wife and mother that help define who she is within the larger social system.[4] This exploration of self-concept will also provide an opportunity to examine some of the theoretical assumptions from developmental theory that might shape an assessment of a successful adjustment to widowhood. Following these more theoretical reflections, I will offer some practical suggestions for the church's ministry with older widows.

My interest in this topic developed as a consequence of both personal and professional experience. In my experience as a church pastor, I often observed older widows gain a sense of accomplishment from mastering tasks and challenges faced for the first time in widowhood. In recent years I have watched two women in my own extended family make this same journey. These women had a quiet pride about their newfound competence and identity. I say "quiet" because they did not talk about it much. It was almost as if talking about the new sense of freedom and competence experienced by these women would somehow diminish the previous marital relationships. At about the same time, I was being introduced to the sociological literature on aging. Here I discovered a number of studies on widowhood that confirmed the anecdotal experience from my family. For the most part, such literature has not been significantly used by pastoral care givers in ministry with older adults.

Definition and Scope of This Study

For the purpose of this study, a widow is defined as "a woman who has married and whose partner has died."[5] The focus of this chapter will be on older widows in heterosexual relationships.[6] I have chosen to focus on this population because of the large number of older women who are widowed and active in local churches. My hope is that this chapter will contribute to the small but growing body of literature on pastoral care of older women.

The population of older people (those over sixty-five), especially women, continues to grow significantly. By the year 2030, 22 percent of the population will be over sixty-five, while the eighty-five-plus group will have tripled in size.[7] Older women outnumber men by a three-to-two ratio and this disparity increases among those over eighty-five. In 1989, there were thirty-nine men for every 100 women over the age of eighty-five.[8]

As of 1990, these older women were also three times more likely to be widowed than their male counterparts, and among women over seventy-five years of age, 65 percent were widowed.[9] Given the reality that many women in the current cohort of older women (over the age of sixty-five) will experience widowhood, the scarcity of attention to this life event is quite striking.[10]

Because widowhood[11] is not experienced by all older women, it cannot be considered a developmental stage through which all women will pass. It is a life experience, however, that a large percentage of older women, particularly those now over the age of sixty-five, will experience. The loss of one's spouse is often experienced as a situational crisis that reawakens and reconfigures developmental issues.

I have chosen to focus on studies that explore the older woman's adjustment to widowhood.[12] This adjustment generally occurs in the final phase of the grief process, what Bowlby calls the "phase of a greater or lesser degree of reorganization."[13] A woman enters this latter phase of grief when she has made significant progress in working through the emotional experience of loss and is beginning to reinvest herself in life.

Although there are common patterns of widowhood, each woman's experience has unique features. Becoming a widow involves real losses and significant challenges in a woman's life that require creativity, flexibility, and the use of a woman's internal and external resources in order to successfully meet these challenges. Women's ability to survive and thrive following widowhood will vary according to different external and internal factors. Some of these factors include the existence of social supports, economic and social situations, ethnicity and race, educational level, economic status, level of independence in the marriage, and other factors that shape the experience of the marriage.[14] A woman's ability to reconstruct her self-concept is also a significant factor in adjustment to widowhood.[15]

Unfortunately, some of the factors that have the potential for shaping a woman's experience of widowhood have received little attention in either the sociological or gerontological research. For example, in many of the studies I reviewed, race or ethnicity does not appear to be a variable that is examined as a factor influencing adjustment to widowhood, even though in some cases the samples are racially mixed. Although the impact of race and ethnicity on widowhood bears further study, other factors, such as economic status, education, health, social support, and social role complexity, seem to play a greater role in the adjustment to widowhood than ethnicity alone.

Another variable that might have an impact on the experience of widowhood is the presence of violence or abuse in a marriage. The consequences of abuse and violence on the experience of widowhood are not entirely clear. Many of the sociological studies on widows do not cite abuse as a variable considered in the research conducted. There are complex issues of power and control and psychological dependence in relationships in which abuse occurs. Violence against women is an experience that does not respect age and an important issue that must be confronted. These factors have the potential to complicate significantly the experience of grief following the loss of one's spouse and deserve further attention and research.

The loss of a life partner is a broader issue than widowhood in heterosexual relationships. The loss of a long-term life partner in a committed lesbian relationship might have features both parallel to and distinct from the experience of widowhood. As more attention is paid to the life issues of lesbian women, partner loss in committed relationships might become the subject of further research.[16]

The Reality of Loss

Women who become widowed experience a significant life transition that requires adjustment and adaptation. Although the loss of the relationship might be the most significant, widowhood also might bring a loss of one's accustomed social role as a wife. In addition, many widows might experience reduction or loss of income following their husband's death. The widow's expectation of the future must change as the prospect of growing old with her spouse is no longer a reality. This loss of anticipated future is an intrapsychic loss, or an internal experience of loss triggered by an external event.[29] One's place in one's family or in the larger social system of friends might also change, bringing about a systemic loss.[30] All these losses might be a part of the experience of bereavement, "a specific state initiated by the death of someone who is close and dear."[31]

Grief is the normal emotional response to loss and bereavement. The experience of grief is unique for each individual and can include a wide range of emotions from sadness and anger to relief. Grief is also shaped by the circumstances of the death. When a death is anticipated, as in the case of a lengthy illness preceding death, the adjustment to widowhood might be eased.[32] This relief is particularly common when death relieves the husband from suffering.[33]

Researchers on grief and mourning, such as John Bowlby, have noted identifiable patterns and movements to the overall process of grief.[34] Progression through the grief process, although potentially an intense emotional experience, generally leads to a resolution of the bereaved's investment in the deceased and adaptation to the loss.

One of the central tasks of widowhood is moving through the process of grieving and adjusting to the losses that accompany this life transition. Normal grief does have an endpoint, and though one's life is never quite the same after a significant loss, life can continue to be enjoyable and have a sense of meaning and purpose.

Widows in the Church

As long as marriage has been a social institution, widowhood has been a reality. Within the Christian tradition, concern for the widowed is expressed in both the Hebrew Scriptures and in the New Testament. Because widows did not have legal or economic status in the ancient world, they were considered vulnerable and in need of protection.[17] As a part of their religious duty, the ancient Hebrews were called on to provide for the most vulnerable, which included the poor, the orphaned, and the widowed.[18] One of the church's first benevolent works was to provide care for widows (Acts 6:1-7).[19] Recent research indicates that not only did the church support its older widows, but by the second century, a clerical order for older widows existed.[20] Older widows, who met the requirements for entrance into this order, held a special place in the life of the church.[21] This order comprised "the most prominent group of women in the first three centuries of the church."[22]

The early Christian church provided for its older widows and honored their place in the church. Today many congregations are made up of largely older women, many of whom are widowed.[23] If the demographics in other mainline Protestant churches are similar to those in the United Methodist Church, then in many churches, congregations have a larger proportion of older people than the general population. A 1994 Survey of United Methodist Opinion indicated that 60 percent of the laity are female and 15 percent of the laity (both male and female) are widowed.[24] In 1994, 61.4 percent of the laity were over the age of fifty, and 32.8 percent were sixty-five-plus, compared to 25.5 percent and 12.6 percent of the general U.S. population.

If these statistics are correct, they suggest that the percentage of older women in the United Methodist Church is fairly high. Because 15 percent of the laity are widowed and 60 percent of the laity are women, we can estimate that there are a fair number of widowed women in the churches. It might well be that the patterns of the early church are being reversed.[25] Although the early church supported its widows, the contemporary church might be economically sustained and led by the widows in its midst.

Images of Older Widows

When I was first widowed, people just did not know what to say. They'd come by and we'd sit and look at each other. I guess they was afraid of saying the wrong thing. People that I'd known for fifty years just couldn't talk to me for awhile. That was the hardest thing, almost harder than losing Bill, was everyone treating me so different-like. It took me longer to get over that than it did to get over his death. Well, you never really get over it, you just go on anyway, 'cause that's what he would have wanted me to do. But anyway, folks finally started comin' round again. . . . So in a way, it's not been as hard as I thought it would be."

—Carrie Jones, age ninety-one

Fifteen seminary students each interviewed an older woman (fourteen of whom were widowed).[26] In almost all cases, the students reported that the particular older woman interviewed was not "typical." Although it was unclear exactly what the image of a typical older woman was, what did emerge was a view that older women who were physically healthy, engaged in life, and enjoying a high level of life satisfaction were somehow not typical. This experience suggests that the intersection of ageism and sexism continues to shape stereotypical images of older women.[27]

A number of the older women in this study, like Carrie Jones quoted above, reported that their own experience of widowhood did not seem to fit their expectations. Several reported that the experience of widowhood was not as bad as had been expected. One woman stated that she thought that she was faring better than others might be. One respondent stated that people often think of a widow as "a little bent over old lady," but that she thought widows were "just like anybody else."[28] These statements suggest that widows themselves are likely to hold and be affected by negative or stereotypical images of widowhood.

Well-Being in Widowhood

The death of one's spouse is presumed to be one of the most stressful life events that can occur. As noted above, this event brings with it multiple losses. Previous research has indicated possible links between the death of one's spouse and higher rates of illness and death.[35] Anecdotal reports often indicate that some older spouses often die within a year or two of their spouse's death.

One way to measure the impact of widowhood is to evaluate a woman's own internal or subjective experience of well-being. To what extent do widowed women rate their own lives as fulfilling and meaningful? This question was explored in a longitudinal study by Lund, Caserta, and Dimond.[36] Lund and his colleagues examined three indicators that measured the impact of bereavement on subjective well-being. Measures of depression, life satisfaction, and perceived health covered "the continuum from specific to global and from transitory to stable dimensions" of subjective well-being.[37]

The outcomes of this study indicated that widowhood had a less severe effect on subjective well-being than anticipated by the researchers.[38] The people in this study did show increased levels of depression in the first few months of bereavement, but after several months their levels of depression were similar to the non-bereaved respondents.[39] Life satisfaction for the bereaved was also lower than for the nonbereaved but only in the first month after death. Perceived health scores were about the same.

Overall, the findings of this study indicate that although the death of one's spouse in later life does affect subjective well-being, the impact is not generally long lasting. Although the authors cite a number of limits to their study, their work indicates that the death of one's spouse in later life might not be as debilitating as expected.[40]

This study by Lund and colleagues is one of a number of studies that support the claim that grief is a normal process following a death.[41] In the process of grieving, individuals experience a wide range of emotions that might include anger, sadness, depression, or relief. Older women might experience a temporary decline in subjective well-being in the first few months of bereavement; however, most are able to move through this grief process and become reengaged in life. This does not mean that the impact of the loss is not felt, but that older women continue to have the capacity to adjust to loss and find new meaning in life.

Surviving and Thriving: Relevant Factors

Although some general patterns can be discerned in the experience of bereavement, the experience of widowhood is different for each woman. Some women are able to move through the mourning process and return to a level of functioning and life satisfaction near, at, or even above preloss levels, but others have more difficulties that might result in complicated grief reactions.

A number of variables might affect a woman's adjustment to widowhood. Some of the variables examined by sociologists include social networks, social supports, coping strategies, religious belief, health, community integration, and the degree to which a woman is able to reshape her self-concept. This literature is quite extensive. The limitations of space, however, only allow for a brief examination of a few representative studies that might be informative for pastoral care providers.

The Importance of Social Networks

One of the pioneering researchers of widowhood is Helen Lopata. Her landmark 1973 study, *Widowhood in an American City*, is an extensive survey of widows in the Chicago area.[42] Although this study was not restricted to older women, the mean age of the widows in the study was sixty-eight.[43] *Women As Widows*, a follow-up study published in 1979, specifically looked at the various support systems available to these women and the extent to which these support systems were used.[44] Many of the widows in this study failed to use "many of the supports deemed beneficial in modern urban environments."[45]

Lopata's study indicated that many of these widows showed limited involvement in support activities and social support systems outside the family.[46] A disturbing finding of her study was the absence of helping professionals, including clergy, who provided assistance immediately before and following the husband's death.[47] When clergy are mentioned, it is usually in terms of their failure to "provide expected and needed help."[48]

Religious Beliefs

More recent studies suggest findings somewhat different from those of Lopata. Her study might have been significantly influenced by the sample, who were primarily urban women, generally of the same generation and of similar age. Kathleen Glass's study of older adults' coping resources indicates that many women found religious beliefs and rituals to be a helpful resource in coping with the husband's death.[49] Women were more likely than men to find church attendance and religious beliefs helpful in adjusting to their husband's death, and "religious belief was a marker associated with the healthy functioning of widows but not widowers."[50] It must be noted that the subjects of Glass's study were identified through "church burial records from Catholic parishes in two Midwestern cities," thus increasing the possibility of the positive influence of religious beliefs and rituals.[51]

Community Integration

Other factors measured to evaluate adjustment to widowhood include the degree to which a woman is integrated into the life of her community and the level of stress and the number of difficulties in daily life. One study that examined these factors began with the hypothesis that widows would be less integrated into their communities, experience higher levels of stress and more daily "hassles," have fewer social supports, and be more likely to seek social supports than nonwidowed women.[52] This hypothesis was not supported by the findings of the study.[53]

Pellman's study indicates that widowhood, by itself, is not an accurate predictor of either community integration or the experience of stress and "hassles" in daily life.[54] A finding of this study, which surprised the researcher, was that those most likely to seek out social support seemed least in need of it. Pellman also found that both widowed and nonwidowed participants who were more integrated into the communities experience fewer "hassles" in daily living and lower stress levels.[55]

Links between Social Networks and Social Support

Schuster and Butler examined the links between social support, social networks, and adjustment to bereavement.[56] This particular study made a distinction between social networks and social support, or types of help received. The findings of this study were consistent with earlier research that indicates long-term adjustment to bereavement is multidimensional. The presence of two of these dimensions, social networks and support, can have a positive impact on adjustment to bereavement.[57] Social support and social networks, however, were not synonymous, and each had a different impact on the adjustment to bereavement. The frequency of social contact had less impact on mental health than the amount of "affective," or emotional, support and assistance with practical tasks, or what researchers called "instrumental social support."[58]

Furthermore, the timing of the help seems critical. Both affective and instrumental help received immediately after death (in the first few days or weeks) had the most influence over later adjustment and functioning.[59] This study shows that the support received at the time of death had a significant impact on mental health and adjustment to the loss.[60] This confirms that pastoral support given during the acute phase of grief can positively affect the later course of bereavement.

Summary

The sociological research reviewed helps provide a more accurate picture of the experience of widowhood. Identifying some of the factors that affect a woman's adjustment to widowhood, such as social support and religious beliefs, can help us develop effective strategies of care. We now turn to the second task of this chapter, examining the reconstruction of self-concept in widowhood in light of developmental theory. I will examine both psychological and sociological dimensions of the redefinition of self that often accompanies widowhood. Both of these dimensions of self are explored in light of feminist critiques of developmental theory.

Psychological Dimensions of the Redefinition of Self

The theoretical assumptions that we hold, whether conscious or unconscious, often shape what we see in a particular situation or how we interpret what we observe. I have chosen to use the rather blunt phrase of "dying off or drying up" to reflect stereotypical expectations for older widows. These stereotypes are reflected in Carrie Jones's quotes earlier in the text. The often articulated fears that an older widow will die shortly after her husband's death or be unable to manage the affairs of her daily life also reflect hidden assumptions. The implicit assumption is that a woman whose sense of self has been significantly identified with her husband does not have a well developed sense of autonomous self. If adult development is defined in terms of a separate autonomous self, then such a woman surely has not made much progress developmentally, and it is not expected that she will do so late in life.

Many developmental theories, including that of Erik Erikson, hold that development progresses through stages, moving from fusion of self and other to an autonomous separate self.[61] In these developmental theories, connectedness reflects a less well developed sense of self. Feminist theorists have challenged theories of the self that emphasize an autonomous, separate self as the goal of development.[62] Jean Baker Miller argues that this autonomous self does not fit women's experience.[63]

Feminist reconstructions of developmental theory have argued that women develop a sense of self in relation to others.[64] Miller, along with Gilligan and

Surrey, suggests that women's experience of self is a "self-in-relation".[65] Surrey states:

> The self-in-relation model assumes that other aspects of self (e.g. creativity, autonomy, assertion) develop within this primary context. That is, other aspects of self-development emerge in the context of relationships, and there is no inherent need to disconnect or to sacrifice relationship for self-development.[66]

The intention of this theoretical framework of "self-in-relation" is not to idealize women's relational capacities, but to provide a way of understanding development that is more descriptive of women's experience.[67] The concept of self-in-relation can help us see the reorganization of self that occurs in widowhood not as a result of earlier developmental failure, but as part of a woman's ongoing development of self within a relational matrix.

The redefinition of self as self-in-relation provides a framework for reevaluating Erik Erikson's developmental theory as it might be applied to older widows. In Erikson' schema, a central developmental stage of late adulthood is "generativity vs. stagnation," whereas identity formation is seen as a task of early adulthood.[68] Generativity is concerned with the care and guidance of the next generation. Erikson also sees generativity as including "productivity and creativity."[69]

From the perspective of Erikson's theory, a widow's redefinition of self could be understood as necessary because she had not adequately accomplished the task of identity formation as a young adult. Thus, instead of attending to the proper task of late adulthood, generativity, she is completing an earlier developmental task.

If, however, we reconfigure Erikson's developmental schema in light of the concept of self-in-relation, we come to a different assessment. All developmental tasks occur within the context of relationships. Older widows, who have spent much of their lives directed toward the care of others in the roles of wife and mother, now are able to direct their creative and generative energies toward their own self-definition and development while still remaining meaningfully connected to others. Widows who are successfully able to reconstruct their self-concept might now define themselves in the context of a broader network of relationships, rather than in terms of a primary relationship with a spouse.

The task of redefining the self-in-relation, although difficult, provides an opportunity for growth. A woman's definition of a self-in-relation during marriage might be significantly shaped by her relationship with her husband. Many women in the current cohort of older women have defined themselves, or been defined, in terms of traditional roles. A number of women, currently in their seventies and older, went directly from the parental (paternal) home to reside with their husbands. The period of widowhood might be the first time a woman has lived alone. Although this new living situation might be a daunting, even frightening prospect, it can also be a time of liberation and self-discovery.

A woman's sense of self-in-relation as a widow might be defined by a more diffuse network of relationships that might include a support group of other widowed women, and relationships with her children, a religious community, and the larger community of which she is a part. Research has also indicated that widows who are more integrated into the community and well related to others report higher levels of subjective well-being. Involvements with this wider network might provide new opportunities for growth and the chance to experiment with new self-understandings.

A woman might come to an understanding of herself that is defined as much by her own interests and internal experiences as well as her relationships to others. A story that illustrates this change was reported to me by a friend who was concerned about how her mother would adjust to widowhood. She perceived her mother's identity as being significantly defined by her relationship with her husband. Her mother's first act of independence was to cancel a magazine subscription that came to her husband, because it reflected his interest and not hers. I have seen such small acts of independence and moves toward a new understanding of self repeated by women relatives and church members who move beyond the initial grief of widowhood to a reengagement of life on their own terms.

Sociological Perspectives on Self-concept

Widowhood brings about a number of changes in a woman's external world that might also lead to changes in both her identity and self-concept.[70] One of the tasks facing the widow is the reconstruction of her self-concept.[71] According to Lopata, the self-concept is composed of several elements.

> It contains packages of pervasive identities, such as woman, black, old, widow (in societies in which it really is a pervasive identity); of social role identities with their idiosyncratic variations, such as wife and friend in couple-companionate relations; and of what I call the "generalized self" images of the self as a certain type of person that transcend role and situational contexts.[72]

While each element has its own boundaries, the entire composition might undergo reconstruction or revision at times of transition or significant life events.[73]

The degree to which a woman's sense of self has been shaped by her social roles as wife and mother will affect her experience of widowhood. If a woman's identity and sense of self have been largely shaped by identification with her husband's identity, the task of reshaping her self-concept following her husband's death might be more difficult. Many women, however, seem able to redefine themselves successfully following the death of their husbands, despite the challenges of this task.[74]

In the current group of women over the age of sixty-five, the earlier reconstruction of the self-understanding at the time of marriage to include the new identity of wife is likely to have been more extensive for a woman than her husband's reconstruction of self-concept as he assumed a new role and identity. Berger and Kellner report that this reconstruction of self-concept is also more extensive for middle- and upper-class women than lower-class women.[75]

Just as marriage requires the reconstruction of self-concept, so too does the death of one's husband. As the role of wife is left behind, a woman "enters temporarily the role of widow."[76] In the current U.S. context, however, the role of widow does not have a stable or pervasive identity. Once the socially accepted period of mourning is over, others might no longer ascribe this role to her; thus, she is left in limbo. She can no longer claim the role of wife or reenter into the identity of a single woman.[77] One way out of this dilemma is to find an identity in which roles and relationships are not defined by marital status. Although the role of mother usually continues, when children are grown it may no longer provide the organizing center it once did.[78] No other role effectively replaces "the set of relations, emotions, and sentiments of the role of wife."[79]

One of the key factors in determining the level of ease or difficulty in the task of reconstructing a woman's sense of self-concept following the death of her husband is the balance of dependence, independence, and interdependence present in the marriage. "Interdependence" is defined as the extent to which the couple's lives and identities were intertwined.[80] In interdependent marriages, couples tend to communicate more frequently, share household and parental tasks, and develop a more companionate form of marriage.[81] A high degree of interdependence is also shown by women who are quite involved in their husband's roles.

In her landmark study of widows in the Chicago area, Lopata found that interdependence was higher for middle- and upper-class couples than working- and lower-class couples. Lopata also found that the higher the degree of interdependence in the marriage, the higher the initial degree of disorganization in the self immediately following the husband's death.[82] In these interdependent marriages, the initial experience of loneliness was also greater following the death of the husband.[83] Women who had a greater sense of identity independent from their husbands and the roles of wife and mother usually showed lower levels of initial disorganization following the husband's death. This lower level of disorganization was also found in marriages in which spouses followed parallel tracks without much overlap.[84] In a more recent (1993) study, Wortman and associates found that the social role complexity, which is present in many African American marriages, acts as a positive factor that might lessen the negative impact of the husband's death.[85]

Widows employ various strategies to deal with this experience of disorganization and the need to reconstruct the self-concept. Some of these strategies include learning new skills in order to complete tasks once done by the husband.[86] Immediately following the death of her husband a woman might feel somewhat less competent as she takes on new tasks; however, women interviewed later in their widowhood were more likely to report an increased sense of competence as a consequence of learning new skills.[87] Women with higher levels of education were more likely to "engage in self-concept reconstruction."[88] This higher likelihood of engagement appeared to be true regardless of when in her life the woman acquired her education. Lopata also identified a connection between education, social isolation, and changes in self-concept.[89]

Our normative assumptions and definitions of self shape how we evaluate the reconstruction of self-concept. If we define self as an autonomous, separate self, then the interdependence that Lopata describes might be seen as problematic. If we define self as self-in-relation, then interdependence simply becomes a category that describes women's experience. Older widows might continue patterns of interdependence within a broader framework of relationships.

Suggestions for Ministry with Widows

Several of the studies reviewed indicate that some of the stereotypical images of widowhood as a time of isolation, loneliness, and low life satisfaction might not represent an accurate picture for many women. Periods of isolation and loneliness might accompany widowhood but are more likely to occur in the early stages of widowhood. The literature also indicates that widowhood is a varied experience. Some women move through the normal process of grief and return to an active engagement with life, while others face complications in this process.

What conclusions might be drawn regarding the church's ministry to and with widows? Can the church reclaim its early tradition in which widows were valued by the church, provided care and support, and given a prominent place in the church's ministry? Here are some specific suggestions for the church's ministry with widows in light of recent research.

1. Clergy are often the first helping professional to attend to the bereaved through their role in conducting funeral services. Clergy and other pastoral care givers need to be educated about the process of normal grief. Knowledge of the factors associated with complicated grief might provide opportunities for earlier intervention and appropriate referral.

2. The impact of the funeral service itself should not be underestimated. Glass's study indicates that for the current group of elderly women, the traditional role of clergy in providing religious rituals following death is still valued. Funerals often mark the official initiation into public dimensions of the grieving process and the role of widow. Clergy who take the time to help older women identify the religious rituals that are most meaningful to them and design funeral services that will respond to the unique religious and emotional needs of widows and their families will offer a valuable service. Thoughtful pastoral care in the acute stages of grief might have a positive impact on the longer term process.

3. Practical help received early in the grief process can make a positive difference in the adjustment to widowhood. Schuster's and Butler's study indicated that both affective (or emotional) and instrumental (or practical) help received early in

the grief process had a significant impact on later mental health and adjustment to bereavement. Many churches provide informal networks for both affective and instrumental help. The most common form of instrumental help in churches is to provide a meal for family members after a funeral. The provision of the post-funeral meal also reminds the new widow that she is a part of a larger community of faith. It reminds her that the church can be an ongoing source of social support. This sharing around the table is also reminiscent of communion, one of the central ritual and liturgical acts of the church that reminds us of the sacred story that shapes us as Christians.

4. The formation of more formal networks to provide both affective and instrumental help to widows early in the grieving process would have a positive impact. This assistance might take the form of instrumental help with financial matters, home maintenance and repair, shopping, and other aspects of daily living. Many laity feel inadequate to provide emotional support at the time of death and are willing to offer instrumental help.[90] It is important that such instrumental help is not devalued. Laity can be encouraged to see the importance of the instrumental help that many are willing to provide. This encouragement might take the form of a bank of volunteers to help widows with specific tasks.

5. The support of others who have experienced widowhood can be a positive factor in adjustment to bereavement.[91] Those who have moved through the normal grief process and found new ways to be engaged in life can be an important resource to those who are newly widowed. One secular model currently in operation is the American Association of Retired Persons' "Widow to Widow" program. The church might also provide opportunities for women to socialize not only with other widows, but with people of all ages through women's societies and Sunday school classes or other support groups. Where possible, women should be encouraged to maintain relationships that were in existence before their husband's death. Many churches now offer short-term grief groups for the recently bereaved. Such groups are valuable not only because they offer a structured environment for constructive grief work, but also because these groups often become the basis of an informal ongoing support network of widows.

6. The church can facilitate or enhance the process of reconstruction of the self-concept through its educational and pastoral care ministries. Women who have a sense of identity in addition to the traditional roles of wife and mother seemed to fare better in this task of self-concept reconstruction. Through its educational and outreach ministries as well as opportunities for leadership, the church might help older women find interests and identities outside of these traditional roles while not diminishing or disdaining the importance of these roles. Churches can actively encourage women to become involved in a variety of ministries within the church community. It is important that these opportunities for ministry expand beyond the traditional roles of volunteer secretarial help. Involvement in various outreach ministries, such as tutoring children or hands-on projects such as

construction of a "Habitat for Humanity" home, might provide the opportunity for women to develop new skills and new competencies that contribute to a new self-understanding.

7. Preventative pastoral care programs can help women understand some of the adjustments to widowhood before the actual event of the husband's death. In many cases, the husband's death can be anticipated. Offering courses that educate women about the grief process might be helpful. The timing of these offerings might be important. Women who are burdened with the daily tasks of caregiving for a critically ill spouse might have a greater need for respite care. Short courses that are directed to all the older adults in a congregation about planning for death, such as presentations dealing with the ethical and legal questions involved in medical power of attorney, advanced directives, and funeral planning might ease difficult decisions near or at the time of death.

8. Offering women opportunities to gain new skills needed to complete tasks once undertaken by their husbands might increase a sense of competence and confidence and lead to a new self-understanding. Such opportunities might involve providing assistance with or instruction in matters such as managing one's finances, small home repairs, or auto maintenance.

9. In addition to providing assistance in the immediate aftermath of death, the church can also provide opportunities for a widow's continued engagement in life and the faith community. In order for this to occur, the church must challenge sexist and ageist attitudes and stereotypes about widowed women. This challenge includes questioning developmental schemas that might shape our expectations about what kind of growth and development are possible for older widows.

10. Given that widowhood often has a negative impact on a woman's economic status, the church might undertake legislative advocacy for widowed women as part of its commitment to social justice. Remembering that commitment to care for the widows has been a part of the church's ministry since its beginning can provide the contemporary church with motivation and a mandate as it seeks to develop a contemporary model of ministry for, with, and by widowed women.

Conclusion

Older women can not only survive but thrive as widows. Widowhood presents both challenges and opportunities for growth. For many women, widowhood presents an opportunity to come to new self-understandings.

In this chapter, I have sought to develop a picture of widowhood that is closer to the lived experience of women than prevalent myths and stereotypes. Such a picture will allow us to design ministries that are more likely to meet the needs and use the gifts of older women.

Part 3

Setting the Pace:
Developmental Issues

Women remain sensitive to certain issues that alter the movement, flow, and the stride of their development. Using five vignettes, Nancy Ramsay shows how issues of power and empowerment, trust, vocation, competence, and embodiment recur in the lives of women and influence their growth and differentiation. Teresa Snorton focuses on the issue of self-care as a developmental issue for African American women, especially when they overextend themselves as the altruistic and all-powerful matriarchs. Snorton's findings become applicable to other women who neglect themselves in an imbalance of care of the other over care of the self. Carroll Saussy, writing in the last third of her anticipated life span, elaborates on the issue of healthy eating in relationship to mind, body, and spiritual development.

The progression of a series of traditional or "natural stages" is often broken by the single lifestyle (Mary Lynn Dell). No single life cycle or model of adult development adequately describes the tasks of adulthood for individuals who do not marry. Furthermore, for women with acquired disabilities and lives interrupted by chronic illness or trauma, no life cycle is predictable (Paula Buford). Disabled women face issues that are more common in older adulthood than in midlife or early transitions. Although Nancy Ramsay, Teresa Snorton, Carroll Saussy, Mary Lynn Dell, and Paula Buford make no claim to exhaust the many developmental issues unique to women, they accent the way women are setting the pace in the emerging patterns of their own development.

Truth, Power, and Love: Challenges for Clergywomen across the Life Span

Nancy J. Ramsay

Recent literature in developmental theory proposes a relational model in which maturity is reflected in the depth and complexity of empathic connections as well as a corresponding depth of self-understanding.[1] Similarly, recent theological literature on the exercise of power also describes its intrinsic relationality and discloses its fulfillment as mutual empowerment.[2] Both these lines of research refute more long-standing, linear constructions of the self that unilaterally support an autonomous self-exercising power. They suggest instead the importance of relational authenticity as an appropriate norm for encouraging women's exercise of power across the life span. Any discussion of women's power and authority must also necessarily address the disempowering effect of sexism and the need for nurturing assistance to counteract both internalized and external forces that constrain women's empowerment.

Relational authenticity relies on the skillful practice of empathic connection. Variously constructed in response to the needs of women at different points in the life span, it includes a dynamic interaction of love, truth, and power. Several case illustrations of women in young adult, midlife, and older adult years disclose this dynamic interaction. These illustrations also include cultural differences as a lens for reflection on expressions of relational power. Predictable themes that will inform reflections here include the paradoxical relation of finitude and empowerment, embodiment, generativity, fear, courage, agency, and hope.

The church's complicity in disempowering and marginalizing women suggests a particular value in paying attention to the experience of clergywomen regarding issues of power and authority. The relational developmental model articulated by theorists at the Stone Center at Wellesley College is particularly useful for clergywomen, because this model explicitly addresses themes of love, power, and truth that are so central for the daily practice of ministry.[3] Moreover, this model identifies relational competence as a motivation and goal for women across the life span in ways that immediately resonate with experience in ministry. If women's development as beings-in-relation[4] is described by the metaphor of conversation, and "voice" refers to the self, then relational competence describes the skillful engagement in conversation in which one's voice is clear, honest, self-aware, and respectful, and one's listening is attentive, respectful, and inviting. Relational competence is experienced as authenticity in relation.[5] Although we will explore authenticity-in-relation as a motivation and goal for clergywomen, it functions normatively in the lives of many women.

Truth, Power, and Love:
Challenges for Clergywomen across the Life Span

Whenever clergywomen gather, our stories disclose the challenging ways truth, power, and love emerge in the daily practice of ministry. We manage current conflicts in the congregation, deal with staff relations, cope with the care needs of congregants, balance professional development and personal needs, and discern ethical issues. Often we must summon the courage to speak truth to power and wonder how to do so in our own voice. Daily we discern how to exercise power authentically, discriminate between behaviors that offer care and those that encourage dependency, and negotiate the call to love self and neighbors.

The five vignettes that follow suggest challenges clergywomen face when practicing ministry authentically as young adults, at midlife, and nearer retirement. We will use these vignettes constructed from many interviews with clergywomen to reflect on the usefulness of feminist developmental theory and theology for enhancing the experience of authenticity in relationships in the practice of ministry.

A Young Adult Clergywoman: Pat

Pat is a twenty-eight-year-old Caucasian woman who is in her second year as pastor of a small, one hundred-year old Presbyterian (U.S.A.) congregation in a county seat community surrounded by a mix of agriculture and light industry. She married shortly before coming to the congregation and is now pregnant. She is the first woman pastor in the congregation. Pat excelled in seminary and at graduation won an award in preaching. There are four other clergywomen serving in the presbytery who range in age from thirty-eight to fifty-six. Pat had hoped for more connection with them but finds herself "not in synch" with their interests. Pat is concerned about how her pregnancy will complicate her growing sense of her professional identity in the congregation.

Pat describes herself as aware that claiming her own voice is a challenge she is growing into. She still finds herself sometimes stepping into the role she believes her responsibilities require, though she does not feel completely at home in it. Claiming her voice is especially needed when she is relating to those two or three times her age who are facing issues of finitude hard to imagine from her more limited experience. Yet she can sense an emerging confidence and congruence in her pastoral identity. She increasingly prefers a more relational style for exercising her authority in ministry. Sometimes her previous need to prove the "correctness" of her point returns when she is in a more public sphere, such as the local ministerial association or planning the community Thanksgiving service, where she was the only clergywoman and the youngest by twenty years. In her preaching she finds she sometimes now allows her own passion for her topic to inform her delivery, but she still frequently wonders about how her sermon will be received and what the congregation will think of it. This dynamic also emerged recently at a meeting of the educational committee, where she proposed using a denominational curriculum for children and youth. A committee member the age of Pat's parents objected. Pat felt this response was condescension about her competence as a young adult and an indirect challenge to her authority as pastor. The curriculum was adopted, but she has questions about the process.

Middle-Age Clergywomen: Gloria, Margaret, and Karen

Gloria is forty-eight. As a pastor in the Christian Methodist Episcopal Church, she is one of the very few African American clergywomen serving in an African American congregation. Gloria is divorced and the mother of two young adult children. She is taking courses in a nearby seminary, serving her congregation, and holding down her job with a local insurance agency. She has the support of her bishop, who recently moved her from her position as an assistant pastor in a downtown church to serve as pastor in a small town congregation in a nearby county while she gets her seminary education. She is keenly aware of the importance of his support, given the opposition of many to the validity of her call. Gloria's involvement in the ministry began with her work as a Sunday school teacher whose gifts became evident as her class grew in size and vitality. Gradually, she began to trust her experience and gained the grudging support of her pastor for her emerging sense of call. She served as assistant pastor for six years. Her status as a divorced woman was more of an issue then, when some thought she was using her activity to search for another husband. She says she tried to downplay her femininity then but is now feeling more confident of herself as a woman and imagines her age is helping others be more at ease as well.[6] She does know she must find more time to care for herself physically and spiritually in the midst of juggling her work, school, and pastoral responsibilities.

Gloria says she has come to imagine herself as a midwife among her parishioners. They are coming to trust her care. She is especially aware that she needs to address issues of both personal and social transformation in their lives, because stories about racism, unemployment, drug abuse, and marital strife are emerging in her conversations with her members.[7] She knows many pastors in her denomination and congregants doubt her authority for ministry, but she has found her increased confidence in the fruits of her relationships in ministry help her not to worry unduly about those who doubt her call. It is still a challenge for her to think her experience is honored in the more public dimensions of ministry. Her gender and recent ordination sometimes mean her life experience and gifts are ignored by clergymen, as happened, for example, at a recent denominational event. She wishes she had more women colleagues with whom to talk or an older mentor to guide her in the decisions, but she is confident about the future of her ministry.

Margaret's experience as a forty-five-year-old Caucasian, Episcopal clergy-woman is different in some ways from Gloria's. Margaret has been an ordained Episcopal priest for three years. Her husband is a college professor in the nearby city where Margaret got her seminary degree. Her children were finishing high school and entering college when she felt her call sufficiently to begin exploring ordained ministry. She left her work as director of a nonprofit agency to attend seminary. As it did for Gloria, the support of her bishop made a big difference in Margaret's journey.

Margaret reports that entering ministry at midlife has complicated her experience of her authority for ministry. She sometimes feels "out of order." She thinks the process of trusting herself in the professional role might be more difficult now than if she had begun when she was twenty years younger. Although the sacramental character of ministry in her denomination has given her authority as a pastor there are uncomfortable moments when she wishes she could borrow the confidence she earned in her earlier career. Through her experience of younger women coming to seminary out of college, she thinks her age and experience allow her to come to ministry not as a career but as a vocation she now can fulfill more fully than in her previous work. Still, it has been hard to become a "junior" colleague among clergy younger than she.

She describes the paradox of being more aware of the authenticity of what she knows and the reality of how much she does not know. It is still something of a challenge to yield the need for control and to trust more fully the authority that arises through relationships. In those relationships, however, she often experiences a level of connection that she and parishioners find helpful. Spiritually, she has found her experience of God enlarging as she regularly engages in the pastoral, teaching, preaching, and sacramental dimensions of her ministry.

Karen is a fifty-five-year-old Caucasian who entered seminary after college. She is the mother of three adult children. She divorced fifteen years ago as she gradually came to trust her sense of her sexual orientation as a lesbian. Eventually she left her original denomination, because she could no longer tolerate the secrecy and division between her personal and professional identity. The fear and secrecy increasingly took its toll on her capacity to minister effectively. She is now in her second parish as a pastor in the United Church of Christ, her denomination for the last ten years. Karen is still discrete about her relationship with another woman in the area, but she feels more authentic and whole. She describes herself as having to do a lot of "catching up" with herself to get rid of the effects of hiding and the silencing consequences of fear. She now revels in the new sense of power and authenticity she feels for sharing her gifts for ministry.

An Older Clergywoman: Irene

Irene is a sixty-two-year-old minister in the United Methodist Church. She is single. She has served five congregations since she entered ministry in her late thirties. Irene has served two working-class congregations in a nearby metropolitan area and is now in a rural setting on the perimeter of that area. She anticipates retirement in the next three to five years.

Irene is a survivor of breast cancer, which was discovered and treated nine years ago. She describes that very real experience with finitude as contributing to changes in her style of ministry in the past decade. Before her illness she reports she waged a losing battle with workaholism and a "superwoman" style of ministry. Paradoxically, a brush with death was freeing. She is much more intentional about her use of her time and commitments relationally. She is careful to sustain her close friendships and ties with family alongside her ministry. In some ways she is still as involved, but she feels more in control of her work rather than being controlled by others' expectations.

She is surprised by how energized she feels in her ministry. Irene describes a deepening intimacy in her connections with parishioners and in her relationship with God. She mentions the calm and peace of Psalm 131 as increasingly descriptive of her sense of herself. This peace seems to be empowering for her ministry. Instead of the control that drove her efforts earlier, she now describes an internal sense of tender strength that leads her to exercise her authority for ministry unselfconsciously and authentically, such as in her worship leadership. At the same time, she also feels freer to use her authority to advocate for her congregants in the community. For example, she recently agreed to a request from area colleagues in ministry to speak before the zoning commission, whose decisions about proposed changes could seriously affect the quality of life of residents and the tax burden on many older adults. Instead of fuming quietly and ineffectively as she might have earlier, she has found it empowering to prepare for her presentation to the commission.

During her recovery from cancer, Irene consulted a nutritionist and describes how differently she experiences her body. She exercises regularly and reports a satisfaction in her experience of herself as a woman that was sorely missing earlier in her life, when her singleness and her gender were a painful combination. Now she feels an empowering integrity between her more positive experience of her embodiment and her pastoral identity.

These clergywomen's reflections describe varied experiences with the dynamic interplay among truth, power, and love. Certainly their developmental differences emerge as they cope with other challenges and contingencies. Each describes herself, however, as exploring issues of authenticity—how to speak in her own voice—

whether as a young woman or at the end of a career. Each acknowledges the challenge of authentic relationality.

How can Pat, at twenty-eight, hold onto her rightful authority when she thinks it is questioned, and at the same time acknowledge the inevitable limitations of her brief life experience? How does Margaret, at forty-five, trust the authorization that congregants offer and previous experience confirms when she is also out of order as a new clergywoman? Can she risk trusting the truth emerging in her connectedness with parishioners? Gloria describes the empowering relation of love and truth as she has trusted a sense of call sufficiently to gain the support of her bishop and the responsiveness of her congregants. How can she find the balance between caring for herself sufficiently with the frenetic demands of her two-career life, so there will be enough of her to share? How can Karen deepen the empowering authenticity-in-relation that her shift to a welcoming denomination has allowed? What steps did Irene take that have allowed the increasing sense of authenticity for ministry she reports? What does her description of the relation between embodiment and authenticity suggest for clergywomen in any developmental era? What does Irene's journey in ministry suggest about the paradoxical relation between finitude and the power of love and relationality? Developmental themes such as power and empowerment, trust, vocation, competence, and embodiment recur in the lives of these women, but their experience of authenticity as selves-in-relation evokes differing challenges across the life span as they experience an increasingly more differentiated sense of identity and relationality.

Feminist Developmental Theory

There are striking convergences in the experiences of these clergywomen and feminist developmental theory. Relationality as an essential feature of identity is the central affirmation of recent feminist research regarding women's development.[8] Building on earlier neoanalytic theory and object relations theorists, these researchers argue that identity is formed in a continuous relational developmental pathway. Identity is shaped through the practice of making and sustaining relationships, often first with one's mother and subsequently with an ever-enlarging web of connections. This notion is in contrast to earlier theories that defined the self as shaped through a linear progression of separation and individuation in which autonomy was the measure of maturity.[9] Rather than focus on this process of separation and individuation, feminist theorists describe the developmental process of relationship differentiation and elaboration. Development happens within relationships. The developmental process is an emotional-cognitive dialogue unfolding in a synchrony of increasingly complex relational being, so that development within the self and her relationships reciprocally inform one other.[10]

Love as mutually respectful care is a primary value in this theoretical model, in which relationality is described as both the goal and motivation for women's development.[11] Self-esteem develops through one's perceived competence in entering and sustaining important relationships of mutual growth and interaction. Competence is not measured by the self-reliance and autonomy of a separate self but by the capacity for relational being in which one's own creativity, insights, and individuality are clear within relationships where those same attributes of the other are also honored.[12] Pat, at twenty-eight, was beginning to know this. Older and midlife clergywomen are more convinced of the centrality of relational skills.

Relational competence requires the integration of personal and relational goals with all the diverse skills this competence entails. First among these is "accurate empathy" that is cognitively and affectively attuned and responsive to the subjective experience of the other.[13] Such attunement discloses the way in which relationality as lifelong conversation is an art to be practiced and refined. It presumes self-awareness that respects the particularity and the limitations of one's own voice and the values and experiences of one's own social location and context. Clarity about one's own voice and context allows one truly to engage nondefensively with the difference represented by the other's cognitive and affective experience. Pat, at twenty-eight, is working hard to be clear that her voice is her own, not that of a daughter or granddaughter. Karen's ability, at fifty, to repudiate secrecy and its silencing effects in her ministry reports a profound difference in her experience in ministry. Conversation in its ideal sense involves a readiness to be affected by, even changed by, the experience of the other. Empathy, as described here, welcomes difference as a resource for expanding one's own self-understanding rather than minimizing difference to preserve the illusion of similarity. Paradoxically, clarity about differences evidenced in each voice in a conversation provides for richer and more useful communication.

Empathy clearly presumes a value for mutuality in relationships with a necessarily reciprocal influence as well as openness to change. If the conversation is to flourish, each participant must bring to the conversation an appropriate vulnerability that includes honesty about one's needs as well as a desire to enhance the experience of the other. Mutuality, however, depends on the ability to balance love, truth, and power.[14] First, difficulty sharing one's own needs or receiving care distorts love, suggesting the importance of trust for the process of empathy. On the other hand, one can so accommodate to the needs of the other that one's own voice is lost or muted, and resentment and a sense of devaluation of one's self is likely. Pat describes this challenge as she continues to worry about how listeners receive her sermons, though she knows she is a competent preacher. This devaluation of her own voice is a distortion of truth. Finally, the experience of dominance by another precludes mutuality, because it signals objectification and manipulation and the silencing effect of the abuse of power.

Themes of power and empowerment arise in the process of mutually empathic engagement. A relational identity development model envisions power as bipolar. That is, the model defines power as the capacity to: be moved, respond, and move another.[15] It assumes power is expansive, rather than a closed or finite phenomenon one needs to hoard. In this developmental model, relational contexts are necessary for personal empowerment at cognitive and affective levels. The interaction creates a synergy that enlarges each party's energy and vision.[16] Agency for relational being is best understood as "agency-in-community."[17] In mutually empathic relationships, we expand one another's ability to affect the world and each other. Empowerment emerges from mutually empathic relationships in which we are truly engaged or heard and experience ourselves as also hearing another. Each woman seemed to have experience with this empowerment.

We need only think of the power that emerges in collaborative ventures in which we genuinely hear and encourage one another to share ourselves and what we know. Rather than using what we know to intimidate or compete, we use ourselves truly to understand and advance the experience of the relationship. Rather than using power to control, we use it to enlarge the resources of all involved. Margaret, forty-five, describes the shift toward this new way of experiencing power. Mutual empowerment is the goal of relational being and a guiding ethic of relational developmental models.

Locating agency in a relational context discloses ethical responsibility in a way different from separative definitions of the self. Responsibility is both redefined and enlarged, because the criteria for agency are no longer simply those of an individual's autonomy. Now responsibility involves the recognition that one has the capacity to act or fail to act on behalf of the interests of the other. We will signal this shift by using the term "response/ability."[18] Here power is defined in the service of care or love for self and other. Relational being presumes the importance of contexts in which people live. Interdependence now defines freedom rather than autonomy. Empathic attunement with the subjective experience of another cannot coincide with strategies that distance us from the consequences of our agency. Freedom is disciplined by relationality. It is also enlarged by relationality, for our own possibilities are expanded by the other's care. For example, both Gloria and Irene, whose ministries encourage agency-in-community, describe the importance of public advocacy for their sense of empowerment for ministry.

Just as the balance intended by mutuality is vulnerable to distortions, so this ethic of response/ability is also challenged by cultural and ecclesial distortions of women's experience of power. This ethic presumes women's agency. Prevailing patriarchal definitions of power have led many women to believe they cannot and perhaps ought not exercise genuine agency. Having internalized a subordinated role early in life, many women cannot imagine it could be appropriate to act in their own interests or that power could be shared. Young women in particular might also think it is dangerous to exercise power, because to do so requires breaking connections and risks the possibly isolating consequences of voicing difference from those with whom they are connected. Ecclesial tradition complicates these fears by its implication in the subordination of women so that, for example, acting on one's own interests could be defined as selfish or proud. An ethic of response/ability also presumes the importance of rightly naming differences in power that help define current relational contexts such as racism, classism, and heterosexism. The long-standing history of marginalization, violence, and devaluation that have accompanied these abuses of power quickly reveal the challenge of empathic attunement for women who seek to connect across these differences or become more aware of the contexts that shape their own identity.[19] Gloria's growing confidence despite the opposition of some clergymen in her denomination suggests the importance of her courage to name rightly her parishioners' needs.

Authenticity in relationship defines maturity in this relational development theory.[20] Authenticity involves a capacity for and a commitment to full affective and cognitive connection in relationships. Authenticity underscores the value of truth in this theory. It takes considerable courage to speak authentically with a readiness to engage the risks and likely conflicts and other challenges accurate empathy will include over time. Authenticity demonstrates the interwoven character of truth, power, and love in relational developmental models, for it presumes a commitment to response/ability in relationships and an appreciation for the empowerment that mutuality offers. Authenticity in relationship is surely a skill that requires practice and remains a goal across the life span. Yet it provides women at various developmental points a way of measuring their progress in relational competence.

Relational authenticity is a primary motivation and goal of pastoral identity. Authenticity assumes a more complex character in ministry, for pastoral identity involves not only relational authenticity as described above, but the clergywoman's evolving interaction with her particular theological tradition and intentional engagement in conversation with the experiences of those who speak in different theological voices. Joretta Marshall has described well the dynamic stability of relational development that is then expanded by another ongoing "conversation" with ministers' evolving understanding of their primary theological tradition.[21] She wisely claims the value of novelty or difference for continuing personal and professional development in ways that are consonant with relational theorists' stress on the role of difference as crucial for promoting personal and relational growth and empowerment. As people stretch to accommodate difference, each person experiences some level of redefinition and expansion of vision.[22] Gloria stretched to accommodate the way her experience challenged her denomination's norms. Karen realized she had to find a denomination that could better accommodate the level of difference her authentic practice required. The motivation and goal of authenticity for pastoral identity helpfully clarifies the complex challenge pastoral identity poses for clergy and certainly for clergywomen.

Authenticity discloses the multiple challenges clergywomen face in constructing truthful practices for exercising authority in a culture that inculcates a subordinated sense of self in women, and in a theological tradition whose teaching and norms for ministry have historically marginalized or silenced women's voices. Authenticity in the practice of ministry reflects an interactive and evolving relational and theological competence. It is felt internally and conferred publicly as the authority to practice ministry as a religious leader among the people of God. Because our experience of relational and theological competence accrues over time, we resolve recurring themes such as authority, power, or finitude differently across the life span. A relational, evolving understanding of authenticity presumes such central issues are never fully resolved but that they are experienced quite differently as we participate in increasingly complex, embodied, and varied relational networks.

Earlier we noted how an ethic of response/ability in the feminist relational developmental model discloses the vulnerability of women to the consequences of hierarchical and abusive constructions of power such as sexism, racism, classism, and heterosexism. We briefly acknowledged how a long-standing history of marginalization, violence, and devaluation for women signals the challenge of differences that are not benign sources of novelty but instead destructive barriers to relational empowerment and authenticity. These four abusive constructions of power often disempower women in at least the following similar ways:

1. We internalize a subordinate status (women clergy or female physician).
2. We pathologize experience ("hysterical" woman).
3. We discount experience ("just being emotional").
4. We deny experience (no right to be angry, have an idea, or express an idea worth sharing).[23]

All four of these experiences are disempowering, given our discovery that our power emerges in mutually empathic relationships in which the value of each is honored and engaging difference is essential for growth. It becomes obvious that skill in managing conflict and a capacity to cope with the emotion of anger are essential for the development of relational competence and authenticity. Yet these sources of disempowerment undermine authentic expressions of anger. For a person in a subordinated status, honesty about anger might be dangerous or self-destructive, especially given this culture's tolerance of violence against women and the economic vulnerability of a person in a subordinate role. In a culture that inculcates a marginalized status in women, anger might be pathologized as signaling a lack of impulse control. Similarly, anger might suggest immaturity because one believes affective experience is inherently inferior to reason. Finally, women often learn to deny their anger because it causes shame and guilt as well as increasing their vulnerability to further devaluation. The internalization of subordinate status for women is especially difficult because we participate in our own disempowerment and undermine the possibilities for authenticity.

Ironically, anger, a feeling many women fear, is a resource for their fuller experience of truth, power, and love. Irene's sense of empowerment and fuller integrity in her ministry because of her choice to protest injustice is suggestive here. Anger is an important resource for authentic relationality. Anger may represent our resources for passion, assertion, vitality, and communion, because it reasserts our power to resist devaluation, objectification, and marginalization either of ourselves or others.[24] Anger suppressed, in fact, endangers relationships, because anger signals the need for relational repair.[25] To rob people of the right to value their anger is to threaten the power of their love to restore, renew, and heal brokenness at personal, relational, and systemic levels. When women experience the denial or trivialization of their anger, their capacity to hope is undermined, for anger is a sign of hope, a resource for resisting devaluation and injustice at personal and systemic levels.[26] Paradoxically, honesty about anger expressed constructively is more likely to repair than break relational connections. Relationships are far more endangered by unspoken anger that fuels distorted connections such as resentment. "The appropriate expression of anger fosters both autonomy and connection, encouraging persons to trust their thoughts and feelings and to dare to be their true selves-in-relation."[27]

Relational development is at once a cognitive and an affective process. The consequences of sexism, racism, and classism are not only affectively disempowering for women. They also often undermine women's ability to experience themselves as able to think about ideas, critique them, and even create their own ideas. In *Women's Ways of Knowing* Belenky, Clinchy, Goldberger, and Tarule demonstrate that "women's self-concepts and ways of knowing are intertwined."[28] Rather than focusing on identity development, these researchers focused on epistemology. They explored how women in this culture predictably develop their views about what is true and by what authority they come to trust what they know. Although they do not make essentialist claims about the differences in women's ways of knowing, they do disclose the ways a patriarchal culture can impede and even silence a woman's ability to trust her experience and value her capacities to engage her ideas with those of others. Their research population included women of diverse ages and socioeconomic, educational, and racial experience, but it yielded a distinctive pattern of five shared epistemological perspectives that demonstrate a common struggle to resist the disempowering consequences of gendered stereotypes that devalue women's authority to know and learn and think creatively.[29] Using phrasing that describes a woman's capacity to imagine the authority of her own agency in knowing, the five perspectives move from an utterly external locus of control to an internal one that is highly self-aware and contextualized. The five perspectives are: silence, received knowledge, subjective knowledge, procedural knowledge (separate or connected), and constructed knowledge.

The researchers helpfully describe the sorts of familial and educational contexts that best foster women's positive sense of mind and voice in ways that once again affirm themes of truth, power, and loving connection. Their findings validate the priority relational development theory places on the cognitive and affective empowerment women experience through empathic connections, especially with their parents and teachers. They found that women were most empowered to learn and know whose families modeled interdependence and mutual care and respect, and whose mothers were intellectually and emotionally available to their children and able to "receive and hear what he or she has to say."[30] Similarly, those who experienced teachers in various settings who invited them to claim their ability to construct ideas and do what they needed to do were empowered to believe they could learn and know in their own voices.[31] One clear learning is that women do not "find our voices autonomously."[32]

From this study of the development of one's own agency in the experience of knowing, we can draw direct implications for seminary education that encourage women's continued development and growth in the practice of ministry. The study is also suggestive for any woman who enters graduate education. Those who begin seminary at midlife might well experience new dissonance as they enter seminary. They have already developed a more reflective sense of self with broader networks of belonging than they had as college graduates, but they might encounter a dis-empowering sense of disconnection in graduate academic contexts. Theological faculty will serve them best who not only build connections of care, but help validate women's life experience as an important resource for their engagement with biblical and theological texts. Younger women, on the other hand, might bring from the immediacy of their college experience skills in procedural knowing—the critical engagement with others' ideas—but need encouragement in developing the distinctiveness of their voice in conversation with those ideas, that is, to move more toward constructed knowing. Each needs encouragement in moving toward authenticity in knowing but is challenged differently by that goal. We can overhear this process in the experiences of Pat at twenty-eight, Margaret at forty-five, and Irene at sixty-two.

Feminist Theology

What is particularly striking about the developmental resources described above is the shared priority for authentic relationality that we find here and in contemporary feminist theological reflection on the interaction of love, truth, and power, especially in relation to the doctrine of the Trinity and in relation to the nature and exercise of power in religious leadership. I will briefly summarize some of this reflection and then explore ways in which these developmental and theological resources extend and correct each other.

The resounding affirmation of feminist theological reflection on the Trinity is that it clearly presents relationality as the primary character of who God is and in so doing affirms for humankind as well the priority of communion over individual being. Catherine LaCugna summarized the significance of the development of the doctrine of the Trinity for our knowledge about God and therefore ourselves, this way: "Love for and relationship with another is primary over autonomy. . . . Personhood, being-in-relation-to-another, was secured as the ultimate originating principle of all reality."[33]

Trinitarian doctrine also asserts the coequality of the three persons of the Trinity, signaling that the power God exercises is not hierarchical but personal.[34] Mutual respect and interdependence are presumed while honoring the uniqueness of each. Scriptural images of friendship are figured here.

A feature of this communion and divine friendship is the personal and relational empowerment that arises from diversity. "The shared life of all persons, whether human or divine, consists in the communion that arises out of genuine diversity among equals."[35] The complexity of God's truth, love, and power emerges more adequately by the synergy of Holy Wisdom generating and continuously sustaining creation and creatures, Jesus' compassionate love reuniting justice and love, and the Spirit's vitalizing and liberating power.[36]

Feminist theologians also find in the Trinity further resources for resymbolizing God's power and love differently from patterns based on hierarchy or omnipotence. Here God's power clearly serves love. It is "the liberating power of connectedness that is effective in compassionate love."[37] The power of God's love is not diminished by mutual interrelation and the vulnerability that accompanies it. Rather, through the creative and sustaining power of the Creator's presence, the solidarity in suffering of Jesus' ministry and death, and the liberating vitality of the Spirit, we come to see the fierce tenderness of God's redemptive love that emerges in compassionate resistance to the seeming finality of evil, suffering, and guilt.[38] Certainly the experiences of Gloria and Irene demonstrate the power of love as their ministries developed to include compassion and resistance. Karen also bore witness to the power of love to sustain resistance.

Yet in this new prizing of relationality as the very nature of God and therefore an interpretive key for creatures in God's image, we are also challenged to recognize that the reciprocity of relation and care God offers creation is also finally asymmetrical, for we are creatures whose lives are dependent on God.[39] Recalling the research sample for this chapter, this theme of mutuality but finally asymmetry also emerges in theological reflections on power in ministry contexts. It is an important theme in dialogue with relational developmental theory and crucial for understanding the complexity of authentic expressions of power by clergywomen. Margaret voiced this well when she described the importance of her symbolic power for authorizing her ministry as a priest as well as the empowerment she experienced in more mutual caring connections.

Postmodernity has helpfully disclosed power not as a commodity but as an intersubjective and dynamic reality that is experienced as an emotional expression of strength that ideally circulates within relationships.[40] A circulating intersubjective expression of strength describes well the ideal for the weblike exchange of power among clergy and congregants, but it is important to acknowledge that the experience for clergywomen is still more complex. Intrapsychically, we find our-selves coping with varying levels of internalized subordination that is the legacy of a patriarchal culture. Many women report that externalizing this internalized sub-ordinate identity so as to diminish its distortions is a lifetime project. Professionally, we function in ecclesial contexts that are highly complicit in this subordination of women, and like our congregants, we are shaped by ecclesial and cultural contexts quite confused about power and suspicious that it could be exer-cised authentically. Yet we function in roles that are historically and publicly authorized as associated with and representative of God's power.[41] This represen-tative influence is further compounded by symbolic power that accrues to clergy via our own self-understanding and the imaginative projections of congregants, especially as we engage in the priestly exercise of ministry in liturgical and caring contexts. Representative or institutional and symbolic features of clerical power are particularly important for understanding the enduring asymmetry in the power of clergy, for these roles qualify what are often experiences of mutuality in ministry. With congregants, our institutional identity is ever present, and the capacity for exercising symbolic power that represents the strength and presence of God's care must be as certain as our human vulnerability to the contingencies of existence. As anyone knows who has witnessed empowerment of a community when its minis-terial leadership exercised institutional power and rightly challenged injustice, or who has felt symbolic power in the skillful exercise of ritual practice to effect heal-ing, asymmetrical power is not in and of itself problematic. The norm for power is love that intends mutuality, not dependency or domination, in the community. Distortions in the exercise of power in congregational contexts might arise through the action and inaction of clergy or congregants or both.

The diverse and complex character of clergywomen's experiences of power is suggested in the trinitarian image of relationality qualified by asymmetry men-tioned earlier. This is especially true when we remember that love is the norm for the exercise of God's power as well as our own.

It is within the Trinity that we understand the divine and dynamic equilibrium embedded in deity. A God who creates, judges, and preserves is also a God who is with us in the incarnation. This person of God informs how one exercises "power over." A God who sustains, surprises, reveals is also a God who enables and requires the kind of discernment necessary for distinguishing between God's Spirit and our own. This person of God informs how one exercises "power within." A God with us, "emmanuel," who befriends, comforts, and challenges, is also a God who shows us how to befriend one another. This person of God informs how one exercises "power with."[42]

The authenticity of God's truth, power, and love prefigured in this trinitarian image of God's relational being is suggestive for an authentic exercise of power in ministry. Such authenticity is first defined by norms beyond our own necessarily more narrow interests. As "power over," it requires our commitment to the criteria of justice and neighbor-love embodied in the life and ministry of Jesus. As "power within," it relies on a willingness to nurture and exercise our gifts and wisdom as disclosed by God's Spirit. As "power with," it presumes our goal of building up the body of Christ through the "coactive" empowerment of all God's people.[43]

Each of these forms of power can yield to distortions. Generative and protective intentions can yield to dominance, encouraging infantilizing dependency or control disguised as efficient management.[44] Charismatic power that does not point beyond itself to the generosity and creativity of God's Spirit disempowers and controls.[45] Coactive power that is indistinguishable from the politically naive and exclusive features of friendship will likely falter in the absence of vision and energizing difference.[46] But it might also falter when it does not value the wisdom and particular experience of the community. Each of these distortions would render the exercise of power inauthentic. Avoiding such distortions points to the importance of relational competence that invites collaboration, mutual accountability, and respect for the limits and possibilities for one's particular voice.

Conclusion

In the stories of Pat, Gloria, Margaret, Karen, and Irene we overhear their efforts to live into a faithful exercise of power that will be consonant with their current sense of personal and pastoral authority and their diverse Protestant ecclesiologies. Each of Stortz's three categories of "power over," "power within," and "coactive power" poses challenges to these women at different points. In fact, there is a reciprocity of influence so that sometimes, for example as Pat described, stretching past an internal comfort level with personal or professional identity to exercise power over when that is needed seems to stimulate a further level of relational being. Similarly, security in the authenticity of one's relational being can also give the necessary courage for exercising power, as Karen, Gloria, and Irene demonstrated particularly well.

The experiences of these clergywomen well disclose how the issues of truth, power, and love arise for women in ministry of all ages. Their stories also suggest how authenticity in relation is a helpful norm for clergywomen at every point in the life span dealing with the challenges of ministry. Whether we are twenty-eight or sixty-two, authenticity helps us discern a truthful, empowering, and loving response. We have focused our reflections on the value of relational development theory for experiences of clergywomen. Much of what we have recognized about the dynamic interaction of truth, power, and love at different points across the life span, however, applies readily to women more generally. Similarly, although the symbolic dimensions of authority are constructed distinctively in the experience of clergywomen, many women would affirm the significance of authenticity in relation and the evolving challenge to embody it when we are young, middle aged, or older.

Self-Care for the African American Woman

Teresa E. Snorton

Self-care—the discipline of attending to one's own physical, mental, emotional, and spiritual needs through consistent activities and behaviors which enable renewal and growth.

Self-care is not the occasional nice, kind thing many of us are inclined to do for ourselves after a period of stress. Self-care is not responding to total fatigue with either vegging out or overindulgent behaviors, justified with thoughts of "I earned this." Self-care is not the desperate attention finally given to one of life's struggles—a failing marriage, an abusive relationship, an addiction, or feelings of depression. Unfortunately, when asked about their self-care, many women cite these as examples of how they care for themselves.

As an African American woman, I am particularly concerned about self-care among my sisters. I have found self-care, as defined above, to be difficult, in spite of what I consider to be my fairly well-developed understanding of self and the essential elements for a physically, mentally, emotionally, and spiritually healthy person. Why is self-care such a challenge for me and for other African American women? What values have we been taught that dissuade us from self-care? What other factors negatively affect such a discipline in our lives?

Several months ago, I was on bed rest for about a week with displaced discs in my back and sciatic nerve pain in my leg. I was in excruciating pain for several weeks. From the very beginning, I "knew" there was something more wrong with me than just a pulled muscle (the doctor's original diagnosis). Strangely enough, though I was in anguish and though I instinctively knew something was drastically different about my body's symptoms, during the initial days of my distress, I actually continued to try to function as usual. I went to work. I did housework and laundry. I walked across the expansive campus of the university where I was employed. I chauffeured my children. I cooked. The insistence of a few friends, and an erosion of my tough exterior, which finally led to tears because I was in such agony, finally enabled me to stop. By then, a new diagnosis had been determined and bed rest mandated.

As I lay in bed (actually in a recliner chair—laying in bed was still too painful), I began to ponder why it had been so difficult for me to stop to take care of myself. I quickly affirmed that as a single parent, I had to do it all. As I became more serious in my reflections, I had to acknowledge that I had a relatively good support system of friends and neighbors who were more than willing to help with errands, child-care needs, and food. My kids had more than enough clothing, so doing laundry was in no way a critical need. Besides, at thirteen and eleven, they were hardly likely really to need more than my coaching and supervision—which I could do from my recliner.

So, I had to ask myself again, why was it so difficult for me to care for myself? This was not a new question for me. It has been a relatively consistent theme in my life's journey. I overextend and overcommit; I neglect basics, such as proper nutrition, rest, and exercise. The dramatic nature of my current injury made me more curious about the strong internal forces that override even my common sense when it comes to self-care.

My grandmother had died a few months before the back episode, and I began to think of her as I ruminated over this notion of self-care. She died at the age of 106. She was a very important person in my life. Recently, I have become clearer about the lessons she taught me about being a woman, an African American woman. These lessons are something of a gospel for me, reinforced by the gospel of biblical texts oft quoted by my grandmother. I thought it fitting to at least think for a moment about what she taught me about self-care. I thought long and hard but could not remember any lessons related to self-care, except for a few directions about pregnancy and gynecological matters. My grandmother was a well-spoken woman (as in, she spoke her mind on any subject), so I had to wonder about this absence of verbal teachings on self-care.

As an alternative, I then chose to ponder the unspoken messages I had learned about self-care from my grandmother and other women in my family and community. As my recollections became clearer about what had been modeled for me, it dawned on me that I had been taught to devalue self-care. The women of my family and community, including my grandmother, modeled a set of values and behaviors for African American women. Self-care was not among those values and behaviors. Assuming my family and those women were not particularly unique among African American women, I finally began to think in broader terms about the lack of self-care among African American women.

Self-care (or the lack thereof) for African American women is shaped by a variety of forces. The individual woman's understanding of self-care and her ability to practice self-care is challenged by these very forces. Therefore, to understand and encourage self-care among African American women, these factors must be clearly understood and attended to by those in personal or professional relation-ships with them. The three primary forces that I identify are cultural influences, socioeconomic influences, and theological influences. In the following sections, I will elaborate on each of these forces, using sayings that were often quoted to me during my childhood and adolescence. These sayings are similar in impact to the notion of "soul stories" described by Anne Wimberly.[1] Without ever saying so, soul stories create and shape reality and become the unconscious beliefs upon which our behaviors are based. The descriptions of the three primary influencers of beliefs about self-care will then be followed by a discussion of the meanings of rest, renewal, and growth. Finally, these meanings will be used to elaborate on self-care as essential for African American women seeking a healthy spirituality.

Cultural Influences: "Every Bucket's Got to Stand on Its Own Bottom"

I am not sure of the origin of the saying, "Every bucket's got to stand on its own bottom," but I heard it a lot as a child. I do not even specifically remember which of my parents or grandparents quoted it—but the message was clear to me. In African American culture, responsibility was typically an important value, likely because of the historical experience of slavery.

In slavery, doing one's share of the work was crucial. Slaves who were slothful were often punished or even sold. Other slaves could be given more work to do if another slave was not doing his or her part. Training young slave children to work hard and pull their own weight became important for community and family. Needless to say, this need to work hard increased in post-slavery days, when freed men and women had to eke out the best life possible with limited resources. Indulging in self-care was just that—indulgent.

In the African American culture, very little distinction was made between men and women. Women slaves were expected to work as hard as men. Black women were rarely described as "delicate" or "weak." Even the occasion of childbirth did not afford the slave woman any luxuries. Narratives tell of many slave women actually giving birth in the fields and then returning to their work within a few hours after delivery.

This history has yielded an ingrained cultural understanding of self and work. For a black woman, I believe the message of self-sacrifice was more intense because of her dual role as worker and a homemaker. "Every bucket's got to stand on its own bottom" captures the idea that every person is responsible for his or her own life and work. Periods of dependence, rest, or withdrawal simply were not permit-ted or embraced as necessary.

African American women, therefore, generally have powerful cultural messages to work hard, do one's own work, and take care of others. Although there was not necessarily a direct edict to abandon self-care, it was not embraced as an essential.

And after working all day and taking care of one's family after work, who had time for any self-care!

Socioeconomic Influences: "We Don't Have Money to Burn"

I am also as unclear about the origins of the phrase, "We don't have money to burn" and who I heard it from. But I do clearly recall this message from my formation years. I grew up in the late fifties and sixties, in pre-integration days, when segregation was gasping its last breath and the Civil Rights era was just beginning to breathe on its own. Socially, there were many places we as "colored" people could not go. Local parks and swimming pools, country clubs with golf and tennis were off limits to us.

A set of values around recreation as an inaccessible luxury, I believe, became a part of the structure of the African American culture. Leisure was more associated with music, dancing, eating, and activities like cardplaying in many African American communities. Like most everything else in the African American context, recreation was a community activity with little emphasis on the needs of any individual. In this context, it seems to me that African American women were again indirectly taught not to consider their personal needs for rest, relaxation, and renewal.

In addition to segregation and inaccessible resources, African American women like me also learned about the proper stewardship of economic resources. Acquiring disposable income for music and ballet lessons for me and my sister was a significant financial achievement in my family's economic life. These were the very things eliminated when money was tight, however. "We don't have money to burn" was the response to a request for what was considered a nonessential expense. Even when accessibility became a nonissue with integration, the expense of recreation was interpreted through a particular set of lenses. For example, in the days before chemical permanents for straightening hair were widely used, I could not go swimming at the newly integrated community pool because my hair would get wet. Wet hair would become dry and nappy (tightly curled) and would necessitate another trip to the beautician, and we surely did not have enough extra money for that. So I never learned to swim. I did learn to look for the hidden costs of doing anything just for fun.

Even though I (and several others of my African American sisters) now have more disposable income than our childhood families did, it still creates an inner struggle in me to invest money in a yearly membership at the YMCA, a spontaneous weekend trip, an expensive vacation, or home exercise equipment. In spite of my professed value for self-care, these can seem to be extravagant and nonessential expenses to me.

Theological Influences: "God Won't Put Anymore on You than You Can Bear"

Religious and theological beliefs also have a profound impact on self-care. How dare I complain or seek refuge from the vicissitudes of life, when God is understood as the monitor of my endurance. The belief that "God won't put anymore on you than you can bear" is a popular tenant in African American religious life. The mandate to be strong in the face of adversity and daily living was reinforced by this cultural gospel text. Author Julia Boyd writes, "I was raised to believe that I was supposed to be strong and handle whatever came my way."[2]

In *Soul Theology*, Nicholas Cooper-Lewter and Henry Mitchell write about the core beliefs of the African American religious tradition. Among the seven core beliefs they identify, one is the belief in the majesty and omnipotence of God.

> If indeed God be God, there can be no outer limit to divine power and no entity capable of opposing it. Nothing can exist that is free of the ultimate control of the Creator and Lord of the universe.... All people need to know at the core of their being is that God's hand holds the whole world.[3]

With the assurance that the power of God is directed towards the ultimate good of humanity, there is no need to fear, worry, be anxious, or be overwhelmed by life's demands.

In this spiritual climate, self-care is a moot point for a couple of reasons. First, God will take care of you. Second, whatever you happen to have to deal with (bear), God will not give you too much. In other words, the belief is that you already have the capacity to handle the volume of responsibility and stress of your life. God has seen to that, so there is no need for periods of respite to retool, refuel, or just rest. Although these beliefs have considerable merit when speaking of faith and its ability to sustain us through life's difficulties, I see a problem in what often ends up as a passive approach to the care of the self.

Self-care is not a passive activity. Truly to care for one's self requires a conscious effort to provide rest for the body and mind and renewal of the soul. To seriously view oneself as a "temple of God"[4] requires a commitment to the care and preservation of this sacred space or being. The temple image presents a new theological foundation for self-care opposed to the implicit message that we are to ignore the self and symptoms of distress based on the mantra, "God will not place any more on you than you can bear."

The Consequences of Poor Self-Care

I am partially concerned about self-care issues for purely selfish reasons. I need to take better care of myself. I want to see my sons become men and fathers. One day I would like to be a grandmother, healthy and energetic enough to play with my grandchildren. I do not want to be preoccupied with illness and doctor visits in my senior years. I hope my mind will maintain most of its clarity until my death. I hope not to become another statistic.

The statistics on black women's health account for the other part of my interest in self-care issues. In my work as a hospital chaplain and counselor, I see too many African American women suffering from the ill effects of poor self-care. As a minister, I see far too many women unable to thrive and grow emotionally, mentally, and spiritually because they have yet to appreciate themselves as worthy of care.

The health statistics are staggering. In her book *Breaking the Fine Rain of Death: African American Health Issues and a Womanist Ethic of Care*, Emilie M. Townes cites these facts:[5]

- Only 64 percent of African American women receive early prenatal care.
- Black women die at a rate two times higher than the national norm from heart disease and stroke.
- Black women have higher death rates and lower five-year survival rates for most types of cancer than white women, primarily because they delay seeking medical attention.
- Black women have an incidence of diabetes two times higher than white women, and black women are more likely to die of its complications.
- About 83 percent of diabetic African American women twenty to seventy-four years old are overweight.
- Racial-ethnic women represent 40 percent (4.6 million) of this country's 11.7 million uninsured women, compromising their access to health care resources.
- Sixty-eight percent of newly reported cases of HIV infection are among black women, and since 1990 AIDS has been the second leading cause of death for black women between twenty-five and thirty-six years old.

The Black Women's Health Book[6] provides a comprehensive look at these and other health issues for African American women.

Not only are health statistics a powerful indicator of problems with self-care, but facts on black women and mental health highlights the problem even more. According to an article on black women and depression in *Essence* magazine, "The rate of clinical depression among Black women is estimated to be almost 50 percent higher than among White women."[7] That same article cites a 1996 study by the National Mental Health Association that found that 63 percent of black respondents believed that depression was a "personal weakness." In that same study "40 percent of the Black people surveyed said denial was a major barrier to treatment for depression and 38 percent cited shame and embarrassment as another obstacle."[8]

Some of the consequences of poor self-care are eventual physical and mental health problems. Neither the body, nor the soul, nor the psyche can remain healthy without proper maintenance, and improvements. In my estimation, the costs of illness, depression, and death are too high a price to pay for poor self-care. New values for rest, renewal, and growth are needed in order for African American women to thrive in their physical, emotional, and spiritual lives.

Self-Care Begins with a Theology of Rest

My theological image for rest is found in the Old Testament. In Genesis 2:2 we find this account of God's activity: "And on the seventh day God finished the work that he had done, and he rested on the seventh day from all the work that he had done." Did God rest simply because of fatigue, or is there a more profound truth in the verse? The larger creation story is about the transformation of chaos into order. God ordered into being the heavens and the earth, the sea and the dry land, the waters and fish, and every living thing. Although the creation story is about the origin of life as we know it, it is also a story about organization, a story about work, and that story culminates with God declaring that what had been created was good. Then God rested.

I think the story points not to God's fatigue, but to God's understanding of creation as a cyclical endeavor. One can only work for so long before rest is necessary for renewal and subsequent re-creation in the next experience. God's work was done, and rest became the prerequisite for God's participation in the next divine-human encounter.

When I rest, it is usually because I am tired, so tired that I can neither reflect on the value of the work I have done nor prepare myself for the next task to be done. My sleep is fitful. My dreams are turbulent. My body aches. My mind is either racing or completely shut down to the point that I cannot think clearly, let alone reflect. I do not think this is what is meant in Genesis by "rest." Genesis 2:3 says, "So God blessed the seventh day and hallowed it, because on it God rested from all the work that he had done in creation." The rest portrayed in this text is blessed, hallowed, sacred. The rest described here is filled with a sense of completion, fulfillment, celebration, reverence.

When moving towards a discipline of rest, African American women need to appreciate and seek these dimensions of rest. How? First, *rest must be viewed as a necessity, not a luxury*. More importantly, rest must be understood as an integral part of the work cycle. My grandmother and other women of her generation would work very hard on Saturday nights—cooking, ironing, housekeeping, fixing hair—because they believed that work should not be done on Sunday. In these postmodern times, Sunday is like any other day of the week, even if we do not go to our jobs away from home. Sunday is a catch-up day: catch up on laundry; catch up on shopping and errands; catch up on visiting friends, socializing, going to the movies, and so on. Rest should not be confused with leisure (or the socially accepted activities that masquerade as leisure). Some of my African American sisters not only need rest from their work, but from their busy social calendars!

Second, rest in its purest form compels one to not only view it as a necessity, but also *to schedule time for rest*. When I was active in an aerobics class, I loved the sequence of the dance activities. First there were the warm-ups, then the real stuff to give the cardiovascular system a good workout. A few exercises to target areas (abdomens, hips, thighs) followed, and then the whole workout ended with a cool-down. Every class session we followed the same routine, the same cycle of activities. Each part of the routine occurred in proper sequence to maximize the benefits of the exercise. Our lives should likewise be cyclical, where periods of intense engagement in life and work are routinely followed by periods of rest.

Two of my professional colleagues have recently told me about circumstances that intervened into their busy lives but ended up affording them some much needed rest. One had a period of unemployment, and another had complications after surgery that prolonged her recovery period. They both spoke of treasuring these unexpected gifts of rest. Here we find the third element of proper rest. *It requires withdrawal from one's usual activities for a discernable period of time.*

God's involvement with creation was not finished. Only the creating activity itself (the work) was done. God's rest was a period of preparation for the next divine-human encounter. Rest begat renewal. The loving God went off to rest and be renewed and left humanity on its own. Too many African American women cannot get rest because they fail to see the value in their going away and leaving others—husbands, lovers, children, parents, siblings—to struggle on their own for a while. It was a renewed, rested God, not a fatigued God, who spoke to Adam and Eve in the subsequent story in Genesis. African American women must resist the seduction of playing the all-powerful matriarch with no needs of her own.[9]

Self-Care as Renewal

I have always liked clothes, and when I was younger, getting dressed was often a high point in my day. My outfit would be chosen to fit my mood. Accessories would be chosen to accent the color, style, or unique feature of the outfit. Clothing was not just covering for my body; it was a message to myself and to the world about my state of mind. Close friends could often tell when I was having a good day just by looking at the clothing I was wearing. There was a lot of intentionality in what I chose to wear.

Self-care should be a process similar to dressing with intention. Self-care should not be just another task to check off a list. Rather, self-care should be tailored to fit the need and the occasion. Just as getting dressed required that I plan and choose, this kind of self-care requires time and attention. It is not something that can be done in a hurry.

Renewal that is fueled by a period of rest is like a process of changing clothes. Renewal involves the shedding of the old to make room for the new (undressing). Then the new must be selected carefully. What are my needs? Are there any wounds that need a special dressing first? What challenges and activities do I need to prepare myself for? What special accessories do I need to acquire?

The process of renewal is a time of refocusing. Whereas rest enables one to reflect on the work previously done, renewal enables one to garner the insight and energy needed to continue on the journey of life. Skipping the renewal process is like going into a snowstorm in a bathing suit! We are ill-equipped because we do not allow time to refocus on the new needs mandated by changing conditions.

Self-Care and Growth

Using this same metaphor—dressing—to speak of self-care, what does growth mean in this context? When rest and renewal are neglected, growth is stunted. True growth, be it spiritual, emotional, or mental, is dependent upon proper rest and renewal.

Growth is possible when periods of reflection (rest), followed by periods of renewal (self-awareness and refocusing), lead one to embrace new attitudes, new stances, new ways of coping, responding, and living. I have never been successful at starting a new fitness routine in the midst of a significant period of stress. In order to grow—to embrace a new routine—I must first slow down, examine what has been going on, make decisions about what to let go of, and move my focus from external demands to internal needs.

When I was dealing with my back injury and the bed rest it demanded, I had to take inventory of a few of my habits. I switched from a large shoulder bag to a much smaller hand-carried purse. I bought several new pairs of shoes with heels no higher than a half an inch. I bought a new mattress with firm support. I learned new stretching exercises to strengthen certain muscles. Growth involves the recognition that something else, or something more, is needed to continue on the journey.

The New Testament speaks of putting new wine into old wineskins.[10] We are cautioned against such an action, because the old wineskins will burst. So it is if we undertake any efforts toward growth without first tending to the prerequisites of rest and renewal. Growth involves facing life's changes without skipping those cycles. I would never consider wearing the same outfits I wore twenty-five years ago when I was a college student, even though some of them are back in style. Why not? I have grown. I am not the same person physically, emotionally, socially, or spiritually as I was then. I see and think of myself differently because of the numerous changes and experiences that have shaped my life over the years.

Growth is the culmination of a good commitment to self-care. I wish I could end with a testimony of my conversion to good self-care, but I cannot. Self-care is still a struggle for me. But now that I recognize the powerful cultural, socioeconomic, and theological influences on my beliefs about self-care, it is easier for me to interrupt my own patterns of self-neglect. It is further tempting for me to end with some suggestions or a prescription for the readers to follow in cultivating self-care. But I will not do that either. That in itself would circumvent the work each individual must initiate to begin a regimen of self-care. However, I believe that the first step is in identifying the cultural, socioeconomic and theological factors influencing one's beliefs about self-care. Once these are named, effective self-care should come easier to those willing to create new metaphors and beliefs about the essential task of caring for the self.

Food, Glorious Food?

Carroll Saussy

"Abba, God in heaven, hallowed be your name!
Give us today the bread of tomorrow." Matthew 6:9, 10[1]

Imagine the number of times a day that *food* is part of your conversation, in your thoughts, gathered and prepared by your hands, or on your fork! Many issues cluster around the topic of food, among them health, enjoyment, celebration, meal; weight, diet, diet pills; animal-product versus plant-based diet; various forms of vegetarian diet; eating disorders: obesity, anorexia nervosa, bulimia nervosa, binge eating, dysfunctional eating; obsession with slenderness, self-esteem, body image; fasting; energy, spirituality. At the same time, there are both more overweight people and more malnourished people in the world today than ever in recorded history.[2]

Food is a central religious issue. Christians and Jews believe in a God who created every good thing, including the human appetite and a vast variety of foods to satisfy it, a God who promised a land flowing with milk and honey, a God who provided manna in the desert. People of many cultures and religions pause to thank the creator of the universe for the food they are about to receive. Christians join in the oft repeated prayer that Jesus taught, a prayer that recognizes God as the giver of bread of today and tomorrow. Religious rituals around the world and throughout history have included food and drink. How profoundly human that Jesus gathered his close friends and followers to feast together the night before he died. In memory of that sacred meal, a shared cup and loaf are at the heart of the Christian tradition. Indeed, eucharist extends from the table where Jesus gave his final thanks and ate his final meal, to the family table where thanks are offered, stories are told, and food is shared. For many Roman Catholics and other Christians, the use of bread instead of the pre-Vatican II pressed wafer, and wine or juice in the communal cup has made a dramatic difference in the experience of God's sacred presence within the sacramental elements. A *loaf* is broken, and a *cup* is shared. Thanks are given. Body and spirit are nourished.

The Bible offers resources for thinking about how people are to relate to food. Humankind is given dominion over the earth and all that it yields. Humans must take responsibility for God's land that flows with milk and honey. Gleaners are to be offered the right to collect what remains in the field. A jubilee year is to be honored as a time for the redistribution of the abundance of food and resources. A caring person shares the last of her oil and meal to provide for a stranger in need. *Eucharistic* people are to be filled with gratitude and known for their table fellowship. Following Jesus, Christians do what he did—they give thanks, break bread, and pass the cup. They are called to widen the circle of those with whom they break bread in their homes "with joyful and sincere hearts" (Acts 2:46). Christians are temples of the Spirit, responsible for the well-being of their bodies. They are called the body of Christ; sadly, however, many members are filled to overflowing, while many sicken and die in critical need of sustenance.

Food is clearly a constant and central need in human life. The purpose of this chapter is to reflect on the complex issues of food and women's physical, emotional, and spiritual development. Clearly, food is a developmental issue for all humankind: without it there is no chance for development—we die. We need food continually and at every stage of life. Women who give birth carry major responsibility for the nurture and health of their children. For centuries, women have carried primary if not sole responsibility for family meals. For women, food is not only a matter of survival; it is a psychosocial issue deeply connected to identity, self-esteem, intimacy, health, community, and celebration.

This chapter begins with reflections on healthy eating and spirituality that grew out of personal experience. Research on that topic brought me face to face with unhealthy eating. Included in unhealthy eating are the dangerous diet industry and a related set of problems, socially promoted eating disorders, all of which are briefly explored. I then discuss the important differences between the messages "be thin" and "be healthy," reviewing current research on food and health. The final section of the chapter explores pastoral responses to those with disordered relationships to food. My interest in the question of healthy eating started when I joined the Women's Health Initiative; food took on heightened importance in my life.

The Women's Health Initiative

A serendipitous decision to join the Women's Health Initiative[3] in 1996 proved to be a grand one in the scheme of my life and gave me a fresh approach to aging. The Women's Health Initiative (WHI) is precisely about the physical development and health of females, particularly during their senior years. Women need more accurate information about the relationship between eating habits and breast cancer, heart disease, stroke, colon cancer, and osteoporosis if they are to enjoy long and healthy lives. One of the central foci of WHI is "diet change" to healthy, low-fat foods; I was assigned a place in a "diet change" group. After several months of a modified regime, basically eliminating most of the high-fat foods that had long been so satisfying, I experienced increased health and vigor in my body and my spirit. I felt like a new person. I found myself more awake, more aware of my body, enjoying increased physical energy, able to concentrate on academic pursuits for longer and more productive periods, more in tune with God's Spirit in my life, and more tangibly convinced of the body/spirit connection. I realized that I had not advanced to a separable chronological stage of life called old age; rather I had been aging since birth. Now, somewhere into the last third of my anticipated life span, I was making fresh new discoveries about wholeness and health and developing a new relationship to my body. Indeed I was dramatically involved in a developmental issue; I was developing a new lifestyle. I wondered if my experience matched that of other women in the program.

Queries among colleagues in our diet change group as well as a half-dozen women in one other group evoked a variety of responses. Several women acknowledged that they lost the taste for the high-fat foods they once loved. Others continue to crave high-fat foods. (I reported to one group that a study suggests that people who maintain a low-fat regime experience less depression. One woman said, "Not so," that when she feels hungry at night it's usually for juicy, high-fat food, and she feels depressed because she can't have it!) Many admit that when they stick to their new regime, they experience better overall health and that when they lapse, they feel guilty. They know they have let themselves down. Most of the women have a sense of generativity, of doing something for women of coming generations who will benefit from discoveries about food, health, and the female body. They also anticipate a longer, more satisfying life. Several gave responses suggesting that the enormous efforts they have made result in a sense of personal satisfaction and well-being. In my own case, I have been able to surrender fear that one day I will suffer a stroke and instead enjoy the assurance that I am doing what I can to prevent that from happening. Although interested in the possibility, none of the women shared my experience of mind/body spiritual renewal that accompanied a low-fat regime.

The WHI diet change group in fact follows no particular diet. The word "diet" usually implies a specific plan about what one eats for various meals and what one avoids. Diets are usually undertaken for the short term and focus on immediate results. (They are meant for the short range, yet ironically women who diet engage in one short-range attempt after another over decades of their lives.) The word "diet" is also commonly used to refer to the types of food one always consumes, the type excluded, as in "vegetarian diet." In order not to confuse issues in this chapter, I use "low-fat regime" when referring to my lifestyle change. The problematic nature of the word "diet" is explored in the next section.

Women at WHI are given no list of forbidden foods. Although the goal of the group is to greatly reduce the number of fat grams consumed in a day, participants are warned against too drastic a reduction in fat. Fat is recognized as fundamental to the body, adding essential nutrients. Fat helps the body maintain temperature and offers protection against environmental changes. Fat cushions vital organs, carries vitamins throughout the body, and supplies essential fatty acids.[4] Fat is good, but we do not need much of it. WHI participants are told to calculate about 20 percent of their energy from fat,[5] keeping their total intake of fat grams down to a very low number—24 grams for my 5'5" stature. WHI suggests that the source of fat should be balanced between animal and plant foods. (Experts such as cardiologist Dean Ornish advise against any animal fat.) Initially, of course, the task is anything but simple. A low-fat regime calls for imagination, willpower, and a bit more time and care in both gathering ingredients and preparing meals. I am indeed more food conscious than I was when entering the diet change group. Perhaps the most negative aspect of the program is the requirement that participants keep a food log three days a month, counting both numbers of portions of fruit, vegetables, and grains, and the fat-gram content in all that they consume. Such recording smacks of obsessive dieting, counting calories, weighing and measuring food. I cope with this annoying task by reminding myself that I am contributing to a research project to benefit future generations. WHI needs the data.

Ironically, once a major shift in regime has been accomplished, some converts find it hard to return to high-fat foods, beyond a few tastes from time to time. The aftereffects of a high-fat meal—for me, intestinal discomfort and troubled sleep—are not worth the rich tastes. Lifestyle change best describes what my low-fat regime has meant—a lifestyle change that included new eating habits and food preferences. With that change, I have experienced great joy and spiritual renewal. Although not yet a true vegetarian, I am moving closer to becoming one all the time. An anonymous poem echoed in my soul:

> Yes, sometimes unusual things happen
> after a switch to a vegetarian diet.
> I've seen a number of cases in which . . .
> people broke out in violent attacks of good
> health, followed by bouts of physical
> exercise and sweet thought.[6]

I am aware of enormous psychological and spiritual benefits available through a low-fat regime. Perhaps some family members and friends would prefer that I keep my happy discoveries to myself; I am inclined to shout them from the rooftop, and I've learned that some people hear my testimony as judgment against them.

Diet: A Problematic Word, Problematic Industry

The word "diet" is understandably a red flag word for many women. Perhaps it has been co-opted by the multibillion dollar diet industry, an industry that fails miserably in its results. Perhaps "diet" is too closely connected for some women with the "tyranny of slenderness"[7] and with prejudice against fat people, body hatred, and eating disorders. Not only is fat judged as unattractive, even repulsive, but the church has linked fat with gluttony, one of the seven deadly sins. Theologian Mary Louise Bringle observes that since Adam's and Eve's first transgression involved the eating of forbidden food, and that forbidden food being the sweetest in the garden, a corollary message is conveyed that the particularly pleasurable must be forbidden.[8]

Women who reject the tyranny of slenderness have celebrated the freedom they experience when they take charge of their body at every level. (I am not convinced, however, that most liberated women's "taking charge" includes paying enough attention to health, specifically to the kinds and quantities of food and drink consumed, and to exercise and relaxation. Women who continue to worship the socially constructed god of thinness "take charge" as well; however, their concern seems to be predominantly weight, with little attention paid to health issues.) Because women have long been so other-focused that they have not taken adequate care of themselves, taking charge of their bodies does not come easily to some of them. Rather than "love thy neighbor as thyself," some well-meaning women have followed "love thy neighbor, not thyself," as if we cannot do both/and. Many older women struggle with the results of body neglect over much of their adult lives.

The diet industry is fed by a patriarchal society that dictates norms for the attractive female body, norms that clearly overlook the diversity of body shapes and sizes, norms that feed the fear of fat and result in women overestimating their body size.[9] Social psychologist Christine Smith notes that the idealized thin female body promotes a weak, childlike woman. The periods in this country's twentieth century when women collectively sought power and control were the very times when thinness was elevated: in the 1920s, after the first wave of feminism; in the 1960s, after publication of Betty Friedan's *The Feminine Mystique*; and in the 1990s, after a third wave of feminism. Weight and body image, Smith concludes, are symptoms of "a larger disease, one that seeks to keep women weak."[10]

The lifetime effects of weight discrimination, especially against women, are tragic. For example, females who are overweight as youth or young adults make less money, complete fewer years of schooling, and suffer higher poverty rates than their normal-weight peers.[11]

Perhaps more insidious but not central to this chapter, is the overemphasis on females being sexually appealing to men. Such an emphasis burdens both those who fit the criteria for attractiveness—whose "features" include large breasts; slim, appealing body shape; youthful, wrinkle-free faces perfectly made up—and those who do not. Lovely-to-look-at, strikingly attractive women often struggle to know who they are besides trophies of patriarchy, that is, objects that are sexually appealing to men and the envy of too many women. Some of those who do not meet the measure have a hard time being at peace in their bodies.

Studies indicate that dieting as we have known it does not work. Ninety-eight percent of those who lose weight on a weight-management program regain the weight within five years; 90 percent gain more than they lost. A noted weight researcher goes so far as to claim that "dieting is the leading cause of obesity in the US."[12] According to Johns Hopkins University Hospital, the costs of treating obesity and its complications was $45.8 billion in 1990.

In the same year, 53 million dieters spent an estimated $33 billion on dieting programs. A survey indicated that 62 percent of adults are dieting; 18 percent are constantly on a diet.[13] Speaking at a Buck Center for Research in Aging, nutritionist Debra Waterhouse said, "One in three Americans is overweight, largely because of dieting." Female children suffer under the same tyranny. Fifty percent of nine-year-olds and 80 percent of thirteen-year-olds have dieted; 90 percent have poor body images.[14] An experiment was done wherein children were asked which kind of people they saw as desirable friends; lowest on the scale were fat children. Even fat children spurn other fat children as friends.[15]

I was challenged by a student in a pastoral care and counseling class who knows well the negative effects of diets. While completing a reading assignment, she took issue with an author's lumping eating disorders and chemical dependency in the same chapter; at the same time she railed against diets. She wrote in her journal:

> Compulsive eating is a coping mechanism that includes overeating, anorexia/bulimia, and dieting. Eating (and not eating) that isn't done because of the body's physical need but because of some external circumstance—time of day, feeling angry/sad/lonely, the arbitrary rules established in a diet by some stranger, categories of "good" and "bad" food—is a self-defeating behavior.

> I was outraged and concerned to see that the resources listed for eating disorder at the end of the chapter were all about dieting. This is irresponsible! Looking to a diet to control one's eating instead of relying on one's own body is itself compulsive. Offering a client a diet book is no more helpful than giving a bulimic the address to the nearest all-you-can-eat buffet. . . . All the reliable scientific evidence tells us that diets don't work for physical and psychological reasons.

Women especially are susceptible to the diet industry, because their fat cells are five times the size of men's. In addition, women have four times as many fat-storing enzymes as fat-releasing enzymes; men have the reverse—four times as many fat-releasing as fat-storing enzymes.[16]

Studies indicate an additional health problem with dieting: those with fluctuating weight increase the risk of dying from heart disease by 70 percent over those who maintained a stable weight, regardless of initial weight, blood pressure, smoking, cholesterol, or physical activity.[17]

Eating Disorders

Although the inspiration to write specifically about a low-fat regime and spirituality because of my experience with the Women's Health Initiative motivated me to write this chapter, research quickly broadened my focus. I soon recognized a connection *but not a necessary link* between the lack of healthy food intake and women's eating disorders. Some people choose to eat unhealthily; many of them do not develop eating disorders, although they may suffer ill physical and emotional health. Some people cannot afford to eat healthy food. An obese woman in the Women's Health Initiative who was motivated to address her food-related health issues found maintaining a low-fat regime nearly impossible. Working as a cook for a very low salary, she took advantage of the fringe benefit of eating the predominantly high-fat food she was ordered to cook. With coaching from a dietitian, she has been able to make slow but minimal progress.

A National Institute of Health study supports a correlation between obesity and "diets of poverty," which generally includes the consumption of high-fat foods and low amounts of fruits and vegetables. In 1991, 50 percent of African American women and 31 percent of European American women living in poverty were obese, and 37 percent of African American women and 21 percent of European American women living at three times the poverty level incomes were obese.[18]

A major reason for my ambivalence about addressing the topic of eating disorders is that I respect the reluctance among feminist theorists and practitioners to speak for the other. I have rarely been overweight and have no firsthand experience of a profound struggle to maintain a healthy weight; hence, I have not contended with obesity and I cannot speak for obese women. Nor have I been tempted to starve myself or to binge and purge; hence, I cannot speak for women suffering with anorexia or bulimia.

At the same time, I am intrinsically interested in food issues and take seriously the health hazards of obesity, anorexia, and bulimia, as well as the dangers of consuming high-fat foods in excess. I also wonder just how far people with eating disorders must be from the experience of receiving the bread of today and tomorrow with thanks, with *eucharist*. Far from being part of an enjoyable daily ritual for which they give thanks to God, food becomes an all-consuming issue that fills them with anxiety and dread. This section will address briefly some of the major eating disorders and a less serious problem, dysfunctional eating.

When is one simply overweight, when obese? There are no easy answers to this question. Johns Hopkins and other sources hold that weighing 20 percent above one's ideal weight constitutes obesity; the Harvard Medical School says 30 percent. Obesity results from too many fat cells. Adults at normal weight have thirty billion fat cells. Moderately obese, those 30 to 69 percent above ideal weight, have one hundred billion fat cells. Severely obese people have as many as two hundred billion. The fat cell theory holds that fat cells are always waiting to fill up with fat.[19]

How does one determine ideal weight, if there is such a thing? Not only are there no easy answers, there may be no answer. Ideally, individuals might determine the weight range their body most enjoys. Only the individual or her doctor would know how healthy she is. Clearly specifications do not fit all shapes. For example, Johns Hopkins offers a formula based on sex, height, and body frame, a formula that is perhaps too fraught with variances to be very useful. Women: start with 100 pounds for the first five feet; add five pounds per inch over five feet; women with a small frame subtract 10 percent of the total; women with a large frame, add 10 percent. Men: begin with 106 pounds for the first five feet; add six pounds per inch over; use the same percentage increase or decrease for frame size. A colleague responds that her calculation comes to 105, which she knows well is not a realistic weight for her. Unrealistic ideals exacerbate the problem of weight for women. Some people, however, find a formula to be a helpful guide when used flexibly.

The print and electronic media have been filled with results of recent studies on excessive weight, considered by many in the medical profession to be an escalating problem in the United States.[20] The National Heart, Lung and Blood Institute, using revised normal weight charts drawn after researchers combed through thousands of health studies, finds 29 million more Americans overweight than previously thought. This suggests that 55 percent of the population, or 97 million American adults, is now considered overweight or obese.[21] Nonetheless, weight charts and the body mass index are open to controversy and can result in what Bringle calls the sin of *weightism*, discrimination based on shape, a lingering prejudice that permeates society.[22]

On the other end of the continuum are women who suffer from an intense fear of becoming fat, even though they are under a healthy or normal weight for people of their age and height. Anorexic people have a distorted body image and feel fat even when they become emaciated. *The Diagnostic and Statistical Manual of Mental Disorders* uses the arbitrary figure of 15 percent below expected body weight as one of the criteria for anorexia nervosa. Bulimia nervosa describes people who engage in recurrent binge eating followed by self-induced vomiting or purging with laxatives. As with anorexia, people suffering with bulimia have distorted perceptions of their bodies and are persistently overconcerned with weight.[23] Some girls and women swing between anorexia and bulimia.

Feminist Naomi Wolf sums up the psychological effects and devastating results of semi-starvation. Anorexia leads to irritability, poor concentration, anxiety, depression, apathy, lability of mood, fatigue, and social isolation. . . . The anorexic may begin her journey defiant, but from the point of view of a male-dominated society, she ends up as the perfect woman. She is weak, sexless, and voice-less, and can only with difficulty focus on a world beyond her plate. The woman has been killed off in her. She is almost not there.[24]

"She is almost not there." A central theme in this volume is body/spirit unity. Both body and spirit are "almost not there" when a woman starves herself. Wolf calls anorexia a prison camp holding a fifth of the well-educated American young women as inmates. Underweight women are an institution in the fashion world and in advertising. The average magazine model is 5'10H" tall, weighs 114 pounds, and wears a size 4 dress; the average woman is 5'4H" tall, weighs 140 pounds, and wears a size 10 to 14 dress.[25] "Average," however, says nothing about the height, weight, or dress size of women who are above or below average.

Only my commitment to explore eating disorders kept me motivated enough to read through Marya Hornbacher's haunting autobiography, *Wasted: A Memoir of Anorexia and Bulimia*.[26] Hornbacher's story is an unending, walking nightmare of a young girl whose eating disorder became full-blown when she was nine years old. I had a hard time believing Marya is only twenty-three at the book's finish, where she acknowledges that she has changed but is by no means cured or of healthy body. Marya's profoundly complicated relationship with her parents is woven throughout her story. Food, alcohol, drugs, and sex are the weapons she used to express her body hatred become self-hatred. Never have I read such a sustained, tragic account of a perverted relationship with food and one's body. Perhaps Hornbacher will tell her story to vulnerable grade-school girls before they slip into a deadly, disordered relationship with food and with their bodies.

The term "dysfunctional eating" describes inappropriate or disordered eating behaviors that are not as serious as clinical eating disorders. Eating is dysfunctional when it is separated from its normal function and not regulated by ordinary inter-nal controls. Instead, one depends upon willpower not to eat, planned diets, count-ing calories or fat grams, or the sight or smell of food.[27] Debra Waterhouse advises, "Eat when you're hungry, eat what you crave and don't overeat it." In contrast, Marya Hornbacher speaks of her hunger this way:

> I do not remember a time when I was ever certain what the word *hungry* sig-nified, or a time when I recall eating because I was *physically* hungry. "Hungry" did not necessarily connote a growling belly. Rather, "hungry" was begging my mother to bake bread, thus securing a proximity to the scent of her perfume, standing on a chair with her hands on my hands as we kneaded the dough. "Hungry" was wheedling my father into taking me for rainbow sherbet, thus securing his jokes and funny voices and solid shoulder to lean my head on and watch pigeons in the park. "Hungry" was the same as lonely, and not-hungry was the same as scared.[29]

I wonder whether anyone can persevere through Hornbacher's story without recognizing the deadliness of the sin of weightism. Weightism is undoubtedly one of the causes of dysfunctional eating, a problem all too close to eating disorders.

Researchers debate the relationship between eating disorders and sexual abuse. In a National Women's Study, a random sample of 4008 adult women in the United States were interviewed three times over one year. This study concluded that bulimics were twice as likely as people free of eating disorders to have been raped or sexually molested, four times as likely to have experienced aggravated assault.[30] Chaplain Jane Dasher reports a high correlation between eating disorders and sexual abuse.[31] Studies on eating disorders and sexual abuse are inconclusive, however, and it is an injustice to women with eating disorders to oversimplify the causes.

Food, Health, and Social Pressure

One feminist believes that the obsession with slenderness has resulted in the acquisition of a lean, fat-free body becoming a religion. This is not a religion that proclaims that "my body is the Temple of the Holy Spirit" or "I am the body of Christ." Rather, its creed proclaims, "I eat right, watch my weight, and exercise." Fatness and flabbiness produce "a hell on earth." The religious rewards include beauty, energy, health, and a long successful life, promoting at least the attitudes if not the incidence of full-blown anorexia.[32]

The truth is that fatness is not a moral failure; fatness is morally neutral. Nor is girth gluttony. Gluttony indeed endangers health; gluttony focuses on the value of food to the exclusion of greater values and becomes a destructive habit. Gluttony is a sin; so is weightism. It is sinful to judge and discriminate against people because of the shape of their body.[33]

One must distinguish between the messages "be thin" and "be healthy," just as one must decouple weight and healthy eating. American society's overconcern with weight began in the 1920s. Although the importance of health and longevity have played a significant role at various times over the decades, having a thin body for the sake of a thin body has become the overriding motivation,[34] and as Christine Smith suggests, the subtext has been to keep women weak. The indisputable truth is that healthy people come in a variety of sizes and shapes, weighing in at numerous points on the scale. Many fat people eat healthy food and live long, productive, healthy lives. Thin people are sometimes undernourished and in poor health. Too many female teenagers suffer under an epidemic of anorexic and bulimic behaviors. Fat is indeed a feminist issue; fat is a social issue; fat is a developmental issue; fat can be both a health issue and a spiritual issue. Maintaining a healthy body and spirit is very important. A healthy body and spirit affect one's sense of identity and capacity for intimacy. Some healthy bodies will be thin; some will be heavy. As Kate Chernin says:

> The size of the body is a matter of highly subjective individual preferences and natural endowments. If we should evolve an aesthetic for women that was appropriate to women it would reflect this diversity, would conceive, indeed celebrate and even love, slenderness in a woman intended by nature to

be slim, and love the rounded cheeks of another, the plump arms, broad shoulders, narrow hips, full thighs, rounded ass, straight back, narrow shoulders or slender arms, of a woman made that way according to her nature, walking with head high in pride of her body, however it happened to be shaped.[35]

"Be healthy" puts women in charge of their own bodies. Taking charge requires an integrated sense of self, a realization of the body/spirit connection. Taking charge implies a movement toward health. I acknowledge my disbelief when women claim that what they call fat and what I see as obesity is beautiful. I judge obesity as neither beautiful nor healthy, and I challenge obese women who object to accepting reasonable medical restrictions. Do some women use their protest against slenderness as an excuse for careless, excessive eating that invites dangerous health risks? Although genes might well determine body type and, to a degree, weight, surely dietary and lifestyle factors are also involved.

There is ample medical evidence that excessive fat is primarily a health issue. With a rise in body mass index (BMI) comes a rise in blood pressure and total cholesterol levels, increasing the risk of heart disease, diabetes, and some cancers.[36] Dean Ornish reports that over 115,000 American women aged thirty to fifty were followed for eight years. Those only 5 percent overweight were 30 percent more likely to develop heart disease. Mildly to moderately overweight people had 80 percent higher risk of coronary disease than lean women; those 30 percent overweight, 300 percent higher risk. The question remains, who determines what is overweight? Nonetheless, evidence links high-fat regimes with obesity, coronary heart disease, stroke, breast cancer, colon cancer, osteoporosis, diabetes, hypertension, and gallbladder disease.[37]

Malnutrition, at the other end of the weight issue, puts especially teenagers in crisis: two-thirds of high school girls are dieting; half are undernourished; one-fifth take diet pills; many girls and boys use laxatives, diuretics, fasting, and vomiting to get slim. When asked, "If you had three wishes, what would you wish for?" nearly every eleven- to seventeen-year-old girl said, "To lose weight." In a different survey, girls indicated more fear of getting fat than of cancer, nuclear war, or loss of parents![38] Young adult women continue the struggle. As Naomi Wolf says, they are "expected to act like 'real men' and look like 'real women.'"[39]

Although eating disorders afflict people of all races, classes, genders, and sexual orientations,[40] African American teens and young adult women tend to be less easily destroyed than their European American peers by the pressure to be slender. Many African Americans define beauty more broadly, appreciating women of many sizes and offering more flexible beauty images.[41] As an African American woman in the Women Health Initiative said, "Our bodies were not built to be slim." Another participant suggested that African American young adult women are increasingly concerned with slenderness, but she believes that the emphasis is more on health than on sex appeal. There is indication, however, that in the seventies and eighties the middle-class European American obsession with slenderness became an "equal opportunity obsession." A Gallop Poll during this period indicated that 41 percent of nonwhites thought they were overweight; moreover, what had been a concern that blossomed in adolescence now surfaced among fourth-grade girls.[42] Native American women are most likely to be overweight or obese: in 1987, 60 percent of Native American women on reservations and 63 percent in urban settings were obese. Asian women have low rates of obesity (12 percent) and major Hispanic subpopulations have high rates (32 to 48 percent). As previously mentioned, in 1991, 50 percent of African American women and 31 percent of European American women living in poverty were obese; 37 percent of African American women and 21 percent of European American women living at three times the poverty level incomes were obese.[43]

The paradox is that people in the United States are constantly bombarded by multiple messages in the media. Illustrations of unblemished, thin bodies cover print media and television screen along with challenges and promises from the dieting industry. At the same time, advertisements for high-fat fast food fill more pages of the print media and flicker across the same television screen, while larger and larger portions of food are piled on restaurant plates. For those who consume high-fat foods or overindulge, over-the-counter medications promise quick relief.

The irreducible fact is that each individual is accountable to herself and her God for knowing, appreciating, and using well the only body she will ever have. Good food is a central resource for keeping both the body and the spirit healthy and their connection vital, and for celebrating life with joy and gladness, with gratitude, with *eucharist*.

Pastoral Responses

People with eating disorders such as anorexia or bulimia need medical, psychological, and spiritual help. They need to understand the complex issues that led them to dysfunctional eating, that is, to recognize the psycho-systemic factors involved in their disordered relationship with food. They need to be helped to see that they did not create their problem in a vacuum. The oppression and trivialization of women, the pressure to measure up to impossible ideals, the control of their bodies in a patriarchal society—all these factors have contributed to the personal problems involved in their eating disorder. In other words, the system is sick, and they need not label themselves as "sick."[44] Personal problems involved in the disorder often include low self-esteem, conflicted relationships within the family, social dysfunction, cognitive distortion, and a rigid personality.[45] A vast majority of people suffering from eating disorders are women. On the other hand, obesity is a health problem belonging to men and women of all ages. Although genetics is a primary factor in obesity, difficult issues involved in anorexia and bulimia are often involved in obesity, problems sometimes deepened by childhood sexual abuse.

Those ready to confront their eating disorders always need medical attention; they can also benefit from supportive pastoral care. The catch is that people with eating disorders have to be motivated to change; they need to want to recover. In efforts to be helpful to relatives, friends, and students struggling with eating disorders or dysfunctional eating, I have learned many times over that a helper cannot "push the river." A person needs to come to her own decision to recover. As a friend who finally made such a decision said, as much as people might want to help or hurry another's process, "The saying is true: it takes as long as it takes." She laments that obese people are often bombarded by their friends and loved ones to "just do it," adding, "[Concerned people] often have no clue about the real complexities of the issue. Negative comments and nagging just fuel the unhealthy relationship between a person and food. I think a great pastoral function would be to educate the family or support unit."

In addition to helping family members back off, pastors can provide safe places where people with eating disorders might explore, without pressure, what they want to do about their perceived problems. These safe places might be offered in one-on-one counseling sessions, through support groups, or through referral to a therapist. There are no quick fixes; there is no cheap grace. A thoughtful, empathic response, however, might help a person want something new for herself. People do not change until they are able to envision a new possibility for themselves, or as pastoral theologian Andrew Lester might say, until they discover a new future story.[46]

A woman who has recently faced her eating disorder writes: "The core of my eating disorder was secrecy. Things that happened to me could be covered up with food. Then I began to cover up what I did with food. Then I finally just began to cover up, locking myself in and others out." Unable to face herself honestly, she was unable to face others honestly. The breakthrough came when she was able to reveal her secrets. A deeply spiritual person, her spirit was able to embrace her body after years of alienation, and with a remarkable sense of integration she rewrote her future story.

Feminist clinician Marcia Hutchinson uses imagery as a clinical tool when treating women with mild body image issues. She works primarily with people who are not eating disordered, are of average weight, but report a "disordered relationship to food and weight." The twelve-week therapy consists of two-and-a-half-hour sessions limited to ten women and uses guided imagery as the major tool. Other elements are journaling, group sharing, movement, and expressive media. She reports that results have been dramatically positive.

Believing that imagery is "the language of the inner self," Hutchinson helps women pay attention to their image making and their sense of self. She believes that women with eating disorders often lack a solid sense of self and are thus less able to confront what society holds as valuable. With new self-images, women are able to create new mental patterns and experience deep emotional healing.[47]

A teaching tool I have used with considerable success is the Ira Progoff method of dialoguing with the body.[48] In courses on the pastor as person, faith and self-esteem, and human sexuality and interpersonal relationships, students are offered the opportunity to engage in such a dialogue early in the semester. When they list important stepping-stones in their lifelong relationship with their body, self-esteem issues invariably surface. Occasionally memories of physical or sexual abuse surface. Without fail, members of the seminar share the struggle the dialogue evokes, with the body angrily responding that it is mistreated. Such mistreatment almost always has to do with poor eating habits, a lack of exercise, and inadequate relaxation. The dialogue requires either a confrontation or a celebration of connection between body and spirit. Sometimes the dialogue results in a conversion.

A student who has struggled with obesity for as long as she can remember finally hit bottom when she dialogued with her body. Immediately after class, she told me that she was ready to face her physical and emotional needs. I knew this student over several years in several classes. At some point in each course she shared with me her desire to lose weight, but she took no concrete steps to do so. For a complex of reasons, the time was right during the sexuality seminar. Her determination continues, supported by a medically monitored weight reduction plan (not a diet) and pastoral psychotherapy; there is clear evidence that her decision has given her respect for her body and lifted her spirit.

Dasher offers other pastoral responses to eating disorders, all of which might break the silence and allow for conversation and connection. One might preach on eating disorders or sponsor an educational series on the significance of food or on theology of eucharist.[49]

Food and Mental/Spiritual Health

My original question was, does a low-fat regime enhance one's sense of self, feelings of physical well-being, and intellectual and emotional capacities? A highly impressionable and intense person, I did not know how much to trust my own experience. Was I finding the results that I sought, in effect manufactured, when I pursued a low-fat regime?

Research conducted in a Welsh city indicated that women (but not men) who consumed large amounts of fruits and vegetables enjoyed better mental health than those who did not. Regardless of age or social background, the women suffered less anxiety or depression. Two possibilities emerged from the study: intake of vitamins and minerals might result in better mental health; or women with higher self-esteem might consume more fruits and vegetables in order to maintain a desirable weight. There is also evidence that micronutrient supplements improve mood, increase scores on intelligence tests, and result in better memory, attention, and eye-hand coordination.[50]

John Robbins, best-selling author of *Diet for a New America* and founder of EarthSave, focuses on the quality of life as the real issue in eating well:

> For a person who is not burdened by clogged and hardened arteries, whose kidneys and skeleton are not under siege from excess protein, and whose cells are not driven to cancerous multiplication by too much fat, the experience of life is thoroughly different from the experience of someone whose diet is based on animal products. The real advantage is not merely a matter of life extension numbers, but can be found in a body that remains strong and supple and a mind that remains clear and flexible as the years go by.[51]

I would add other advantages, namely a spirit that remains hopeful and joyful, and a body/mind/spirit connection that celebrates the bread of tomorrow with *eucharist*, with gratitude. In answer to all three parts of my original question: Yes. I believe that a low-fat regime does enhance one's sense of self and physical well-being, as well as intellectual and emotional capacities. In my case, food never tasted better. And although I might have much to learn about eating ethically, I believe a low-fat regime also makes me a better citizen of a world in need of justice in food production and distribution.

Conclusion

Along with earth, air, fire, and water, food is a common and essential element in the lives of all human beings. No one can live without it. In several parts of our bountiful world, many people die tragically because food is not available to them. During the same hours, however, people all over the world die because of unhealthy foods eaten in superabundance: high-fat foods kill them. All adults living above the poverty level share responsibility for the distribution of food and are individually responsible for what they take into their body as well.

The partaking of food can be one of the most body- and spirit-enhancing rituals enjoyed by human beings. When my husband and I prepare a gourmet meal for family or friends, and when the food is enjoyed at a leisurely celebration filled with shared stories and interesting conversation, we have all the energy we need to do the clean-up once the party is over and still enjoy what we sometimes call "the magic" of the evening. Life is at its best when a family or group of friends gather to relax and share their stories around a carefully prepared table of delicious, healthy food savored at a leisurely pace. The joining of hands in a grace before meals can be precisely that: an awareness of grace and the increased flow of grace, God's life and love, moving from hand to hand and heart to heart in communion, in eucharist, the giving of thanks. This is what food is all about. "Abba, God in heaven, hallowed be your name! Give us today the bread of tomorrow."

Will My Time Ever Come?
On Being Single

Mary Lynn Dell

As I sit at my computer to try to put into words the fruits of my research, practical experience, and reflections on singleness and the Christian female, I am reminded that as much as I pride myself on clarity and objectivity of thought, one's writing can never truly be divorced from the reality of one's life. Ironically, I am composing this chapter in the spring of my thirty-ninth year of a very single life, just days before I am to be married. I am caught in a flurry of emotions, confident that the covenant into which I am about to enter freely and enthusiastically is indeed right and pleasing to God. Yet I am very much aware of the blessings, joys, toils, challenges, prejudices, trials, stimulation, and spiritual, emotional, and professional growth I have experienced as a single person over the last twenty years. I have struggled with the vulnerabilities of singleness and emerged at peace and very content in single life. As a physician and psychiatrist, I have the clinical experience of evaluating and treating single women of all ages and backgrounds and the gift of being allowed into their deepest, most private thoughts, fears, and dreams for their future. As a clergywoman, I see both the opportunities and the challenges for individual Christians and the church striving to enter into complete, unconditional communion with single men and women of all ages and circumstances. Indeed, only for a few more days will I have this unique vantage point as a *single* psychiatrist and *single* clergywoman and enjoy the particular credibility it affords. I am extremely cognizant of the joys of singleness I am about to leave behind, and at this watershed time (according to everyone's developmental schemas!) have definite opinions about singleness, marriage, family, and pastoral care!

Before exploring this developmental category further, certain basic premises need to be made explicit regarding the subject population. First, single women comprise a heterogeneous group and one must not generalize too readily. Women might be single because of divorce or death of spouse or an unfulfilled desire to marry that might or might not be fulfilled in the future. Or they might have made and continue to make the decision not to marry for one or more personal or professional reasons. Singleness has implications for women in their early adult years different from those for women in their forties, sixties, or eighties. Some unmarried women are lesbians, others are heterosexuals who live with other heterosexual women for companionship or, more often, to share expenses. Single women might share living space with men to whom they might or might not be romantically attached. Increasingly, single daughters of all ages are returning home to live with parents, perhaps indefinitely. The implications of being a single woman also vary tremendously according to race, ethnicity, religion, socioeconomic status, educational level, and geographic location. Although there is no typical single woman, for practical purposes this chapter will focus primarily on heterosexual women over the age of twenty-one with a minimum of a high school education who reluctantly find themselves single in a predominantly married culture, and women who consciously choose to be single in a society often inhospitable to those who do not conform to the demographics of the American nuclear family.

Self-Denial and Self-Sacrifice: The Measure of a Good Christian Woman

I will never forget the day after Christmas in 1998. Although David and I knew, as did all our friends and family, that we would eventually marry, December 26 was the day when we called those close to us to share our good news and the date of the wedding. I was taken aback by one particular response I received from a close female relative who has chosen not to work outside the home as she raises her two sons. "Are you really sure you want to do this? After all those years of only having to think about yourself and being able to do what you want when you want to do it, you aren't going to be able to be nearly as selfish as you have been."

I was stunned by her words initially, then somewhat irritated. After all, as a physician I had spent more nights staying up with sick children than any mother I knew, and I had canceled so many personal plans due to medical emergencies and church obligations that it was little wonder I was still single. Not to mention the fact that I was the first person this individual and scores of others called when children were ill, a question about medication arose, or any kind of school or child-rearing concern presented itself. Indeed, I lived and acted more settled and married than many married parents I know. Why was I perceived as being self-centered as a single person, and why did the possibility of marriage change that perception?

I believe two related principles to be operative here. First is the prevailing image or stereotype of singles living carefree lives, indulging themselves materially and behaviorally in all types of activity that no responsible—that is, married—person would consider. The second, and undoubtedly the most problematic for married and single women alike, is the equating of self-sacrifice and self-denial with true and genuine Christian love and servanthood. Brita Gill-Austern has written insightfully on this topic in her essay in *Through the Eyes of Women*. Gill-Austern offers six psychological, cultural, and theological roots for the tendency of women to express love and care in self-sacrificial forms and explains why these qualities and behaviors are reinforced. Although all six are important and have implications for single women, three are especially relevant to the self-perception of single women and how they are viewed by the predominantly married world and the family-oriented institution of church.

First, such behavior is deeply rooted in women's experience that identity is essentially defined in connectivity and relation; and in a culture that substantially informs this sense of self by raising women to consider the needs of others, to take care of men, and to care for children.[1] Females are not as children divided into two groups—those who will marry and those who shall remain single. All receive essentially identical education and socialization in schools, churches, and for the most part, at home. If a woman's self-identity is tied up largely in caring for men and children, and if marriage is the most acceptable vehicle to fulfill that expectation, what does that say to and about the self-esteem and self-worth of single women with these same societal expectations who do not have husbands and families? The degree to which most people in society have knowingly or unknowingly subscribed to marriage and motherhood as the preferred channels of connectivity and relation cannot be underscored too heavily. Eighty hours or more a week of caring for other people's children and subjugating a personal life to the unpredictability of emergency calls from families in crisis was not enough to erase the perception that I was, by virtue of my single marital status, somehow selfish, the complete master of my schedule all the time, and perhaps even self-indulgent. Stronger in some family and religious circles than others, the message that a woman's identity is connected to self-sacrifice and self-denial in the care of her husband and family is not necessarily healthy for married women, but it can be used as a handicapping indictment against unmarried women. If one is single, there are no husband and children to sacrifice for; hence, one cannot really know the redeeming virtues of this sacrificial love. Certainly these messages, though often covert, serve to perpetuate stereotypes of unmarried women as selfish and insensitive to the needs of others.

Second, women are motivated toward self-sacrifice because they have grown up in a culture that gives them a message that in order to remain connected and maintain relation they must sacrifice themselves and their needs.[2] A close corollary of Gill-Austern's first premise at initial reading might look like just a rephrasing of the obvious. For the single female, the concern is how "to remain connected and maintain relation" without "sacrificing themselves and their needs." Unlike many feminist theorists and therapists, I would remind singles and others that one cannot avoid some self-sacrifice and delayed gratification of needs—that is part of sharing, being attuned to the needs of others in a healthy and uplifting way, and being a part of a caring community. The concern for certain unmarried women is that the anxiety and fear of being alone or severed from human connection to the extent they desire might compel them to deny themselves and behave in ways that compromise mutually healthy relationships with others and diminish what they have to offer at work, to the church, and to the larger society.

Women are motivated toward self-sacrifice because their identities as women and Christians have been shaped by a theological tradition that views self-denial and self-sacrifice as the defining attributes of Christian love.[3] Simply said, the church has too often subscribed to the same views as secular culture that in order to be a "good Christian woman," a pious individual sacrifices her needs and desires for the welfare of her husband and family. If there is no husband or children, how does one define these qualities, and how is an unmarried person to manifest them publicly? Is it even possible to overcome the negative stereotypes rooted in the "opposites" of qualities one desires in a good Christian spouse—responsibility, wholesomeness, thoughtfulness, and consideration? What does it mean that the dominant culture in the United States has ingrained these and similar positive attributes in virtually all of modern psychology's developmental schemas and in the core of the great institutions of marriage, family, employment, and the church? Let us examine the effects of stereotypes about singles and developmental, psychodynamic, and biological factors in the lives of unmarried people; their relationships within family, culture, and religious institutions; and their efforts to be grown up in a world oriented toward married grown-ups.

The Intrapersonal Issues

Similar to other categories of individuals who share a lone common descriptor, in this case singlehood, unmarried women are such a heterogeneous group that it is difficult, if not perilous, to generalize without risking misunderstanding. This danger is perhaps most real when considering personality styles, psychodynamics, and therapy issues of single women. At the outset, I will underscore that singleness in and of itself is not a pathological condition, disease state, or cause for worry about one's mental health. The overwhelming majority of single women are functioning well in their work, leisure, and relationships, and share the same biopsychosocial protective and risk factors for physical and psychiatric illnesses as others of their same ethnicity, age, and socioeconomic status. What follows is a brief discussion of my experiences as a psychiatrist and psychotherapist working with this group of adults.

Although it is true that most single women are free of major psychopathology, it is also true that many of the more severe psychiatric illnesses either have their onset or most severe episodes during the twenties, thirties, and early forties. For example, schizophrenia and bipolar disorder have typical onsets in the late teens through the early thirties, eating disorders are prevalent during the twenties and thirties, and many individuals with personality disorders lead quite chaotic lives through their forties. Serious illnesses might involve recurrent periods of intensive treatment, perhaps up to and including inpatient, day patient or intensive outpatient care. In these instances, singleness is not the primary focus of treatment, but an aspect of the patient's life to consider in individualized treatment planning. The degree of physical and financial dependence on older parents and the extent of continued parental involvement and supervision in the lives of their adult children can be tough issues for all involved. Relationships between parents and offspring, between the single adult and his or her siblings and friends can be stressed and require continual adjustment and attention, as do numerous day-to-day practical matters that are best handled when interpersonal relationships are healthy and flexible. Too often, those involved in the care and decision-making processes with these singles neglect to consider the effects of extreme dependency or "protracted adolescence" on the spirits and self-esteem of these adults. Many of these same issues are struggles for singles with chronic or acute medical illnesses necessitating extreme or long-term dependency on others. Whether confined to a wheelchair and requiring special nursing needs or struggling with chronic mental illness, the implications, positive and negative, of the single marital status should be recognized and considered thoroughly for all involved.

I have noted recurring themes in psychotherapy with single women. Often a single woman is compelled to enter psychotherapy when messages she has internalized from her family of origin and traditional society have convinced her that she is a failure because she has not married, and that if she could only find and fix the flaws, she would be "good enough" to attract a "good enough" man and marry. The belief that she is flawed, even incomplete, as a single person can lead to low self-esteem and perhaps depressive symptoms if other significant risk factors are present. The failure to accomplish such a "natural" developmental task such as marriage can be mistaken by the woman and others as a sign of immaturity, unattractiveness, or being undesirable or uninteresting to men. Several women claimed to feel temporary or transient, as if their adult lives would not or could not begin until after marriage. In one instance, this feeling of being transient, waiting for life to start when she walked down the aisle, lessened considerably when the forty-something-year-old woman purchased her own home and took charge of planning for her financial needs after retirement.

Some women express discomfort at having to negotiate in both the private, feminine realm of their living space and traditional household responsibilities, and the more public domain of outside employment, financial matters, and the more typical male concerns. Car selection and maintenance are classic examples requiring a female to cross gender lines and feel comfortable and competent in both worlds. Often, the same women who are quite successful and confident with traditionally masculine tasks resent attempts by others to "masculinize" them, to attribute to them assertiveness and certain leadership or organizational skills historically valued in men but not necessarily in women.

Some women do avoid serious relationships and marriage because of difficulties with emotional or physical intimacy. Although these individuals do occasionally seek psychotherapeutic help, they comprise the minority of calls. Other women need to deal with past failed romantic relationships or their relationships with emotionally and physically abusive fathers before they were capable of serious dating and marriage. A few women have such idealized and romantic preconceptions of marriage that any real relationship disappoints them greatly, decreasing the likelihood that they will commit to marriage. As a group, however, few single women initiate contact with a therapist to address these issues. In my clinical experience as a psychiatrist, women are most likely to seek out or be referred to therapy when the anxiety about not marrying has grown disproportionately, overwhelming her coping skills. Being single is a problem or huge disappointment in their lives, and the undesired single state totally defines and dictates most aspects of their lives. I have also treated a significant number of women for whom single marital status is not the core issue or identified problem. Instead, they are most concerned about and desire help in dealing with family, friends, workplaces, and social institutions (including the church) that are not yet sure what to do with single adults. This is especially true for women who either acknowledge they might never marry or have decided to live full, complete lives as competent single women until they do marry. In the process of examining their feelings about and reactions to those individuals and events they find challenging, frustrating, discriminatory, even maddening in their daily lives, these women emerge with greater insight and knowledge of themselves, and more often than not, are better prepared and equipped for committed relationships.

The Family Issues

In addition to experiencing oneself as out of step with the wider society, the adult who remains single beyond the standard age range might also feel out of step with the norms of his or her own family. . . . Most families define the eventual marriage of the children as part of the natural evolution of the family. Marriage can signal to parents that they have successfully reared their children to "mature adulthood," especially in the eyes of the surrounding culture. The change in status from single to married often provides the impetus or context to realign relationships from parent/child to adult/adult, which then has an impact on all family relationships. Within the family, the shift from child to adult can be more difficult to negotiate without the boundary-making ritual of marriage and the creation of a new nuclear family.[4]

This passage from Natalie Schwartzberg, Kathy, Berliner, and Demaris Jacob's *Single in a Married World* nicely summarizes the pivotal developmental task for single adults and their parents. It is understandable that parents of single adults, often in their sixties and older, struggle with attributing full maturity, responsibility, even trust and confidence, to their unmarried adult children. Until recently, all developmental paradigms and all constituents of responsible society, especially the church, preached that the normal course of events is for adult children to marry and begin their own nuclear families within an acceptable age range determined by biology, education, career constraints, and societal norms for marriage and childbearing. Middle-aged unmarried individuals were called "old maids," "spinsters," or more politely, "bachelors," and if their parents were still alive they simply were not mentioned unless the older generation was being cared for by the single adult child. Once again, the majority of single adults do achieve satisfying relationships with their parents in time, but usually not without renegotiation of roles and a recasting of the strengths, abilities, and actual needs of the adult child. An understanding of the process of redefining that relationship and some common pitfalls might prove helpful to those working with single adults.

Parents of single adults often feel like they have failed as parents when their single offspring do not marry. This perceived failure might be further personalized if they understand the adult child's single status to be a negative comment on the parental marriage and home life. All too often, marriage is the only parameter both parents and single adults use or believe should be used as the measure of adult maturity and responsibility. Even when the single adult achieves some degree of success according to typical societal markers—for instance, education, income, or leadership—the unmarried person can find that the pressures and expectations for marriage from the family of origin exceed even those of society at large. The dichotomy between what has been and is expected and the reality is usually only highlighted if siblings have married and are engaged in lifestyles and activities more closely identified with traditional American family life. Singles can feel caught between the proverbial rock and hard place when they are alienated from a family of origin that does not seem to understand lifestyle, choices, and even adult work responsibilities, yet is resentful of time and emotional energy the unmarried adult must invest in outside friendships, work, and other activities that are fulfilling and help provide the senses of purpose and accomplishment not available in relationships within the family.

A previously unrecognized time when single adults seek out or are referred to therapists or clergy for psychotherapy or pastoral counseling is when the unmarried adult child approaches mature adulthood or middle age and is facing the declining health or imminent death of parents with whom these issues have not been resolved. One must deal with anticipatory mourning over loss of one's parents, not unlike that of married offspring of elderly parents. For many well-adjusted, even happy single adults, however, the relationship with their parents is the primary and most intense they have experienced in their lives, and they might experience a particular anxiety as they face the reality of parental aging and eventual death. Regardless of the quality and ups and downs of the parent/child relationship, and particularly if single adults are not close emotionally to siblings or extended family members, the helping professional can be immensely valuable as the single adult child seeks ways to gain parental affirmations of love, approval, and respect—sentiments commonly expressed on unique and monumental occasions such as weddings and the birth of children. It is on these occasions that single adult children often do the true emotional work of "leaving home" that is neglected by young adults who make the traditional progressions from parental home to college dormitory to a home with a new spouse and, eventually, children.

Life in the Outside World

Reflecting on the many and varied constituencies that comprise and inform her worldview as a Protestant theologian, wife, and mother with feminist leanings, Bonnie Miller-McLemore has noted the following in her pioneering work *Also a Mother: Work and Family as Theological Dilemma:*

> I stand upon several thresholds, caught between cultures. I am neither inside nor wholly outside the traditions and cultures that have held me and those that have liberated me. On one hand, despite my best intentions, I still wrestle with the resilient ideals of the "Father-Knows-Best" family that gripped the heart of America in the 1950s. At the same time, I live, albeit uneasily, with the new, still sketchily drawn ideals of working women. I feel caught in a vicious circle that the women's movement identified: women's stories have not been told and have not shaped cultural myths; without them a woman is lost; in order to forge ahead, women need stories that value their experiences. For the most part, the task of arbitrating the contradictions between cultures has been up to individuals.[5]

If such standing upon several thresholds is true for a married mother of three young sons, surely unmarried women today straddle even more cultures and must be conversant in the languages of more lifestyles than their married counterparts. For instance, an unmarried woman in her late thirties or early forties was a little girl during the original run of "Ozzie and Harriet" and "The Donna Reed Show." She grew up with the notions, at least in early and middle childhood, that a good wife and mother baked cakes from scratch and always dried clothes outside on the clothesline because the clothes would be crisper and smell fresher than if they were dried in a dryer. If her mother did work outside the home, it is statistically unlikely that she did so until her youngest child was in elementary school. The same females who were immersed in that particular culture before their tenth birthdays were, over ensuing years, encouraged by other elements of culture to pursue education and employment skills, so that they might not be dependent upon husband or family during adulthood. They have been told and taught in more recent decades that women are equal to men and numerous opportunities are open to them that their mothers and older sisters could never have imagined. Still, the values instilled at formative ages were from mothers and wise women of a previous era. Many single women have responsible leadership positions five days a week in the business world, yet hear theology on Sundays that is inconsistent with the way they must live and move and be the rest of the week in order to take care of themselves outside the walls of their homes and church sanctuaries. These struggles and culture clashes between what one was raised to expect and daily reality as an independent adult are more poignant, even ironic, for single women who are not in leadership positions and feel as if they have no influence or voice in the workplace and no one to hear their voice and opinions at home. Few people understand that the dilemmas and angst of culture clashes and competing expectations do not inquire about one's marital status or living situation before striking, let alone that unmarried women might have fewer resources and supports for coping than their married counterparts.

As a single woman I found work to be both a blessing and a healthy, generative outlet, though at times the little things in my professional life seemed to be a caricature for the trials and tribulations of singlehood. Independent of marital status, I confirmed many times that nothing serves to highlight life's ultimate truths and the true character of one's colleagues like the call schedule. As a medical student, intern, and resident, I was happy to volunteer for the "big holidays"—Christmas, Thanksgiving, New Year's, Memorial Day, and Labor Day—so that my married buddies could spend some time with their spouses. Soon, more and more of my peers were starting families, increasing the unspoken expectation that we single folks would let the married people have time with their spouses and kids; after all, we could relax and have fun anytime, right? Soon the newborns were in school, and their parents wanted the entire week of Christmas off to coincide with school breaks, not just a day or two here or there. My married colleagues were to be admired for their sincere efforts to coparent with their spouses, often busy professionals themselves. When it is the physician-parent's time to drive in the five o'-clock carpool to soccer practice, working up a new patient at four or even later puts not only the carpool in peril, but has a domino effect on anywhere from ten to thirty innocent soccer players and, in some communities, an entire township's junior athletic league (or so one would be led to believe!). So the single physicians were at risk not only for greater numbers of unevenly distributed call shifts, but inequities of work distribution during the regular week. This situation sneaked up gradually over the years on people like me who are very profamily and generally want to get along well with coworkers. Bucking the covert pressure to sacrifice my preferences for the convenience of parents and children would have seemed not only unpatriotic, but in opposition to the value for families implicit in pediatrics and child psychiatry, and even adversarial toward the "family values" singles unwittingly endorse by associating with Protestant churches in the 1990s. Ironically, the situation most unfair to single women is the pregnancy of a married colleague. As a woman, one feels obligated to close ranks with other women and compensate for the lost staff during a maternity leave, so that the men will have no reason to complain about women in medicine or being taken advantage of by working mothers. In actuality, many single females pick up the surplus workload, wondering if their "time will ever come" or silently resenting the fact that they will probably not be repaid for their extra efforts.

Of course, most professions have comparable scenarios, and I am certainly not saying that physicians are the only professionals who make personal sacrifices, but this example does illustrate some struggles all single women face at some point if they work outside their home. First, most workplaces and employee schedules and benefits are organized and maintained with the married, family person as the pro-totypical worker. Second, although my married colleagues would have denied this and felt sincere about their denial, a single person's time outside the workplace is not valued in the same way as a married person's or parent's time. This reality is a variation on the theme that single people are self-indulgent and focused only on their needs and desires. Therefore, for a single person to spend extra hours at work is not the same magnitude of travesty as for a married person, because the single person is not pulled away from spouse and children. Herbert Anderson and Freda A. Gardner write in *Living Alone*:

> If someone lives alone, she or he is usually viewed by the rest of the world as someone with no responsibilities and lots of free time. People who live alone might not feel they have a good excuse to say no to any request for help. People who are married or live with others are less free because they appear to have more obligations. While it is true that single people are often ex-cluded socially in a "corporate society," it is paradoxical that because more is expected of them in the work arena, they have even less time to develop the types of relationships they might want and that would certainly make them more socially acceptable."[6]

Finally, when employers, coworkers, and promotion systems look at singles in the workplace only in terms of how the single employee can make the greatest con-tributions in the least amount of time to the organization, the meaning of work in the life of the single person might be trivialized. "For the single person, the con-nection of work life to personal meaning is essential. . . . Personal meaning comes in many forms—pride in earning one's living, giving to society, creating something enduring, power. . . . Since the work system is highly significant to single people as a source of livelihood and as a socialization network, potential problems in this area can become quite threatening to their well-being. When, as too often is the case, work systems are not sensitive to their needs, single people feel different, excluded and sometimes even exploited."[7]

Pastoral psychotherapists and clergy working with single women of all ages should also remember that the culture in which their relationship with the indi-vidual is initiated and grows is not necessarily the only culture in which the woman is dealing with her singleness. Rural areas and small towns are not always hos-pitable to this population, so single women sitting in large urban congregations on

Sunday mornings might be caught between the cultures of their families and hometowns, and the cultures of their present metropolitan lives. The implications of singleness for Jewish and Asian American women are different from those for Protestant women of European descent. Certainly, single African American women considering dating and marriage face issues different from other ethnic groups.[8] A full discussion of these cultural considerations is beyond the scope of this chapter, but clergy and therapists ministering to single adults should familiarize themselves with these concerns.

Special Topics

A number of issues and decisions faced by unmarried women span two or more of the relationship categories of self, family, and larger culture, or perhaps do not fit neatly into any of these groupings. Much ink has been spilled on some of these topics, such as sexuality, whereas I have seen little material formally addressing the interpersonal dynamics between single women and their married counterparts. What follows here is not intended to be an exhaustive and definitive discourse on these potentially controversial issues but points out to readers the opportunity for further discussion inside and outside the pastoral psychotherapy paradigm and the greater church. The six areas we will address in this chapter include sexuality, women who choose not to marry, relationships between single women and married women, physical health and medical concerns, childlessness, and adoptions by single women.

Sexuality and Sexual Expression

Not only has significant time and energy been devoted to this subject over the past three decades by all religious traditions and denominations at the national, regional, and congregational levels, but individuals, religious professionals, ethicists, and churches remain as polarized as ever about acceptable moral standards and conduct. One can easily identify devout Christians in congregations and more vocal individuals in the national spotlight who are adamant in their beliefs that no form of sexual expression outside of marriage is acceptable. Others think that certain behaviors are permissible between responsible adults in caring relationships free of power differentials or abuse. Many individuals fall on a continuum between these divergent viewpoints. James B. Nelson has written extensively from a liberal perspective.[9] James C. Dobson champions the traditional view of complete and total celibacy outside of heterosexual marriage,[10] and Lewis B. Smedes has offered guidelines less permissive than Nelson but more flexible than Dobson.[11]

I will not recapitulate the extensive discussions and debates addressed by the above authors and other thinkers; readers are undoubtedly quite familiar and conversant with one or more of those standard dialogues. Instead, I wish to highlight two different considerations relevant to single women, sexual expression, and the church. First, we must acknowledge that unmarried women are in a bind when it comes to these discussions in the religious community. The quagmire is often not related to any deep psychological, spiritual, or sexual identity issues. The awkwardness is simply about being able to talk about sexuality as a single person when the conversation partners include young, old, men, women, married, or unmarried—the full diversity of the church. Many single women remain silent on the subject outside a small circle of same-sex single friends, believing that if they talk about a subject that the church has traditionally maintained is the exclusive or near exclusive property of married people, they risk being seen as loose, immoral, or unprincipled. With labels like these hanging over their heads, single women think they risk losing not only the respect of other Christians and church members, but jeopardize opportunities for service and leadership in the church that add meaning and fulfillment in their lives. Still today, even in congregations and denominations viewed as liberal and inclusive on this topic, single women think that some clergy and lay leadership equate initiating or participating in conversations about singles' sexuality with inappropriate assertiveness on the part of a single female. Single women who handle the label "assertive" with ease in the workplace might be reticent to be seen that way in private life and the church setting, especially if hope exists for establishing meaningful heterosexual relationships in a congregational setting. Not to participate or be included in discussions of sexuality or to have some outlet for sexual expression, however, perpetuates the all-too-common feeling that one is not "fully adult" until marriage or involvement in a committed relationship. These concerns are not uncommon or outdated; indeed, these are issues that inevitably arise at some point in the psychotherapy of single female clergy and laywomen. They should also serve as a reminder that the church still has work to do in this area, lest we become complacent and assume that every constituency feels comfortable voicing opinions and concerns regarding sexuality.

A second observation is not unique to singles or the topic of sexuality in the church, but is nonetheless worth highlighting. Often, a particular church's or religious institution's stance on sexual morality and behavior is inconsistent with its general theological bent on most other issues. For instance, religious professionals and churches that pride themselves on liberal theology, use of higher biblical criticism, and support for social justice practices can become biblical literalists and closed to divergent viewpoints when it comes to sexuality, period, let alone sexual expression by Christian singles. Clergy who are otherwise open-minded and receptive, and seemingly tolerant of many forms of sin, can become uncharacteristically rigid and judgmental when this topic is broached. In my experience, it is not one position or another, liberal or conservative, permissive or reserved, that is problematic in and of itself. In fact, there is merit to any clearly defined, consistently stated opinion about singles' sexuality, for singles then know the position of the church and pastoral staff and can make an informed decision about how they want to relate to the prevailing moral teachings. Difficulties arise when the attitudes, opinions, and teachings about sexuality and sexual expression and the theologies that inform them are internally inconsistent with the hermeneutics and style of scriptural interpretation applied to other moral and ethical issues in that particular congregation or religious group. For the church to be most helpful to singles, to hold them accountable while being simultaneously supportive and prophetic, as much consistency as possible across the life entire of the church is necessary.

Single by Choice

The church really has a tough time with women who are single by choice! The Roman Catholic church is equipped to handle single woman who become professional religious, but the expectations that young adult women will not only marry but want to marry and organize their lives in pursuit of that goal are still resoundingly strong in church communities and society as a whole. For a small minority of women, the deliberate decision not to marry or encourage relationships that could eventuate in marriage is a decision formed from difficult past experiences or fear of what committed relationship might entail. "The choice of singleness—deciding never to marry or being the person to leave a relationship—might lessen the element of pain or cause the grief and pain to occur at a different time in the process than the pain of an involuntary single. But the pain of making even a necessary decision to leave a marriage or not to marry might involve the death of dreams and expectations of lifestyle. It might also involve the judgment of family, friends, church, and society."[12] Increasing numbers of unmarried women, however, perceive they have alternatives to the traditional expectations and lifestyles, might enjoy heterosexual dating relationships, even experience times in their adult development when they wish for more companionship and other aspects of married life, but after weighing the pros and cons, continue to make the informed decision not to marry or pursue marriage. For the numbers of women in this category who are psychologically and spiritually healthy, growing, contributing to the lives of others, and celebrating their choice of lifestyle, the greatest handicap is outdated stereotypes applied to them by other individuals, society, and the church.

Single Women and Their Married Sisters

Like most single women, I experienced a gradual but noticeable decline in my extracurricular life that coincided with the attrition of my single female friends due to marriage. In some relationships each of us has worked diligently to maintain close ties, but I now only exchange occasional e-mails and Christmas cards with some others, and I am satisfied to see still others at five-year reunions and keep tabs on them through mutual friends. God continues to bless me with new friends and acquaintances. For some singles, however, rifts in important relationships with other women might occur when one individual marries, or at a later point in time if values shift and priorities and lifestyles shift. These relational changes can be

devastating for singles who might not be as fulfilled as they would like in other aspects of their lives, are shy or socially reticent, or have been overly dependent in
these peer relationships. Tensions with married coworkers might arise over family
needs of women who are married with children, or the perception that single
women are necessarily more ambitious and have more time for job-related pursuits
than those who go home to husbands and offspring. This phenomenon has been
replicated on a larger societal level as a result of the resurgence of religious and political conservatism during the past two decades, too often pitting working women,
married and unmarried, against married women and mothers dedicated to maintaining the ideals of the American nuclear family via many traditional methods.[13]
Pastoral psychotherapists need to remember the importance of female friendships
in healthy adult psychological life, and maintain vigilance that differences in marital status are not the sole reason for diminishing interaction with previous friends
or an excuse for limiting contacts with other women in the present and future.

Single Women, Health, and Medicine

Regrettably, the church has been silent for too many years on the issue of physical
health as good stewardship. The parish nurse and church clinic movements are
welcome corrective measures, but much greater use of these and other private and
public healthcare resources by unmarried women needs to be encouraged. Without
the usual developmental milestones of marriage and childbirth and often without
significant others to provide reminders, unmarried women can be notoriously neglectful of routine maintenance and preventative healthcare. Ironically, this neglect
might coexist with stringent attention to maintaining a steady weight and exercising enough to keep a good appearance, rendering it difficult to persuade women
there is more to staying fit than exercising for a half hour three times a week!

Clergy and pastoral psychotherapists might be especially helpful in two ways.
First, many single women need to be reminded that routine care is an investment
in their futures, and they should have one physician they see for check-ups according to recommended schedules. Without as many immediate family and social supports as some married people, singles need to identify a physician who will
claim them as a patient and be able to coordinate and deliver care in case of an accident or sudden onset of illness. If a serious mental illness or set of emotional
symptoms leads a single woman to seek evaluation or treatment, a referral should
be made to a primary care physician for a physical evaluation simultaneous to or
even before the psychological evaluation to determine whether physical problems
might be causing or exacerbating the psychiatric symptoms. This inquiry into a
single's medical care has become even more valuable today as managed care plays
musical benefits and musical doctors, increasing frustration and the likelihood that
patients will postpone or neglect care out of pure frustration. One used to be able
to depend on the church and the family physician for continuity in life. Now the
church might be the more reliable of those two faithful institutions!

Second, clergy, the church, healthcare professionals, family, and friends too often underestimate the effects on single women of particular physical events and illnesses, especially gynecological issues. I remember treating a single major depressive episode in a nun who was quite enthusiastic about her chosen vocation, had no regrets about her thirty years in the order, no personal history of medical illness, no family psychiatric history, and no depressive symptoms until she faced menopause. When that link was recognized, she remarked, "Although I don't mind kids, I've been perfectly happy in my order and have never thought I short-changed myself by not marrying and having a family. No one has ever accused me of being maternal, and I was never one of those females who wanted to be a mother, even when I was a girl playing with dolls. And I wouldn't change a thing about being a nun now. It's just that knowing it's no longer my choice not to have children, that now it's out of my hands and I couldn't even if I wanted to, that is the loss I have to deal with now." Menopause, an event many might take for granted or not think is relevant to the emotional life or health of a celibate nun, put this individual in touch with a number of other issues she benefited from dealing with in therapy.

I recall the experience of a thirty-one-year-old, never-married nurse who was diagnosed with a pelvic mass, detected initially on a routine pelvic exam. Although she was comfortable and not anxious in a hospital setting, she voiced feeling extremely awkward when scurried off to the ultrasound department within minutes of finding the mass. On the inside she was trying to keep from panicking and jumping to conclusions that the mass was cancerous, would require a hysterectomy, and destroy her future childbearing capability. She felt very alone and the experience seemed surreal as she waited in the reception area of the ob/gyn ultrasound facility of a large urban teaching hospital with fifty pregnant women in their third trimesters. The tumor was surgically excised a few days later and the pathology report indicated it was benign, but due to the nature of the surgical repair, she will likely experience difficulty becoming pregnant or carrying a baby to term. This is a poignant example of a medical condition and related surgical event that will affect this young woman's self-concept, dating relationships, and future decisions regarding marriage and childbearing. Until encouraged to do so by her psychiatrist, she had not considered discussing any of her feelings or experiences with her local pastor, nor had the clergyperson any idea that a woman did not need to be married to be so deeply affected by this condition and treatment. This area clearly requires more work and consciousness-raising by those individuals who do appreciate and understand these multifaceted issues.

Single and Childless

"I love kids; it's men I can't stand!" What a common sentiment in the ranks of single women who are not married, are not ready for marriage, or just plain do not want to be married but do desire to have children and be mothers. Many people in the church do not appreciate that although in the best of circumstances marriage and motherhood are related, it can be perfectly natural to shun the former while very much wanting to mother and be a mother. Once again, reproductive ability and the desire to exercise that ability as an adult, to bear and nurture children, are not determined solely, if at all, by one's marital status, yet have great influence on how both married and single women live their lives. "The acknowledgment of a woman's reproductive capacity is an important component of her sense of identity and femininity, regardless of whether she actually bears children. The knowledge that there is a finite time for reproduction also influences her concept of time and her own life cycle. She must make decisions about career and family in a way that is different from that for men."[14]

At the dawn of the twenty-first century, single women have more options for dealing with childlessness than in the past. First, because of improved health care and societal changes, it is more acceptable now than in years past to postpone childbearing until a woman is in her late thirties or early forties. This artificially provides an extra alternative for childless women by increasing the acceptable upper age limits for pregnancy and childbirth. Adoption, considered in greater detail below, and pregnancies outside of marriage are now more common and less rigorously censored and opposed in many religious communities. Every single woman I have spoken with who has sought out motherhood in nontraditional fashions , however, has described great soul-searching; conversations (in some cases, deliberations!) with family members about emotional, practical, and financial support; and considerable apprehension about their judgment from friends and, of course, the church. Most single women raised in the church are not themselves yet comfortable with becoming pregnant in nontraditional circumstances, opting instead for adoption or other ways to exercise their creativity and generativity, perhaps by working with children in other settings, or birthing projects and worthwhile activities in the workplace or community. It is important to recognize, however, that the issue of childlessness never disappears. Instead, childlessness takes on additional meanings and sheds others over the course of years. Older unmarried women might deny regretting that they did not marry but will often admit regretting they did not experience motherhood. Pastoral psychotherapists must remember to inquire about these feelings as they work with unmarried women of all ages who do not have children, biological or adopted.

The Single Woman and Adoption

A discussion of adoption would have been appropriate in the previous section on childlessness, but I have chosen to segregate this topic from the others as a reminder to pastoral care providers that adoption is not only about a parent and a child, but also about the *relationship* between those two individuals. The implications of the adoption change with time, and the developmental stages of both the adult and child, and their unique dyadic relationship will mean different things at different times to each individual. These changing dynamics should be thought through deliberately with a faithful diligence that might not be necessary in two-parent families or other single parent families in which adoption is not part of the story.

In recent years, the numbers of singles applying to adopt healthy newborn infants has skyrocketed. Given that the supply of healthy American babies has not kept pace with the demand by prospective parents, the number of foreign adoptions has also increased. In many cases, adoption by unmarried parents, especially single women, is a win-win situation for both mother and child. Single adoptive parents tend to be in their late thirties or forties, well educated, financially independent and secure, and established enough in their professional lives to devote time to home and family without significant risk to job and future security. By the time the adoption is finalized and the child is actually in the arms of the mother, the candidate has endured considerable investigation and scrutiny, and invested enough time, money, and energy in the process that her determination and dedication have usually been demonstrated for the world to see. Five years is not an atypical length of time between initial inquiry and completed adoption, giving prospective grandparents, other family members, and friends more than enough time to adjust to the idea and, it is to be hoped, provide emotional and other supports for the adoptive mother. Adopting and raising a child can be a very healthy, fulfilling outlet for a single woman's generative needs and nurturing gifts, and certainly many infants benefit from placement in a caring home and reception into an extended family and church community.

On the other hand, I have worked with several unmarried adults, male and female, who have unrealistic expectations about adoption, convinced that a child and family will fill voids in their lives or correct injustices done to them in earlier years. As a solo parent, one is always "on call"—a formidable responsibility, especially if the new adoptive parent has little experience with infants or young children. In many if not most adoptions, especially foreign, the receiving parent is not provided with much information about the family medical and psychiatric history of the child, or few details are known about the child's life between his or her birth and the time of the adoption. Adoptive parents should be aware that adopted children are disproportionately represented in inpatient and outpatient psychiatric populations when compared to age-matched nonadopted children. Schwartzberg, Berliner, and Jacob make the following observation: "Despite the growing number of single people having children, being a single parent is not easy and it should not be romanticized. Not only is it difficult to be at odds with societal expectations, but there is the need for greater financial stability and social resources when raising children on one's own. If support networks, friendship and family, have been developed and finances have been taken seriously leading up to the decision, the transition to parenthood will be easier."[15] Clergy should be aware of referral resources in their community when problems in this special population exceed the pastor's training or available time.

Single Women and Adult Developmental Models

Feminists and nonfeminists across all disciplines have long agreed that no single life cycle or model of adult development adequately describes the tasks of adulthood for individuals who do not marry, especially females. The stages espoused by Sigmund Freud and other psychoanalysts are too sexual and stereotyped to be practical, and feminist theories, although describing thought processes, moral development, and interpersonal relationships in a helpful fashion, do not lend themselves to daily therapeutic work with both genders as well as many would like.

Over the past forty years, pastoral psychotherapists have been particularly drawn to the epigenetic continuum and developmental model of Erik Erikson. It is easy to understand why this has been the case. Erikson's "eight stages of man," outlined in his 1963 landmark book *Childhood and Society*, was the first developmental theory to run from birth to death.[16] Stages 6, 7, and 8 cover the adult years. In stage 6, spanning twenty to thirty-five years of age, the fundamental issues are intimacy versus isolation. The positive byproducts of that stage are affiliation and love. Stage 7, encompassing ages thirty-five to sixty-five, is concerned with generativity versus stagnation, with the favorable results being productivity and care. Stage 8 is achieved at approximately age sixty-five, and the fundamental issues are ego integrity versus despair. From the successful negotiation of that stage comes reconciliation and a sense of integrity. Erikson's theory represents both an advancement and alternative to the psychosexual theories of development of Freud and like-minded thinkers, which had dominated psychological and therapeutic strategies until that time.

In *Also a Mother: Work and Family as Theological Dilemma*, Bonnie Miller-McLemore offers a thorough, very balanced critique of the contributions and potential pitfalls of Erikson's developmental stages as they are frequently applied to contemporary women, especially women who mother or are mothers.[17] Three of Miller-McLemore's observations regarding Erikson have particular implications for single women. First, she correctly points out that qualities of caring and caregiving necessary for generativity do not appear mysteriously when a woman turns thirty-five years of age and finds herself in the roles of wife and/or mother. Empathy, gentleness, kindness, sensitivity to the feelings and needs of others, and self-sacrifice are nurtured and positively reinforced in female children by family, church, and greater society from very young ages. As Miller-McLemore puts it, "the fruition of generativity and care does not appear suddenly out of a vacuum, in a mid-life crisis, but appears after a long and steady process of concern about the practice of care-giving."[18] Her second observation is that in Erikson's schema, a woman's ascendancy through the developmental phases, and therefore her generativity, is by necessity dependent upon yielding attachments to her family of origin and her adult attachments to a man and offspring. Finally, Miller-McLemore sees continued possibilities in Erikson's conceptualization of generativity: "In this single word we find embodied the human aspiration for a fulfilling adulthood which includes at least two aspects of human life that various theological traditions have long honored: (1) meaningful vocation; and (2) fruitful procreation. In a nutshell, generativity means an encompassing orientation to a life of productivity, creativity, and procreativity."[19]

The most obvious problem with the application of Erikson's stages to single women is that negotiating the ladder is dependent on traditional events such as marriage and childbearing. Not to marry or have a child is to stymie the "achievement" of the virtues of successive stages. Conversely, one can lay claim to the full expression of a virtue of a stage one's life events have not allowed admission. Miller-McLemore's observation of the nurture of generative qualities in female children confirms this, and validates the ethic of generativity in single women—an ethic with origins as deep and drives as strong as the most nurturant of women who are or become wives and mothers. The second concern, that a woman's progression through life stages is dependent on her relationship to a male, particularly in her early adult life, is not a new criticism, having sparked much reactionary study and theory in feminist circles in the last twenty to thirty years. Many women, this author included, interpret this fact of gender bias as just that—a fact of gender bias from a generation not in tune with this particular concern—and as the most compelling reason for revision of adult developmental theories. Miller-McLemore's third point, noting consistencies in Erikson's theory and historical theological understandings of generativity, should be affirming for singles about the potential of full life in a caring, theological community, as well as encouragement in future endeavors at better understanding of the lives of single women in the church. While for many individuals, generativity may include biological procreativity, it is not limited to childbearing and child-rearing. True generativity rightfully encompasses work, occupation, vocation, and other expressions of calling, creativity, and productivity.

An Alternative Model: Stages of the Single Adult Life Cycle

In *Single in a Married World: A Life Cycle Framework for Working with the Unmarried Adult*, Schwartzberg, Berliner, and Jacob wrestle with the psychological, family, work, and cultural struggles of singles from a nonreligious (although not necessarily "non-pastoral"!) perspective. They concur that new models and paradigms for healthy adult development are needed that do not depend upon marriage, parenting, and other traditional expectations as the only gauges of maturity and robust psychosocial health. Drawing upon their vast clinical experiences as therapists of unmarried individuals, they have developed a paradigm they call "Stages of the Single Adult Life Cycle".[20] The cycle consists of five life cycle stages comprised of certain emotional tasks. The cycle stages are characterized by chronological time periods instead of traditional milestones, that is, marriage, that are not truly limited to specific ages.

Stage	Emotional Process
Not yet married	1. Shifting the relationship with the family, dependent to independent 2. Increased autonomy in the world outside the family (work and friendships)
The thirties: "twilight zone" of Singlehood	1. Facing single status for the first time 2. Expanding to include other possibilities in addition to marriage

Midlife (40s to mid-50s)	1. Addressing fantasy of Ideal American Family
	  a. accepting possibility of never marrying
	  b. accepting possibility of not having biological children
	2. Defining meaning of current and future work
	3. Defining an authentic life within the single status
	4. Establishing adult role in family of origin

Later life (50s until failure of physical health)	1. Decisions about work life 2. Enjoying fruits of one's labors and benefits of singlehood 3. Acknowledging physical diminishment 4. Facing disability and death of loved ones
Elderly (between failing health and death)	1. Confronting mortality 2. Accepting life as it has been lived

This developmental model is operates on the premise of dealing with life as it is in reality and totality, whereas others have concentrated on certain aspects of life (family of origin, sexuality, and marriage are examples) to the exclusion of important dimensions of an individual's development. Therefore, this model is much more comprehensive than others, and lends itself to a more complete, richer, fuller understanding of the individual. As such, it is clearly a much more valuable therapeutic and pastoral tool, if it is applied in those contexts. It is also flexible enough to be adapted for use by and for men, women, never married individuals, divorced, widowed, and gay and lesbian singles. It provides enough structure to understand typical, healthy life events, assess and diagnose various problems, and conceptualize comprehensive biopsychosocial treatment plans when interventions are indicated. It also allows for the retention and inclusion of aspects of other developmental schemas, such as Erikson's, when those ways of thinking about developmental issues may make positive contributions.

So Where Do We Go from Here?

This chapter has sought to broaden the understanding of single women by describing the diversity of individuals carrying this designation, their challenges and struggles within themselves, with their families, church settings, and culture. Yes, single woman have unique challenges and may sometimes wrestle with feeling "one down," but in reality they share most of the daily, often mundane struggles of their married peers. We have focused on the specific issues inherent to the unmarried state in an effort to increase understanding among pastoral psychotherapists, clergy, and others who interact with unmarried women, particularly those dealing with important life issues.

Important work is yet to be done in many respects. Churches, especially those of the mainline Protestant variety, have struggled with the role of singles, and single women have seemed especially perplexing. Continued thought and prayer needs to be accorded regarding how singles are integrated into the full life of the body of Christ, at times as recipients of ministry, at other times as the sowers, harvesters, laborers, prophets, teachers, and healers. Singles have much to contribute to the health and support of the faith community. On another note, an increased understanding of the stresses and vulnerabilities, psychological and otherwise, will contribute to the pastoral care of unmarried persons and foster spiritual growth.

As for me—I had better return to my packing. I'll have time and opportunities in the days ahead to savor the joys of Christian marriage and the challenges and work of maintaining and growing in my union with David. Right now I need to remember and give thanks for the blessings of people and experiences bestowed upon me as a single woman.

Women with Acquired Disabilities:
Constructing New Lives
in a Strange Land

Paula Buford

Listen to the voices of eight women with disabilities:

Beyond a doubt, the church has been the most harmful [place for me to be as a disabled person]. . . . A lady at church told me I should be pleased that I was diagnosed with Lupus because scientists might learn something from my illness to help others. . . . [After several periods of increased disease activity], somebody just decided that I wasn't going to teach Sunday school anymore. Didn't tell me. Didn't ask me. Just took my name off the Sunday school room [door].
 Kathleen Lewis

Herein lies one of the great problems of having an "invisible" illness: people expect you to do as much as the average person, usually as much as a full-time professional, when one may, due to side effects of medication or symptoms of the illness, be unable to hold . . . any full-time job. One wants to explain, but in my case [with manic-depressive illness], it is not advisable, as I could decrease my options even further.
 Grace Little

I don't feel like I'm a healthy person because I'm not able to function on the level that the human body was created to function . . . [but] there are ways I can make myself healthier as an unhealthy person.
 Kathy Berry, discussing her multiple sclerosis

I hate it when I tell someone about my disability, and they respond, "Well, the whole world's disabled!"
 Paula Buford, referring to a traumatic brain injury

In a way, this accident was a blessing because it made me see who was really going to be there for me and who was dysfunctional and couldn't be there.
 Francene Passantino, commenting on her traumatic brain injury

[After my two strokes] I was shuffling around the house with my shoulders bent over. . . . [I] told myself I was acting like an old woman who had forgotten how to walk. . . . I started acting as if I could walk and found I could still do it. I told myself about things I could do instead of things that I thought I couldn't.

Bernie Blanton

Society allows you the "sick role": You look sick; you are depressed, non-directive, childlike, submissive. But if you live with a chronic illness for a lifetime, you can't constantly live out of the sick role. If you look good, are independent or happy, are responsible for yourself, people aren't going to believe you are sick. So, you are caught in a double bind. . . . And the emotional reaction can be more disabling and crippling than the actual physical limitation.

Kathleen Lewis[1]

I am getting disability [insurance payments] and I thought, 'Gosh, I'm not doing anything for it!'. . . . I guess it's a works/righteousness kind of thing. . . . Now that I'm making some progress [physically and vocationally] I don't feel quite as guilty or bad.

Tamara Puffer, discussing her traumatic brain injury

Some people think we [addicts] use [drugs] just because we want to use. You think we enjoy not taking a bath for a week, not having nothing to eat, living in a dope house with no lights, . . . living under bridges? Nobody wants to live like an animal.

Kimberly Thomas, recovering cocaine addict

Women's marginalization in our culture is no longer debatable. *Fact*: Women, as a social group, are dis-abled by patriarchal culture. *Uncomfortable fact:* Millions of women are doubly dis-abled by chronic illness and trauma.[2] *Fact to be denied*: If we live long enough, most of us will experience some form of disability. *Embarrassing fact:* Many disabled persons spend years getting accepted for Social Security disability benefits.[3]

Fiction: Disabled persons are easily identified. Fiction: Most disabled persons are too lazy to work and do little to help themselves.[4] Fiction: The disability movement has always advocated for persons with mental disabilities.[5] Fiction: The church leads the way in helping persons with disabilities. Fiction: Disabled women have figured prominently in feminist research and women's studies.[6]

In many areas of feminist research, as with this book on women's life cycle, new paradigms presented might apply only to women in the mainstream. Note feminist Joan Borysenko's disclaimer in her 1996 book, *A Woman's Book of Life: The Biology, Psychology, and Spirituality of the Feminine Life Cycle:*

> This book is based on life cycles common to all women, and issues that pertain to the majority of us. The special concerns of women of color, women . . . from other cultures, disabled women, and lesbian women are important . . . but were simply beyond . . . my expertise (author's notes, n.p.).

In this chapter, I will describe what it is like for an adult woman to have her life turned upside down by an acquired or hidden disability.[7] I will focus on disabilities from which a woman will not be restored to her former state. Everything about her life changes including identity, sometimes personality[8], self-esteem, significant relationships, spirituality, income, vocation, and future goals and dreams. Attempts to live her preinjury lifestyle or to compare herself with a woman in good health result in sabotage and self-blame. Her life is fragmented and must be reexamined, reconstructed, and renamed not once but often for a lifetime. She has suddenly been cast into a strange, barren land[9]—lost, terrified, alone—with no maps, provisions, or survival training for the journey. How can she learn to sing God's song in a strange land?[10]

This challenge is put before millions of women with acquired disabilities. Eight of us—seven conversation partners (whose narratives were developed through personal and phone interviews[11]) and I—will be tour guides through this strange land for the "temporarily able-bodied." Because of our unique life circumstances, we have become experts, or "patient professionals,"[12] in disability and chronic illness. We do not wish to be pitied, blamed, ignored, nor promoted to sainthood. We simply wish to be heard as women who are reconstructing lives interrupted by chronic illness or trauma.[13]

Overview of Women's Lives

In this section, I will introduce these eight women with acquired disabilities to the reader. In subsequent sections, I will describe the devastation of initial diagnosis and early progression of the dis-ease,[14] show how these women are constructing new lives on a daily basis; explore how their significant relationships have shifted; name social structures that help and harm them in their recovery process; and offer suggestions for ministering to women with disabilities.

Grace Little (pseudonym), forty-four-year-old part-time secretary and former missionary, married, was diagnosed with manic-depressive illness twelve years ago. Paula Buford, forty-six-year-old, divorced, former pastoral counselor and now potter and writer, is on Social Security disability; onset of a traumatic brain injury was six years ago. Bernie Blanton, seventy-three-year-old retired widow with grown children, experienced two strokes four years ago while she was still married. Kathy Berry, forty-three-year-old part-time associate pastor on Social Security disability (former writer and editor for denominational publications), is married with two children. Kathy was diagnosed with multiple sclerosis at age thirty-five. Kimberly Thomas, thirty-six-year-old divorced mother of a twelve-year-old son, was an alcoholic by age twenty-one and moved into crack cocaine addiction; she has been a "recovering" addict (in remission) for three and a half years and works as a nurse. Francene Passantino, thirty-seven years old and recently married, incurred a traumatic brain injury nine years ago. Now, she is on Social Security disability and does volunteer editing. Fifty-three-year-old Kathleen Lewis, a nurse who is divorced from a Baptist minister and has two grown sons, is on Social Security disability. She writes, counsels, and lectures on chronic illness out of twenty years experience with Lupus and other rheumatic diseases. Tamara Puffer, thirty-six-year-old former associate minister and professional violinist, is on Social Security and private insurance disability. She sustained a traumatic brain injury two years ago, three months after she was married. She is currently doing volunteer ministry at an intentional Christian community providing services to the homeless and at an assisted living facility.

Moving into the Strange Land of Chronic Illness and Disability

As can be seen from the above descriptions, there are many ways to move into the strange land of chronic illness. Kathleen Lewis, Grace Little, Kathy Berry, and Kimberly Thomas had symptoms of their diseases in young adulthood, but diagnosis and treatment eluded them for scores of years from initial onset. Some diagnoses were delayed because symptoms were elusive or doctors minimized their significance.

As a teenager, Kimberly Thomas hid her recreational drinking from strict parents who were active in church. At age twenty-one, she married an alcoholic who "taught [her] to drink" (to binge drink and stay out all night). When alcohol no longer satisfied her, she moved onto crack cocaine.[15]

Grace Little, diagnosed with manic-depressive illness in 1987 at age thirty-three, had her first hypomanic episode (a milder form of mania in which one is euphoric) while serving in a two-year post-college missionary program when she became infatuated with a member of her Sunday school class who was several years her junior. After her overseas assignment, she enrolled in seminary because of her own interest in theology and because of her parents' wish to "get [her] in a context where [she] would meet some nice, eligible men."[16]

Unlike these women, who had vague symptoms years before diagnosis, some women's onset of illness was in the blink of an eye. One evening, says sixty-nine-year-old Bernie Blanton, "I noticed that my right hand wasn't doing like it was supposed to do. Immediately, I looked in the mirror and discovered that the right corner of my mouth was drawn downward, and I knew I'd had a stroke." Calling for help, she noticed her garbled speech.[17]

Tamara Puffer and Michael Galovic, newlyweds of three months, were enjoying a leisurely evening together when, "Pow! We got hit!" In a coma, Tamara was hospitalized and then went through intense rehabilitation for about a year. Diagnosed with a traumatic brain injury (TBI), she had to relearn language skills and learn compensatory strategies for poor attention, memory, concentration, organization, dizziness, poor motor skills in her right hand, fatigue, double vision (partially corrected by surgery), hypersensitivity to noise and light, and inability to process information rapidly.[18]

Sometimes trauma instantly changes women's lives, but it may take months, even years, for this injury to be diagnosed and treated. Twenty-eight-year-old Francene Passantino was at work inventorying boxes when a fifty-pound box of books fell on her temple, dislocating her jaws and a vertebra in her back, and causing a mild TBI (undiagnosed). Though "I didn't go unconscious. . . . I felt very strange. . . . There was internal swelling [in the brain] that I had no idea was going on. . . . I went to doctors and they said, 'Oh, you're alright.'" Francene continued to have horrible pain, crushing fatigue, inability to read or stay on task, disorientation, poor memory, emotional lability.[19] Though her family thought she was malingering and she began to think she was crazy, she signed up to be a research subject at a hospital studying mild TBI. A year post-injury, she was diagnosed and sent to rehab, and Worker's Comp finally accepted responsibility for her treatment.

I had two car accidents in 1992 while traveling to professional conferences out of state. In each, I hit my head but was released from emergency rooms with no diagnosis. Aged forty, I had a full-time counseling practice and was close to completing a doctorate. Over a period of two years, I experienced similar symptoms to Francene's and Tamara's: fatigue; emotional lability; poor concentration, attention, and memory; and an overwhelming need to sleep. I knew I was suffering from post–traumatic stress disorder, depression, and whiplash, but that did not account for the strange changes in my body and mind. After seeing alternative and traditional doctors for two years and stopping my work as a pastoral counselor one year post-injury, I was finally fully diagnosed: mild TBI (and organic mood disorder),[20] Graves' disease (a thyroid disorder), and post–traumatic narcolepsy (a neurological sleep disorder).[21]

Even women with decades of mysterious symptoms experienced a health crisis that changed their lives forever. Twenty years ago, Kathleen Lewis, a thirty-three-year-old nurse, started throwing blood clots to her lungs while at work: "It was like I went off a cliff. . . . I went straight from work to the hospital and never returned to work. . . . And I lived for the first two years from the couch to the bed to the hospital, with an occasional venture out to the church." Her initial response to her Lupus diagnosis was, "I'd rather die than live like this for the rest of my life."[22]

Although Kimberly Thomas had been moving toward addiction for many years, her life changed forever when she first tried crack cocaine in 1988: "Little did I know that when you first hit the crack, you are immediately addicted to it." Obsessed with crack, she stole money from her parents and stayed away from home for weeks at a time. Despite four inpatient treatments for addiction, Kimberly's illness continued to progress. She was banned from both her husband's and her parent's homes and eventually lived in a crack house, "an empty house with no lights, no running water, no food, no furniture. . . . Just a house with candles and everybody [up to ten or fifteen people] is using [crack]." Desperate, she began having "homicide and suicide thoughts. One time I wanted to kill my son and my husband 'cause I thought I was gonna die and I wanted to take them with me." Mouthing off to a drug dealer while high, she had a gun pulled to her head. That was her "bottom."[23] In 1995, she surrendered to police officers. After fifteen months in jail and prison, she was released and continues in recovery.

In 1990, Kathy and Bill Berry and their two children moved from Atlanta to Richmond for her to take a position as a writer for the Foreign Mission Board of the Southern Baptist Convention (SBC). Six years earlier, she had suffered blurred vision, which eventually cleared. For all of 1990, her left side was less functional. In February of 1991, when she was thirty-five, Kathy "woke up one morning and from [her] ankles down [she was] numb; the next morning from the knees down; the next morning, from the thighs down; and the next morning, from the waist down." When her doctor explained that she had multiple sclerosis (MS), a progressive and relapsing neurological disease, she was relieved: "[A]t least I knew what it was....You can deal with something you know about, whether it's horrible or not." After a week in the hospital, Kathy returned to full-time writing.[24]

Grace Little experienced her first acute manic episode in 1987, when she and her husband were missionaries. They had just attended a musical presentation about the movement of the Holy Spirit through history.

> [Suddenly] I was experiencing events that we [my husband, Don, and I] went through as coming together. . . . I saw myself as being part of a plan for bringing in the Second Coming of Christ. . . . There was going to be a peace conference with all the world religions, and I was going to be there. . . . Steven Spielberg was going to make a movie out of all of this and everybody who saw it . . . was going to believe [in God].

Within days, Grace and Don flew back to the United States for her treatment, and they never returned to their work as missionaries. Being on a locked psychiatric ward was confusing and strange. Grace remembers having

> a sense of being a prisoner . . . in a padded cell . . . pounding the walls. I was sad about being locked up . . . [and later] about leaving India and not being able to say good-bye to people. . . . At first I didn't understand that I had this illness. Plus it was threatening to someone who's a Phi Beta Kappa to have anything wrong with their brain. I was in denial.

Finally, after taking lithium, she began to get better.

Constructing New Lives in a Strange Land

How did these women find ways to not only survive in a strange land but have meaningful lives? They did so slowly and with a lot of mistakes, broken dreams, and broken relationships.[25]

I offer two metaphors from my experience. The first is that of a tightrope walker who is constantly given new weights to carry and from whom old ones are removed at random. She maintains a constant balancing act just to survive, whereas in the past moving forward just meant putting one foot in front of the other and walking on solid ground. People do not understand why she is so unbalanced because they cannot see the tightrope.

Recurring dreams inform my psychic struggle for a meaningful life, and they offer a second metaphor for living in a strange land. In the first few years of recovery, I dreamed of myself as a brain injured person who kept getting lost and ending up at the seminary I graduated from in 1979, with no clear idea of a career path. After I completed my Th.D. degree in pastoral counseling in 1997, I had another dream sequence. I was told that my college degree was never completed, and I was sent back to Georgia Southern University to take psychology and history. Twenty years had passed since I had been on campus; everything was different. I had difficulty finding my dorm, my dorm room, and my classrooms. When I finally arrived at the last session of Psychology 101, the professor asked me to explain my absence. Upon learning my background, he said, "I'll pass you if you can give us an oral summary of all of the teachings of Sigmund Freud."

The metaphor of being a pastoral counselor with a Th.D. who is sent back to a Psychology 101 class in college is an apt one for a woman with an acquired disability who is reconstructing her life. All of the women in my study had achieved significant educational, vocational, and relational goals, only to be sent back to the tasks of adolescence and early adulthood where one's whole life is a question mark.

For all the women studied, the first several years of living with an acquired disability were hell. Learning and relearning new terrain as the landscape constantly shifted pushed these women into survival mode. All eight women had poor self-esteem from their lowered abilities "to love and to work."[26]

In the grieving process, each woman had to come to terms with her dis-ease and "make a peace treaty." Most have chosen to accept illness with hope, to "integrate it into their lives and live alongside it" so that illness becomes a part of who they are; not the enemy (Kathleen Lewis). Paradoxically, having a healthy respect for the dis-ease actually diminishes its power: "I know it [my addiction] has a lot of power if I use [drugs or alcohol]. But as long as I don't use, it don't have any power over me" (Kimberly Thomas).

Because of the mystery and tenacity of chronic illness, grief is ongoing. The devastating losses these women have sustained, and will continue to sustain, require drastic responses: care of the self at all costs, devising daily rituals for rest and energy, revising relationships and letting go of those that are not life-affirming, developing new networks of support, changing life goals, and developing a spirituality for a strange land. Passively letting the illness take over their lives is a choice that none of these women have made; therefore, they work diligently at their recovery: "I have had enough [physical] therapy to realize that any further changes will be up to me, and I accept this" (Bernie Blanton).

Daily Rituals and Self-Care

Women with hidden disabilities have to learn to make the most of what they are given. "At first it's like trying to learn to drive a car," says Kathleen Lewis. "You have to focus on every little thing; later, it becomes second nature." To take care of herself, Kathleen gets

> at least 10–12 hours of sleep a night. . . . I have to constantly have water or chewing gum or my throat sticks to itself. . . . I put drops in my eyes . . . every hour. . . . I take alternative medicine. . . . I gear my diet to the level of activity that day….[I do] prayer journaling every morning and evening…..[I listen to] spiritual or upbeat music. . . . I wear sunscreens and opaque makeup and long sleeves and hats. . . . I claim "breath prayers" (a scriptural affirmation of 6 or 7 syllables).[27]

Kathy Berry, with MS, also has to be careful of being outdoors and of getting overheated. Like Kathleen, Kathy begins her day with prayer and meditation. During the morning she writes at home or works at her part-time job as an associate minister. She rests for five hours in the afternoon before her children and husband come home. Because she has difficulty using her hands (for activities that require fine motor skills), her family does many of the homemaking tasks.

Bernie Blanton is still able to live alone, with part-time domestic help. During the day, she does a little housework, watches television, writes e-mail, reads her Bible and other books, rests, does hand exercises, and writes on her memoirs. She usually doesn't dress until the afternoon, unless she goes out with friends, because dressing takes hours (her right hand was severely affected by her stroke).

To deal with my own disability, brain injury, and post–traumatic narcolepsy, a sleep disorder, I get about eleven hours of sleep at night and take several scheduled naps during the day. I get up around noon; work a couple of hours on something left-brain, like writing, reading, or getting on the Internet. After a nap and lunch, I make pottery, or watch videotaped movies, activities which engage my right brain. After another nap, I usually watch TV, listen to music, cook, or do chores. Before I go to bed at night, I play contemplative religious music and throw pots on the wheel. Some days, I schedule activities with friends and go to church, but I have to be careful about being around too many people because my brain gets overstimulated and I "hit the wall."[28] During the last year, I moved into my own home and have cautiously expanded my activities.

Kimberly Thomas centers her life around her job, N.A. (Narcotics Anonymous), the church, being with her son, and helping other "suffering addicts." She speaks of the hard work of recovery, introspection, and personal change:

We [addicts] work hard. . . . We do whatever's necessary for us not to use [drugs] . . . . I believe that I don't have to use, one day at a time, for the rest of my life. . . . [So] if it's going to three or four meetings a week; if it's going over to my sponsor's house; whatever it takes, I do it. I have two primary purposes in life: getting as close to God as I can and staying clean. And with those two purposes, seems like everything else around me goes very, very smoothly.

Though they know these rituals are necessary for survival and sanity, some women, particularly those who are mothers and wives, feel guilty or selfish about their needs. For Kathy Berry, "[Guilt is] a daily thing." She feels guilty about not being with her children more, not working full time, or not doing most of the homemaking. Francene Passantino, newly married, wishes that she had more energy to be emotionally available to her husband.

Revising Relationships and Developing New Networks of Support

Grace Little likes an image she recently heard on National Public Radio about "the need for margins in our lives—emotional and physical cushions—so that when a crisis comes up we are not completely without reserve." But women with hidden disabilities, as can be seen from the above examples, have to maintain huge margins on a daily basis because they have little reserve on which to draw. Furthermore, the maintenance of these margins does not guarantee consistent energy. Every day is unpredictable and different. Pushing oneself one day may result in a collapse or exacerbation of symptoms several days down the road. Or, having several good days in a row might lead a woman into a misguided belief that her disease is in remission. Because of these energy swings and accompanying emotional responses, women with wide margins may easily become marginalized by others. Grace, who makes margins in her life by working as a part-time secretary in the mornings and resting in the evenings, is devalued by her peers who are now in professional positions: "When I meet someone who learns about my seminary background . . . I tell them I work at the University, they ask me what I teach. When I say I'm a secretary, they usually look disappointed, surprised, or as though they have an instant loss of respect for me."

Because Grace is "in the closet" about her manic-depressive illness at work and at church, she has no close friends besides her family. She finds that without having a career or children or the energy to keep up with current events, many people "don't have anything to talk with me about."

Most women with hidden disabilities need positive, honest relationships with others just to hold their ground emotionally and physically, but renegotiating relationships can be difficult and costly. When asked what was the most difficult thing about having Lupus, Kathleen Lewis responded, "Relationships." Reflecting on her traditional marriage, Kathleen commented: "My illness allowed me to grow up. Even though I had the adult caretaking (codependent) role emotionally, the family rules would not allow me to be an adult, assume responsibility for myself, and say 'No.'" Paradoxically, in her illness Kathleen says, "I began to move out of the victim role. . . . My healing emotionally and physically upset the balance of our marriage. [Jim] felt threatened and had to leave."

For most women, the strange land is moving into a disease. For Kimberly Thomas, who began moving into addiction at age thirteen, the strange land is sobriety and healthy relationships.[29] She has learned to be more honest with herself and others about her feelings and is teaching her son to do the same. She also had to overcome destructive attitudes of self-centeredness, irresponsibility, and possessiveness in relationships.[30]

Tamara Puffer and Michael Galovic are currently in marital counseling. The focus of their therapy is learning about the new world of the other: how Tamara has different coping styles and energy and has to process things in a way different from before; how Michael has had to carry a lot of the load for the last few years. Along with processing changes in their relationship, they are pursuing a common goal of learning how to relax and have more fun.

Naturally reticent to ask for help or clarification, Tamara has learned to do things for herself that at first were embarrassing, such as asking for help from bus drivers[31] or wearing earplugs when she goes out to filter out noise, or resting after several hours of work.

Francene Passantino broke off relationships with most of her family of origin and significant others about two years after her traumatic brain injury because they were not supportive of her attempts to rebuild her life. Her neuropsychologist, she explains, pointed out, 'If you don't address this disruptiveness in your personal life, you are never going to get better'. . . . So, literally, I packed my bags and left everybody behind that wasn't by my side, and I felt good about it. And that was the beginning of my recovery."

Francene moved to an apartment to live alone, began an intensive day program of rehabilitation, and began the task of making new friends: "I decided . . . to seek out people that were healthy. . . . [A]s far as men were concerned, I had a complete checklist. And if they didn't conform to that checklist, they were out. . . . Here I was—disabled . . . like [running on] one cylinder—and I'm doing the picking and the choosing!"

Though she was growing, Francene still felt like a victim. At a support group, Francene met Mimi, a woman mute from a stroke but still full of life: "I said to myself, 'I can talk! And this woman is doing more than me'. . . . And I said, 'My feeling sorry for myself is wrong!'" With Mimi's mentoring, Francene says, [I] "started helping others because I realized I had a lot left. . . . That was a big turning point."

I was injured a few months before my father was diagnosed with lung cancer, so I hid my symptoms from my family. Later, after I stopped working, my mother helped me financially, and she had difficulty seeing me as the grown woman I had been before the accident. I was only marginally able to live independently, and we both knew it. I felt like I was a teenager again—wanting to be grown up but still needing an "allowance" from my mother.

I also had to make new friends, because many of my friendships were work related. Some persons who knew me well before my accident seemed uncomfortable around me because of my personality changes and huge losses. To rebuild my support networks, I initiated psychotherapy,[32] spiritual direction, joined a foyer group in my church, and found a woman in my church, Judy Fiocco, to pray with me weekly who later became my closest friend. For months I corresponded with another female pastoral counselor out of state who also had a TBI. Early in my recovery, I took pottery lessons and hung out at the studio for hours at a time; later, I joined a monthly "Spiritual Autobiography with Visual Expression" group, led by pastoral counselor, Mary Logan.

Women with disabilities not only have to rework old relationships and find new ones, but also have to develop whole new *networks* of support. All eight women interviewed have some involvement in support groups geared to their dis-eases; all are active in their churches; all have learned to work new systems: medical providers, insurance carriers, disability pensions with former employers, and Social Security disability systems. Unfortunately, the very systems that are supposed to be in place to help with chronic illness may be a hindrance to women's healing.

All of the women describe a maze of medical systems which might misdiagnose or minimize them, and that they may not be able to afford. In the early years of recovery or during relapses, women have to focus on their symptoms, often running from doctor to doctor. This enormous preoccupation with symptoms, which is necessary for their survival, often moves them into depression.

Francene Passantino, Paula Buford, and Kathy Berry all had adversarial relationships with Social Security disability systems; Francene and Paula also had to sue their former employers for benefits. Describing going to court with her employer, Francene said, "I thought they were going to have to take me out on a stretcher in that friggin' courtroom!"

My own case never got to court, but it was one of the most difficult emotional processes I have ever experienced. I would never have initiated litigation if my lifetime survival were not at stake.

Paula Buford, Kathy Berry, and Kathleen Lewis had hearings for Social Security disability benefits; Paula and Kathy felt demeaned by a judge who treated them as though they were liars and cheats. Kathy said, "It was the worst day of my life." The judge and vocational expert suggested to her that she could work as a ticket collector at a movie theater, be a supervisor at a factory, or work in a gift shop, even though her hands were barely functional and she could only stand a few minutes at a time.

I felt like a rape victim on trial for her previous sexual activity. The intrusive questions from the judge began with, "How often do you take a bath?" Though my doctors and a vocational expert said I was disabled, the disability judge felt I could work because I had almost completed a doctorate. I finally won my benefits after years of appeals, but I was having suicidal thoughts by the time I got them. Earlier, when I explored options for alternative living, I could not even find a religious community to join, because I could not carry a "normal" workload, and I had huge needs for sleep.

Even the church and associations founded for specific medical problems are not always supportive. Many times people are well-intentioned; they just don't know how to respond to disabled persons. In their fear, they run away, patronize, or engulf the persons they are trying to help.

Some women, however, had positive experiences with maintaining relationships and with social institutions. Tamara Puffer easily got Social Security and private disability benefits. Once on Social Security disability, Francene Passantino initiated a work trial. When she was unable to work, she got back into the disability system. Grace Little and Kathy Berry both name their nuclear families and families of origin as offering them the most support. Before her stroke, Bernie Blanton was the sole caregiver for her invalid husband for seven years, so she had already reworked her friendships. She speaks glowingly of how friends and the church came to her aid, both in her strokes and in her husband's death in a nursing home in 1996: "I don't feel my condition has impacted [good] relationships [with family and friends]. . . . I appreciate my friends more because they have been so considerate. . . . My church is a very caring fellowship."

Bernie has enlarged her social systems by joining a covenant group at her church, where she "spent the first two meetings weeping a lot [from her husband's recent death]." She has also joined the Widowed Persons organization, the Atlanta Writers' Club, and the Stroke Club. She does fear, however, that she will never have a romantic relationship: "I did not become asexual when I became a widow [at age 71], but I don't feel I have much to offer anyone."

Tamara Puffer feels that she has actually gained friends since her injury: "My workaholism got in the way with friendships before the accident. . . . Now I'm more honest. Believe it or not, I'm easier to get to know."

Revising Long-Term Goals and Vocations

Women with acquired disabilities need to establish new daily rituals, rework old relationships and build new ones, and learn new systems of support, and they also have to revise long-term goals for themselves and their families. For most of the women, disability means that they are unable to carry out the vocations for which they are trained; many are unable to support themselves financially. Grace Little has chosen not to have children because of her limited energy; Tamara Puffer and her husband have postponed having children.

For many women, full-or part-time work is not possible, because they cannot work under a superimposed schedule. Many supplement their Social Security benefits by working out of their homes on a limited basis. Self-employment and part-time work seldom offer health insurance, however. None of the women in this study would be eligible for individual health policies except those with astronomical prices and exclusion riders for their preexisting conditions.[33]

Some women, like Kathleen Lewis and Grace Little, have gone back to school for retraining. As a Lupus patient, Kathleen did not have the stamina or a stable enough immune system to work as a nurse around sick people. Therefore, at a very slow pace, she went back to school and earned a masters in vocational rehabilitation counseling with a specialty in chronic illness and studied family systems and pastoral counseling. She has written two books, lectures, and has a counseling ministry in her home.

Grace Little has tried unsuccessfully to find meaningful work for herself. Unfortunately, the medicines she takes make her drowsy and slow down her mental processes. Also, she has to pace herself, rest, and limit her stress to keep from exacerbating her condition. She has had four acute manic episodes without warning, and she says, "[I fear] not always being in control of my behavior…It's just a very thin-ice feeling when you know that you can't always be counted on to be a responsible adult." She completed a year toward a masters in speech therapy before realizing she could not maintain a professional pace, and she began to worry about liability issues when working with children. Jobs teaching English as a second language appeal to her, but most of them are part-time. So, she continues her employment as a part-time secretary, but dreams of moving into more meaningful work.

Two years after her injury, Tamara Puffer is working toward finding a part-time position in ministry. She left her full time position as associate pastor with children and youth because of the many organizational tasks involved and because of her desire to pursue a calling in other pastoral directions. Presently, she is getting weekly supervision from me on her volunteer work as a chaplain to senior adults.

Kathy Berry longs to be a writer again; however, her difficulty with her hands keeps her from writing full-time. After her MS diagnosis, she transferred from a writing job into a public relations position at the Foreign Mission Board of the SBC. After two years, she had to leave that position as well. Presently, she works ten hours a week as associate pastor at a small church, but her heart is still in writing. She and Bill always planned to be missionaries overseas, but that goal is now out of their reach.

Francene Passantino worked office jobs for many years before attending college. She was just completing a bachelors degree when she had her injury. After several years of disability, she went back to part-time and later full-time office work but was unable to continue because, as she says, "every symptom I ever had screamed out at me." Back on Social Security disability, she is volunteer editor of *Ahead of the Times*, a newsletter for persons with TBI and their families.[34]

Kimberly Thomas is the only woman of those interviewed who is supporting herself in her chosen profession—nursing. From age twenty-one to thirty-four, however, she was unable to keep a job because of her irresponsibility and addiction. Her dreams for the future include marriage and creating a halfway house for female addicts.

Finding a paid vocation is not an issue for Bernie Blanton. At seventy-three, she is retired, but she longs to write, find more creative outlets, increase her mobility, and she longs for a companion with whom to share her life.

I have looked into doing scores of things: teaching, part-time pastoral counseling or chaplaincy, research writing and freelance journalism, selling health food products or books, assembling products or stuffing envelopes at home, transcribing, interior decorating. In each job I investigate, my inability to control anxiety, pace myself, work without napping and resting, and drive long distances has interfered. Jobs that I can do are those I create myself where I work at my own pace. Most of these pay less than minimum wage or cost me money to do them.

Several years ago, I applied for a part-time chaplaincy position, only to be denied a personal interview or a follow-up phone call after telling them of my disability.[35] Within the last year, I moved to a new home with a pottery studio and a psychotherapy office. Pottery is a therapeutic hobby that I hope will pay for itself. My current vocational goal, therefore, focuses not so much on supporting myself as feeling that I am making a contribution to society, having a ministry, and continuing to grow. Keeping on this path for my avocation may result in a paid vocation.

A Spirituality for a Strange Land

A woman who lives in the strange land of disability rebuilds her life by listening to that still small voice inside of her. Spirituality is not a luxury; it is essential for survival. Now on the boundaries of life, a woman can see more clearly the dysfunction that was present in the former land. Because of limited energy and finances, she simplifies her lifestyle and constantly reassesses: What is essential in my life? What things must be changed? What needs to be added or redefined in my spiritual life? What needs to be grieved and let go?

All of the women interviewed pray daily for themselves and for others who are suffering. Only Kathleen Lewis prays specifically and regularly for physical healing.[36] Others pray for emotional healing, strength, patience, and wisdom. Many believe that God can work miracles, but they are not demanding one for themselves. Most think that their illness is just a part of life; they do not think they have been singled out by God for punishment or for a life lesson.[37] They use varying forms of prayer and meditation. Some pray at a regular time every day; others maintain an openness to God and a prayerful attitude throughout the day; some meditate on Scripture, and others create visual images for their prayers.

Most of the women realize that they are only steps away from death, home-lessness, or total dependency on others for daily needs, so each woman nurtures hope and expresses gratitude for each gift of healing and friendship in her life.

As shown in the previous section, theirs is not a passive spirituality. These women "work out their own salvation".[38] They maintain daily rituals of self-care which nurture hope and healing; work on maintaining positive relationships with others, themselves, God, and their illnesses; seek a vocation and meaning for their lives. Many are now doing advocacy work because of their heightened awareness of marginalized persons. Many of these women also use journaling and prayer to voice their ongoing griefs to God. I write Psalms of Lament and prayers to God on the computer. Most women also listen to music throughout the day and find their pets encouraging.

Humor is also a spiritual gift for women with disabilities. Kathy Berry watches funny movies, reads funny books, and collects jokes. When she's going through a relapse, she refers to her "injury du jour" (like pricking her finger when she's try-ing to cook). Bernie Blanton is "the bunny with batteries who keeps going and going." I'm "retired," "an eccentric potter," or "the old woman who wears purple and spits."[39]

I asked every woman what chronic illness had taught them. The gifts are many for those who have eyes to see: empathy, value of friendships, power of self-reflec-tion, importance of honesty, patience, tolerance for others, ability to "see people as people" (rather than based on their outward appearances), learning to ask for help from others and to be one's own person without embarrassment, slowing down, identifying with marginalized persons, learning to blaze new trails and "color out-side the lines" by creating new structures of support for themselves and others, and developing a renewed vision of how God works in the world with our help.

Ministering to Women with Acquired/Hidden Disabilities

There is much to be done within the church to offer women a place of recovery and to help ministers and congregations heal in their assumptions about chronic illness and disability. Listen to your feelings when you read these suggestions about ministry by, with, and for persons with disabilities. It is likely that you will be over-whelmed. No one person or church could possibly do what is suggested here. Honor your feeling of being overwhelmed. Living with limited energy, resources, and often fragile egos in a complex world that moves at a breakneck speed is the task put before women with acquired disabilities.

There are four areas of suggestions for ministering to women with hidden disabilities. Making buildings handicapped-accessible is a given, though only a first step.[40]

1. Listen and learn from women with disabilities; educate the congregation about disability (especially mental illness and addiction).

- Listen to women with disabilities. Do not make any assumptions about their lives. If you have emotional baggage that prevents you from entering into their worlds, get supervision and/or therapy for your own healing.
- Avoid stereotypical remarks such as, "If you feel as good as you look, you must be doing great!" Or "God is giving you this illness to teach you patience."
- Be aware that your attitudes toward persons with disabilities might speak louder than your words. Be careful to be neither patronizing nor idealizing.
- Do not judge someone's overall functioning by the way she relates in church for several hours a week. One outing a day is all that some women are capable of doing.
- Educate yourself about what resources and support groups already exist in your community.
- Educate your congregation about chronic illness in general and about specific diseases. Provide seminars, bibliographies, information about support groups, and denominational information and speakers.
- Offer brainstorming or consciousness-raising sessions where disabled persons can educate others and where nondisabled persons can voice misconceptions and discomfort that they have about disability.
- Attend A.A., N.A., or other support group meetings that are geared to specific dis-eases that church members have.
- Avoid using loaded words like "crazy" from the pulpit. You may have many parishioners (and their family members) with invisible disabilities who are still "in the closet."
- Realize that disabled women may be teaching you or a family member how to deal with a disability that is in the future for your family.
- Be careful about equating God's judgment against sin through illness. Many disabled persons already have low self-esteem and blame themselves for not getting better.
- Be a part of early intervention in disability. When counseling parishioners with depression, fatigue, stress, have them get a physical. Many physical illnesses have psychological components.[41]

2. Anticipate crises, meet concrete needs, and be ready to offer lifetime support.

- In times of crisis, provide concrete care, such as food, child care, transportation, visits, prayer, or money, but do not make assumptions about how you can best offer care. *Ask.*
- Minister to family members as well as to the woman who is in crisis. No one is disabled in isolation. Family systems are in constant change when one member is disabled, and many marriages cannot stand the strain of chronic illness.
- Offer to pray with and to help find consistent, ongoing support for a woman

with a disability. Consider a prayer partner, deacon, friend, spiritual director, pastoral counselor, or ongoing support group.

- Help women with disabilities develop small goals for themselves; do not support unrealistic expectations. Beware of preaching that if you just have enough faith anything is possible. This mindset can be disastrous for a disabled person. Realize that women with disabilities may make some poor choices when recovering, especially during the first two to four years of their illness. Offer them a place to grieve when new dreams are not realized.
- Throw a party for some disabled members of your church who might be living in poverty. Take them to a movie, concert, or art exhibit. Invite them to a meal at your home or take them to a restaurant.
- Offer pastoral care rituals to disabled women and their families at significant life events: onset of diagnosis; periods of relapse or remission of symptoms; coming home from the hospital; receiving Social Security or other disability benefits (often bittersweet to the recipient); anniversaries of diagnosis; severed family relationships; termination of paid employment; loss of home or independent living; holidays; return to paid employment; purchase of a new home; and so forth.

3. Reincorporate women with disabilities back into the life of the church.
- Be flexible with women with disabilities. Sometimes they may have to cancel an appointment because they are having a bad day and need to take care of themselves. If they miss a church event, do not take it personally.
- Evoke gifts of disabled women in worship, preaching, pastoral care, and in leadership roles in the church. Many women with disabilities have had their vocations shattered and need to find places to give as well as to receive from the church.
- Consider assigning a person with a disability as a pastoral care deacon. Be prepared to tailor some church positions for persons who have lowered energy.
- Be specific in your guidance when preaching or offering pastoral care. Do not just tell persons to "trust God" or "put God first" but help them to develop practices that will enable them to be more aware of God and nurture faith. Ask women with disabilities and their families to help you and the congregation by sharing what they have learned from living their lives on the margins. They might be more keenly aware of self-defeating patterns, hectic lifestyles, dysfunctional work habits and relationships now that they have to listen more carefully to their bodies.

4. Advocate for women with disabilities, offer preventive care, and create new structures of care where there are voids.
- Sponsor support groups in your church for specific target populations. Offer a general support group for persons in transition and invite a person with a disability to be a cofacilitator. Utilize the coping skills and empathy that persons

with disabilities have developed to aid you in your own pastoral care efforts with others in crisis. Educate your congregation about the dynamics of grief.

- Help persons with disabilities to have a voice in local schools, particularly in educating youth about physical, emotional, and spiritual health, family dynamics, physical, mental, and emotional abuse, and drug/alcohol addiction.
- Help disabled women access a larger world. Provide funds for computer technology and training. Start an e-mail list of church members to share jokes, prayer concerns and celebrations, and church events.
- Encourage bartering or cooperative efforts among persons with little income for child care, grocery shopping and cooking, and creative hobbies and vocations that can be done out of their homes.
- Set up soup kitchens, halfway houses, educational grant programs, or vocational rehabilitation, health, and legal services; found agencies to help persons to gain access to low-income housing and low-interest loans that will enable disabled persons to purchase a home or start a home business. Many disabled persons are only a step away from homelessness. Early intervention might help them be independent as long as possible.[42]
- Initiate or support legislation to help disabled persons. (In 1998, Georgia passed a law adding a 10 percent fine for drunk drivers which should raise two million dollars annually for a Brain Injury and Spinal Cord Trust Fund. Other states need to follow suit.)

Summary

In this chapter eight women with disabilities have spoken. Seven said that the greatest thing the church could offer them was to listen. Active listening takes courage, emotional stamina, and the ability to move into worlds of fear, uncertainty, and emotional and physical pain. But also in these worlds are wisdom, patience, empathy, creativity, humor, a heightened awareness of the body, a spirituality in the desert, and many rewarding accomplishments not measured by the world's standards, nor past standards before disability, but by each woman's present standards and goals.

Women with acquired disabilities have lives that fork in the middle and dramatically change course. While no life cycle is predictable, disabled women often face issues that are more common in older adulthood than in midlife or early transitions.[43] No two women with acquired disabilities are alike, even those with the same dis-ease. Singing God's song in a strange land is hard. Women with disabilities welcome supportive companions for a lifetime of journeying.

Afterthoughts

In their own time, eighteen women writing for this volume have begun the re-formulation of developmental theory in pastoral care. In order to do so, we have paid attention to the impact of the culture and the body in addition to the role of the mind and soul in development. We have kept in our minds' eye survivors of intimate violence and trauma, members of underprivileged socio-economic and racial-ethnic groupings, women with disabilities, older widows, non-traditional women, mothers, women whose bodies are marking time, women who have not been in circles of power. With these foci, our work has become distinctive even as we gratefully acknowledge the work of many others on development. We have heeded our predecessors.[1]

How have we proceeded in our research and writing into the reformulation of developmental theory when the images have been painful and provocative as well as joyful and sustaining? Networking with other scholars, listening to narratives of our clients, patients, and parishioners, being supported by male and female colleagues, feeling encouraged by the Society of Pastoral Theology, taking care of our bodies, listening when our souls speak, and watching for God has been our process. We have circulated our individual chapters, enjoyed working dinners together, edited for one another, and revised our research with shared insight and wisdom.

We began our conversation in *Women in Travail and Transition: A New Pastoral Care*. We expanded the roundtable dialogue of issues and concerns in *Through the Eyes of Women: Insights for Pastoral Care*. Now, in this last volume of the trilogy, we conclude with a re-envisioning of developmental theory. In all three works, we have been celebrating women's strengths.

A forerunner in our field, Frances Gillespy Wickes (1875–1967), tells this story in her trilogy which included *The Inner World of Choice*. "A woman physician, whose vocational life had been dedicated to scientific research on occupational hazards, was asked how she could, when fighting for the passage of a better labor law, face 50 or more antagonistic men and hold clearly and decisively to her point without arousing those negative undercurrents that the animus never fails to awaken in the masculine psyche. She said, 'I keep before my inner vision a scene I once witnessed—a thin tired bewildered child sitting with loving patience beside a father who was dying of lead poisoning. Then I remember the meaning of my research in terms of human life.'[2]

We keep before our inner vision the images we have seen and remember the meaning of our research in terms of women's lives.

Notes

Introduction

1. A critique has been offered of Lawrence Kohlberg's sequence of moral development by Carol Gilligan in *In a Different Voice* (Cambridge, Mass.: Harvard Univ. Press, 1982.

2. Women's psychological, spiritual, and biological development has been recently configured by Joan Borysenko. In *A Woman's Book of Life: The Biology, Psychology, and Spirituality of the Feminine Life Cycle* (New York: Riverhead, 1996), the female life cycle is organized into twelve seven-year periods, with the thirteenth part as death. There are three seven-year periods in each quadrant of life: childhood and adolescence; young adulthood; midlife; and elder years.

3. This term, *self-in-relation*, has been the subject of numerous research papers through the Stone Center, Wellesley College. It implies a connectedness that begins in utero and continues through authenticated development of the self.

4. Eccl. 12:6

5. Luke 2:52

6. Genesis 21 contains the account of Sarah becoming the mother of Isaac, father of Jacob. Although some women claim Sarah as a predecessor, others claim Hagar, the Egyptian slave woman who was cast out of the household by Sarah (Genesis 21:9ff). Hagar had born a son, Ishmael, to Abraham before Sarah gave birth to Isaac. Some African American women have claimed identification with Hagar. Thus the image in this preface has been reshaped as Sarah and Hagar's circle.

7. "We Are Dancing Sarah's Circle" is sung to the tune of "We Are Climbing Jacob's Ladder." This song was (re)written by Carole Etzler and sung on her album, *Sometimes I Wish* (Atlanta: Samray Music/Sisters Unlimited, 1976).

8. Jean Baker Miller, *Toward a New Psychology of Women* (Boston: Beacon, 1976), 53.

9. Ibid.

10. James E. Loder, *The Logic of the Human Spirit: Human Development in Theological Perspective* (San Francisco: Jossey-Bass, 1998), 46–54.

11. Ibid., 53.

12. Susan Wolf, "Martha C. Nussbaum: Human Capabilities, Female Human Beings," in *Women, Culture, and Development,* ed. Martha Nussbaum and Jonathan Glover (Oxford: Clarendon, 1995), 113–14.

Chapter 1

1. Charles Gerkin, *The Living Human Document: Re-Envisioning Pastoral Counseling in a Hermeneutical Mode* (Nashville: Abingdon, 1984), 39.

2. Ibid., 30.

3. Ibid., 63.

4. Ibid., 70-71.

5. Dorothee Soelle, *The Strength of the Weak: Toward a Christian Feminist Identity* (Philadelphia: Westminster, 1984), 45.

6. Ibid.

7. Ibid., 46.

8. Jaroslav Pelikan, *Mary through the Centuries: Her Place in the History of Culture* (New Haven, Conn.: Yale Univ. Press, 1996), 91. "Woman of Valor thus became a striking formula for the motif and the metaphor of Mary as warrior and champion, as conqueror and leader." One of the most powerful evidences of this motif in Western Christendom is found in the eventual Latin translation of the words of punishment addressed by God to the serpent: "I shall put enmity between you and the woman, and between your seed and her seed; she [ipsa] will crush your head." See p. 91.

9. Ibid., 84.

10. Rosemary Radford Ruether, *Mary: The Feminine Face of the Church* (Philadelphia: Westminster, 1977), 79.

11. Anne E. Carr, *Transforming Grace: Christian Tradition and Women's Experience* (San Francisco: Harper & Row, 1988), 190.

12. Pelikan, *Mary through the Centuries,* 50.

13. Ibid., 55.

14. Helen Flanders Dunbar, *Emotions and Bodily Changes: A Survey of Literature on Psychosomatic Interrelationships, 1910–1953* (New York: Columbia Univ. Press, 1954), 56.

15. Bruno Bettelheim, *Freud and Man's Soul* (New York: Vintage, 1982). In understanding Sigmund Freud's use of the psyche and soma, Bruno Bettelheim has made a crucial contribution. For Freud, psyche meant mind or intellect. "When Freud speaks of the soul he is talking not about a religious phenomenon but about a psychological concept . . ." (77). Soul becomes the seat of the mind and passions.

16. Dunbar, *Emotions and Bodily Changes,* 31.

17. Maya McNeilly, "Study: Racism has effect on health," *Atlanta Journal/Constitution,* July 23, 1996.

18. Dunbar, *Emotions and Bodily Changes,* 355.

19. McNeilly, "Study." Psychologist McNeilly documented the effects of racist provocation on African Americans as the heart rate and blood pressure of her sample shot up during the racially charged experience.

20. Ibid.

21. Elisabeth Moltmann-Wendel, *I Am My Body* (London: SCM, 1994), 42.

22. Ibid., ix.

23. Ibid., xii.

24. Ibid., xii.

25. Ibid., 85.

26. Ibid., 77.

27. Christine Northrup, *Women's Bodies, Women's Wisdom* (Des Plaines, Ill.: Bantam, 1994), 27.

28. Jean Baker Miller, *Toward a New Psychology of Women,* 2nd ed. (Boston: Beacon, 1986), xxii.

29. "Post-Traumatic Stress Disorder" (Princeton: Films for the Humanities & Sciences, 1991).

30. Carol Gilligan, *In a Different Voice: Psychological Theory and Women's Development* (Cambridge, Mass.: Harvard Univ. Press, 1982), 74.

31. Mary Pipher, *Reviving Ophelia: Saving the Selves of Adolescent Girls* (New York: Ballantine, 1994).

32. Erik Erikson, *Identity: Youth and Crisis* (New York: W. W. Norton & Company, 1968). Cultural consolidation, introduced in the works of Erikson, is also difficult for the woman who is generally not part of the dominant culture. The fragmentation of cultural identity into distinct cultural components is cultural dissolution. See Jeanne Stevenson Moessner, "Cultural Dissolution: 'I Lost Africa,'" *Missiology: An International Review* 14, no. 3 (July 1986): 313–24. In this article I develop the phenomenon of cultural dissolution: "An inner and outer discontinuity disturb the organization of personal sameness" (315). Women receive messages from the culture that objectify, falsify, and belittle them.

33. Judith Hauptman, "Images of Women in the Talmud," in *Religion and Sexism,* ed. Rosemary Radford Ruether (New York: Simon and Schuster, 1974), 196.

34. Nel Noddings, *Women and Evil* (Berkeley, Calif.: Univ. of California Press, 1989), 10.

35. Judith Romney Wegner, *Chattel or Person? The Status of Women in the Mishnah* (Oxford: Oxford Univ. Press, 1988), 158: "The exclusion of women from precisely those aspects of mishnaic culture that nurture the life of mind and spirit inevitably reduced the quality of women's life and personhood."

36. The Rev. Amy Fowler found the image of the double helix, the structure of the DNA molecule, for me. The linear, vertical model was used by Erik Erikson, the pyramid by Abraham Maslow.

Chapter 2

1. Havighurst, Robert, "Social and Developmental Psychology: Trends Influencing the Future of Counseling," *The Personnel and Guidance Journal* 58 (January 1980): 332.

2. J. Eugene Wright, *Erikson: Identity and Religion* (New York: Seabury, 1982), 23.

3. Erik Erikson, *Childhood and Society* (New York: W. W. Norton, 1950, 1963).

4. Jean Piaget, *The Moral Judgement of the Child* (New York: The Free Press, 1932); *Six Psychological Studies* (New York: Viking Books, 1968); *Structuralism* (New York: Basic, 1970).

5. Robert White, foreword to *Forms of Intellectual and Ethical Development in the College Years: A Scheme*, by William Perry (New York: Holt, Rinehart and Winston, Inc., 1970), v.

6. Perry, *Forms of Intellectual and Ethical Development*, 7.

7. Carol Gilligan, *In a Different Voice: Psychological Theory and Women's Development* (Cambridge, Mass.: Harvard Univ. Press, 1982).

8. Mary Field Belenky, Blythe McVicker Clinchy, Nancy Rule Goldberger, and Jill Matuck Tarule, *Women's Ways of Knowing* (New York: Basic, 1986), 10.

9. Perry, *Forms of Intellectual and Ethical Development*, 177–200.

10. Jane Loevinger, *Ego Development* (San Francisco: Jossey-Bass, 1976).

11. Lawrence Kohlberg, *The Philosophy of Moral Development* (New York: Harper & Row, 1981); *The Psychology of Moral Development* (New York: Harper & Row, 1984).

12. James Fowler, *Stages of Faith: The Psychology of Human Development and the Quest for Meaning* (San Francisco: Harper & Row, 1981).

13. Loevinger, *Ego Development*, 24–25.

14. Jane Loevinger and Ruth Wessler, *Measuring Ego Development I* (San Francisco: Jossey-Bass, 1970).

15. Elizabeth Liebert, *Changing Life Patterns: Adult Development in Spiritual Direction* (New York: Paulist, 1992).

16. Kohlberg, *The Psychology of Moral Development*.

17. Gilligan, *In a Different Voice*.

18. Belenky et al., *Women's Ways of Knowing*, 11.

19. Ibid., 15.

20. Ibid., 15–16.

21. Ann Stanton, "Reconfiguring Teaching and Knowing the in College Classroom," in *Knowledge, Difference and Power: Essays Inspired by Women's Ways of Knowing*, ed. N. Goldberger, J. Tarule, B. Clinchy, and M. Belenky (New York: Basic, 1996), 25.

22. Nancy Goldberger, "Introduction: Looking Backward, Looking Forward," in *Knowledge, Difference and Power*, ed. Goldberger et al., 12.

23. Loevinger, *Ego Development*, 309.

24. Vanessa Bing and Pamela Trotman Reid, "Unknown Women and Unknowing Research: Consequences of Color and Class in Feminist Psychology," in *Knowledge, Difference and Power*, ed. Goldberger et al.

25. Loevinger, *Ego Development*, 409–10.

26. Jane Loevinger, "Theories of Ego Development," in *Clinical Cognitive Psychology: Models and Integrations*, ed. L. Breger (Englewood Cliffs, N.J.: Prentice-Hall, 1969), 85.

27. Robert Kegan, *The Evolving Self: Problem and Process in Human Development* (Cambridge, Mass.: Harvard Univ. Press, 1982).

28. Liebert, *Changing Life Patterns*.

29. Loevinger, *Ego Development*, 199.

30. Perry, *Forms of Intellectual and Ethical Development*, 88.

31. Ibid., 200.

32. Laurent A. Daloz, Cheryl H. Keen, James P. Keen, and Sharon Daloz Parks, *Common Fire: Lives of Commitment in a Complex World* (Boston: Beacon, 1996).

33. Perry, *Forms of Intellectual and Ethical Development,* 200.

34. Kegan, *The Evolving Self.*

35. Ibid., 256.

36. Liebert, *Changing Life Patterns.*

37. See, for example, Lyn Mikel Brown and Carol Gilligan, *Meeting at the Crossroads: Women's Psychology and Girls' Development* (New York: Ballantine, 1992); James Fowler, *Weaving the New Creation: Stages of Faith and the Public Church* (San Francisco: Harper & Row, 1991); Fowler, *Faithful Change: The Personal and Public Challenges of Postmodern Life* (Nashville: Abingdon, 1996); Mary Field Belenky, "Public Homeplaces: Nurturing the Development of People, Families and Communities," in *Knowledge, Difference and Power,* ed. Goldberger et al.; Nancy Goldberger, "Introduction: Looking Backward, Looking Forward," in *Knowledge, Difference and Power;* Robert Kegan, *In Over Our Heads: The Mental Demands of Modern Life* (Cambridge, Mass.: Harvard Univ. Press, 1994); Laurent A. Daloz, *Effective Teaching and Mentoring: Realizing the Transformational Power of Adult Learning Experiences* (San Francisco: Jossey-Bass, 1986); and Daloz et al., *Common Fire.*

38. Kegan, *In Over Our Heads* (1984).

39. Ibid., 1–11.

40. Daloz et al., *Common Fire,* 107.

41. Ibid., 3.

42. Douglas K. Huneke, *The Moses of Rovno* (Tiburon, Calif.: Compassion House, 1985).

43. Ibid., 177–87.

44. Daloz et al., *Common Fire,* 5.

45. Ibid., 108.

Chapter 3

1. The topic of working-class women's life span development was first addressed by this author in *Psychological and Moral Development of Working Class Women with Implications for Pastoral Counseling* (UMI, 1990). This chapter develops some of those ideas further. The earlier work includes a copy of the interview questionnaire in the appendix.

2. See Pauline Bart, "Review of Chodorow's *The Reproduction of Mothering*," *Mothering: Essays in Feminist Theory,* ed. Joyce Trebilcot (Totowa, N.J.: Rowman & Allanheld, 1983), 147–52. Also Judith Lorber et al., "On The Reproduction of Mothering: A Methodological Debate," *Signs* 6 (1981): 482–514.

3. Carol Gilligan, "In a Different Voice: Women's Conception of Self and Morality," *Harvard Review of Education* 47 (1977): 481–517.

4. Tex Sample discusses four groups of working-class people: winners (skilled labor), respectables (some white-collar labor; value order, decency, doing things right), survivors (semiskilled labor, ongoing financial struggle), and hard-living people (unskilled labor; rootless, tough) in *Blue-Collar Ministry: Facing Economic and Social Realities of Working People* (Valley Forge, Penn.: Judson Press, 1984), 59–103.

5. E. O. Wright, "American Class Structure," *American Sociological Review* 47 (December 1982): 709–26, uses a Marxist perspective.

6. Marjorie Fiske notes four kinds of developmental theories: stage theories, self-actualization theories, eclectic social change theories, and dialectic theories, in "Changing Hierarchies of Commitment in Adulthood," *Themes of Work and Love in Adulthood,* ed. Neil J. Smelser and Erik H. Erikson (Cambridge, Mass.: Harvard Univ. Press, 1980), 241–42. For further description of the dialectical theory used here, see Klaus Riegel, "Toward a Dialectical Theory of Development," *Human Development* 1–2 (1975): 50–64.

7. Rhea V. Almeida, Rosemary Woods, and Theresa Messineo, "Child Development: Intersectionality of Race, Gender, Class, and Culture," *Journal of Feminist Family Therapy* 10, no. 1 (1998): 23–47.

8. All twenty women interviewed were American Midwesterners. Their self-identified ethnic backgrounds were German, Italian, Scottish, Irish, English, Hispanic, and African American. Their religious self-identifications were Catholic, Protestant, and agnostic. Most worked for pay outside the

home, although some understood themselves primarily as homemakers. They were married, divorced, widowed, and single, although a disproportionate number of the working-class women were divorced. There were slightly more children on average among the working-class women. Interviews were 2 to 2 1/2 hours in length and guided by preset questions regarding life review, life-shaping experiences and relationships, values and commitments, and religion. Because all people interviewed were adults, information about childhood and adolescence was based on recollection. Because the number of women interviewed was small and no claims of a random sample are being made, interview results are suggestive for further study rather than conclusive.

9. Phases are different from stages, which focus on universal, invariant, and hierarchical structures, and from ages, which focus on culturally relative and socially influenced expectations, obligations, and status in role-related time blocks, according to John Snarey, Lawrence Kohlberg, and Gil Noam, "Ego Development in Perspective: Structural Stage, Functional Phase, and Cultural Age-Period Models," *Developmental Review* 3, no. 13 (1983): 303–38. Phases focus on the interaction of universal structures and culturally relative contents to produce new functional tasks.

10. Salvador Minuchin and H. Charles Fishman, *Family Therapy Techniques* (Cambridge, Mass.: Harvard Univ. Press, 1981), 18–19.

11. Barbara Rogoff et al., "Age of Assignment of Roles and Responsibilities to Children: A Cross-Cultural Survey," *Human Development* 18 (1975), 353–69.

12. I am suggesting that Gloria Powell's idea of hybrid identity, which she applies to African Americans, might be extended to any who are marginal to white bourgeois culture. See Gloria Johnson Powell, "Growing Up Black and Female," in *Becoming Female: Perspectives on Development*, ed. Claire B. Kopp (New York: Plenum, 1979), 29f.

13. Almeida, Woods, and Messineo, "Child Development."

14. Sallie Westwood, *All Day, Every Day: Factory and Family in the Making of Women's Lives* (Chicago: Univ. of Illinois, 1985), 6.

15. See, for example, Ravenna Helson et al., "Lives of Women Who Became Autonomous," *Journal of Personality* 53 (1985): 261; Mary L. Walshok, *Blue Collar Women* (Garden City, N.Y.: Anchor, 1981), 50–55; and C. R. Robinson, in "Black Women: A Tradition of Self-Reliant Strength," *Women Changing Therapy*, ed. Joan H. Robbins and Rachel J. Siegel (New York: Haworth, 1983), 136.

16. According to Jerome Kagan and Robert Klein, "Cross-Cultural Perspectives on Early Development," *American Psychologist* 28 (1973), 949, 958, all children are capable of concrete operational thinking and will develop those skills by the age of ten or eleven.

17. Kathleen Gerson, *Hard Choices: How Women Decide About Work, Career, and Motherhood* (Berkeley, Calif.: Univ. of California Press, 1985), 47–67.

18. An early study that included a female sample of adolescents is Elizabeth Douvan and J. Adelson, *The Adolescent Experience* (New York: Wiley & Sons, 1966).

19. Ruth Josselson, "Ego Development in Adolescence," in *Handbook of Adolescent Psychology*, ed. J. Adelson (New York: Wiley, 1980), 188–221.

20. Daniel J. Levinson, *The Seasons of a Man's Life* (New York: Knopf, 1978).

21. Judith Bardwick, "The Seasons of a Woman's Life," in *Women's Lives: New Theory, Research, and Policy*, ed. Dorothy G. McGuigan (Ann Arbor, Mich.: Univ. of Michigan Press, 1980), 35–57.

22. These four suggestions of identity resolution may be found in J. E. Marcia, "Development and Validation of Ego Identity Status," *Journal of Personality and Social Psychology* 3 (1966): 551–58.

23. See David H. Demo and Ritch C. Savin-Williams, "Early Adolescent Self-Esteem as a Function of Social Class: Rosenberg and Pearlin Revisited," *American Journal of Sociology* 88 (1983): 763–74.

24. Sasha G. Lewis, *Sunday's Women: Lesbian Life Today* (Boston: Beacon, 1979), 24, notes studies done in 1969 (40 percent) and in 1976 (55 percent).

25. In a study of two groups of thirty-nine children over a fourteen-year period, one group raised by lesbian mothers and one group by heterosexual mothers, Tasker and Golombok found that class and education were more of a factor than lifestyle in influencing attitudes toward broader social issues. Additionally, there were no significant differences between the groups in their capacity to find and maintain intimate relationships or in their levels of anxiety, depression, and pursuit of mental health assistance. See Jane Ariel, "Review of *Growing Up in a Lesbian Family* by Fiona Tasker and Susan Golombok," *Journal of Feminist Family Therapy* 10, no. 3 (1998): 75–78.

26. Arthur Shostak, *Blue Collar Life* (New York: Random House, 1969).

27. Michael E. Lamb, Margaret Tresch Owen, and Lindsay Chase-Lansdale, "The Father-Daughter Relationship: Past, Present, and Future," in *Becoming Female: Perspectives on Development*, ed. Claire B. Kopp (New York: Plenum, 1979), 107.

28. Walshok, *Blue Collar Women*, 8–34, 40, 50–86.

29. Lillian Rubin, *Worlds of Pain: Life in the Working Class Family* (New York: Praeger, 1976), 60, notes that 44 percent of the seventy-five couples she interviewed got married because the woman was pregnant.

30. John Allen Bruce, "The Role of Mothers in the Social Placement of Daughters: Marriage or Work?" *Journal of Marriage and the Family* 36 (1974): 494–95.

31. J. Thomas Butler, "Early Adolescent Alcohol Consumption and Self-Concept, Social Class, and Knowledge of Alcohol," *Journal of Studies on Alcohol* 43 (1982): 606.

32. Joseph T. Howell, *Hard Living on Clay Street: Portraits of Blue Collar Families* (New York: Doubleday/Anchor, 1973).

33. Kristin Moor, Margaret C. Simms, and Charles L. Betsey, *Choice and Circumstance: Race Differences in Adolescent Sexuality and Fertility* (New Brunswick, N.J.: Rutgers Univ. Press, 1986).

34. Norma Haan, "Adolescents and Young Adults as Producers of Their Development," in *Individuals as Producers of Their Development: A Life Span Perspective*, ed. Richard M. Lerner and Nancy A. Busch-Rossnagel (New York: Academic, 1981), 163.

35. Rubin, *Worlds of Pain*, 73.

36. Christine Griffin, "Broken Transitions: From School to the Scrap Heap," in *Women and the Life Cycle*, ed. Patricia Allatt et al. (New York: St. Martin's, 1987), 81, 86.

37. Melvin L. Kohn and Carmi Schooler, "Class, Occupation, and Orientation," *American Sociological Review* 34 (1969): 666.

38. Peter Conrad and Rochele Kern, eds., *The Sociology of Health and Illness* (New York: St. Martin's, 1981), 109.

39. Daniel Berman, *Death on the Job* (New York: Monthly Review Press, 1978), 46.

40. Studs Terkel, *Working* (New York: Avon, 1974), xxiv.

41. Andrew Cherlin, "Postponing Marriage: The Influence of Young Women's Work Expectations," *Journal of Marriage and Family* 42 (1980): 363.

42. U.S. Bureau of the Census, *Current Population Reports: A Statistical Portrait of Women in the U.S. 1978*, 66.

43. Myra Marx Ferree, "Between Two Worlds: German Feminist Approaches to Working Class Women and Work," *Signs* 10 (1985): 531.

44. R. A. Berk and S. F. Berk, *Labor and Leisure at Home: Content and Organization of the Household* (Beverly Hills, Calif.: Sage, 1979).

45. Rae Lesser Blumberg, "A General Theory of Gender Stratification," in *Sociological Theory, 1984*, ed. Randall Collins (San Francisco: Jossey-Bass, 1984), 68f.

46. Peggy R. Sanday, "Female Status in the Public Domain," in *Woman, Culture and Society*, ed. Michelle Rosaldo and Louise Lamphere (Stanford, Calif.: Stanford Univ. Press, 1974).

47. Daniel Rossides, *The American Class System* (Boston: Houghton Mifflin, 1976), 177.

48. Karen Gail Lewis, "A Life Stage Model Should Include Single Women: Clinical Implications for Addressing Ambivalence," *Journal of Feminist Family Therapy* 10, no. 2 (1998): 1–22.

49. Ellen Rosen, *Bitter Choices: Blue Collar Women In and Out of Work* (Chicago: Univ. of Chicago Press, 1987), 47.

50. Jeanne Stillman and Mary Sue Henifin, "No Fertile Women Need Apply: Employment Discrimination and Reproductive Hazards in the Workplace," in *Biological Woman: The Convenient Myth*, ed. Ruth Hubbard, Mary Sue Henifin, and Barbara Fried (Boston: Schenkman, 1982).

51. Elizabeth Douvan, "Employment and the Adolescent," in *The Employed Mother in America*, ed. F. I. Nye and Lois W. Hoffman (Chicago: Rand McNally, 1963).

52. Levinson, *The Seasons of a Man's Life*.

53. Bardwick, "The Seasons of a Woman's Life," 37.

54. Tillie Olsen, "I Stand Here Ironing," in *Tell Me a Riddle* (New York: Dell, 1976), 9.

55. Rubin, *Worlds of Pain*, 93, notes that middle-class women mention none of these but rather intimacy values (sharing and communication) and status values (comforts and prestige of husband's job).

56. Rosen, *Bitter Choices*, 89.

57. Patricia Zavella, "'Abnormal Intimacy': The Varying Work Networks of Chicana Cannery Workers," *Feminist Studies* 11, no. 3 (1985): 553.

58. R. L. Hill, "Life-Cycle Stages for Types of Single-Parent Families: Family Development Theory," *Family Relations* 35 (1986): 28.

59. Stephanie A. Demetrakopoulos, "Life Stage Theory, Gerontological Research, and the Mythology of the Older Woman: Independence, Autonomy, and Strength," *Anima* 8 (1982): 90.

60. Corinne Azen, "Ethnic Culture, Religion, and the Mental Health of Slavic Women," *Journal of Religion and Health* 18, no. 4 (1979): 298–307.

61. Bernice L. Neugarten et al. *Personality in Middle and Late Life* (New York: Atherton, 1964), 12.

62. Albert Szymanski, *Class Structure: A Critical Perspective* (New York: Praeger, 1983), 301.

63. Evelyn Kitagawa and Philip Hauser, *Differential Mortality in the U.S.* (Cambridge, Mass.: Harvard Univ. Press, 1973), 71, 91.

64. Szymanski, *Class Structure*, 298, 305.

65. Joseph Veroff, Lou McClelland, and David Ruhland, "Varieties of Achievement Motivation," in *Women and Achievement: Social and Motivational Analysis* (Washington, D.C.: Hemisphere, 1975), 200.

66. Almeida, Woods, and Messineo mention four competencies: trust, interdependence, tolerance, and expanded identity.

Chapter 4

1. "Donaldson, Lufkin and Jenrette Newsletter," May 3, 1996, 13.

2. Margi Laird McCue, *Domestic Violence: A Reference Handbook* (Santa Barbara, Calif.: ABC-CLIO, 1995), 81.

3. Ibid., 79.

4. Patrick Langan and Christopher Innes, "Preventing Domestic Violence against Women," *Bureau of Justice Statistics—Special Report* (August 1986): 1.

5. McCue, *Domestic Violence*, 77.

6. Cynthia Costello and Anne J. Stone, *The American Woman, 1994–95* (New York: W. W. Norton, 1994), 121.

7. Marianne Zawitz, "Violence Between Intimates," *Bureau of Justice Statistics* (Washington, D.C.: U.S. Government Printing Office, 1994), 2.

8. J. E. Kesner, T. Julian, and P. C. McKenry, "Application of Attachment Theory to Male Violence toward Female Intimates," *Journal of Family Violence* 12, no. 2 (1997): 212.

9. McCue, *Domestic Violence*, 77.

10. Larry Kent Graham, "Responding to Victims and Perpetrators of Abuse: Panel Discussion," *Pastoral Psychology* 41, no. 5 (1993): 298.

11. Alberta Wood and Maureen McHugh, "Woman Battering: The Response of Clergy," *Pastoral Psychology* 42, no. 3 (1994): 191.

12. Ibid., 192.

13. Carol Adams and Marie M. Fortune, eds., *Violence against Women and Children: A Christian Theological Sourcebook* (New York: Continuum, 1995).

14. John McClure and Nancy Ramsay, *Telling the Truth: Preaching about Sexual and Domestic Violence* (Cleveland: United Church Press, 1998).

15. Toinette Eugene and James Poling, *Balm for Gilead* (Nashville: Abingdon, 1998).

16. Daniel Linz, Edward Donnerstein, and Steven Penrod, "Sexual Violence in the Mass Media: Social Psychological Implications," in *Sex and Gender*, ed. Philip Shaver and Clyde Hendrick (Newbury Park, Calif.: Sage, 1987), 114.

17. Edward Donnerstein and Daniel Linz, "Mass Media, Sexual Violence and Male Viewers," in *Men's Lives*, 3rd ed., ed. Michael S. Kimmel and Michael A. Messner (Boston: Allyn and Bacon, 1995), 381–92.

18. Nicole Benokraitis and Joe Feagin, *Modern Sexism: Blatant, Subtle, and Covert Discrimination* (Englewood Cliffs, N.J.: Prentice Hall, 1986), 10.

19. Andrea Blum, Jule Harrison, Barbara Ess, and Gail Vaschon, eds., *WAC Stats: The Facts about Women* (New York: New Press, 1993).

20. Gary Brooks and Louise Silverstein, "Understanding the Dark Side of Masculinity: An Interactive Systems Model," in *A New Psychology of Men,* ed. Ronald Levant and William Pollack (New York: Basic Books, 1995), 287.

21. Women's Action Coalition, *WAC Stats.*

22. Jean Kilbourne, "Beauty and the Beast of Advertising," in *Race, Class, and Gender in the United States,* 2nd ed., ed. Paula Rothenberg (New York: St. Martin's, 1992), 348–51.

23. Tom Dorsey, "Girls Searching for Role Models Get Little Help from Television," *The Courier Journal* (Louisville, Ky.), July 22, 1996.

24. An earlier version of this section on atonement appears in *The Care of Men,* ed. Christie Cozad Neuger and James Newton Poling (Nashville: Abingdon, 1997), chap. 1.

25. Annie Imbens and Ineke Jonker, *Christianity and Incest,* trans. P. McVay (Minneapolis: Fortress Press, 1992).

26. Mary Daly, quoted by Joanne Carlson Brown, "For God So Loved the World?" in *Christianity, Patriarchy, and Abuse,* ed. Joanne Carlson Brown and Carole Bohn (New York: Pilgrim, 1989), 3.

27. Marie Fortune, "Forgiveness: The Last Step," in *Violence against Women and Children,* ed. Adams and Fortune, 202.

28. For example, see Pamela Cooper-White's discussion of forgiveness in *The Cry of Tamar* (Minneapolis: Fortress Press, 1995), 253–62.

29. Hedwig Meyer-Wilmes, "Excessive Violence against Women in the Name of Religion," in *Concilium—Religion as a Source of Violence,* ed. William Beuken and Karl Josef Kuschel (Maryknoll, N.Y.: Orbis, 1997), 56.

30. Sandra Lipsitz Bem, *The Lenses of Gender* (New Haven, Conn.: Yale Univ. Press, 1993), 138.

31. Lyn Mikel Brown and Carol Gilligan, *Meeting at the Crossroads: Women's Psychology and Girls' Development* (Cambridge, Mass.: Harvard Univ. Press, 1992), 216.

32. Maria Harris, "Women Teaching Girls: The Power and the Danger," *Religious Education* 88, no. 1 (winter 1993): 56.

33. Tracy Robinson and Janie Victoria Ward, "A Belief in Self Far Greater than Anyone's Disbelief: Cultivating Resistance among African American Female Adolescents," in Carol Gilligan, Annie Rogers, and Deborah Tolman, eds., *Women, Girls, and Psychotherapy: Reframing Resistance* (New York: Harrington Park, 1991), 87–103.

34. Beverly Jean Smith, "Raising a Resister," in Gilligan, Rogers, and Tolman, eds., *Women, Girls, and Psychotherapy,* 144–45.

35. Introduction to *A New Psychology of Men,* ed. Ronald Levant and William Pollack (New York: Basic, 1995), 1.

36. James O'Neill, Glenn Good, and Sarah Holmes, "Fifteen Years of Theory and Research on Men's Gender Role Conflict: New Paradigms for Empirical Research," in *A New Psychology of Men,* ed. Levant and Pollack, 171.

37. Ibid., 188–91.

38. Richard Eisler, "The Relationship between Masculine Gender Role Stress and Men's Health Risk: The Validation of a Construct," in *A New Psychology of Men,* ed. Levant and Pollack, 207–25.

39. Brooks and Silverstein, "Understanding the Dark Side of Masculinity," 284.

40. Michael Cascardi and Daniel O'Leary, "Depressive Symptomatology, Self-esteem, and Self-blame in Battered Women," *Journal of Family Violence* 17, no. 4 (1992): 255.

41. Lora Bex Lempert, "A Narrative Analysis of Abuse: Connecting the Personal, the Rhetorical, and the Structural," *Journal of Contemporary Ethnography* 22, no. 4 (January 1994): 428.

42. Piera Serra, "Physical Violence in the Couple Relationship: A Contribution toward the Analysis of the Context," *Family Process* 32, no. 1 (March 1993): 25.

43. Lempert, "A Narrative Analysis of Abuse," 432.

44. Serra, "Physical Violence in the Couple Relationship," 29.

45. Carol Ember and Melvin Ember, "War, Socialization, and Interpersonal Violence," *Journal of Conflict Resolution* 38, no. 4 (December 1994): 633.

46. Paul Yelsma, "Affective Orientations of Perpetrators, Victims, and Functional Spouses," *Journal of Interpersonal Violence* 11, no. 2 (June 1996): 141–61.

47. Wayne Ewing, "The Civic Advocacy of Men's Violence," in *A New Psychology of Men,* ed. Levant and Pollack.

48. Ibid., 304.

49. Ibid.

50. Michael Kaufman, "The Construction of Masculinity and the Triad of Men's Violence," in *Men's Lives,* 3rd ed., ed. Kimmel and Messner, 17.

51. Joseph Pleck, "Men's Power with Women, Other Men, and Society: A Men's Movement Analysis," in *Men's Lives,* 3rd ed., ed. Kimmel and Messner, 5–12.

52. Marie Fortune and James Poling, "Calling to Accountability: The Church's Response to Abusers," in *Violence against Women and Children,* ed. Adams and Fortune, 454.

53. Joseph Pleck, "Men's Power," 8–10.

54. Wayne Ewing, "The Civic Advocacy of Men's Violence," 301.

55. Martha McMahon and Ellen Pence, "Replying to Daniel O'Leary," *Journal of Interpersonal Violence* (September 1996): 452–55.

Chapter 5

Thanks to June Fulton, Connie Goldberg, Chris Stephenson, and Cynthia Stone for their helpful suggestions during the process of writing this chapter.

1. Erik Erikson, *Childhood and Society,* 2nd ed. (New York: W. W. Norton, 1963).

2. Robert Kegan, *The Evolving Self: Problem and Process in Human Development* (Cambridge, Mass.: Harvard Univ. Press, 1982). See also Robert Kegan, *In Over Our Heads: The Mental Demands of Modern Life* (Cambridge, Mass.: Harvard Univ. Press, 1994).

3. James W. Fowler, *Stages of Faith: The Psychology of Human Development and the Quest for Meaning* (San Francisco: Harper & Row, 1981).

4. Carol Gilligan, *In a Different Voice: Psychological Theory and Women's Development* (Cambridge, Mass.: Harvard Univ. Press, 1982).

5. Florence Rush, *The Best Kept Secret* (Englewood Cliffs, N.J.: Prentice Hall, 1980).

6. Judith Herman, *Father-Daughter Incest* (Cambridge, Mass.: Harvard Univ. Press, 1981).

7. Roland Summit, "The Child Abuse Accommodation Syndrome," *Child Abuse and Neglect: The International Journal* 7, no. 2 (1983): 177–93.

8. David Finkelhor, *Sexually Victimized Children* (New York: Free Press, 1979); *Child Sexual Abuse: New Theory and Research* (New York: Free Press, 1984).

9. Ruth S. Kempe and C. Henry Kempe, *Child Abuse,* in The Developing Child Series, ed. J. Bruner, M. Cole, and B. Lloyd (Cambridge, Mass.: Harvard Univ. Press, 1978).

10. Diana Russell, *The Secret Trauma: Incest in the Lives of Girls and Women* (New York: Basic, 1986).

11. Gail Wyatt, "The Sexual Abuse of Afro-American and White Women in Childhood," *Child Abuse and Neglect: The International Journal* 9 (1985): 507–19.

12. Diana Russell, *The Secret Trauma,* 70; Gail Wyatt, "Sexual Abuse"; Diana Russell, Rachel A. Sherman, and Karen Trocki, "The Long-Term Effects of Incestuous Abuse: A Comparison of Afro-American and White American Victims," in *Lasting Effects of Child Sexual Abuse,* ed. Gail Wyatt (Beverly Hills, Calif.: Sage, 1988); Anthony Urquiza and Lisa Marie Keating, "The Prevalence of Sexual Victimization of Males," in *The Sexually Abused Male,* ed. Mic Hunter (New York: Lexington, 1990); David Finkelhor, "Risk Factors in the Sexual Victimization of Children," *Child Abuse and Neglect* 4 (1980): 265–73.

13. A number of writings have come from researchers connected with this project. See, for example, C. Gilligan, J. V. Ward, and J. M. Taylor, eds., *Mapping the Moral Domain: A Contribution of Women's Thinking to Psychological Theory and Education* (Cambridge, Mass.: Harvard Univ. Press, 1988); Lyn Mikel Brown and Carol Gilligan, *Meeting at the Crossroads: Women's Psychology and Girls' Development* (New York: Ballantine, 1993); Jill McLean Taylor, Carol Gilligan, and Amy M. Sullivan, *Between Voice and Silence: Women and Girls, Race and Relationship* (Cambridge, Mass.: Harvard/Belknap, 1996). Books on special topics by authors related to this group also include Dana Crowley Jack, *Silencing the Self: Women and Depression* (Cambridge, Mass.: Harvard Univ. Press, 1991); and Annie G. Rogers, *A Shining Affliction: A Story of Harm and Healing in Psychotherapy* (New York: Viking, 1995). A closely related, pioneering text is Mary Belenky et al., *Women's Ways of Knowing: The Development of Self, Voice, and Mind* (New York: Basic Books, 1976, 1986); and more recently, Nancy Goldberger et al., *Knowledge, Difference and Power: Essays Inspired by Women's Ways of Knowing* (New York: Basic, 1998).

14. Jean Baker Miller, *Toward a New Psychology of Women* (Boston: Beacon Press, 1976, 1986); Judith V. Jordan et al., eds., *Women's Growth in Connection: Writings from the Stone Center* (New York: Guilford, 1991); Judith Jordan, ed., *Women's Growth in Diversity: More Writings from the Stone Center* (New York: Guilford Press, 1997); Jean Baker Miller and Irene Pierce Stiver, *The Healing Connection: How Women Form Relationships in Therapy and in Life* (Boston: Beacon, 1997). See also the Works in Progress Series, papers available from the Stone Center, Wellesley College, Wellesley, MA 02181.

15. Sigmund Freud, *Three Essays on the Theory of Sexuality*, trans. J. Strachey (New York: Basic, 1962). (*Standard Edition*, vol. 7, 145–248).

16. Erik Erikson, "The Eight Stages of Man," in *Childhood and Society*, 2nd ed. (New York: W. W. Norton, 1963), chap. 7, 247–74.

17. For example, Lenore Terr, *Too Scared to Cry* (New York: Basic, 1990); Judith Herman, *Trauma and Recovery* (New York: Basic Books, 1992). This definition also conforms to the definition used for Post-Traumatic Stress Disorder in the *Diagnostic and Statistical Manual of Mental Disorders (DSM-IV)*, 4th ed. (Washington, D.C.: American Psychiatric Association, 1994), 424–28.

18. Erikson, "The Eight Stages of Man," 147.

19. Ibid.

20. Ibid., 250.

21. John Bowlby, *A Secure Base: Parent-Child Attachment and Healthy Human Development* (New York: Basic Books, 1988).

22. Bessel van der Kolk and Alexander McFarlane, "The Black Hole of Trauma," in *Psychological Trauma*, ed. B.A. van der Kolk (Washington, D.C.: American Psychiatric Press, 1987) 32; Jody Messler Davies and Mary Gail Frawley, *Treating the Adult Survivor of Childhood Sexual Abuse: A Psychoanalytic Perspective* (New York: Basic, 1994) 46.

23. Robert Kegan, *The Evolving Self: Problem and Process in Human Development* (Cambridge, Mass.: Harvard Univ. Press, 1982), 133–60.

24. Anna Freud, "The Concept of Developmental Lines," *Psychoanalytic Study of the Child*, 18 (1963) 245–65.

25. This concept is somewhat like that of "domains" used by infant observation researcher Daniel N. Stern in his *Interpersonal World of the Infant: A View from Psychoanalysis and Developmental Psychology* (New York: Basic, 1985). Stern considers that a "phase" model of development in which phases are only revisited via regression is useful in understanding cognitive tasks but not an infant's sense of self. In Stern's conception, which is focused on the first eighteen months of life, "All domains of relatedness remain active during development." (31).

26. The notion of an "object" was derived from Freud but departed from Freud's theory that all motivation is grounded in biological instincts, the "drives" of sex and aggression, and another person becomes the "object" or target for satisfaction of the drives.

27. D. W. Winnicott, *Playing and Reality* (New York: Basic, 1971).

28. It should be noted that the idea that an infant comes into the world as a blank slate appears to be disproved by recent work in the field of infant observation, particularly Daniel Stern, *The Interpersonal World of the Infant*, and the temperament studies of Stella Chess and Alexander Thomas, *Temperament in Clinical Practice* (New York: Guilford, 1986); Thomas and Chess, *Temperament and Development* (New York: Brunner/Mazel, 1977); Thomas and Chess, *Dynamics of Psychological Development* (New York: Brunner/Mazel, 1980).

29. M. J. Marks, "Conscious/Unconscious Selection of the Psychotherapist's Theoretical Orientation," *Psychotherapy; Theory, Research and Practice* 15, no. 4 (winter 1978): 354–58.

30. This process is eloquently described in Leonard Shengold, "Child Abuse and Deprivation: Soul Murder," *Journal of the American Psychoanalytic Association* 27 (1979): 539. See also Shengold, *Soul Murder: The Effects of Childhood Abuse and Deprivation* (New York: Fawcett/Ballantine, 1991).

31. Bruce Perry et al., "Childhood Trauma: The Neurobiology of Adaptation and Use-Dependent Development of the Brain—How States Become Traits," *Infant Mental Health Journal*, in press, available at www.trauma-pages.com/perry96.htm; Bessel van der Kolk, *Psychological Trauma* (Washington, D.C.: American Psychiatric Press, 1987); van der Kolk, "The Body Keeps the Score: Memory and the Evolving Psychobiology of Post Traumatic Stress," in press, available at www.trauma-pages.com/vanderk4.htm; Allan Schore, *Affect Regulation and the Origin of Self* (New York: Lawrence Erlbaum, 1994).

32. This view is similar to that detailed by Jody Messler Davies and Mary Gail Frawley in *Treating the Adult Survivor of Childhood Sexual Abuse*. It can also be understood from a Piagetian developmental perspective: the traumatic experience has remained at the sensorimotor level, and needs to be brought into representation, through language, for growth and integration to occur.

33. Neuropsychological research appears to validate this process as even aiding in making positive changes in brain chemistry that help undo some of the early negative effects of trauma. See Van der Kolk, "The Body Keeps the Score"; Perry, "Childhood Trauma."

34. Mary Belenky et al., *Women's Ways of Knowing*.

35. Ibid., 3.

36. Nelle Morton, *The Journey Is Home* (Boston: Beacon, 1985).

37. See writings from the Stone Center, cited above.

38. These theories differ in a number of respects. One important difference is the relative degree of attention paid to conscious vs. unconscious material in the therapeutic relationship. This difference is partly due to the intellectual and clinical heritage of each theory. Interpersonal and feminist-relational theorists trace their work back to Sullivan and Frieda Fromm-Reichman; relational theorists, to object relations; and intersubjective theorists, to self psychology. Interpersonal and feminist-relational theorists tend to work more in the sphere of conscious interactions between patient/client and therapist, and relational and intersubjective theorists are analysts who tend to focus on apparent manifestations of unconscious dynamics in the transference-countertransference relationship between the therapist and patient. These differences are not absolute, however, and vary from one practitioner to another.

39. For example, see interviews with incest survivors by Annie Imbens and Ineke Jonker, *Christianity and Incest*, trans. P. McVay (Minneapolis: Fortress Press, 1992).

40. Jane Grovijahn, "A Feminist Theology of Survival," unpublished Ph.D. dissertation, Graduate Theological Union, Berkeley, California, 1997.

41. See also Elisabeth Moltmann-Wendel, *I Am My Body: A Theology of Embodiment* (New York: Continuum, 1995).

42. Ana-Maria Rizzuto, *The Birth of the Living God: A Psychoanalytic Study* (Chicago: Univ. of Chicago Press, 1979).

43. Ibid., 90.

44. Fowler, *Stages of Faith*, 121.

45. D. W. Winnicott, *Maturational Processes and the Facilitating Environment* (London: Hogarth, 1965).

46. Fowler, *Stages of Faith*, 133.

47. Ibid., 173.

48. Ibid., 172.

49. There is some parallel here to D. W. Winnicott's notion of a "False Self" and a "True Self." (See "The Theory of the Parent-Infant Relationship" and "Ego Distortion in Terms of True and False Self" in *Maturational Processes and the Facilitating Environment*. The so-called False Self conforms to rigidly enforced expectations of caretakers, and the true spontaneous self is suppressed in the service of survival. I prefer the term *ambulatory self* or *coping self* to *false self*, in recognition of the constructive and at times even heroic task of carrying on, coping, and succeeding that is performed by this aspect of the personality.

50. Studies by Finkelhor and J. Landis, summarized in Herman, *Father-Daughter Incest*, 13; also extrapolated from statistics for female perpetrators in Russell, *The Secret Trauma*, 218, also citing Finkelhor, *Sexually Victimized Children* (New York: Free Press, 1979). For further discussion of prevalence of abuse and the myth of the rarity of abuse, see Pamela Cooper-White, *The Cry of Tamar* (Minneapolis: Fortress Press, 1995), 152ff.

51. Two excellent resources for male survivors are Mike Lew, *Victims No Longer: Men Recovering from Incest and Other Sexual Child Abuse* (New York: Harper & Row, 1990); and *The Sexually Abused Male*, ed. Mic Hunter.

52. Pamela Cooper-White, *The Cry of Tamar: Violence against Women and the Church's Response*. See also in this anthology chapter 4 on developmental narratives of violence by Christie Cozad Neuger.

53. Bonnie Miller McLemore, "The Living Human Web: Pastoral Theology at the Turn of the Century," in *Through the Eyes of Women: Insights for Pastoral Care*, ed. Jeanne Stevenson Moessner (Minneapolis: Fortress Press, 1996), 9–26. See also Pamela Couture, "Weaving the Web: Pastoral Care in an Individualistic Society," in *Through the Eyes of Women*, 94–106.

54. Emilie Buchwald, Pamela Fletcher, and Martha Roth, eds., *Transforming a Rape Culture* (New York: Milkweed, 1993).

Chapter 6

1. John Putnam Demos, *Entertaining Satan: Witchcraft and the Culture of Early New England* (New York: Oxford Univ. Press, 1982), 157.

2. The research for this article was funded by the Henry Luce III Foundation through the Association of Theological Schools, and presented to the faculty of Perkins School of Theology and at the 1998 Conference of Luce Fellows. I am grateful for many helpful insights from those who have heard or read an earlier version and especially for the wisdom of M. Shawn Copeland, Paula Buford, Carolyn Bohler, Kathleen Greider, and Jeanne Stevenson-Moessner.

3. When she identifies herself in the story, Nilla chooses a male figure. She might perhaps be unusual in that regard. She is not unusual, however, in describing powerful figures in male language. Nearly all of the girls interviewed in my study named God as "he." (See Patricia H. Davis, *Counseling Adolescent Girls* [Minneapolis: Fortress Press, 1996], 39–49, for more discussion of this phenomenon. Also see Carol Saussy, *God Images and Self Esteem: Empowering Women in a Patriarchal Society* [Louisville, Ky.: Westminster John Knox, 1991], for a discussion of the negative effects of an exclusively male God-image for women and girls.)

4. A few recent titles include: *Chamber of Fear* (New York: Golden, 1998); *Cheerleaders: The New Evil* (New York: Pocket Books, 1994); *The Hitchhiker* (New York: Scholastic, 1993); *Scream* (New York: Golden Books, 1998); and *Forbidden Secrets* (New York: Pocket, 1996).

5. Recent titles include: *Darkest Hour* (New York: Pocket, 1993); *Hidden Jewel* (New York: Pocket, 1995).

6. Melvin Burgess, *Smack* (New York: Holt, 1998).

7. Robert Cormier, *Tenderness* (New York: Delacorte, 1997).

8. Brock Cole, *The Facts Speak for Themselves* (Arden, N.C.: Front Street, 1997).

9. Norma Fox Mazer, *When She Was Good* (New York: Arthur A. Levine, 1997).

10. Sara Mosle, "The Outlook's Bleak," *The New York Times Magazine*, August 2, 1998, 34, 36; Alison Lurie, "Reading at Escape Velocity," *The New York Times Book Review*, May 17, 1988.

11. Jennifer M. Brown and Cindi Di Marzo, "Why So Grim?" *Publishers Weekly*, February 16, 1998, 120–23.

12. David Finkelhor, *Childhood Sexual Abuse* (New York: The Free Press, 1984); Gail Wyatt, "The Sexual Abuse of Afro-American and White Women in Childhood," *Child Abuse and Neglect* 9 (1985): 507–19.

13. Diana Russell, *The Secret Trauma* (New York: Basic, 1986).

14. U. S. Department of Justice, "Female Rape Rates, by Race and Age of Victim, 1993," *National Crime Victimization Survey, 1992–1993* (Washington, D.C.: U.S. Department of Justice, Bureau of Justice Statistics, 1993).

15. Federal Bureau of Investigation, *Supplementary Homicide Report, 1992.* (Washington, D.C.: U.S. Department of Justice, Bureau of Justice Statistics, 1993).

16. Robert Kegan, *In Over Our Heads: The Mental Demands of Modern Life* (Cambridge, Mass.: Harvard Univ. Press, 1994), 15–36. In Kegan's earlier work, *The Evolving Self* (Cambridge, Mass.: Harvard Univ. Press, 1982), he builds on the work of Piaget and his followers, extending Piaget's cognitive theory to include the affective, interpersonal, and intrapersonal along with young adult and adult psychologies.

17. Ibid.

18. Myra and David Sadker show the particular ways girls are silenced in their school environments in their volume *Failing at Fairness: How America's Schools Cheat Girls* (New York: Charles Scribner's Sons, 1994).

19. Carol Gilligan, "Teaching Shakespeare's Sister: Notes from the Underground of Female Adolescence," in *Making Connections: The Relational Worlds of Adolescent Girls at Emma Willard School*, ed. Carol Gilligan, Nona P. Lyons, and Trudy J. Hanmer (Cambridge, Mass.: Harvard Univ. Press, 1990), 6–27.

20. Mark Edmundson, *Nightmare on Main Street: Angels, Sadomasochism, and the Culture of Gothic* (Cambridge, Mass.: Harvard Univ. Press, 1997).

21. Ibid., 5.

22. Ibid., 67.

23. We could easily identify other instances of "facile transcendence" in other kinds of spirituality/healing movements.

24. Edmundson, *Nightmare on Main Street*, 75.

25. See Jeanne Stevenson-Moessner's article on embodied theologies in this volume.

26. Excellent resources are available on issues of abuse and healing for girls and women. See Christie Neuger's article in this volume, and other resources such as Carol Adams and Marie Fortune, *Violence against Women and Children: A Christian Theological Sourcebook* (New York: Continuum, 1995); Linda H. Hollies, *Inner Healing for Broken Vessels* (Nashville: Upper Room, 1992); Barrie Levy, ed., *Dating Violence: Young Women in Danger* (Seattle: Seal, 1991); Davis, *Counseling Adolescent Girls*, 66–81; and S. Amelia Stinson-Wesley, "Daughters of Tamar: Pastoral Care for Survivors of Rape," in Jeanne Stevenson Moessner, ed., *Through the Eyes of Women: Insights for Pastoral Care* (Minneapolis: Fortress Press, 1996), 222–39.

Chapter 7

1. Delores Williams, *Sisters in the Wilderness: The Challenges of Womanist God-Talk* (Maryknoll, N.Y.: Orbis, 1993), ix.

2. Megan McKenna, *Not Counting Women and Children: Neglected Stories from the Bible* (Maryknoll, N.Y.: Orbis, 1997), 41.

3. Luke 18:15-17; see also Matthew 19:13-14 and Mark 10:13-14.

4. John 13:33

5. Galatians 4:19; 1 John 2:1, 12, 28; 3:7, 18; 4:4, and 5:21.

6. Mark 5:21-43; see also Matthew 9:18-26 and Luke 8:40-56.

7. Lloyd deMause. "The Evolution of Childhood, " in *The History of Childhood*, ed. Lloyd deMause (Northvale, New Jersey: Jason Aronson, 1974), 1.

8. J. M. Hawes and N. R. Hiner, "History of Childhood," in *Encyclopedia of Bioethics*, revised edition, ed. W. T. Reich (New York: Simon and Schuster Macmillan, 1995), 351–52.

9. John Boswell, *The Kindness of Strangers* (New York: Vintage, 1988), 24, 428–31.

10. Hawes and Hiner, 352.

11. Ibid., 353.

12. D. M. Bernstein, "The Discovery of the Child: A Historical Perspective on Child and Adolescent Psychiatry," in *Child and Adolescent Psychiatry: A Comprehensive Textbook*, 2nd ed., ed. M. Lewis (Baltimore: Williams and Wilkins, 1996), 1247–49.

13. Ibid., 1249.

14. Hawes and Hiner, 353–54.

15. David J. Vandermeulen, letter, February 1, 2000. Also, several pastoral theological works have examined the roles of children in families and the church and the roles of females as wives and mothers (hence the value regarding the study of children). Two relevant texts are: Janet Fishburn, *Confronting the Idolatry of Family: A New Vision for the Household of God* (Nashville: Abingdon, 1991), and Bonnie J. Miller-McLemore, *Also a Mother: Work and Family as Theological Dilemma* (Nashville: Abingdon, 1994).

16. M. L. Dell and M. K. Dulcan, "Childhood and Adolescent Development," in *Human Behavior: An Introduction for Medical Students*, 3rd ed., ed. A. Stoudemire (Philadelphia: Lippincott-Raven, 1998), 261–317; M. D. Levine, W. B. Carey, and A. C. Crocker, ed. *Developmental-Behavioral Pediatrics*, 3rd ed. (Philadelphia: W. B. Saunders, 1999); M. D. Lewis and F. Volkmar, *Clinical Aspects of Child and Adolescent Development*, 3rd ed. (Philadelphia: Lea and Febiger, 1990); D. B. Pruitt, ed., and the American Academy of Child and Adolescent Psychiatry, *Your Child: What Every Parent Needs to Know About Childhood Development from Birth to Preadolescence.* (New York: HarperCollins, 1998).

17. Dell and Dulcan, 261–317; B. S. Zuckerman, D. A. Frank, and M. Augustyn, "Infancy and Toddler Years," in *Developmental-Behavioral Pediatrics*, 3rd ed., ed. M. D. Levine, W. B. Carey, and A. C. Crocker (Philadelphia: W. B. Saunders, 1999), 30–36.

18. Dell and Dulcan, 275–76; Zuckerman, Frank, and Augustyn, 25–30.

19. Dell and Dulcan, 276–77; Zuckerman, Frank, and Augustyn, 34–35.

20. Zuckerman, Frank, and Augustyn, 24–26.

21. E. F. Krug and K. C. Mikus, "The Preschool Years," in *Developmental-Behavioral Pediatrics*, 3rd ed., ed. M. D. Levine, W. B. Carey, and A. C. Crocker (Philadelphia: W. B. Saunders, 1999), 38; E. F. Ziglar and E. D. Gilman, "Day Care and Early Childhood Settings," *Child and Adolescent Psychiatry Clinics of North America*, 7, no. 3 (July 1998), 484.

22. Dell and Dulcan, 281–84; Krug and Mikus, 38–42.

23. Dell and Dulcan, 283–87; Krug and Mikus, 40–42; M. Lewis, "Overview of Infant, Child, and Adolescent Development," in *Textbook of Child and Adolescent Psychiatry*, 2nd ed., ed. J. M. Wiener (Washington, D.C.: American Psychiatric Press, 1997), 44–56.

24. Dell and Dulcan, 287–92; Krug and Mikus, 40–43; M. Lewis and F. Volkmar, *Clinical Aspects of Child and Adolescent Development*, 3rd ed. (Philadelphia: Lea and Febiger, 1990), 170.

25. L. Combrinck-Graham, "Development of School-Age Children," in *Child and Adolescent Psychiatry: A Comprehensive Textbook*, 2nd ed., ed. M. Lewis (Baltimore: Williams and Wilkins, 1996), 271; L. B. Inderbitzin, A. C. Furman, and M. E. James, "Psychoanalytic Psychology," in *Human Behavior: An Introduction for Medical Students*, 3rd ed., ed. A. Stoudemire (Philadelphia: Lippincott-Raven, 1998), 143; Charles Sarnoff, *Latency* (Northvale, N.J.: Jason Aronson, 1976), 33.

26. Dell and Dulcan, 293–95.

27. M. D. Levine, "Middle Childhood," in *Developmental-Behavioral Pediatrics*, 3rd ed., M. D. Levine, W. B. Carey, and A. C. Crocker (Philadelphia: W. B. Saunders, 1999), 51–67.

28. T. Shapiro and W. Becker, "The Early Grade-School Child: Introduction," in *Handbook of Child and Adolescent Psychiatry*, 2, ed. J. D. Noshpitz (New York: John Wiley and Sons, 1997), 4.

29. Robert Coles, *The Spiritual Life of Children* (New York: Houghton Mifflin Company, 1991).

30. James W. Fowler, *Stages of Faith: The Psychology of Human Development and the Quest for Meaning* (San Francisco: Harper & Row, 1981).

31. David Elkind, "Piaget's Semi-Clinical Interview and the Study of Spontaneous Religion," *Journal for the Scientific Study of Religion* 4, (1964), 40–46; David Elkind, "The Origins of Religion in the Child," *Review of Religious Research* 12, (1970), 35–42; David Elkind, "The Development of Religious Understanding in Children and Adolescents," in *Research on Religious Development: A Comprehensive Handbook*, M. P. Strommen, ed. (New York, Hawthorn, 1971), 655–85; Ronald Goldman, *Religious Thinking from Childhood to Adolescence* (New York: Seabury, 1964); E. Harms, "The Development of Religious Experience in Children," *American Journal of Sociology* 50, (1944) 112–22; Ralph Hood Jr., Bernard Spilka, Bruce Hunsberger, and Richard Gorsuch, *The Psychology of Religion: An Empirical Approach*, 2nd ed. (New York: Guilford, 1996), 62–68; and Fritz K. Oser, "The Development of Religious Judgment," in *Religious Development in Childhood and Adolescence*, ed. F. K. Oser and W. G. Scarlett (San Francisco: Jossey-Bass New Direction for Child Development, 1991), no. 52, 5–25.

32. L. A. Kirkpatrick and P. R. Shaver, "Attachment Theory and Religion: Childhood Attachments, Religious Beliefs, and Conversion," *Journal for the Scientific Study of Religion*, 29, (1990), 325–34; and L. A. Kirkpatrick, "An Attachment Theory Approach to the Psychology of Religion," *International Journal for the Psychology of Religion*, 2, (1992), 3–28.

33. P. L. Benson, K. S. Masters, and D. B. Larson, " Religious Influences in Child and Adolescent Development," in *Handbook of Child and Adolescent Psychiatry* 4, J. D. Noshpitz, ed. (New York: John Wiley and Sons, 1998), 208; D. Hellner, *The Children's God* (Chicago: Univ. of Chicago Press, 1986); Ana-Maria Rizzuto, *The Birth of the Living God: A Psychoanalytic Study* (Chicago: Univ. of Chicago Press, 1979); and L. M. Wagener, "Clinical Pastoral Care," in *Handbook of Child and Adolescent Psychiatry* 6, J. D. Noshpitz, ed. (New York: John Wiley and Sons, 1998), 592–94.

34. Benson, Masters, and Larson, 209.

35. Barry L. Bandstra, *Reading the Old Testament: An Introduction to the Hebrew Bible* (Belmont, Calif.: Wadsworth Publishing Company, 1995), 454; and Kathleen M. O'Connor, "Lamentations," in *The Women's Bible Commentary*, ed. C. A. Newsom and S. H. Ringe (Louisville, Ky.: Westminster John Knox, 1992), 179–80.

36. B. L. Bandstra, 342; Katheryn Pfisterer Darr, "Ezekiel," in *The Women's Bible Commentary*, ed. C. A. Newsom and S. H. Ringe (Louisville, Ky.: Westminster John Knox, 1992), 183–88.

37. Leviticus 15:19-33.

38. L. William Countryman, *Dirt, Greed, and Sex: Sexual Ethics in the New Testament and Their Implications for Today* (Philadelphia: Fortress Press, 1988), 26, 28–29.

39. Leviticus 20:18.

40. Countryman, 22–32; Suzanne Pinckney Stetkevych, "Sarah and the Hyena: Laughter, Menstruation, and the Genesis of Double Entendre," *History of Religions* 36, (1996), 29–30; Judith Romney Wegner, "Leviticus," in *The Women's Bible Commentary*, ed. C. A. Newsom and S. H. Ringe (Louisville, Ky.: Westminster John Knox, 1992), 29–30; and Richard Whitekettle, "Levitical Thought and the Female Reproductive Cycle: Wombs, Wellsprings, and the Primeval World," *Vestus Testamentum* 46, (1996) 380–91.

41. Leviticus 12:1-7.

42. Countryman, 29; Wegner, 30.

43. Wegner, 30.

44. Ibid., 43.

45. Mary Jane Lupton, *Menstruation and Psychoanalysis* (Urbana, Ill.: Univ. of Illinois Press, 1993), 95; and Carole A. Rayburn, "The Body in Religious Experience," in *Handbook of Religious Experience*, R. W. Hood Jr., ed. (Birmingham, Ala.: Religious Education Press, 1995), 485.

46. Lisa Sowle Cahill, *Sex, Gender, and Christian Ethics* (New York: Cambridge Univ. Press, 1996), 135; and Mary Ann Tolbert, "Mark," in *The Women's Bible Commentary*, ed. C. A. Newsom and S. H. Ringe (Louisville, Ky.: Westminster John Knox, 1992), 267–68.

47. Countryman, 74; Luke Timothy Johnson, *The Writings of the New Testament: An Interpretation*, rev. ed. (Minneapolis: Fortress Press, 1999), 244–45.

48. C. N. Jacklin and L. J. Martin, "Effects of Gender on Behavior and Development," in *Developmental-Behavioral Pediatrics*, 3rd ed., ed. M. D. Levine, W. B. Carey, and A. C. Crocker (Philadelphia, Pa.: W.B. Saunders, 1999), 100–01; R. L. Rosenfeld, "Puberty and its Disorders in Girls," *Endocrinology and Metabolism Clinics of North America* 20, (1991) 15–16; and J. S. Sanfilippo and S. P. Hertweck, "Physiology of Menstruation and Menstrual Disorders," in *Comprehensive Adolescent Health Care*, 2nd ed., ed. S. B. Friedman, M. Fisher, S. K. Schonberg, and E. M. Alderman (St. Louis, Mo.: Mosby, 1998), 990.

49. L. P. Plotnick, "Puberty and Gonadal Disorders," in *Principles and Practice of Pediatrics*, 2nd ed., ed. F. A. Oski (Philadelphia, Pa.: J. B. Lippincott, 1994), 1968–71; and M. D. Wilson, "Menstrual Disorders," in *Principles and Practice of Pediatrics*, 2nd ed., ed. F. A. Oski (Philadelphia, Pa.: J. B. Lippincott, 1994), 779.

50. P. K. Braverman and S. J. Sondheimer, "Menstrual Disorders," *Pediatrics in Review* 18, (1997), 17–25; L. S. Neinstein, "Menstrual Problems in Adolescents," *Medical Clinics of North America* 74, (1990), 1182; Rosenfeld, 15–20; Sanfilippo and Hertweck, 990.

51. C. A. Ford and W. L. Coleman, "Adolescent Development and Behavior: Implications for the Primary Care Physician," in *Developmental-Behavioral Pediatrics*, 3rd ed., ed. M. D. Levine, W. B. Carey, and A. C. Crocker (Philadelphia, Pa: W. B. Saunders, 1999), 71–72; D. Offer, K. A. Schonert-Reichl, and A. M. Boxer, "Normal Adolescent Development: Empirical Research Findings," in *Child and Adolescent Psychiatry: A Comprehensive Textbook*, 2nd ed., ed. M. Lewis (Baltimore, Md.; Williams and Wilkins, 1996), 280; and Neinstein, 1181–82.

52. Plotnick, 1968.

53. S. M. Coupey and P. Ahlstrom, "Common Menstrual Disorders," *Pediatric Clinics of North America* 36, (1989), 551; and Wilson, 777.

54. Coupey and Ahlstrom, 567–69; and Sanfilippo and Hertweck, 1010–11.

55. Coupey and Ahlstrom, 554–55; Sanfilippo and Hertweck, 1008–09; and Wilson, 777–78.

56. S. E. Carpenter, "Psychosocial Menstrual Disorders: Stress, Exercise, and Diet's Effect on the Menstrual Cycle," *Current Opinion in Obstetrics and Gynecology* 6, (1994), 538; Rosenfeld, 30–33; Sanfilippo and Hertweck, 1004–06; and Wilson, 778–79.

57. Wilson, 780–81.

58. Lupton, 3.

59. D. C. Cumming, C. E. Cumming, and D. K. Kieren, "Menstrual Mythology and Sources of Information about Menstruation," *American Journal of Obstetrics and Gynecology*, (1991), 472–75; and Lupton, 5–7, 187–88.

60. Maurice R. Green, ed. *Interpersonal Psychoanalysis: The Selected Papers of Clara M. Thompson* (New York: Basic Books, 1964), 244–45.

61. Rosemary Radford Ruether, "Feminist Interpretation: A Method of Correlation," in *Feminist Interpretation of the Bible*, ed. Letty Russell (Philadelphia: Westminster Press, 1985), 113–14.

62. Brita L. Gill-Austern, "Pedagogy under the Influence of Feminism and Womanism," in *Feminist and Womanist Pastoral Theology*, ed. Bonnie J. Miller-McLemore and Brita L. Gill-Austern (Nashville, Tenn.: Abingdon, 1999), 155.

63. Kathleen J. Greider, Gloria A. Johnson, and Kristen J. Leslie, "Three Decades of Women Writing for Our Lives," in *Feminist and Womanist Pastoral Theology*, ed. Bonnie J. Miller-McLemore and Brita L. Austern. (Nashville, Tenn.: Abingdon, 1999), 34.

64. See Inderbitzin, Furman, and James, 144–55; M. Lewis, "Overview of Infant, Child, and Adolescent Development," in *Textbook of Child and Adolescent Psychiatry*, 2nd ed., ed. J. M. Wiener (Washington, D.C.: American Psychiatric Press, 1997), 39–66; and I. F. Litt and J. A. Martin, "Development of Sexuality and its Problems," in *Developmental-Behavioral Pediatrics*, 3rd ed., ed. M. D. Levine, W. B. Carey, and A. C. Crocker (Philadelphia, Pa.: W. B. Saunders, 1999), 457–70.

65. See Brenda Munsey, ed., *Moral Development, Moral Education, and Kohlberg: Basic Issues in Philosophy, Psychology, Religion, and Education* (Birmingham, Ala.: Religious Education Press, 1980); and F. Clark Power, Ann Higgins, and Lawrence Kohlberg, *Lawrence Kohlberg's Approach to Moral Education* (New York: Columbia Univ. Press, 1989).

66. See Carol Gilligan, *In a Different Voice* (Cambridge, Mass.: Harvard Univ. Press, 1982); Carol Gilligan, Nona P. Lyons, and Trudy J. Hanmer, eds., *Making Connections: The Relational Worlds of Adolescent Girls at Emma Willard School* (Cambridge, Mass.: Harvard Univ. Press, 1990); and Carol Gilligan, Janie Victoria Ward, and Jill McLean Taylor, eds., *Mapping the Moral Domain* (Cambridge, Mass.: Harvard Univ. Press, 1988).

67. See R. B. Brooks, "Self-Esteem During the School Years: Its Normal Development and Hazardous Decline," *Pediatric Clinics of North America* 39, (1992), 538–40; Dell and Dulcan, 285–86; Jacklin and Martin, 100–6; Litt and Martin, 457–70; T. F. Murray, "Gender Identity and Gender Identity Disorders," in *Encyclopedia of Bioethics*, rev. ed., ed. W. T. Reich (New York: Simon and Schuster Macmillan, 1995), 901–907; A. Yates, "Childhood Sexuality," in *Child and Adolescent Psychiatry: A Comprehensive Textbook*, 2nd ed., ed. M. Lewis (Baltimore, Md.: Williams and Wilkins, 1996), 221–35; and K. J. Zucker and R. Green, "Gender Identity and Psychosexual Disorders," in *Textbook of Child and Adolescent Psychiatry*, 2nd ed., ed. J. M. Wiener (Washington, D.C.: American Psychiatric Press, 1997), 657–76.

Chapter 8

1. Mary Pipher, *Reviving Ophelia: Saving the Selves of Adolescent Girls* (New York: Ballentine, 1994).

2. Ibid., 44.

3. Ibid., 19.

4. Ibid., 13.

5. Lewis Carroll described Alice in a note for a stage production of Alice in Wonderland in these terms: youth, audacity, vigor, swift directness of purpose. (Lewis Carroll, *The Annotated Alice: Alice's Adventures in Wonderland and Through the Looking Glass*, [Cleveland: The World Publishing Company, 1960], 37.) Unfortunately, the March 1999 television production of "Alice in Wonderland" showed Alice to be somewhat slow moving and ponderous, even worried, with furrowed brow.

6. Carroll, *The Annotated Alice*, 161.

7. It was because I had a fifteen-year-old daughter that so many mothers spoke to me about Pipher's book. The use of Alice as a metaphor for these girls did not come to mind until I was analyzing the data.

8. This interview process was not objective in a technical sense. I interviewed fully aware of my own subjectivity. When I asked the questions, I sought simply to acknowledge that I had heard or to offer an empathic response. Occasionally I asked a follow-up question for clarification. I did not share from my own experience. If a girl talked to me about something other than what I had asked, I let her finish before proceeding with the next question.

9. Ancestry is often more mixed than it appears, and definitions of race are complex. I did not ask specifically how each girl defined herself racially, though several included race in their self-descriptions.

10. I wrote letters to eight of the girls, explaining this work and asking to interview them. In the letter I explained that if they did not want to participate, they could simply throw away the letter. If they did want to, they would need to discuss the project with a parent or guardian and contact me with

the agreement they and their parents signed. Before I could choose two more girls to ask, two asked to be included! Every one said yes within a week. The interviews occurred the week after school let out for summer, in my office at the seminary.

I did not make huge attempts to keep secret who was involved in the interviewing, for it was not crucial to the project. I did not share anything that one girl said in the interview with another, however. I informed the girls that I would pay them $10 for their time in sharing with me, and I paid them in cash at the interview itself.

11. I did not ask for details about family situations, but I did learn that three have two younger siblings, one has two much older siblings, two have one younger sibling, one is the oldest of five, another has ten siblings, and several have step-siblings with whom they do not currently live.

12. I am not aware of the group's economic make-up. All are cared for in homes or apartments and are apparently able to participate in the arts or recreational activities as well as school functions. Probably their families would be classified as between upper low- to middle-income families.

13. Pipher, *Reviving Ophelia,* 265.

14. I explained that I would audiotape the session in order to have the sessions transcribed and that only the faculty secretary would hear those tapes. I shared the rules I had set out for myself and asked whether they had any rules to add, or questions. The sessions averaged forty-five minutes in length.

Rules I shared:

You can choose not to answer anything that you wish to skip or decline.

You can change any question to suit you.

You can ask me any questions you want, even about why I might ask that question.

You can add ideas or comments if you want to.

You won't be cited by name at all, unless you choose to be quoted with your name.

I'll use a tape recorder so I don't have to take notes, but your voice won't be shared with any group.

If you want, I can share the results with you as a group in about a year, or just give you the chapter to read.

We don't have to get through all the questions in the interview.

15. Toccarra Cash and Charelle Johnson.

16. Carroll, *The Annotated Alice,* 37.

17. I believe that this comment and Jane's were the only references to race mentioned by a European American girl. As in all segments of American society, whites in this interview process did not have to deal with race as consciously as blacks. Whites can try to avoid the issue.

18. Having blonde hair is noteworthy in a setting in which she might be one or one of two with blonde hair in a classroom.

19. Carroll, *The Annotated Alice,* 32.

20. The Dayton public schools are based on a magnet system, so a student ranks the schools she wishes to attend. All of the girls who are students of the magnet school for the visual and performing arts chose to attend that school; however, they also were required to audition for their arts magnet. The three girls who are now in private schools made choices, with their families' involvement, which led them to those schools. These school choices might increase the girls' sense that they are choice-makers (as well as "chosen").

21. Carol Gilligan, *In a Different Voice: Psychological Theory and Women's Development* (Cambridge, Mass.: Harvard Univ. Press, 1982). Also, Carol Gilligan, Nona P. Lyons, and Trudy J. Hanmer, *Making Connections: The Relational Worlds of Adolescent Girls at Emma Willard School* (Cambridge, Mass.: Harvard Univ. Press, 1990). Gilligan discusses a shift away from using "I" toward the pronoun "it" and movement away from claiming one's own authority in adolescent girls around the age of twelve to thirteen. Often females regain their voice, reclaiming their "I" pronoun at middle age.

22. Erik H. Erikson, *Identity: Youth and Crisis* (New York: W. W. Norton, 1968). Erikson argued that boys develop in adolescence a self that initiates, is autonomous, and forges an identity, while a female holds her identity "in abeyance" as she prepares to attract the man by whose name she will be known and whose status will define her.

23. Joen Fagan and Irma Lee Shepherd, eds., *Gestalt Therapy Now: Theory, Techniques, and Application* (New York: Harper and Row, 1970), 5, 17, 27, 212, 237. Gestalt therapists discuss projection as disowning aspects of self. One can see through another's eyes rather than one's own. This is sometimes referred to "giving one's eyes away."

24. Carroll, *The Annotated Alice,* 58.

25. Many people have written on developing and maintaining one's identity and relationships. Gilligan, cited above, and Jean Baker Miller, *Toward a New Psychology of Women* (Boston: Beacon, 1976) are classics. Recent pastoral theology volumes that discuss this issue are: Bonnie F. Miller-McLemore, *Also a Mother: Work and Family—A Theological Dilemma.* (Nashville: Abingdon, 1994); Jeanne Stevenson-Moessner and Maxine Glaz, *Women in Travail and Transition: A New Pastoral Care* (Minneapolis: Fortress Press, 1991); and Jeanne Stevenson Moessner, *Through the Eyes of Women: Insights for Pastoral Care* (Minneapolis: Fortress Press, 1996).

26. These girls are not unique in their priorities. Asked what their most compelling long-term need in life is, almost four times more college students polled by KPMG Peat Marwick chose achieving outstanding success in their chosen field over finding a mate. In fact, finding a mate also trailed achieving financial security and finding job fulfillment. *Dayton Daily News,* November 22, 1998.

27. For example, in addition to art options at the magnet school itself, the girls actually mentioned during the interviews these other events: mock trial competitions; district and state art contests; speech competitions; a Wright Step program for females interested in science based at Wright State. One girl had come from the program just that day, after building a car from scratch.

28. Carroll, *The Annotated Alice,* 37.

29. Patricia Davis, "Horror and the Development of Girls' Spiritual Voices," chapter 6 in this volume.

30. Harold S. Kushner, *When Bad Things Happen to Good People* (New York: Avon, 1981).

31. There are ample resources for exploring ways to name God. I suggest these options: Nancy L. Eisland, *The Disabled God: Toward a Liberation Theology of Disability* (Nashville: Abingdon, 1994); Major J. Jones, *The Color of God: The Concept of God in Afro-American Religious Thought* (Macon, Ga.: Mercer Univ. Press, 1987); Carroll Saussy, *God Images and Self-Esteem: Empowering Women in a Patriarchal Society* (Louisville, Ky.: Westminster John Knox, 1991); Marjorie Hewett Suchocki, *In God's Presence: Theological Reflections on Prayer* (St. Louis: Challis, 1996); Delores S. Williams, *Sisters in the Wilderness: The Challenge of Womanist God-Talk* (Maryknoll, N.Y.: Orbis, 1993); Brian Wren,. *What Language Shall I Borrow? God-Talk in Worship—A Male Response to Feminist Theology* (New York: Crossroad, 1989); Carolyn Bohler, "God as Jazz Band Leader: Divine and Human Power and Responsibility," *Journal of Theology* 51 (summer 1997), 53–78; Carolyn Bohler, *God Is Like a Mother Hen and Much, Much More* (Louisville, Ky.: Presbyterian Publishing Corporation, 1996), a resource for children.

32. Carroll, *The Annotated Alice,* 152.

33. Ibid., 133.

34. I did not manage to ask each girl every question. I have not omitted minority responses, though I have occasionally not included repetitious ones.

35. Carroll, *The Annotated Alice,* 37.

36. Ibid., 109.

37. "The central developmental question of a girl's adolescence becomes 'Where do I begin and other people end?'" Joan Borysenko, *A Woman's Book of Life: The Biology, Psychology, and Spirituality of the Feminine Life Cycle* (New York: Riverhead, 1996), 71.

38. Carroll, *The Annotated Alice,* 91.

39. Borysenko, *A Woman's Book of Life,* 72.

40. Carroll, *The Annotated Alice,* 30.

41. John B. Cobb Jr. and David Ray Griffin, *Process Theology: An Introductory Exposition.* (Philadelphia: Westminster, 1976) 65, 83.

42. Carroll, *The Annotated Alice,* 122, 161, 109.

43. Pipher, *Reviving Ophelia,* 183.

44. Carroll, *The Annotated Alice,* 64.

45. Patty Davis, in this volume, illustrates the horror that girls live with and the absurdity of simplistic religious answers to their concerns. These irrelevant and even harmful answers are dominant among those given by the church and so-called religious adults. Davis suggests that girls are not accepting at face value either the naive sex education or the simplistic theology that is thrust upon them. She implies that adults should grow up and face ambiguity, entering into genuine and realistic dialogue with girls.

Chapter 9

1. First described in print in Carolyn Treadway, "Birth and Grace," *The Friendly Woman* 5, no. 2 (spring 1981).

2. Helen Reddy, "I Am Woman," Capitol Records.

3. For a fuller description of experiential or subjective knowing, see Mary Belenky et al., *Women's Ways of Knowing: The Development of Self, Voice, and Mind* (New York: Basic, 1986).

4. For a fuller explanation of these concepts, please see Arthur and Libby Colman, *Pregnancy: The Psychological Experience* (New York: Herder and Herder, 1971). See also Penelope Washbourn, *Becoming Woman: The Quest For Wholeness and Female Experience* (New York: Harper & Row, 1977), chap. 7.

5. See Bonnie Miller-McLemore, *Also a Mother: Work and Family as Theological Dilemma* (Nashville: Abingdon, 1994), chap. 7.

6. Kahlil Gibran, "On Children," from *The Prophet* (New York: Alfred A. Knopf, 1961), 17.

7. I have addressed some of the physical dimensions of mothering more thoroughly in *Also a Mother: Work and Family as Theological Dilemma* (Nashville: Abingdon, 1994), chapter 6.

8. These changes are not recent in the United States. See Nanette M. Roberts, "American Women and Life-Style Change," in *Christian Feminism: Visions of a New Humanity*, ed. Judith L. Weidman (New York: Harper & Row, 1984), 95–116.

9. Iris Marion Young, "Making Single Motherhood Normal," *Dissent* (winter 1994): 91.

10. Sandra Pollack, "Lesbian Parents: Claiming Our Visibility," in *Motherhood: A Feminist Perspective*, ed. Jane P. Knowles and Ellen Cole (New York: Haworth, 1999), 181–82.

11. Frank A. Johnson and Colleen L. Johnson, "Role Strain in High Commitment Career Women," *Journal of the American Academy of Psychoanalysis* 4, no. 1 (1976): 15–16.

12. Mirra Komzrovsky, *Women in College: Shaping New Feminine Identities* (New York: Basic, 1986), 253.

13. Eloise Stiglitz, "Caught between Two Worlds: The Impact of a Child on a Lesbian Couple's Relationship," in *Motherhood: A Feminist Perspective*, ed. Knowles and Cole, 107.

14. See Philip Blumstein and Pepper Schwartz's extensive study of thousands of couples, *American Couples* (New York: Morrow, 1983), 115, 324, cited by Susan Moller Okin, *Justice, Gender and the Family* (New York: Basic, 1989), 140.

15. See Victor Turner, *The Ritual Process: Structure and Anti-Structure* (Ithaca, N.Y.: Cornell Univ. Press, 1969), 94–96, and Arnold Van Gennep, *The Rites of Passage*, trans. Monika B. Vizedom and Gabrielle L. Caffee (Chicago: Univ. of Chicago Press, 1960), 10–11. See also Robbie Davis-Floyd, "Pregnancy and Cultural Confusion: Contradictions in Socialization," in *Cultural Constructions of "Woman,"* ed. Pauline Kolenda (Salem, Wis.: Sheffield, 1988), 9–57.

16. See Mircea Eliade, *The Sacred and the Profane: The Nature of Religion* (New York: Harper, 1961).

17. Julia Kristeva, "Stabat Mater," in *The Kristeva Reader*, ed. Toril Moi (New York: Columbia Univ. Press, 1986), 166, 178–79.

18. Kathryn Allen Rabuzzi, *Mother with Child: Transformations through Childbirth* (Bloomington, Ind.: Indiana Univ. Press, 1994), vii. See also her earlier book, *Motherself: A Mythic Analysis of Motherhood* (Bloomington, Ind.: Indiana Univ. Press, 1988).

19. Penelope Washbourn, *Becoming Woman: The Quest for Wholeness in Female Experience* (San Francisco: Harper & Row, 1977), 97.

20. Tikva Frymer-Kensky, "Birth Silence and *Motherprayer*," *Criterion* (spring/summer 1995): 28. See *Motherprayer: The Pregnant Woman's Spiritual Companion* (New York: Riverhead, 1995).

21. See Thelma Aldcroft, "Childbirth, Liturgy, and Ritual—A Neglected Dimension of Pastoral Theology," in *Life Cycles: Women and Pastoral Care*, ed. Elaine Graham and Margaret Halsey (London: SPCK, 1993), 180–91; and Joan Laird and Ann Hartman, "Women, Rituals, and Family Therapy," in *A Guide to Feminist Family Therapy*, ed. Lois Braverman (New York and London: Harrington Park, 1988), 157–73.

22. Adrienne Rich, *Of Woman Born: Motherhood as Experience and Institution* (New York: W. W. Norton, 1976), 11.

23. *Also a Mother*, chap. 2.

24. Daniel N. Stern and Nadia Bruschweiler-Stern with Alison Freeland, *The Birth of the Mother: How the Motherhood Experience Changes You Forever* (New York: Basic, 1998), 5.

25. Erik H. Erikson, "Womanhood and the Inner Space (1968)," in *Woman and Analysis: Dialogues on Psychoanalytic Views of Femininity*, ed. Jean Strouse (Boston: G. K. Hall, 1985), 295; *Childhood and Society*, 35th Anniversary Edition (New York: Norton, 1963), 267.

26. Mary Field Belenky, Blythe McVicker Clinchy, Nancy Rule Goldberger, and Jill Mattuck Tarule, *Women's Ways of Knowing: The Development of Self, Voice, and Mind* (New York: Basic, 1986), 27, 35–36, 142–43.

27. Carol Gilligan, *In a Different Voice: Psychological Theory and Women's Development* (Cambridge, Mass.: Harvard Univ. Press, 1982), 64–105.

28. For related comments, see Bonnie J. Miller-McLemore, "Produce or Perish: Generativity and the Question of New Reproductive Technologies," *Journal of the American Academy of Religion* 59, no. 1 (spring 1991): 39–69; "Produce or Perish: A Feminist Critique of Generativity," *Union Seminary Quarterly Review* 43, nos. 1–4 (1989): 201–21.

29. Brita Gill-Austern, "Love Understood as Self-Sacrifice and Self-Denial: What Does It Do to Women?" in *Through the Eyes of Women: Insights for Pastoral Care*, ed. Jeanne Stevenson Moessner (Minneapolis: Fortress Press, 1996), 316.

30. Rhona Mahony, *Kidding Ourselves: Breadwinning, Babies, and Bargaining Power* (New York: Basic, 1995), 106, 113–14. Emphasis in text.

31. Sallie McFague, *Models of God: Theology for an Ecological, Nuclear Age* (Philadelphia: Fortress Press, 1987), 104.

32. Ibid., 105. See also Margaret L. Hammer, *Giving Birth: Reclaiming Biblical Metaphor for Pastoral Practice* (Louisville, Ky.: Westminister John Knox, 1994).

33. Margaret Hebblethwaite, *Motherhood and God* (London: Geoffrey Chapman, 1984), 1.

34. Elizabeth Ann Dreyer, "Asceticism Reconsidered," *Weavings: A Journal of the Christian Spiritual Life* 3, no. 6 (1988): 14.

35. For suggestive possibilities, see Wendy M. Wright, *Sacred Dwelling: A Spirituality of Family Life* (Leavenworth, Kan.: Forest of Peace, 1994).

36. Sara Ruddick, "Maternal Thinking," in Joyce Treblicot, ed., *Mothering: Essays in Feminist Theory* (Totowa, N.J.: Rowman and Allanheld, 1983), 215.

37. Ibid., 217, 223–24.

38. Anne B. Abernethy, "When the Minister Has a Baby," in *Creative Ministries in Contemporary Christianity*, ed. Perry LeFevre and W. Widick Schroeder (Chicago: Exploration, 1991), 3–28.

39. Sheri Fenster, Suzanne B. Phillips, and Estelle R. G. Rapoport, *The Therapist's Pregnancy: Intrusion in the Analytic Space* (Hillsdale, N.J.: The Analytic Press, 1986).

40. Ibid., 39.

41. Abernethy, "When the Minister Has a Baby," 6.

42. Ibid., 18.

Chapter 10

1. In the United States in 1998, women's average life expectancy is eighty years, making a woman's fortieth year the demographic starting point of midlife. Midlife is variously defined, however, and years included in "midlife" by various authors range from thirty-five. In this essay, I am addressing what some authors call "early" midlife, approximately ages thirty-five to fifty.

2. By "wholistic" awareness and response, I mean awareness of and response to the compound connectedness of body/mind/spirit/relationship/culture/nature that gives rise to human being and experience. Wholistic awareness and response focuses less on the multiplicity of these domains and more on care for their interrelatedness. Therefore, wholistic awareness and response seeks to reconcile and knit together our knowledge about the multiple dimensions of human experience—body and mind and spirit and relationship and culture and nature and on and on—into wisdom for living whole lives together. Although many disciplines and professionals are responsible for specialization in one or another of these domains (for example, physicians are required to be specialists in the body, psychologists are required to be specialists in the mind, theologians are required to be specialists in the S/spirit, etc.), my assumption in this essay is that pastoral theologians and caregivers are called to study and nurture wholeness of life. Such an integration is so difficult that it at first seems unfeasible, but it has long been the special gift and responsibility of spiritual seekers and spiritual caregivers to identify such soulful, centering, collective wisdom. This chapter stands in that long tradition of soul care.

3.   Dr. Patricia Allen, as quoted by Gail Sheehy, *The Silent Passage: Menopause,* rev. ed. (New York: Simon and Schuster, Pocket, 1998), 23.

4.   Susan M. Love, with Karen Lindsey, *Dr. Susan Love's Hormone Book: Making Informed Choices about Menopause* (New York: Random House, Times Books, 1997), 1. Because menses normally fluctuates before it completely stops, the event of menopause can be reliably identified only retrospectively, that is, after the event. Diagnostically, women are usually said to be "menopausal" when twelve months have passed since their last menstrual cycle.

5.   New England Research, Inc., *Women and Their Health in Massachusetts: Final Report 1991* (Watertown, Mass.: New England Research Institute, 1991). As cited by Judith Reichman, *I'm Too Young to Get Old: Health Care for Women after Forty* (New York, Random House, Times Books, 1996).

6.   The earliest literature tends to use the term "perimenopause" to refer not to the whole hormonal transition, but only to the period when a woman experiences signs and symptoms. Because women's average age when signs and symptoms become observable is 47.5 years, and the average age at menopause is 51.3, according to this usage, the average length of perimenopause is 3.8 years. Later literature, however, emphasizes that hormonal fluctuations are occurring and affecting women's bodies in important ways beginning in the mid-thirties, even if there are no signs and symptoms. I prefer use of "perimenopause" to refer to the whole hormonal transition, because it emphasizes the importance of hormonal fluctuations and of preventive health care in a woman's thirties and early forties (and not only in response to uncomfortable or distressing symptoms in a woman's late forties and fifties).

7.   As long as women carry primary responsibility for the twenty-four-hour-a-day task of managing households and nurturing children and family relationships, midlife will pose special challenges for women. See Janet Zollinger Giele, ed., *Women in the Middle Years: Current Knowledge and Directions for Research and Policy* (New York: John Wiley & Sons, 1982).

8.   That information about perimenopause is expanding so rapidly is likely due to the confluence of at least two factors: increasing numbers of women researchers and writers, and increasing numbers of women in perimenopause. The information is no longer buried in scholarly literature but has moved into the mainstream. Between 1994 and 1998, at least twelve self-help health books were published on perimenopause. (See the chapter's annotated bibliography.) Additionally, many search programs can locate information about perimenopause on the Internet (see, for example, women's health Web pages, on-line summaries of newspaper and television stories, and chat groups).

9.   Sheehy, *The Silent Passage,* xv.

10.   James E. Houston and L. Darlene Lanka, *Perimenopause: Changes in Women's Health after 35* (Oakland, Calif.: New Harbinger, 1997), 5.

11.   For helpful Christian reflections on issues in women's spirituality in and after midlife, see: Kathleen Fischer, *Autumn Gospel: Women in the Second Half of Life* (New York: Paulist Press, Integration Books, 1995); Janice Brewi and Anne Brennan, *Mid-Life: Psychological and Spiritual Perspectives* (New York: Crossroad, 1982). For books that explore menopause (but contain helpful inferences for perimenopause) with an emphasis on spirituality, see Christine Downing, *Journey through Menopause: A Personal Rite of Passage* (New York: Crossroad, 1987; Marian Van Eyk McCain, *Transformation through Menopause* (New York: Bergin and Garvey, 1991). Three chapters address midlife, spirituality, and health issues in Joan Borysenko, *A Woman's Book of Life: The Biology, Psychology, and Spirituality of the Feminine Life Cycle* (New York: Riverhead, 1996). General literature on the spirituality of midlife is too extensive to be cited here in full. One recent and helpful addition to this literature is Joyce Rupp, *Dear Heart, Come Home: The Path of Midlife Spirituality* (New York: Crossroad, 1997).

12.   The value and meaning of the term "soulfulness" for pastoral theology and care is developed in Kathleen J. Greider, Gloria A. Johnson, and Kristen J. Leslie, "Women Writing for Our Lives," in *Feminist and Womanist Pastoral Theology,* ed. Bonnie J. Miller-McLemore and Brita L. Gill-Austern (Nashville: Abingdon Press, 1999), 39–42.

13.   Jung published "Die seelischen Probleme der menschlichen Altersstufen" in 1930. Revised, it first appeared in English in 1931 as "The Stages of Life," in C. G. Jung, *Modern Man in Search of a Soul,* trans. W. S. Dell and Cary F. Baynes. Citations in this chapter are from C. G. Jung, "The Stages of Life," in *The Structure and Dynamics of the Psyche,* vol. 8 of *The Collected Works of C. G. Jung,* ed. Herbert Read, Michael Fordham, and Gerhard Adler, trans. R. F. C. Hull (New York: Pantheon, 1970), pars. 749–95. In addition to its role in the emergence of psychological theories of midlife, the essay is sometimes cited as one of the earliest examples of contemporary developmental psychology.

14. The almost exclusive focus of "Stages of Life" on only one stage is reasonably attributable to the fact that Jung conceptualized the essay while in midlife. He was fifty-five when the essay was published.

15. Jung, "Stages of Life," pars. 778 and 784.

16. He might also be corrupting his argument by failing to make sufficient distinction between his own psychic needs and those of others. The specific complements he prescribes seem biased in the direction of resolving Jung's own midlife struggles. In addition to "Stages of Life," see C. G. Jung, *Memories, Dreams, Reflections,* ed. Aniela Jaffé, trans. Richard and Clara Winston (New York: Random House, 1963).

17. Eugene C. Bianchi, *On Growing Older: A Personal Guide to Life after Thirty-five* (New York: Crossroad, 1985), 36.

18. "Stages of Life," par. 787.

19. For a similar point of view, see Mary James Dean and Mary Louise Cullen, "Woman's Body: Spiritual Needs and Theological Presence," in *Women in Travail and Transition: A New Pastoral Care,* ed. Maxine Glaz and Jeanne Stevenson Moessner (Minneapolis: Fortress Press, 1991), 91.

20. Bianchi, *On Growing Older,* 37.

21. Because "perimenopause" is relatively new and unfamiliar terminology, some authors speak of "menopause" when they are referring to matters that could be or are relevant to perimenopause. Where I rely on literature on menopause that is relevant to perimenopause, I indicate my extension of those findings through use of the formulation "peri/menopause."

22. For extensive bibliographic references for cross-cultural studies of menopause, see Love, *Dr. Susan Love's Hormone Book,* 318, 334–35.

23. M. Lock, P. Kaufert, and P. Gilbert, "Cultural Construction of the Menopausal Syndrome: The Japanese Case," *Maturitas* 10 (1988): 317–32. Cited by Love, *Dr. Susan Love's Hormone Book,* 20.

24. Carol Turkington, *The Perimenopause Handbook: What Every Woman Needs to Know about the Years Before Menopause* (Lincolnwood, Ill.: Contemporary, 1998), 43–44.

25. Love, *Dr. Susan Love's Hormone Book,* 20–21; Turkington, *The Perimenopause Handbook,* 43–44; Reichman, *I'm Too Young to Get Old,* 205–6.

26. Sheehy's interviews provide anecdotal evidence.

27. M. Flint and R. S. Samil, "Cultural and Subcultural Meanings of the Menopause," in *Multidisciplinary Perspectives on Menopause,* ed. M. Flint, F. G. Kronenberg, and W. Utian, *Annals of New York Academy of Sciences,* 1990, 134–48, cited by Love, *Dr. Susan Love's Hormone Book,* 21.

28. Bernard J. Cortese, *What You Need to Know about Perimenopause* (Freedom, Calif.: The Crossing, 1998), 6.

29. Sheehy, *The Silent Passage,* 44.

30. "The majority of women regard menopause as a short-term event and do not connect it with long-term health problems in postmenopausal life. . . . Less than half the women in a recent Gallup survey related the Change to these important issues, and more than one in four did not see a doctor at all, because they felt their symptoms were a natural part of menopause." Sheehy, *The Silent Passage,* 9. Many sources discuss physicians' lack of knowledge about perimenopause. For example, see Turkington, *The Perimenopause Handbook,* xi–xii.

31. Sheehy, *The Silent Passage,* 18. Immediate and excessive use of HRT and other pharmaceuticals can be another form of overtreatment. See Love, *Dr. Susan Love's Hormone Book.*

32. Stephanie DeGraff Bender, with Treacy Colbert, *The Power of Perimenopause: A Woman's Guide to Physical and Emotional Health during the Transitional Decade* (New York: Harmony, 1998), 2.

33. Love, *Dr. Susan Love's Hormone Book,* 3.

34. Sheehy, *The Silent Passage,* 10.

35. Reichman, *I'm Too Young to Get Old,* 10.

36. Sheehy, *The Silent Passage* 43.

37. Nancy Lee Teaff and Kim Wright Wiley, *Perimenopause: Preparing for the Change: A Guide to the Early Stages of Menopause and Beyond* (Rocklin, Calif.: Prima, 1995), 21.

38. Reichman, *I'm Too Young to Get Old,* 21.

39. Turkington, *The Perimenopause Handbook,* 2.

40. Teaff and Wiley, *Perimenopause,* 3, 168. Like many other researchers, Teaff and Wiley report that women with a history of PMS and other menstrual complications report more severity in perimenopausal symptoms.

41. Sheehy, *The Silent Passage,* 6.

42. Marcia Lawrence, *Menopause and Madness: The Truth about Estrogen and the Mind* (Kansas City, Mo.: Andrews McNeel, 1998).

43. Sheehy, *The Silent Passage,* 177.

44. Limitations of both space and expertise prevent me from discussing the complications and controversy surrounding hormone replacement therapy. To get a sound introduction to the issue, two books that offer extended, careful, and distinct discussions of this important issue are Love, *Dr. Susan Love's Hormone Book,* and Reichman, *I'm Too Young to Get Old.*

45. Sheehy, *The Silent Passage,* 168.

46. Teaff and Wiley, *Perimenopause,* 77.

47. Some women are "menophobic," unsympathetic or even hostile toward the signs and symptoms of menopause in themselves or other women (Sheehy, *The Silent Passage,* 6). This results from a woman's inattention to her internalization of the social stigma directed against menses and menopause.

48. Bender, *The Power of Perimenopause,* 69.

49. Turkington offers extensive aid for finding a physician.

50. Sheehy, *The Silent Passage,* 165.

51. John 10:10.

52. This story is found in all four gospels: Luke 7:36-50; Matthew 26:6-13; Mark 14:3-9; John 12:1-8.

53. Psalm 126.

54. Bender, *The Power of Perimenopause,* 49–50, 65.

55. Ibid., 152.

Chapter 11

1. Psalm 139:14.

2. C. Sue Furman, *Turning Point: The Myths and Realities of Menopause* (New York: Oxford Univ. Press, 1995), 36.

3. Gail Sheehy, *The Silent Passage: Menopause* (New York: Random House, 1992), 8.

4. American Medical Association, *Essential Guide to Menopause* (New York: Pocket, 1998), 13.

5. I had remembered the title of the book as being "Betwixt and Between the Gatepost," which served as a seed for the title of this chapter. It turns out I had combined the title of two books by the same author. The original titles were *Twixt Twelve and Twenty* and *Between Me, You and the Gatepost* by Pat Boone (Englewood Cliffs, N.J.: Prentice-Hall, 1960).

6. American Medical Association, *Essential Guide to Menopause,* 6.

7. Susan Davis, *The Healthy Woman: Menopause and Other Things We Don't Talk About* (New York: Brunner/Mazel, 1996), 10.

8. Ibid., 10.

9. American Medical Association, *Essential Guide to Menopause,* 5.

10. Furman, *Turning Point,* 36.

11. Alan Silverstein and Cynthia Cotton, *Menopause: A Basic Guide for Women* (Freemont, Calif.: Jain, 1996), 2.

12. American Medical Association, *Essential Guide to Menopause,* 15.

13. Furman, *Turning Point,* 36.

14. Davis, *The Healthy Woman,* 15.

15. Ibid., 14.

16. All books listed in the bibliography have information regarding estrogen loss and replacement options. Some books support one option over the other but generally claim their bias and rationale for it early in the book. Other books present an unbiased look at all options. There are ample resources available to help women make well-informed, individualized choices for addressing the issue of estrogen loss.

17. *Fried Green Tomatoes,* dir. Jon Avnet, prod. Jon Avnet and Jordan Kerner. Universal Studios, 1991, videocassette.

18. Other movies that I have used with women's groups dealing with empowerment issues, aging, and intergenerational relationships between women include *Something to Talk About* (Warner Home Video, 1995), *The Spitfire Grill* (CastleRock Entertainment, 1996), *The Trip to Bountiful* (Bountiful Film Partners, 1985), and *Hope Floats* (20th Century Fox Film Corp, 1998).

19. Maria Harris, *Dance of the Spirit: The Seven Steps of Women's Spirituality* (New York: Bantam Books, 1989), 1–21. Awakening is the first stage of Harris's seven-stage process of developing women's spirituality.

20. Maria Harris has written two books on women's spirituality that are very useful for individual or group work in this area. Both books contain suggestions for personal reflection and group discussion. In addition to the book referenced above, see also *Jubilee Time: Celebrating Women, Spirit and the Advent of Age* (New York: Bantam Books, 1995), which is specifically designed for midlife and aging women. Both books also combine a woman's spirituality with her sexuality and creativity.

21. Reinhold Niebuhr. Most people are familiar with the serenity prayer: "God grant me the serenity to accept the things I cannot change, courage to change the things I can, and the wisdom to know the difference." Reinhold Niebuhr reportedly delivered this in 1934 as a closing to s spoken prayer. It was later used by AA, but was never published by Niebuhr.

22. I am not sure who to credit for the origin of this notion of "power surge," but it has become an increasingly popular euphemism for the hot flashes associated with estrogen loss and menopause.

23. Althea Horner, *The Wish for Power and the Fear of Having It* (Northvale, N.J.: Jason Aronson, 1989).

24. Matthew 5:15.

25. Ellen Cole, "Over the Hill We Go: Women at Menopause," in *Women in Context: Toward a Feminist Reconstruction of Psychotherapy*, ed. Marsha Mirkin (New York: Guilford, 1994), 322–23.

26. This list of common symptoms and physical changes associated with the body's response to hormonal changes due to menopause can be found in various forms in the collection of literature referenced in the bibliography.

27. Marcia Woodruff, "Love at Fifty," in *When I Am An Old Woman, I Shall Wear Purple*, ed. Sandra Martz (Watsonville, Calif.: Papier-Maché, 1987), 93.

28. Gretchen Henkel, *The Menopause Sourcebook* (Los Angeles: Lowell House, 1996), 81.

29. See Genesis 17:15-22; 18:9-15; 21:1-7 for Sarah's story. See Luke 1:5-25, 39-66 for Elizabeth's story.

30. Furman, *Turning Point*, 40.

31. An excellent resource for helping pastors begin to deal with their own sexual issues as a prerequisite for learning to hear and attend pastorally to the sexual issues of others is William Arnold, *Pastoral Responses to Sexual Issues* (Louisville, Ky.: Westminister John Knox, 1993). The first three chapters are written as guides for personal reflection for the pastor as a way of increasing self-awareness of one's own sexuality.

32. Joshua 24:15.

33. John 10:10.

Bibliography (Chapter 11)

American Medical Association. *Essential Guide to Menopause*. New York: Pocket, 1998.

Barbach, Lonnie. *The Pause: Positive Approaches to Menopause*. New York: Dutton/Penguin, 1993.

Cole, Ellen. "Over the Hill We Go: Women at Menopause." In *Women in Context: Toward a Feminist Reconstruction of Psychotherapy*. Ed. Marsha Mirkin. New York: Guilford, 1994.

Davis, Susan. *The Healthy Woman: Menopause and Other Things We Don't Talk About*. New York: Oxford Univ. Press, 1995.

Furman, C. Sue. *Turning Point: The Myths and Realities of Menopause*. New York: Oxford Univ. Press, 1995.

Gitleman, Ann. *Super Nutrition for Menopause*. New York: Pocket Books, 1993.

Harris, Maria. *Dance of the Spirit: The Seven Steps of Women's Spirituality*. New York: Bantam Books, 1989.

———. *Jubilee Time: Celebrating Women, Spirit and the Advent of Age*. New York: Bantam Books, 1995.

Henkel, Gretchen. *The Menopause Sourcebook*. Los Angeles: Lowell House, 1996.

Horner, Althea. *The Wish for Power and the Fear of Having It*. Northvale, N.J.: Jason Aronson Inc., 1989.

Horrigan, Bonnie. *Red Moon Passage: The Power and Wisdom of Menopause*. New York: Harmony Books, 1996.

Judelson, Debra, and Diana Dell. *The Women's Complete Wellness Book*. The American Medical Women's Association. New York: Golden Books, 1998.

Martz, Sandra, ed. *When I Am An Old Woman, I Shall Wear Purple.* Watsonville, Calif.: Papier-Maché, 1987.

Moquette-Magee, Elaine. *Eat Well for a Healthy Menopause.* New York: John Wiley & Sons, Inc., 1996.

Paige, Judith, and Pamela Gordon. *Choice Years: Health, Happiness, and Beauty through Menopause and Beyond.* New York: Villard Books, 1991.

Sheehy, Gail. *The Silent Passage: Menopause.* Rev. Ed. New York: Pocket Books, 1998.

Silverstein, Alan, and Cynthia Cotton. *Menopause: A Basic Guide for Women.* Freemont, Calif.: Jain Publishing Company, 1996.

Voda, Ann M. *Menopause, Me and You: The Sound of Women Pausing.* New York: Harrington Park Press, 1997.

Chapter 12

1. E. H. Erikson, *Identity and the Life Cycle* (New York: International Universities Press, 1959).

2. E. H. Erikson, *Childhood and Society*, 2nd ed. (New York: W. W. Norton, 1963); "Reflections on Dr. Borg's Life Cycle," in *Adulthood*, ed. E. H. Erikson (New York: W. W. Norton, 1978).

3. R. Butler, "The Life Review: An Interpretation of Reminiscence in the Aged," *Psychiatry* 26 (1963): 65–76.

4. M. Walaskay, *The Construction and Validation of an Ego-Integrity Interview*, unpublished doctoral dissertation by M. Glaz (under author's previous name), The University of Rochester, Rochester, New York, 1981.

5. David Gutmann, *Reclaimed Powers: Men and Women in Later Life* (Evanston, Ill.: Northwestern Univ. Press, 1994), 9.

6. Ibid., 1–22.

7. Ibid., 133–84.

8. Z. Schachter-Shalomi, *From Age-ing to Sage-ing* (New York: Warner, 1997), 58–59.

9. M. S. Mahler, "On Child Psychosis and Schizophrenia: Autistic and Symbiotic Infantile Psychosis," *Psychoanalytic Study of the Child* 7 (1952): 286–305; "Autism and Symbiosis: Two Extreme Disturbances of Identity," *International Journal of Psychoanalysis* 39 (1958): 77–83.

10. M. S. Mahler, F. Pine, and A. Bergman, *The Psychological Birth of the Human Infant* (New York: Basic, 1985).

11. F. Pine, *Developmental Theory and Clinical Process* (New Haven, Conn.: Yale Univ. Press, 1985), 42–49; D. N. Stern, *The Interpersonal World of the Infant* (New York: Basic , 1985), 19–21.

12. Gutmann, *Reclaimed Powers*, 1–22.

13. I. A. Wilson, *Consilience* (New York: Alfred A. Knopf, 1998), 181–209, most clearly describes the difficulties in social science theory and research. Briefly stated (183), Wilson suggests: "Such is the paradox of the social sciences. Familiarity bestows comfort and comfort breeds carelessness and error. Most people believe they know how they themselves think, how others think too, and even how institutions evolve. But they are wrong. Their understanding is based on folk psychology, the grasp of human nature by common sense—defined (by Einstein) as everything learned to the age of eighteen—shot through with misconceptions, and only slightly advanced over ideas employed by the Greek philosophers." Out of context, this criticism might seem heavy handed, but it describes very well the situation in gerontology research.

14. D. I. Templer, "The Construction and Validation of a Death Anxiety Scale," *The Journal of General Psychology* 32 (1970): 165–77.

15. Walaskay, *Ego-Integrity Interview.* A copy of the research interview (124, 133–36 in the dissertation) may be found in appendix A of this chapter.

16. J. Marcia, "Development and Validation of Ego Identity Status," *Journal of Personality and Social Psychology* 3 (1996): 551–58; S. K. Whitbourne and C. S. Weinstock, *Adult Development: The Differentiation of Experience* (New York: Holt, Rinehart, Winston), 1979.

17. M. Walaskay, *Ego-Integrity Interview*, 18–31. See appendix B for page 30 from the dissertation, "Summary of Hypothetical Characteristics on Dimensions."

18. Ibid., 93.

19. N. S., raw score differences on the Death Preparation Scale were: Integrity Achieving 28.90, SD 3.31, and Foreclosed 30.50, SD, 6,55. Ibid., 58.

20. Ibid., 60.

21. Ibid., "Results," chap. 3, 56–96.

22. Ibid., 60.

23. M. Walaskay, S. D. Whitbourne, and M. F. Nehrke, "Construction and Validation of an Ego-Integrity Interview," *The International Journal of Aging and Human Development* 18, no. 1 (1983–84): 61–72. Reprints available: M. Glaz, P. O. Box 275, Fraser, CO 80442.

Chapter 13

1. The names in this story have been changed. These quotations are taken from a research interview for the course "Counseling Women in the Church" at Saint Paul School of Theology, Kansas City, Missouri, conducted by Kathy Leclere. Used by permission of interviewer and interviewee. Carrie Jones is a ninety-one-year-old, white woman who lives in rural Missouri.

2. Helena Z. Lopata, *Current Widowhood: Myths and Realities* (Thousand Oaks, Calif.: Sage, 1996), 43.

3. Ibid., 120.

4. Ibid.

5. Ibid. 1.

6. Although younger women also face widowhood, there are significant differences in their experience that deserve attention but that cannot be given in this brief chapter. A separate literature deals with this population.

7. *Aging in America: Trends and Projections* (Washington, D.C.: U.S. Government Printing Office, 1991), 11.

8. Ibid., 17.

9. Cathi M. Taeuber and Jessie Allen, "Women in Our Aging Society: The Demographic Outlook," in *Women on the Front Lines,* ed. Jessie Alan and Alan Pifer (Washington, D.C.: Urban Institute, 1993), 26, 29.

10. Sara Arber and Jay Ginn, *Gender and Later Life: A Sociological Analysis of Resources and Constraints* (London: Sage, 1991), 1, 20.

11. A widow is defined here as a "woman who has been married and whose husband has died" (Lopata, *Current Widowhood,* 1). Although research on widowhood is somewhat limited, literature on women who have experienced other forms of partner loss, such as homosexual or heterosexual women in long-term committed relationships, is scarce. Because such a high percentage of women in the current cohort of older women are widowed, I have chosen to focus on widowhood. Further work is needed on older women and other forms of partner loss.

12. An extensive body of literature explores the shape and nature of grief. See Kenneth Mitchell and Herbert Anderson, *All Our Losses, All Our Griefs* (Philadelphia: Westminster, 1983); Ester Shapiro, *Grief as a Family Process* (New York: Guilford, 1994); John Bowlby, *Attachment and Loss,* vol. 3, *Loss, Sadness and Depression* (New York: Basic, 1980).

13. John Bowlby, *Attachment and Loss,* has divided the experience of grieving into four phases: (1) numbing, (2) searching and yearning for the lost figure, (3) disorganization and despair, and (4) greater or lesser degree of reorganization.

14. Lopata, *Current Widowhood.*

15. Ibid.

16. There are currently very few articles on this topic. See Graham J. McDougall, "Therapeutic Issues with Gay and Lesbian Elders," in *The Forgotten Aged: Ethnic, Psychiatric, and Social Minorities,* ed. T. L. Brink (New York: Haworth, 1993).

17. Bonnie Bowman Thurston, *The Widows: A Women's Ministry in the Early Church* (Minneapolis: Fortress Press, 1989), 10–13.

18. Ibid., 14.

19. Ibid., 7.

20. Ibid., 7.

21. Ibid.

22. Ibid., 8.

23. Based on demographic data as well as anecdotal information from students at Saint Paul School of Theology serving rural charges. In many cases, the average age of the congregation is over sixty, and a large percentage of the members are women. A significant number of these women are widowed.

24. *A Profile of United Methodists Based on the Survey of United Methodist Opinion* (Dayton: The Office of Research, General Council of Ministries of the United Methodist Church, 1995).

25. Ibid., 8.

26. A course entitled "Counseling Women in the Church" was taught at Saint Paul School of Theology, Kansas City, Missouri, during the fall semester, 1997. Students conducted a sixty- to ninety-minute interview with an older woman as an assignment in the course. Permission to use the material collected was obtained.

27. Evelyn R. Rosenthal, "Women and Varieties of Ageism," in *Women, Aging, and Ageism,* ed. Evelyn Rosenthal (New York: Haworth, 1990), 1.

28. Edith, age eighty-six.

29. Mitchell and Anderson, *All Our Losses, All Our Griefs,* 40.

30. Ibid., 35–46.

31. Phyllis R. Silverman, *Widow-to-Widow* (New York: Springer, 1986), 3.

32. Shirley L. O'Bryant, "Forewarning of a Husband's Death: Does It Make a Difference for Older Widows?" *Omega* 22, no. 3 (1990–91): 227–39.

33. Ibid., 237.

34. Bowlby, *Attachment and Loss.*

35. Ibid., 3.

36. Dale A. Lund, Michael S. Caserta, and Margaret F. Dimond, "Impact of Spousal Bereavement on the Subjective Well-Being of Older Adults," in *Older Bereaved Spouses,* ed. Dale A. Lund (New York: Hemisphere, 1989), 3, 11.

37. Ibid., 4.

38. Lund, Caserta, and Dimond, "Impact of Spousal Bereavement," 3, 11. Although this study included men as well as women, 78.9 percent of the sample were women.

39. Ibid.

40. Ibid., 3, 11, 12.

41. Ibid.

42. Lopata, *Widowhood in an American City* (Cambridge, Mass.: Schenkman Publishing Company, 1973).

43. Lopata, *Women as Widows* (New York: Elsevier, 1979).

44. Ibid.

45. Ibid., 355.

46. Ibid., 356.

47. Ibid., 357.

48. Ibid., 358.

49. Kathleen A. Glass, "Appraisal, Coping and Resources: Markers Associated with the Health of Aged Widows and Widowers," in *Older Bereaved Spouses,* ed. Lund, 91.

50. Ibid.

51. Ibid., 81.

52. Julie Pellman, "Widowhood in Elderly Women: Exploring Its Relationship to Community Integration, Hassles, Stress, Social Support, and Social Support Seeking," *International Journal of Aging and Human Development* 35, no. 4 (1992): 253.

53. Ibid., 259, 260.

54. Ibid.

55. Ibid.

56. Tonya L. Schuster and Edgar W. Butler, "Bereavement, Social Networks, Social Support, and Mental Health," in *Older Bereaved Spouses,* ed. Lund, 55–66.

57. Ibid., 65.

58. Ibid.

59. Ibid.

60. Ibid.

61. Judith V. Jordan, Alexandra Kaplan, Jean Baker Miller, Irene P. Stiver, and Janet L. Surrey, *Women's Growth in Connection: Writings from the Stone Center* (New York: Guilford, 1991), 1.

62. See Carol Gilligan, *In a Different Voice: Psychological Theory and Women's Development* (Cambridge, Mass.: Harvard Univ. Press, 1982); also Jordan et al., *Women's Growth in Connection.*

63. Jordan et al., *Women's Growth in Connection,* 11.

64. See ibid.

65. See Miller, "The Development of Women' Sense of Self"; and Surrey, "The Self-in-Relation: A Theory of Women's Development," in ibid.

66. Surrey, "The Self-in-Relation," in ibid., 52.

67. Ibid., 54.

68. Erik Erikson, *Childhood and Society,* 2nd ed. (New York: W. W. Norton, 1963), 266, 268.

69. Ibid., 267.

70. Ibid.

71. Lopata, *Current Widowhood,* 120.

72. Ibid., citing Lopata, *Widows and Dependent Wives: From Social Problem to Federal Program,* 1986a.

73. Lopata, *Current Widowhood,* 120.

74. Ibid., 120–24.

75. Ibid.

76. Ibid.

77. Ibid., 121.

78. Ibid.

79. Ibid.

80. Ibid., 103.

81. Ibid.

82. Ibid., 104.

83. Ibid., 105.

84. Ibid., 104.

85. Ibid., 109.

86. Ibid., 122.

87. Ibid., 122.

88. Ibid., 123.

89. Ibid.

90. This statement is based on my experience in ministry. Many lay people are afraid they will not "say the right thing" to a grieving person and often belittle the instrumental help given as unimportant.

91. Silverman, *Widow to Widow.*

Chapter 14

1. See especially Mary Field Belenky et al., *Women's Ways of Knowing: The Development of Self, Voice, and Mind* (New York: Basic, 1986); Judith Jordan et al., *Women's Growth in Connection* (New York: Guilford, 1991); and Judith Jordan, ed., *Women's Growth in Diversity* (New York: Guilford, 1997).

2. See especially Catherine Mowry LaCugna, ed., *Freeing Theology* (New York: Harper Collins, 1993); Elizabeth Johnson, *She Who Is* (New York: Crossroad, 1992); Rebecca S. Chopp, *The Power to Speak* (New York: Crossroad, 1989); Carol S. Robb, ed., *Making the Connections: Beverly Wildung Harrison Essays in Feminist Social Ethics*(Boston: Beacon, 1985); Kyle Pasewark, *A Theology of Power* (Minneapolis: Fortress, 1993); Letty Russell, *Household of Freedom* (Philadelphia: Westminster, 1987); and Martha Ellen Stortz, *Pastor Power* (Nashville: Abingdon, 1993).

3. See Jordan et al., *Women's Growth in Connection*; Jordan, ed., *Women's Growth in Diversity;* and Jean Baker Miller and Irene Pierce Stiver, *The Healing Connection* (Boston: Beacon, 1997).

4. Judith V. Jordan, "A Relational Perspective for Understanding Women's Development," in Jordan, ed., *Women's Growth in Diversity,* 20.

5. Janet L. Surrey, "The Self-in-Relation: A Theory of Women's Development," in Jordan et al., *Women's Growth in Connection.*

6. Vashti McKenzie, *Not without a Struggle: Leadership Development for African American Women in Ministry* (Cleveland: United Church, 1996), 110–11.

7. Cheryl J. Sanders, *Empowerment Ethics for a Liberated People* (Minneapolis: Fortress Press, 1995), 101, 102, 105.

8. See Surrey, "The Self-in-Relation," 61–62, for a fuller discussion of the emotionally and cognitively intersubjective definition of relationality that includes continuous psychological connection and

recognizes the significance of the relationship as a reality larger than the sum of the selves participating in it and lending vitality to each participating self.

9. Janet L. Surrey, "The Relational Self in Women: Clinical Implications," in Jordan et al., *Women's Growth in Connection*, 36.

10. Surrey, "The Self-in-Relation," 62–63.

11. Jean Baker Miller, "The Development of Women's Sense of Self," in Jordan et al., *Women's Growth in Connection*, 15.

12. Judith Jordan, "A Relational Perspective for Understanding Women's Development," in Jordan, ed., *Women's Growth in Diversity*, 20.

13. Judith Jordan, "The Meaning of Mutuality," in Jordan et al., *Women's Growth in Connection*, 82; and Surrey, "The Self-in-Relation," 54.

14. Jordan, "The Meaning of Mutuality," 90.

15. Janet Surrey, "Relationship and Empowerment," in Jordan et al., *Women's Growth in Connection*, 168.

16. Ibid., 164.

17. Miller, "The Development of Women's Sense of Self," 17.

18. Surrey, "Relationship and Empowerment," 167.

19. For an excellent discussion of the challenges of critical engagement by women across boundaries of cultural difference, see Linda Moody, *Women Encounter God* (Maryknoll, N.Y.: Orbis, 1996).

20. Surrey, "The Self-in-Relation," 60–61.

21. Joretta Marshall, "Toward the Development of a Pastoral Soul: Reflections on Identity and Theological Education," *Pastoral Psychology* 43, no.1 (1994): 11–28.

22. Jordan, "The Meaning of Mutuality," 89.

23. Jean Baker Miller, "The Construction of Anger in Women and Men," in Jordan et al. *Women's Growth in Connection*, 182.

24. Kathleen Greider, *Reckoning with Aggression* (Louisville, Ky.: Westminster John Knox, 1997), 56–76.

25. Beverly Harrison, "The Power of Anger in the Work of Love," in *Making the Connections*, ed. Robb, 14–15.

26. Carroll Saussy, *The Gift of Anger* (Louisville: Westminster John Knox, 1995), 58.

27. Ibid., 43.

28. Belenky, *Women's Ways of Knowing*, 3.

29. Ibid., 15.

30. Ibid., 189.

31. Ibid., 195.

32. Janet Stiver, "Discussion Summary," in *Women's Growth in Diversity*, ed. Jordan, 47.

33. Catherine LaCugna, *Freeing Theology*, 86–87.

34. Ibid., 94.

35. Ibid., 92.

36. Johnson, *She Who Is*, 229.

37. Ibid., 270.

38. See especially Wendy Farley, *Tragic Vision and Divine Compassion: A Contemporary Theodicy* (Louisville: Westminster John Knox, 1990); and Nancy J. Ramsay, "Compassionate Resistance: An Ethic for Pastoral Care and Counseling," *Journal of Pastoral Care* 52, no. 3 (1998): 217–26.

39. Johnson, *She Who Is*, 228.

40. See Michel Foucault, "Two Lectures," in *Power/Knowledge*, ed. Colin Gordon (New York: Pantheon, 1980), 98; Pasewark, *A Theology of Power*; Richard Sennett, *Authority* (New York: Random House, 1980); and Stortz, *Pastor Power*.

41. For a further discussion of this issue of symbolic authority, see Nancy J. Ramsay, *Pastoral Diagnosis* (Minneapolis: Fortress, 1998), 109–26.

42. Stortz, *Pastor Power*, 42.

43. Ibid.

44. Ibid., 68.

45. Ibid., 93.

46. Ibid., 109.

Chapter 15

1. Anne Streaty Wimberly, *Soul Stories: African American Christian Education* (Nashville: Abingdon, 1994).

2. Julia A. Boyd, *Can I Get a Witness? For Sisters, When the Blues Is More than a Song* (New York: E. P. Dutton, 1998).

3. Nicholas C. Cooper-Lewter and Henry H. Mitchell, *Soul Theology: The Heart of American Black Culture* (San Francisco: Harper and Row, 1986), 43–44.

4. 1 Corinthians 3:16-17 (NRSV) says, "Do you not know that you are God's temple and that God's Spirit dwells in your. If anyone destroys God's temple, God will destroy that person. For God's temple is holy, and you are that temple."

5. Emily M. Townes, *Breaking the Fine Rain of Death: African American Health Issues and a Womanist Ethic of Care* (New York: Continuum, 1998), 115–17, 129–30.

6. Evelyn C. White, ed., *The Black Women's Health Book: Speaking for Ourselves* (Seattle: Seal, 1994).

7. Rosemarie Robotham, "Out of the Dark," *Essence* 30, no. 2 (June 1999): 94.

8. Allison Abner, "When You're Feeling Low," *Essence* 30, no. 2 (June 1999): 96.

9. An in-depth discussion of "matriarch" can be found in Teresa E. Snorton, "The Legacy of the African-American Matriarch: New Perspectives for Pastoral Care," in *Through the Eyes of Women,* Jeanne Stevenson Moessner, ed. (Minneapolis: Fortress Press, 1996).

10. Matthew 9:17 says, "Neither is new wine put into old wineskins; otherwise, the skins burst, and the wine is spilled, and the skins are destroyed; but new wine is put into fresh wineskins, and so both are preserved." See also Luke 5:37-38.

Chapter 16

1. Scripture citations are from *The Inclusive New Testament* (Brentwood, Md.: Priests for Equality, 1994).

2. John Robbins, *May All Be Fed: Diet for a New World* (New York: Avon, 1992), 13.

3. WHI, sponsored by the National Institutes of Health beginning in 1991, studies post-menopausal women ages fifty to seventy-nine who attend forty centers in fourteen cities across the country. Participants stay in the program for ten years.

4. "Making Wise Choices: Women's Health Initiative Dietary Change Group News" 8 (summer 1998): 1.

5. Robbins, *May All Be Fed,* 68.

6. Kate Chernin, *The Obsession: Reflections on the Tyranny of Slenderness* (New York: Harper & Row, 1981).

7. Mary Louise Bringle, *The God of Thinness: Gluttony and Other Weighty Matters* (Nashville: Abingdon, 1992), 53–54.

8. Bringle concludes that almost 95 percent of adult women have a distorted sense of their body size. Among adults who are within what is considered an ideal weight range, 75 percent think they need to lose weight. Ibid., 25.

9. Christine A. Smith, "Women, Weight, and Body Image," in Joan C. Chrisler, Carla Golden, and Patricia D. Rozee, eds., *Lectures on the Psychology of Women* (New York: McGraw-Hill, 1996), 97, 101.

10. Frances M. Berg, *Afraid to Eat: Children and Teens in Weight Crisis.* 2nd ed. (Hettinger, N.D.: Healthy Weight Publishing Network, 1997), 94, 1997.

11. Dawn Atkins, "Weight Loss: Fact and Fiction." See Dawn Atkins, "Killing Us for Our Own Good: Dieting and Medical Misinformation," audio and video tape, Box 934, Santa Cruz, CA 95060.

12. Ibid.

13. Debra Waterhouse, "Nutrition Expert Calls Dieting 'Dangerous,'" at seminar sponsored by the Buck Center for Research in Aging, Novato, Calif., June 20, 1996.

14. Bringle, *The God of Thinness,* 105.

15. "Nutrition expert," 2.

16. The Framingham study published in *New England Journal of Medicine* 1991.

17. National Institutes of Health, *Women of Color Health Data Book,* 1998, pub. no. 98–4247, 46–47.

18. "What Causes Obesity?" in InteliHealth. Johns Hopkins Univ., 1996–1999 (May 13, 1998). Last updated July 15, 1999, www.intelihealth.com.

19. Obesity has reached epidemic proportions around the world, increasingly among the poor, resulting in a surge of people suffering from diabetes and cardiovascular disease. "Obesity at Epidemic Levels Globally," UPI Science Network. United Press International, 1998. (September 1, 1998) www.arec.umd.edu/arec365/upi083198.htm.

20. "Think You're Thin? Think Again," CBS Worldwide Corp., Intelihealth, June 1998, http://www.intelihealth.com.

21. Bringle, *The God of Thinness,* 103–4.

22. *Diagnostic and Statistical Manual of Mental Disorders,* 4th ed. (American Psychiatric Association, 1994), 539–50.

23. Naomi Wolf, "Hunger," in Patricia Fallon, Melanie A. Katzman, and Susan C. Wooley, *Feminist Perspectives on Eating Disorders* (New York: Guilford, 1994), 99–100, 105.

24. "Nutrition expert."

25. Marya Hornbacher, *Wasted: A Memoir of Anorexia and Bulimia* (New York: Harper Collins, 1998).

26. Berg, *Afraid to Eat,* 51–52.

27. "Nutrition expert."

28. Hornbacher, *Wasted,* 26–27.

29. Berg, *Afraid to Eat,* 79.

30. Jane Dasher, "Manna in the Desert: Eating Disorders and Pastoral Care" in *Through the Eyes of Women: Insights for Pastoral Care,* ed. Jeanne Stevenson Moessner (Minneapolis: Fortress Press, 1996) 183.

31. Roberta P. Seid, "'Too Close to the Bone': The Historical Context for Women's Obsession with Slenderness," in Fallon, Katzman, and Wooley, *Feminist Perspectives on Eating Disorders,* 4.

32. Bringle, *The God of Thinness,* 119, 139.

33. Dasher, "Manna in the Desert: Eating Disorders and Pastoral Care," 181.

34. Chernin, *The Obsession,* 28.

35. "Think You're Thin?"

36. Dean Ornish, *Eat More, Weigh Less* (New York: HarperCollins, 1993), 4, 5, 28. In addition to the diseases mentioned above that affect both women and men, prostate cancer is also on the list.

37. Berg, *Afraid to Eat,* 16, 17.

38. Wolf, "Hunger," 107.

39. Dasher, "Manna in the Desert: Eating Disorders and Pastoral Care," 180.

40. Berg, *Afraid to Eat,* 39.

41. Bringle, *The God of Thinness,* 24.

42. NIH, *Women of Color Health Data Book,* 46–47.

43. Dasher, "Manna in the Desert: Eating Disorders and Pastoral Care," 185.

44. Paul A. Mickey, "Bulimia and Anorexia: Signs of the Times," in Robert J. Wicks, Richard D. Parsons, and Donald Capps, eds., *Clinical Handbook of Pastoral Counseling,* vol. 2 (New York: Paulist, 1993), 521–42.

45. Andrew Lester, *Hope in Pastoral Care and Counseling* (Louisville, Ky.: Westminster John Knox, 1995).

46. Marcia Germaine Hutchinson, "Imagining Ourselves Whole," in Fallon, Katzman, and Wooley, *Feminist Perspectives on Eating Disorders,* 157–58.

47. Ira Progoff, *At a Journal Workshop: The Basic Text and Guide for Using the Intensive Journal Process* (New York: Dialogue House, 1975).

48. Dasher, "Manna in the Desert: Eating Disorders and Pastoral Care," 189.

49. R. Cook and D. Benton, "The Relationship between Diet and Mental Health," *Personality and Individual Differences* 14, no. 3 (March 1993), 397–403.

50. Robbins, *May All Be Fed,* 85.

Chapter 17

1. Brita Gill-Austern, "Love Understood as Self-Sacrifice and Self-Denial: What Does It Do to Women?" in Jeanne Stevenson Moessner, ed., *Through the Eyes of Women: Insights for Pastoral Care* (Minneapolis: Fortress Press, 1996), 305.

2. Ibid., 306.

3. Ibid., 308.

4. Natalie Schwartzberg, Kathy Berliner, and Demaris Jacob, *Single in a Married World: A Life Cycle Framework for Working with the Unmarried Adult* (New York: W. W. Norton, 1995), 7.

5. Bonnie J. Miller-McLemore, *Also a Mother: Work and Family as Theological Dilemma* (Nashville: Abingdon, 1994), 30.

6. Herbert Anderson and Freda A. Gardner, *Living Alone.* Family Living in Pastoral Perspective series (Louisville, Ky.: Westminster John Knox, 1997), 58–59.

7. Schwartzberg, Berliner, and Jacob, *Single in a Married World,* 28, 89.

8. R. Staples and L. B. Johnson, *Black Families at the Crossroads: Challenges and Prospects* (San Francisco: Jossey-Bass, 1993).

9. James B. Nelson, *Between Two Gardens: Reflections on Sexuality and Religious Experience* (New York:Pilgrim, 1983); *Body Theology* (Louisville, Ky.: Westminster John Knox), 1992; *Embodiment: An Approach to Sexuality and Christian Theology* (Minneapolis: Augsburg Publishing House, 1978).

10. James C. Dobson, *Love for a Lifetime: Building a Marriage That Will Go the Distance* (Portland: Multnomah, 1987).

11. Lewis B. Smedes, *Sex for Christians: The Limits and Liberties of Sexual Living* (Grand Rapids, Mich.: William B. Eerdmans, 1994).

12. Kay Collier-Stone, *Single in the Church* (Washington, D.C.: Alban, 1992), 7.

13. Nancy A. Schrepf, "Feminism and the Rearing of Children," in Joseph D. Noshpitz, ed., *Handbook of Child and Adolescent Psychiatry,* vol. 7 (New York: John Wiley and Sons, Inc., 1998), 84–85.

14. Malkah T. Notman and Carol C. Nadelson, "Gender Development and Psychopathology: A Revised Psychoanalytic View," in Mary V. Seeman, ed., *Gender and Psychopathology* (Washington, D.C.: American Psychiatric Press, 1995), 11.

15. Schwartzberg, Berliner, and Jacob, *Single in a Married World,* 80.

16. Erik H. Erikson, *Childhood and Society* (New York: W. W. Norton, 1950, 1963).

17. Miller-McLemore, 41–53, 180–81.

18. Ibid, 181.

19. Ibid, 22.

20. Schwartzberg, Berliner, and Jacob, 56.

Chapter 18

1. For resources with a sociological and ethical perspective, see Michelle Fine and Adrienne Asch, *Women with Disabilities: Essays in Psychology, Culture, and Politics* (Philadelphia: Temple Univ. Press, 1988); Arthur Kleinman, *The Illness Narratives: Suffering, Healing, and the Human Condition* (New York: Basic, 1988); Susan Sontag *Illness as Metaphor* (New York: Farrar, Straus and Giroux, 1978), and *AIDS and Its Metaphors* (New York: Farrar, Straus and Giroux, 1989). See also the resources in note 7 that deal with the more visible disabilities and those in note 40 from a spiritual, theological, and pastoral care perspective.

2. Eight million working-age adults in the United States receive some kind of disability benefits. Of these 1 percent have jobs (Federal EEO Advisor, LRP Publications, vol. 2, no. 11, December 16, 1999), 1.

3. The 1994 statistics show that 34 percent of disabled persons are granted benefits on their first application; only 13 percent more receive benefits on first appeal. Many continue with hearings and additional appeals for many years (Nancy G. Shore, ed., *Social Security Forum,* vol. 18, no. 2:11 [Midland Park, N.J.: National Organization of Social Security Claimants Representatives, February 1996]).

4. A 1999 survey by the National Organization on Disabilities showed that 76 percent of disabled persons wanted to work, but only 25 percent were actually employed. Only 1 percent of the 8 million working-age adults who receive Social Security disability benefits have jobs (Federal EEO Advisor, CRP Publications).

5. Kathy Black, who has researched the deaf community, theorizes that persons with deafness are often assumed to be "crazy"; thus, they distance themselves from mental health advocacy.

6. At present, books are being written about women and disabilities, but they might not be required reading in general pastoral care classes. The field of pastoral care has tended to focus on persons with terminal illness or acute episodes of chronic illness, rather than long-term issues with disabilities.

7. Bernie Blanton's disability is not hidden because she walks with a cane. I have included her because of her age and the high incidence of strokes.

For sources on the more visible disabilities, see the following: Nancy L. Eiesland, *The Disabled God: Toward a Liberatory Theology of Disability* (Nashville: Abingdon, 1994); Susan Lonsdale, *Women and Disability: The Experience of Physical Disability among Women* (New York: St. Martin's, 1990); Marsha Saxton, and Florence Howe, *With Wings: An Anthology of Literature by and about Women with Disabilities* (New York: The Feminist Press at the City Univ. of New York, 1987); and Joni Eareckson Tada, *Her Story* (Anthology of *Joni, A Step Further,* and *Choices . . . Changes*) (New York: Inspirational, 1994).

8. This is particularly true of acquired brain injury (which includes stroke, tumor, and traumatic brain injury) and mental illness.

9. Although the image of a "strange land" came out of my own experience with disability, it is also used by many writers with chronic illness.

10. "How can we sing the Lord's song in a strange land?" is a question, a lament to God by the Israelites after their exile to Babylon (Psalm 137:4). I have changed "Lord" to "God" to be more inclusive.

11. Five women were referred to me by church members and self-help groups; two are writers and disability advocates; I included myself as the eighth woman. I conducted these interviews in person or by phone from August 24–October 9, 1998. In addition, several persons sent me e-mail messages, and Bernie Blanton wrote out her responses to my questions so that her answers would be more accurate.

Eight women are too small a sample to be representative of the general population. For sources on women of other races, classes, and cultures, see Diane Driedger, and Susan Gray, eds., *Imprinting Our Image: An International Anthology by Women with Disabilities* (Charlottetown, P.E.I.: Gynergy, 1992); Diane Driedger, Irene Feika, and Eileen Giron Batres, eds., *Across Borders: Women with Disabilities Working Together* (Charlottetown, P.E.I.: Gynergy, 1996).

12. Term used by Kathleen Lewis in her interview with me. She prefers to think of herself as a "patient professional" rather than as a "professional patient."

13. When I asked how ministers could help women with disabilities, seven of the eight interviewed said, "*Listen.*"

14. I use the term *dis-ease* to include medical conditions and injuries as well as diseases.

15. For more about addiction, see Barbara Gordon, *I'm Dancing as Fast as I Can* (New York: Perennial Library, 1989); *The Big Book (Alcoholics Anonymous)*, 3rd ed. (New York: Alcoholics Anonymous World Services, 1976); and the movies, "When a Man Loves a Woman" (Burbank, Calif.: Touchstone, 1994) written by Ronald Bass and Al Franken, prod. Jordan Kerner and Jon Avnet, dir. Luis Mandoki; and "Losing Isaiah" (Hollywood, Calif.: Paramount, 1995), prod. by Howard W. Koch Jr. and Naomi Foner, dir. by Stephen Gyllenhaal, screenplay by Naomi Foner; based on the novel by Seth Margolis. For stories of drug addicts, see *The Basic Text (Narcotics Anonymous)*, 5th ed. (Van Nuys, Calif: Alcoholics World Services, 1988): 153–273.

16. For more about manic-depressive illness, see Kay Redfield Jamison, *An Unquiet Mind: A Memoir of Moods and Madness* (New York: Alfred A. Knopf, 1995); David A. Karp, *Speaking of Sadness: Depression, Disconnection, and the Meanings of Illness* (New York: Oxford Univ. Press, 1996).

17. For more about stroke, see Bonnie Sherr Klein, *Slow Dance: A Story of Stroke, Love and Disability* (Berkeley, Calif.: Page Mill, 1998).

18. For more about traumatic brain injury, see Claudia L. Osborn, *Over My Head: A Doctor's Own Story of Head Injury from the Inside Looking Out* (Kansas City, Mo.: Andrews McMeel, 1998); and the movie, "Regarding Henry" (Hollywood, Calif.: Paramount, 1991) written by Jeffrey Abrams, prod. Scott Rudin and Mike Nichols, dir. Mike Nichols. For mild traumatic brain injury, see Diane Robert Stoler, and Barbara Albers Hill, *Coping with Mild Traumatic Brain Injury* (Garden City Park, N.Y.: Avery, 1998).

19. A person with emotional lability can rapidly shift from one emotion to another with little warning or provocation.

20. Organic mood disorder is a catch-all diagnosis that describes psychological disorders with an organic, or physical, origin that are caused by a number of neurological disorders as well as drug addiction. With traumatic brain injury, energy swings can be accompanied by mood swings. One may also have more difficulty with impulsive behavior and emotional lability because of a lowered frustration tolerance.

21. Mild TBI (traumatic brain injury) can be difficult to diagnose because it mimics symptoms of healthy grief and post–traumatic stress disorder. For a comparison of symptoms, see Stoler and Hill (*Coping with Mild Traumatic Brain Injury*, 219). Mild TBI often does not show up on a CT scan or MRI. A person does not have to lose consciousness or even have a severe blow to the head to incur an injury. A person suffering from mild TBI may have difficulty recognizing the severity of the injury because mild TBI effects the executive functioning of the ego, including organization, judgment, and complex problem solving.

22. Lupus is an aphasic autoimmune disease, which can be fatal. For more about Lupus, see Kathleen L. Lewis, *Celebrate Life: New Attitudes for Living with Chronic Illness* (Atlanta: Arthritis Foundation, 1999); Joanna Baumer Permut, *Embracing the Wolf: A Lupus Victim and Her Family Learn to Live with Chronic Disease* (Atlanta: Cherokee, 1989).

23. An addicted person's "bottom" is the low point to which she gets before she asks for help.

24. For more about multiple sclerosis, see Nancy Mairs, *Remembering the Bone House: An Erotics of Place and Space* (New York: Harper & Row, 1989); and *Waist-High in the World: A Life among the Non-Disabled* (Boston: Beacon, 1996).

25. Socologist Arthur Frank believes that illness calls for a restructuring of life stories in three possible narratives: the restitution narrative, the chaos narrative, and the quest narrative (*The Wounded Storyteller: Body, Illness, and Ethics* [Chicago: The Univ. of Chicago Press, 1995]).

26. Freud contended that healthy adults (males, of course) need to be able "to love and to work."

27. See Lewis, *Prayer without Ceasing: Breath Prayers* (Lafayette, La.: Prescott, 1998) and *Celebrate Life* (1999).

28. "Hitting the wall" is when the body/mind shuts down often unexpectedly and in varying ways. The only remedy is rest.

29. Experts in addiction believe that a person's development is arrested at the age of the onset of the addiction.

30. See chapter five, "How It Works" in the *Big Book of AA* for the twelve steps for recovering from an addiction. These steps have been appropriated by many different populations because they offer a practical way to live a spiritual life.

31. In the last year, Tamara has begun driving again.

32. I did short-term hypnotherapy with Henry Close, who included a metaphor about my life as chap. 9, "The Fallen Tree," in *Metaphor in Psychotherapy: Clinical Application of Stories and Allegories*, Practical Therapy series. vol. 4 (San Luis Obispo, Calif.: Impact Publishers, 1998), 59–66.

33. Since the writing of this chapter, the law has made it easier for disabled persons to return to work. On December 17, 1999, the president signed the Ticket to Work and Work Incentives Improvement Act of 1999. Social Security disability beneficiaries may receive a "ticket," if they wish, which they can redeem for vocational rehabilitation, employment, or other support services. Additionally, persons with disabilities can maintain their Medicare coverage after they go back to work. The flaws with this law are that the states are not required to implement all of these provisions; many of them are time limited; and there are still great needs for improving education, transportation, and *employment bias against persons with disabilities* ("Fact Sheet: Ticket to Work and Work Incentives Improvement Act of 1999," Social Security Administration Web site <www.ssa.gov/work/-factsheet.htm> and Federal EEO Advisor, LRP Publications, vol. 2, no. 11, December 16, 1999), 1–2.

34. For a subscription, write to "Ahead of the Times," Box 1094, Woodbridge, New Jersey 07095; e-mail: aheadof123@prodigy.net.

35. I cannot prove that their lack of response was due to my disability.

36. Kathleen sees emotional, spiritual, and physical healing as being inseparable.

37. Francene Passantino, the exception, believes that God allowed her injury "to get my attention."

38. In Phil. 2:12-13, Paul says to "Work out your own salvation with fear and trembling, for God is at work in you." (RSV). Faith must be lived out, with God's help.

39. In the poem, "Warning," Jenny Joseph exclaims that when she is "old" she will dispense with social graces: "When I am an old woman I shall wear purple with a red hat that doesn't go, and doesn't suit me and [I will] learn to spit. . . . " (Sandra Martz, ed., *When I Am an Old Woman I Shall Wear Purple*, [Watsonville, Calif.: Papier-Maché, 1987]).

40. These suggestions are compiled from my own experiences and from the interviews with the other seven women. None is gender-specific. Men and children with disabilities should be given the

same consideration. For additional references on how the church can learn from and minister to persons with disabilities, see Kathy Black, *A Healing Homiletic: Preaching and Disability* (Nashville: Abingdon, 1996). Nancy L. Eiesland, *The Disabled God: Toward a Liberatory Theology of Disability* (Nashville: Abingdon, 1994), and "Changing the Subject: Toward an Interfaith Theology of Disability," *Journal of Religion, Disability, & Health.* Vol. 3, no. 1:55–62. William A. Blair and Dana Davidson Blair, eds. (Binghamton, New York: Hayworth, 1999); Nancy L. Eiesland, and Don Saliers, eds., *Human Disability and the Service of God* (Nashville: Abingdon, 1998); Stewart D. Govig, *Strong at the Broken Places: Persons with Disabilities and the Church* (Louisville: Westminster John Knox, 1994); Gary Gunderson, *Deeply Woven Roots: Improving the Quality of Life in Your Community* (Minneapolis: Fortress Press, 1997); Judy Griffith Ransom, *The Courage to Care: Seven Families Touched by Disability and Congregational Caring* (Nashville: Upper Room, 1994); John T. Vanderzee, *Ministry to Persons with Chronic Illnesses: A Guide to Empowerment through Negotiation,* Guides to Pastoral Care Series (Minneapolis: Augsburg Books, 1993); Brett Webb-Mitchell, *Dancing with Disabilities: Opening the Church to All God's Children* (Cleveland, Ohio: United Church, 1996); Ann Weems, *Psalms of Lament* (Louisville, Ky.: Westminster John Knox, 1995); and Rachel Naomi Remen, *Kitchen Table Wisdom: Stories that Heal* (New York: Riverhead, 1996). For books on theodicy, see Dorothee Soelle, *Suffering* (Philadelphia: Fortress Press, 1975); Harold S. Kushner, *When Bad Things Happen to Good People* (New York: Avon, 1981); Charles Ohlrich, *The Suffering God: Hope and Comfort for Those Who Hurt* (Downers Grove, Ill.: InterVarsity, 1982). For ministers, chaplains, or pastoral counselors who want a medical family-systems approach, see the book by psychiatrist John S. Rolland, *Families, Illness, & Disability: An Integrative Treatment Model* (New York: Basic, 1994). For the families of those with disabilities see Greta Rey, *For Caregivers with Love* (Grand Rapids, Mich.: Baker, 1996), and Rosalyn Carter, *Helping Yourself Help Others* (Time Warner, 1996). For books on the grieving process see JoAnn LeMaistre, *After the Diagnosis: From Crisis to Personal Renewal for Patients with Chronic Illness.* (Berkeley, Calif.: Ulysses, 1995); Helen R. Lambin, *From Grief to Grace: Images for Overcoming Sadness and Loss* (Chicago: ACTA, 1997); Lewis Tagliaferre and Gary L. Harbaugh, *Recovery from Loss: A Personalized Guide to the Grieving Process* (Deerfield Beach, Fl: Health Communications, 1990); Stephanie Ericsson, *Companion through the Darkness: Inner Dialogues on Grief* (N.Y.: HarperPerennial, 1993).

41. See James Morrison, *When Psychological Problems Mask Medical Disorders: A Guide for Psychologists* (New York: Guilford, 1997).

42. My church offers a year-long alcohol and drug recovery program for homeless men who live at the church and are incorporated into the life of the church. Most members agree that we have received far more from the men than they from us. After going to his first "graduation" ceremony (for these men), one church member exclaimed, "It's like being back at an old-fashioned [Baptist] revival meeting and hearing testimonies!"

43. Problems that many elderly persons and most disabled women face are impending death, a need for life review, an increased need to care for their bodies, lower income and ability to engage in paid or meaningful vocation, role changes or reversals with family members and friends, and being patronized by society. It would be stereotypical to say that *all* elderly persons have to deal with these issues. See Joan Borysenko, *A Woman's Life: The Biology, Psychology, and Spirituality of the Feminine Life Cycle* (New York: Riverhead, 1996), and the numerous other books on women's life cycles cited throughout this volume for the issues faced by senior adults.

Afterthoughts

1. As an example of the emerging literature, see Paula Buford, "The Lost Tradition of Women as Pastoral Caregivers from 1925 to 1967: A 'Dangerous Memory,'" unpublished dissertation, Columbia Theological Seminary, 1997.

2. Frances G. Wickes *The Inner World of Choice* (New York: Harper & Row, 1963). Wickes, an American analytical psychologist, had been a student of Carl Gustav Jung.